P9-EMF-102

THE FAMILY IN VARIOUS CULTURES

The Family In Various Cultures

Fourth Edition

Stuart A. Queen
Washington University, Emeritus

Robert W. Habenstein
University of Missouri

J. B. Lippincott Company

PHILADELPHIA   NEW YORK   TORONTO

Copyright © 1974, 1967, 1961 by J. B. Lippincott Company

Copyright 1952 by J. B. Lippincott Company

This book is fully protected by copyright and, with the exception of brief excerpts for review, no part of it may be reproduced in any form by print, photoprint, microfilm, or by any other means without the written permission of the publishers.

ISBN: 0-397-47297-8

Library of Congress Catalog Card Number 73-21517

Printed in the United States of America

7 9 10 8

Library of Congress Cataloging in Publication Data

Queen, Stuart Alfred, 1890-
    The family in various cultures.

    Includes bibliographies.
    1. Family. I. Habenstein, Robert Wesley, 1914-
joint author. II. Title.
HQ503.Q4   1974   301.42   73-21517
ISBN: 0-397-47297-8

CONTENTS

FOREWORD TO THE FOURTH EDITION

This book combines the comparative and the historical approaches to the study of family systems for the benefit of college students and others whose interest is real, but whose time may be limited. First published in 1952, THE FAMILY IN VARIOUS CULTURES has since gone through several editions, with each revision adding new material and modifying or updating old material in response to suggestions from readers and incorporating new findings.

Thus the second edition in 1961 featured new data concerning the unusual organization of family life in the *kibbutzim* of Israel. More significantly, Robert W. Habenstein joined Stuart A. Queen as collaborator, replacing John B. Adams, who had assisted with the original edition.

The third revision in 1967 saw the addition of a new chapter on the Black American family, helping to provide greater depth to the reader's understanding of family life in the United States today.

The present fourth edition maintains the organization of earlier editions, updating older chapters where necessary and adding two new chapters: the first deals with several major forms of the Canadian family, and the second examines the contemporary Mexican American family. The Canadian chapter is divided into two sections, the first covering the family system in the Newfoundland fishing village, and the second in rural and to a lesser extent urban French-Canadian provinces.

Many professional colleagues and others have helped with advice and counsel through the various editions of this book, including Ernest W. Burgess and Robert K. Merton. In the first edition Cora Alice Du Bois kindly read Chapter IV, and Kazuya Matsumiya was similarly helpful with the interpretation of Japanese family life. Allan Coult, Sarah Feder, and Robert G. Spier generously assisted with advice at the time of the second edition.

For this edition, the authors wish to thank William Dyson,

Director of the Vanier Institute of the Family, Ottawa, and his staff for invaluable assistance and numerous courtesies. Frederick Elkin, York University, well-known in the field of family and socialization and an expert on the Canadian family, and Parvez A. Wakil, University of Saskatchewan, were most helpful, as were Ellen H. Biddle, Donald Cowgill, Anthony G. Dworkin, William Hays, Charles Mindel, and Ulla Svensson, colleagues at the University of Missouri.

Jane Habenstein, a veteran of the wars of revision and reprinting, has rendered her usual invaluable services. Office space, secretarial help, and encouragement were forthcoming from Bruce J. Biddle, Director, Center for Research in Social Behavior, University of Missouri, Columbia. Richard Heffron, Lippincott editor who has seen the work through several editions and many printings, has in the process become the incumbent of a new role—authors' friend.

Stuart A. Queen
Robert W. Habenstein

January, 1974

1 Introduction

There are many notions about the origin and development of marriage and the family. Some are obviously fanciful; some are symbolic; some are supported by historical and other evidence. One of the most charming stories about the beginnings of marriage is the Sanskrit myth made available to us through Bain's translation.[1]

In the beginning, when Twashtri came to the creation of woman, he found that he had exhausted his materials in the making of man, and that no solid elements were left. In this dilemma, after profound meditation, he did as follows. He took the rotundity of the moon, and the curves of creepers, and the clinging of tendrils, and the trembling of grass, and the slenderness of the reed, and the bloom of flowers, and the lightness of leaves, and the tapering of the elephant's trunk, and the glances of deer, and the clustering of rows of bees, and the joyous gaiety of sunbeams, and the weeping of clouds, and the fickleness of the winds, and the timidity of the hare, and the vanity of the peacock, and the softness of the parrot's bosom, and the hardness of adamant, and the sweetness of honey, and the cruelty of the tiger, and the warm glow of fire, and the coldness of snow, and the chattering of jays, and the cooing of the *kokila*, and the hypocrisy of the crane, and the fidelity of the *chakrawaka*, and compounding all these together, he made woman and gave her to man. But after one week, man came to him and said: Lord, this creature that you have given me makes my life miserable. She chatters incessantly and teases me beyond endurance, never leaving me alone; and she requires incessant attention, and takes all my time up, and cries about nothing, and is always idle; and so I have come to give her back again, as I cannot live with her. So Twashtri said: Very well; and he took her back. Then after another week, man came again to him and said: Lord, I find that my life is very lonely, since I gave you back that creature. I remember how she used to dance and sing to me, and look at me out of the corner of her eye, and play with me, and cling to me; and her laughter was music, and she was beautiful to look at, and soft to touch; so give her back to me again. So Twashtri said: Very well; and gave her back again. Then after only three days, man came back to him again and said: Lord, I know not how it is; but after all I have come to the con-

1. F. W. Bain, *A Digit of the Moon* (1905), pp. 32-34. By permission of G. P. Putnam's Sons.

1

clusion that she is more of a trouble than a pleasure to me; so please take
her back again. But Twashtri said: Out on you! Be off! I will have no more
of this. You must manage how you can. Then man said: But I cannot live
with her. And Twashtri replied: Neither could you live without her. And
he turned his back on man, and went on with his work. Then man said:
What is to be done? for I cannot live either with her or without her.

Another is the well-known narrative found in the second
chapter of Genesis.[2]

And the Lord God said, It is not good that the man should be alone;
I will make him a help meet for him. And out of the ground the Lord God
formed every beast of the field, and every fowl of the air; and brought
them unto Adam to see what he would call them: and whatsoever Adam
called every living creature, that was the name thereof. And Adam gave
names to all cattle, and to the fowl of the air, and to every beast of the field;
but for Adam there was not found a help meet for him. And the Lord God
caused a deep sleep to fall upon Adam, and he slept; and he took one of
his ribs, and closed up the flesh instead thereof; and the rib, which the Lord
God had taken from man, made he a woman, and brought her unto man.
And Adam said, This is now bone of my bones, and flesh of my flesh: she
shall be called Woman, because she was taken out of Man. Therefore shall
a man leave his father and his mother, and shall cleave unto his wife: and
they shall be one flesh.

Curiously both of these stories have it that man appeared
first and that woman was created to be his companion. Actually there is no ground for assuming priority of *either* sex *on
the human level*. In simpler forms of life the facts indicate
that family life often started with a tie between female and
offspring, the male being the later addition to the group.
Perhaps the priority of man in both the Sanskrit and Hebrew
accounts reflects male dominance in India and Arabia at the
time these stories were composed.

Theories About the Family
as an Institution

Neither of the stories just recited can be treated as the
product of scientific and historical research or of philosophi-

2. Genesis 2:18-24.

cal speculation. Both apparently grew up over long periods in the dim and shadowy past. Gradually each became an established part of the formal tradition of a great people. Ultimately they were set down in writing. How seriously they were taken in the days of long ago we can hardly say. Even yet they are subject to varied interpretations. But, whatever else may be said, both narratives imply that marriage and the family began at a particular time and place in a form that has continued until the present. The notion of a definite origin lasted until very recently, but the conception of uniformity was challenged long ago. Travel, trade, and war brought contacts with strange people whose systems of family life differed greatly. The reaction to these new experiences and observations was often that "our" ways are right and proper while "their" ways are queer and wrong. Even when it came to the point of trying to impose "our" institutions upon "them," at least there was recognition of the fact that there are other forms of family life than ours, just as there are other forms of religion, government, and art, other food habits and modes of dress. A corollary of this proposition was apparently slow to emerge. It is this: *inasmuch as patterns of family life vary, no single form need be regarded as inevitable or more "natural" than any other.* And, paraphrasing the anthropologist Levi-Strauss, while the family is found practically everywhere, *there is no natural law making the family universal.*[3]

With the formulation of the general theory of evolution by Darwin and others and with its application to human society by Herbert Spencer, scholars began to talk about the evolution of marriage and the family. They not only noted the existence of many varied types of domestic arrangements; they observed that some seemed to be quite the "opposite" of their own, while others appeared to represent intermediate stages. So they arranged them into what looked like a logical series and expounded the doctrine that the family must pass

3. Claude Levi-Strauss, "The Family," in Harry L. Shapiro, ed., *Man, Culture, and Society* (1960), Chapter XII, p. 266.

through a fixed sequence of variations to reach a given level. During the nineteenth century there were vigorous arguments about which stage came first and the order in which the others appeared. Sir Henry Maine held that the earliest form of the family was "patriarchal," or father-centered. Bachofen insisted that it must have been "matriarchal," or mother-centered, a theory that early in the present century was revived and restated by Briffault. The studies of Spencer and Gillen in Australia suggested to some that there may have been an early stage of "group marriage," in which several men mated with several women. Earlier McLennan had maintained that the beginnings of marriage are to be found in unrestricted, temporary sexual unions. Out of these and other propositions the evolutionary theory of marriage tended to take form somewhat as follows:

In the beginning was promiscuity in which only the mother-child relationship was certain and stable. This was followed by somewhat more lasting ties between several men and several women, a sort of primitive horde whose members remained together for protection, companionship, and sexual satisfaction. Such "group marriage" then gave way to polyandry, in which a number of men were attached fairly permanently to a single woman. Polyandry, of course, assumed an excess of males, hence a small number of mothers, and a low rate of reproduction. It may also have involved female infanticide, or extreme poverty and scarcity of the means of subsistence. With the development of more adequate food supplies and greater security, the sex ratio approached unity. Polyandry might then have given way to monogamy, but powerful men took unto themselves several wives, and thus polygyny arose. The extra males were either killed, enslaved, or forced to wait for a chance to mate. Finally, with the emergence of higher ethical standards, monogamy was established.

Now it is not held that anyone ever seriously proposed just this series of stages as the evolutionary process. It is a composite of several theories, differing in detail, but alike in holding that there is an unvarying sequence through which the institution of marriage must pass. These theories imply, too, that each successive form of family life is better than its predecessor; in other words, that progress is consistent and inevitable. It is sometimes suggested that permanent monogamous unions based on romantic love and equalitarian in spirit, as (allegedly) maintained in contemporary America, represent the acme of human achievement. But a skeptical note is often added by those who point to the "rising tide of divorce" and similar distressing symptoms. Perhaps after all the "golden age" is in the past or, possibly, it is still in the future.

Although these ideas are intriguing and plausible enough, it happens that they lack supporting evidence. Hence, despite some grains of truth, we must reject the theory of straight-line evolution of marriage and the family. This does not mean a return to the doctrine that the family was established in final form at a particular time and place by divine or other fiat. There is plenty of support for the proposition that marriage and the family as we know them in contemporary America, for example, have developed out of other patterns and in connection with other changes in culture. *We assume that all forms of the domestic institution are in process, having grown out of something different and tending to become something still different. But there is no acceptable evidence of a single, uniform series of stages through which the developing family has passed and must pass.*

Cultural Variations in the Family

We may nevertheless take as established the proposition that the family (described for the moment as a group of kinsmen living intimately together, its members mating, bearing, and rearing offspring, growing up, and protecting one another) is rooted in the past, built on our prehuman, biological heritage as well as on our human experience. It is a way of life shared not only by mankind, but by many other species as well. It is a complex of impulses and habits imbedded in our very nature and an integral part of every culture. The living together of man and woman, of parents and children, in an intimate relationship is so firmly established that we need give little thought to the likelihood of its disappearance. Yet, as we have seen, this way of life has no single, uniform pattern. Despite some elements in common, it displays an enormous variety in structure, life cycle, controls, and functions.

One of the important variations has to do with the relation of the nuclear family (mates and their offspring) to the extended family (including grandparents, uncles, aunts, cousins, etc.). In our culture the nuclear family receives most attention. It usually has a separate residence; it is commonly a self-supporting unit. In fiction, in drama, and in everyday living it is accorded the place of honor. More distant relatives are considered, too, but they are usually outside the inner circle of our closest ties, our most intimate experiences, and our basic obligations. But in some other cultures it is very different. Among the Hopi, ancient Chinese, Hebrews, and Romans the wider, more inclusive kinship groups are dominant. Mating is arranged by the head of the kin, who continue to exercise some control over young people even after their marriage. Economic responsibilities are shared throughout the larger group. Often several married couples—elders, children and their spouses, and grandchildren—literally live together in the same household.

Bound up with these differences in the relative importance of the nuclear family and the extended family are the modes of marital selection. In the United States today it is not uncommon for a young man and a young woman to meet, woo, and marry almost without the knowledge of their respective kin. To be sure, their freedom is not absolute. In most states they must secure a license and go through a simple ceremony; if they are first-cousins, in some states, they are forbidden to marry. But as compared with other cultures ours offers a wide range of choice and a minimum of control. Indeed, it appears that marriage in accordance with arrangements made by family heads is very common outside our system. Among the ancient Greeks and until recently among the Chinese many a bride and groom did not even see each other before their wedding. Romantic love as a basis for marriage is relatively new and is dominant mainly in the Western world, chiefly in the United States and Canada. As we go from culture to culture, several of which are dealt with in this book, we find a wide variety of rules concerning who may marry whom. Among the Todas of South India cross-cousin marriages (e.g., daughter of a man to his sister's son) are preferred, while among the Manus of New Guinea they are forbidden.

Descent and inheritance are frequently patrilineal (in the male line from father to son), but among the Hopi, Crow, and Haida of North America they are matrilineal. In the Trobriands of the South Pacific a man inherits from his mother's brother. In many cultures personal effects are handed down, while land belongs to the kinship group. With us almost anything may be left to almost anyone by making a will. The line of descent and inheritance may or may not correspond to the place of residence. Thus the Chinese and Japanese families have been both patrilineal and patrilocal (living with the man's parents), but the Hopi are matrilocal (living with the wife's parents).

In most cultures, it appears that children are desired, but in others, such as the Marquesan, quite the opposite is indicated. Also among the Baganda the first child, after it is weaned, is often sent to live with its father's brother. On the other hand, the birth of twins, considered a catastrophe in Toda society, is an occasion for great rejoicing among the Baganda. In the majority of cultures, both "primitive" and "historical," children's education is usually informal and acquired partly in the family and partly in the larger group. Adult authority may be concentrated, as in the Roman *pater familias,* or it may be diffused among all kinsmen older than the child, as in Samoa. Among many preliterate peoples lactation continues for several years, while with us babies are weaned within a few weeks or months; more likely the infant is bottle-fed from the start. Discipline is mild in most preliterate groups, but among some of our European ancestors it has been harsh and severe. Infanticide is reported in many cultures, including the highly civilized Greeks and Romans.

In most of the cultures about which we have information, women are subordinate to men. Some of the most extreme cases are those of the Todas and the ancient Greeks. On the other hand, the status of women is relatively high among the matrilineal Haida and the patrilineal Kwoma. Among the Hopi, women might almost be described as dominant. Despite these varied patterns of domination and subordination, and even plural marriage, the relations of husbands and wives do not appear to involve much hostility; mutual affection is shown under conditions that would seem intolerable to us. But in some tribes, such as the Kwoma, there is a great deal of friction, and among the Manus marriage seems to be regarded as a necessary evil. Whether the status of the sexes is determined by their economic importance is a moot point. Toda men do practically all the work of any consequence, while the Mundugumor of New Guinea leave most of the work to their women; in both cultures women are definitely subordinate. Among the matrilineal Hopi, men do most of the gardening and herding, while "women's place is in the home." Yet the relative status of the sexes is not what would be expected in conventional society in the United States. Likewise there is some question as to the possible relation between status of the sexes and breadth of the culture base (number and variety of traits which make up a culture). Curiously there have been approaches to equality of the sexes in cultures as diverse as those of contemporary Scandinavia and the Crow Indians.

Some provision for divorce is made in almost every known culture. Men usually initiate the proceedings, but in Dahomey and the United States the great majority of divorces are secured by women. Among the Hopi both men and women may seek divorce at will. Among the ancient Hebrews the husband could dispose of his wife by giving her a "bill of divorcement." The Roman husband had to call a family council before putting away his wife. Among the early Christians divorce was a private family affair. With us it is controlled by the state. The Catholic Church has forbidden complete divorce, while for a time Russia made it relatively free and easy.

In no culture do we find absolute promiscuity, but there are wide differences in the sex mores. Young people in Samoa and the Trobriand Islands enjoy great freedom and enter numerous liaisons, some of which lead to marriage. In the Israeli *kibbutz* there is also great freedom, but there are comparatively few liaisons. Against all this the Christian code is adamant. Among the Arunta and some of the Eskimos hospitality includes wife-lending; among the early Romans extramarital relations of all kinds apparently were rare. Among the Crow Indians, as in Christian Europe and America, there has really been a double standard. Girls and women were expected to remain "pure" while boys and men "sowed their wild oats." Prostitution seems to be rare among the preliterates, but common in urban civilizations. Birth control has been practiced in many lands, but is still a matter of dispute in our country. The general attitudes toward sex range from the Samoan, where sex is a matter of art and recreation, to the early Christian, where all sex was vile and even marriage was looked down upon. *Thus we find an amazing variety of practices, rules, and sentiments in the domestic institutions of different peoples, indicating that human nature is capable of adapting itself to and through a wide range of customs and controls.*

But through all the varied forms of family life four facts stand out rather clearly. First, there is everywhere a relatively strong tie between mother and child, at least during the child's early years.

Second, some approximation to monogamy has been the dominant, if not the ideal, form of marriage, partly because of the near equality in numbers of the sexes, partly because of the smaller expense and fewer obligations involved.

Third, nowhere do we find evidence of unregulated pro-miscuity. From the standpoint of our mores the sex relations of some peoples seem to be indiscriminate and uncontrolled, but on closer study they are always found to be regulated. The rules may be very different from those in our culture, but there are always some rules, and they are often more effec-tively enforced than ours.

Fourth, in nearly all cultures about which we have infor-mation the institution we call the family is identified with four functions: procreation, orientation, division of labor between the sexes, and status-giving. To be sure, many chil-dren are born out of wedlock, and there are childless couples in many lands. But the great majority of families include the offspring of the adult members, and most children enter the world as members of families. It is also true that children learn a great deal about the world from persons outside their families, but for most children everywhere the initial orienta-tion to life and its setting is acquired within the family. Like-wise, status—particularly that involved in sex, age, familial relations, class, caste, and "race"—is acquired from the family into which one is born.

Some Definitions

Perhaps it is time we stopped to define some of the terms we have been using in our discussion. The term family itself has been employed in several different ways. In the simplest biological sense it consists of those individuals who are related by mating and descent, regardless of whether there be any other connection or not. But the biological conception of the family also takes account of a parent or parents caring for offspring. On the human level the interaction between man and woman, parents and children, is not only physical; it involves the development of feelings and ideas, attitudes and sentiments, mutual awareness, and a sense of belonging together. Hence in the sociological sense we think of the family as an intimate social group of persons, most of whom are usually related by ties of blood, and who are regarded by their associates as a distinctive social unit. The limited biological family and the sociological family usually coincide in our culture, but even with us such a procedure as adoption may remove an individual from one family group and attach him to another. He is still the offspring of his biological parents, but he becomes legally and socially the child of his foster parents. Adoption, incidentally, is found in a great many different cultures. Divorce is another procedure through which a biological family may cease to be one sociologically. Even without such legal action as we have mentioned, persons who are not related by blood may live together in a communal manner that will give them the status of a family group.

In our previous discussion we have already noted different kinds of family groups. It is now in order to identify them more precisely. *Nuclear family*, sometimes called conjugal group or marriage group, is made up of husband and wife together with their children born or adopted. *Composite family* is made up of two or more nuclear families which share a common husband or wife. This involves polygyny (one man with two or more wives), or polyandry (one woman with two or more husbands), or concubinage (extra sexual partners who are recognized members of the household, but who do not have the full status of wives). *Extended family*, sometimes called kinship group, is an extension of the parent-child relationships through three or more generations, thus including grandparents and grandchildren, cousins, uncles, and aunts. *Sib* is a more inclusive body of kinsmen, presumably descended from a common ancestor. It is sometimes called a consanguineal group. *Clan* might be called a compromise group since it involves both consanguinity and residence as basic principles. An example is the Toda clan, described in Chapter II, which includes members of a male consanguineal group, or sib, living in one area as a residential group, who are integrated into an operating political and social unit. *Household* includes persons who reside together, "put their feet under the same table," but are not necessarily kin. It might correspond to a composite family; it might be a nuclear family minus members away from home, or plus relatives, in-laws, or boarders living together.

At this point it might be well also to distinguish certain other terms that are sometimes confused. *Patriarchal* means that power is centered in a man, usually the father or grandfather in a family group. *Matriarchal* means that power is centered in a corresponding woman. *Patrilineal* means that descent is traced in the male line; *matrilineal* means that it is traced in the female line. *Patrilocal* means that a family resides with or near relatives of the husband; *matrilocal* means that residence is with or near relatives of the wife.

There are two additional terms of which we will make little or no use. But since they appear in some works dealing with the family, we will add them to our list. A *family of orientation* is the nuclear or composite family into which one is born and in which he is reared, i.e., "socialized" or "oriented." A *family of procreation* is the nuclear or composite family which one joins in establishing through marriage.

In cultures which, like ours, trace kinship and descent bilaterally, we may belong to three different kinship groups, the father's, the mother's, and the spouse's. But in many cultures one line of descent receives major, if not exclusive, attention. In such cultures one may be a member of only one kinship group, his mother's if the system be matrilineal, his father's if it be patrilineal.

Finally, *marriage* is a term often applied to the ceremonial which is appropriately called wedding. It is also applied to the relationship between spouses, referring either to a particular pair (a larger number of individuals in plural marriages) or to the institutionalized pattern of relationship, not the ceremonial, and we shall deal especially with the generalized pattern of relationships between mates rather than the specific adjustments made by particular couples.

Reasons for Comparative Study of the Family

It is understood now that we do not expect to find a direct line of evolution through which the family has come to its present state in our own or any other culture. Neither are we looking for data to support the belief that ours is the most satisfactory form this institution has ever assumed. Nor are we seeking standards of domestic behavior and arrangements which might conveniently be labeled "normal" or "natural" or "right." From the study of the family in various cultures we hope to gain perspective on the possible variety of patterns. We are bound to be impressed by the wide range of forms. We may also get a hint of probable limits to such variation. If we confined our observations to our own culture, we might easily be misled into the notion that certain familiar sentiments, practices, and relationships are instinctive or otherwise inevitable. By viewing the institutions of other cultures we discover that there are substitutes or alternatives for most, perhaps all, of these traits. Instead of being automatic products of our biological makeup, they are seen to vary with other culture complexes and with general environmental conditions. Any number of utterly divergent arrangements are found to "work" in divergent settings. However, we shall find little support for the idea that a custom can be picked up out of one culture and set down in the midst of another without causing some disturbance. For example, the adolescent "experimentation" of Samoans is followed by rather stable marriage in their culture; similar behavior in the United States has often been associated with instability and unhappiness. Thus another aspect of our perspective lies in the appreciation of the interrelatedness of traits. The Samoan family institution is not merely the sum of child-tending by little girls, sex freedom in adolescence, large households containing many kinsmen, and other separate traits. It is all of these taken together and viewed in their relation to the social system as a whole. No one of them can be understood apart from the rest, nor can the family be understood apart from its general cultural setting. Hence instead of starting with a comparison of marriage or inheritance or child care in many cultures, we shall examine in some detail the family system of one culture after another. At the end we shall turn to contemporary North American family systems.

Proceeding on the assumption that every type of family institution has a history of its own, we shall be on the lookout for evidence of changes that have taken place and other events which may be associated with them. In the case of the so-called "historical" cultures, as distinct from the "primitive" or nonliterate cultures, we shall note not only changes but also continuities.

Historical Backgrounds of Our Own Family System

For the purposes of this part of our study we shall begin with the ancient Hebrews, Chapter VII, whose family system displays both contrasts and similarities to our own. Some of their traits have come down fairly directly to us. Thus we still quote with approval "Honor thy Father and thy Mother." We hold to certain Old Testament rules about incest and perversions. We have not quite given up the "double standard" of sex morals. Some of us still take pride in our paternal family trees. But we have shifted our concern pretty largely from the extended to the nuclear family. We are witnessing the decline of male dominance and the almost complete disappearance of arranged marriages.

The Roman family in days of the Republic was much like that of the early Hebrews, the chief difference being strict adherence of the Romans to monogamy, while the Hebrews indulged in polygyny and concubinage. But after the Punic Wars and especially under the Empire came many changes. In the upper classes at least there was a partial emancipation of women; there were many unmarried adults and childless couples against whom various laws were directed; sexual license and divorce became notorious.

Against such conduct among their social "betters," the early Christians reacted vigorously. Being on a level somewhat akin to that of present-day millennial sects, they not only condemned the orgies of the elite; they called all sex vile. They sought to put women back "in their place." Anticipating the Second Coming of Christ, they looked upon marriage as either unimportant or distracting from "things of the spirit." Now it should be pointed out that the foregoing represents teachings of some Church Fathers. How far the rank and file followed them we do not know. But these teachings have not been without influence even in our own day.

Before pursuing further the influence of the Mediterranean world, we must note some of the contributions of northern Europe. It happens that the Anglo-Saxons were like the Hebrews and Romans in stressing the kinship group, male dominance, and rigorous discipline and control over children, but they carried none of these to the same extremes. Their families had perhaps equally inclusive functions. They had rather definite fiscal arrangements in connection with marriage which were carried over into the feudal system and, with modification, into modern England and colonial America.

Medieval England continued a semipatriarchal family system, but experienced some innovations. In importance the clan gave way to the household, which was still much larger than the marriage group. The economic emphasis increased. The Church claimed more and more authority over marriage, divorce, and all matters involving sex. Chivalry put some women on a pedestal and introduced a vogue of romantic love, though not in relation to marriage. Although chivalry was upper class, extramarital, and formalized, it left a literary heritage which has affected the status of women in later centuries. As a matter of fact, from the days of chivalry until now there has been considerable confusion in both the ideologies and the practices involving the status of the sexes. To the

Church woman represented both the Mother of God and the temptress of men. To the knights and ladies marriage was a duty, but love was a pleasure. To the masses of common people wives were apparently taken more or less for granted as helpers and mates. Among these same common people children apparently shared the privations, hardships, and toils of their elders. On socially higher levels they were often placed out to learn trades or the duties of knights and ladies, depending on their status. In all of this we see a mingling of Norman and Anglo-Saxon elements, the former being drawn in part from the classical antiquity already discussed.

Between the Reformation and the Industrial Revolution there were again innovations and continuities. The typical English family was still semipatriarchal, there was great concern about economic aspects of marriage, the double standard was still in vogue, children had rather formal relations with their elders, and the family continued to perform an inclusive array of functions. But the status of woman was slowly changing—apparently there was more rough-and-ready comradeship; romantic love occasionally led to marriage; there were a few protests against the subordination of women; chivalric adoration of the lady was replaced by Platonic love. Amid the conflict of Church and State for control of marriage divorce practically disappeared, although annulment and legal separation left ways out for the rich. Also there were many "clandestine" marriages of couples that circumvented or ignored the onerous formal requirements of the day.

This gives some notion of the state of affairs at the time English colonists were coming to North America. Naturally they established on these shores a semipatriarchal type of family life, with male dominance over fairly large households. In the North rebellion against the established church was reminiscent of the early Christians with their rigid code of sex mores. The New England revolt involved making civil marriage the rule and reestablishing divorce. But it did not eliminate the economic emphasis in domestic arrangements, nor did it discard Old Testament rules concerning kinship and affinity. Also as in old England, children were rather severely treated. However, the necessities of colonial existence broke down some of the old controls. There was increasing freedom in choice of mates, and romantic love more frequently led to matrimony.

In the South there were similarities and differences. The large, semipatriarchal household was usually on a plantation instead of in a town. Vestiges of chivalry lingered on. In the back country a scarcity of clergymen and magistrates made "common law" marriage quite general, continuing the tradition of "clandestine" marriage in England, though in somewhat different form. The presence of slaves was the occasion of interracial concubinage and of mother-centered, unstable families among the Negroes. In both North and South the functions of the family were quite inclusive: procreation; orientation; status-giving; economic organization and production; protection of the young, aged, and handicapped; control of personal conduct; and, increasingly, affection.

REFERENCES

Adams, Bert N., *The American Family*. Chicago: Markham Publishing Company, 1970.

Bain, F. W., *A Digit of the Moon*. New York: G. P. Putnam's Sons, 1905.

Christensen, Harold T., ed., *Handbook of Marriage and the Family*. Chicago: Rand McNally, 1964, Chapter I.

Kephart, William M., *The Family, Society, and the Individual*. Boston: Houghton Mifflin Company, 1966, Chapter I.

Levi-Strauss, Claude, "The Family," in Harry L. Shapiro, ed., *Man, Culture, and Society*. New York: Oxford University Press, 1960, Chapter XII.

Murdock, George Peter, *Social Structure*. New York: Macmillan Company, 1949.

Nimkoff, Meyer F., *Comparative Family Systems*. Boston: Houghton Mifflin Company, 1965.

Reiss, Ira L., *The Family System in America*. New York: Holt, Rinehart and Winston, 1971, Part One.

Part One

2 The Polyandrous Toda Family

The Todas, a pastoral, polyandrous Indian tribe numbering between five and six hundred members, are found in small villages scattered across the plateau of the Nilgiri Hills in South India. The highest peak in this range, Makurti, which rises to a height of 8,760 feet, is considered the domain of the chief Toda god, *Ön*. Surrounding it are the undulating hills and fertile valleys that provide pasture ground for the Toda buffalo. These hills average about 7,000 feet above sea level.

The origin of the Todas is obscure. Centuries of geographical and social isolation have permitted the indigenous growth of a culture, social organization, and genetic stock different in striking respects from these features of nearby hill tribes and from the general cultural patterns of the peoples of the plains of South India.

Physically the Todas are an impressive people. The men are tall, light-brown complexioned, robust, and bearded. Both men and women let their luxuriously black hair grow long down their backs, and both wear distinctive cloaks, their major garment, vertically striped with intricately embroidered edges. They are peaceful, intelligent, dignified, and regal in bearing. They place themselves definitely above the three neighboring hill tribes, which stand in a service relation to them. Their distinctive appearance and customs have made them an object of tourist curiosity as well as a subject of anthropological study.

Toda social organization is complex. The tribe is divided into two endogamous moieties or major divisions, one called

Tarthar and the other *Teivali*.[1] Each of these divisions is further subdivided into a number of exogamous clans, ten for the *Tarthar* and six for the *Teivali*.[2] Clans, by our usage, are characterized by rules of descent *and* residence; thus it is the clans that occupy the many little villages which dot the Nilgiri Hills.

A second major order of Toda social organization exists in the form of nonresidential exogamous sibs or consanguineal groups. These sibs, six of which are patrilineal and five matrilineal, cut across all Toda society, including the major divisions or moieties. Inasmuch as both forms of sib groupings are operative, the kinship system of the Todas is technically recognized as one of dual descent.[3]

Stewardship of the buffalo is the theme which permeates and orients Toda social organization. In the creation myth of the Todas it is said that the great god, *Ön*, brought forth a large number of buffalo out of the earth. *Ön's* wife, *Pinârkûr*, in turn brought forth a larger number of buffalo. Behind *Ön's* buffalo there came out of the earth a man, holding the tail of the last buffalo. This was the first Toda. *Ön's* buffalo were sacred; those of *Pinârkûr* were ordinary. In its elaboration, the myth establishes the sacredness of some buffalo, the dominant position of the male, the stewardship of buffalo as the task of the Toda, and the image of a static society. In the centuries of Toda existence, these elements have never lost their saliency.

The herds of sacred buffalo are maintained by the larger

1. W. H. R. Rivers, *The Todas* (1906). This monograph with corrections and amplifications by Emeneau and Mandelbaum constitutes the basic reference for the chapter. A summary of Toda culture is found in George P. Murdock's *Our Primitive Contemporaries* (1934).

2. See Murray B. Emeneau, "Toda Culture Thirty-five Years After: An Acculturation Study," *Annals of the Bhandarkar Oriental Research Institute*, 19 (1938); "Toda Marriage Regulations and Taboos," *American Anthropologist*, 39 (1937); also "Language and Social Forms: A Study of Toda Kinship Terms and Dual Descent" in A. I. Hallowell, et al., *Language, Culture and Personality* (1941).

3. The matrilineal sib, missed by Rivers, *op. cit.*, was identified and described by Emeneau, *op. cit.* (1935), (1937), and (1941).

divisions of the tribe. The *Tarthars* are stewards of the most sacred buffalo and perform, with a priest drawn from the *Teivali* ranks, the more elaborate dairying ritual. The sacred dairies themselves are located apart from the villages and on sacred ground. Around these dairies has emerged the stylized dairying ritual in which an all-male order of dairy priests performs the sacred tasks of churning and clarifying the butter, or *ghi*. For it is only as *ghi* that the milk of the sacred buffalo can be touched by a nonpriest.

A village consists of several small, parabola-shaped huts, a dairy where the milk of the ordinary buffalo is processed as food, several buffalo pens, and possibly a shed for the buffalo calves. The ordinary buffalo graze in herds on the hills near the villages and are owned by family groups. Even in the villages dairying is performed ritualistically and is restricted to male members of the families, who must also cook any food in which milk or milk products are used.

As the seasons change the buffalo herds are moved to the best pastures, and the Todas may move to new villages in other parts of the plateau. Although there are perhaps ninety villages, not more than two thirds will be occupied at any one time.

In addition to neighboring hill tribes there has been in the last century an influx of people from the plains area below. Although the Todas live in an area of less than 500 square miles, they have at various times found in their midst British governmental officials who established summer provincial headquarters there, other Europeans, Anglo-Indians, Mohammedans, a variety of lowland Hindus, and, of course, the inevitable tourists. The cool summer months on the plateau make the Nilgiri Hills a haven for those who otherwise would swelter in the torrid heat of the Madras plains.

Unlike the Hopi, whose plateau keeps them isolated from outsiders, the Todas have been unable to escape physical contiguity and social contact with other groups carrying diverse cultures. But despite the ubiquitous outsider, the Todas have maintained remarkable cultural integrity and cohesion. The British authorities respected the territorial claims of the Todas and kept their grazing lands intact through government edict. Buffalo herds were kept up and the sacred dairying places were maintained in good order by the Todas without interference or the competition of agriculture or industry. Emeneau's restudy of the Toda people thirty-five years after Rivers' could show only one distinct item of social change: the young men of one sib grouping had taken to wearing gaily colored neckerchiefs![4]

As formidable as has been the Toda resistance to the ways of the outside, the passing years, especially those since World War II, have seen both a decline in Toda population and the beginnings of cultural change. Survival alone in the face of diseases that threaten to decimate the tribe has forced the Todas to seek medical help from the outside. B. N. Das, Indian anthropologist, who "has not been content to treat the Todas as a museum piece," reports recent changes, some of which he has helped bring about. Among the more notable are the beginnings of a Toda agriculture, the decline of dairying and the attendant reduction in number of sacred and ordinary dairying sites, the conversion of some Todas to Christianity, the transformation of polyandry into what he has termed "brittle monogamy," the emergence of progressive-minded Toda youth, and the intervention in the affairs of the tribe by the Indian government.[5]

4. David G. Mandelbaum in a study of the Nilgiri Hills tribes underscored Emeneau's conclusions as to the resistance of the Todas to cultural change. See his "Cultural Change Among the Nilgiri Tribes," *American Anthropologist*, 43 (1941).

5. B. N. DAS, "The Toda in Changing Times," *The Rotarian* (May, 1957). In *Primitive India* (1954), Vitold de Golish, leader of a team of architects studying ancient and primitive Indian structures, reports a generalized sense of despair among the Todas, reinforced by the ravages of disease which at the time was decimating the tribe. Das holds a much more optimistic outlook, feeling that an intelligently directed welfare program of the Indian government including medical care, modern education, agricultural innovation, and, presumably, conversion to Christianity and monogamy through missionary activities would go far to revitalize the flagging Toda culture.

Family Structure

Marriage Institutions: Polyandry

Polyandry, reported in earliest written records of outside observers over 300 years ago and probably existing for centuries before, has been the characteristic marriage institution among the Todas. Since there are many varieties of heterosexual unions which have been misnamed polyandrous, it is worthwhile examining in closer detail the almost classic form in which polyandry is expressed in Toda culture.

The Toda female marries one male and at the same time becomes the wife of his brothers. Should other brothers be born subsequently they will also share equally in marital rights. Insofar as only brothers share a wife, the union may more precisely be termed fraternal polyandry. This form has predominated, but on occasion the marriage will include classificatory brothers—those of the same sib and age group—who may reside in the same or in other villages. Family life arrangements differ accordingly. When all live in one household and one of the brothers is with the wife, he places his cloak and staff outside the hut as a warning to the rest not to disturb him. The marital privileges rotate equitably among the brothers, and there is remarkably little friction or jealousy engendered by the arrangement.

When a wife becomes pregnant, there is no call to determine the biological father. Instead a rather remarkable practice is carried out to give the child a "social" or "legal" father. In a ceremony held about the seventh month of pregnancy, one brother, usually the eldest, is chosen to "give the bow." The pregnant woman retires to a wood accompanied ·by the chosen husband. There he fashions a ceremonial bow and arrow from twigs and grass and, in front of the relatives, presents these objects to the wife.[6] By this gesture he becomes the

6. The ceremony is actually much more involved, with gift exchange, fasting, and a variety of rituals which last through daybreak. See Rivers, *op. cit.,* pp. 319-323.

recognized, "legal" father of the unborn child, and should other children be born he will be their recognized father as well. However, usually after two or three children are born another brother will give the wife the bow and be the recognized father of all children born thereafter.

In cases when those sharing a wife are classificatory brothers the marital arrangements of necessity become more complicated—especially so if husbands live in separate villages. The rule generally applied in such cases is that the wife shall live with each husband in a turn of one month's duration. The selection of a recognized father proceeds by arrangement of the brothers as to who shall give the bow. The child's kinship or "blood" identification will vary, however, with the sib attachment of the recognized father.[7]

Female infanticide, cruel and harsh sounding to Western ears, has customarily been practiced by many nonliterate and some ancient peoples. The Todas not only engaged in this practice but by legend were said to have effected it by placing newly born female babies in the buffalo pens to be trampled. That they actually did this is doubtful, but the symbolism of sacrifice of the inferior female is clear enough and may have provided the rationale for the smothering of some newly born females. Whatever the motivation, the practice did exist until the present century and has been responsible for a sharp numerical discrepancy between the sexes. It would be unscientific to say any female infanticide *caused* polyandry among the Todas. However, once given a surplus of males over females, polyandry becomes a cultural innovation to insure heterosexual unions for all or nearly all male members of the tribe.

The close relationship of the two practices, female infanticide and polyandry, is underscored by their covariation. As the former declined and a realignment of the sex ratio took place, more wives became available to the male Todas. Brothers formerly sharing one wife found it possible each to marry and

7. For an elaboration, see *ibid.*, pp. 516-518.

consequently to share a number of spouses. The result has been a combination of polyandry and polygyny, in effect a form of group marriage. Should the sex ratio equalize, it is not unlikely—as Rivers hazarded a half century ago—that the polyandry-polygyny combination will be replaced by monogamy.[8]

Marriage Institutions: Wife Transfer

Many Todas are first married as children. It is, then, quite possible that when infant marriages occur in considerable number there will be later periods during which there are few females available for marriage. Widowers in a polyandrous society are always more numerous than widows. The Todas, who highly value heterosexual unions which supply a maximum of sexual outlets for males, have instituted a secondary marriage form which, in effect, amounts to wife transfer.

The Toda male in search of a wife is permitted by this practice to seek a mate from among those already married. Having selected one, he may, with permission of the girl's father, of two elders, and of the husband who has given her the bow, exchange a number of buffalo for the latter's wife. The number of buffalo agreed upon varies with the wealth of the wife-seeker.

Often in such exchanges the wife will be much younger than the new husband. For the husband left behind there is less iniquity in the situation than seems apparent. The younger man has now increased his fortune, his prestige is enhanced rather than damaged, and he is in a better competitive position than those older to find a young wife or to marry a child bride. A practice which might seem a threat to the marriage institution actually operates to insure an increased number of marriages and as a device to make available marriage partners for nearly all members of the tribe.

8. In the opinion of Das the preponderance of today's marriages among the Todas is monogamous. The Christian influence in the matter should not be overlooked.

Marriage Institutions: Consort-Mistress

A third custom permitting the union of men and women among the Todas brings together sexual partners from the two moieties. Inasmuch as these two divisions are endogamous the relationship cannot have the legitimacy of regular marriage. The arrangement corresponds roughly to what we would designate as "consort-mistress"; however, the Todas, in contrast to the Americans or the British, for example, have institutionalized the usage.

Such union may take the form of a woman living with a man as if she were his real wife with the exception that the children, if any, would be regarded as those of the legal husband, and in default of a legal husband she would be given the bow by some male member of her husband's sib. The second and more usual form finds the man paying visits to the woman at her husbands' house. Their consent is, of course, first secured, the agreement is confirmed by a third party, and an exchange of money or gifts is effected. A ceremony on the order of real marriage is held, and the new consort may either claim marital privileges in scheduled visits or assume what actually amounts to a husband's role and live with the cohusbands.

That these unions are not merely a variant of wife-lending is indicated by the fact that both consort and mistress have definitely assigned ceremonial duties, especially at funeral ceremonies, Thus, in addition to fraternal polyandry and wife transfer, the Todas have in a fashion almost incomprehensible to the American mind added a third institutionalized quasi-marriage form.

Family and Kinship

The Toda family is a composite of several nuclear, husband-wife marriage linkages in which one female is married to a number of brothers and to which are added the offspring and, usually, the parents of the brothers. The form of marriage already described is fraternal polyandry, while the family form is patrilocal, composite, and extended in the sense that brothers usually do not leave their families of orientation to marry. Rather the wife enters the family of the brothers. Thus two, three, or more generations are likely to be found in the typical Toda family.

The family may also increase in size by the addition of other wives. However, with the decrease in infanticide and consequent increase in proportion of females in the tribe, it has become a growing practice for a Toda male to marry, leave the family, and establish an independent household, either in the same village or in another village occupied by his clan.

The kinship system of the Todas is technically described as the Iroquois type.[9] The features exhibited by the Todas are: the classificatory manner of reckoning kinship, the use of both terms of reference and direct address, age-group differences expressed in terms of reference, and dual descent through sib or consanguineal organization. Such a system uses reference terms to indicate a *class* of persons, e.g., their equivalent of "father" not only includes the Toda's own male parents, but also his paternal uncles and all males of the father's clan and generation. In addition it includes the husbands of his maternal aunts. "Mother" similarly embraces his maternal aunts and other women of the same clan and generation, as well as the wife or wives of his various fathers.

The following make up the kinship reference terms for the Todas: great-grandfather, great-grandmother, grandfather, grandmother, father, mother, son, daughter, grandson, granddaughter, elder brother, younger brother, elder sister, younger sister, mother's brother and wife's father, father's sister and wife's mother, sister's son, sister's daughter, child of mother's brother or of father's sister, husband, wife, male relatives of wife, and son's wife. With the exception of the first two and the next to the last these terms of reference have attached to them a special derivative term for use in direct address.

9. See Emeneau, "Language and Social Forms: A Study of Toda Kinship Terms and Dual Descent," p. 161.

The list is larger than ours but modest by comparison with many other nonliterate groups. Some features may be noted; age differences are indicated for siblings, e.g., elder brother, younger brother, elder sister, and younger sister. Moreover, by virtue of the classificatory principle, all parallel cousins would be "brother" or "sister." Todas generally prefer to marry cross-cousins. In fact, when an unmarried Toda dies he is married after death to a cross-cousin. There are no bachelors in the Toda afterlife. Thus special terminological distinction is given to "child of mother's brother or of father's sister." Inasmuch as they are potentially spouses, cross-cousins instead of calling each other "brother" or "sister" call each other "husband" and "wife." In the same frame of reference "mother's brother" and "father-in-law" on the one hand, and "father's sister" and "mother-in-law" on the other, may use the same terms. This is a natural consequence of the regulation which ordains that the proper marriage for a man is one with the daughter either of his mother's brother or father's sister,[10] i.e., with a cross-cousin.

Descent, as indicated, follows both male and female lines. Patrilineal sib membership regulates a variety of Toda activities including ownership, rights, and duties with respect to the sacred herds of buffalo, pastures, dairies, and priorities in inheritance. Identification, however, is by major clan group. On the face of things the patrilineal sib seems to channel most behavior attributable to kinship; nevertheless, the role of the matrilineal sib is substantial inasmuch as it has equal weight with respect to rules of marriage. Clan membership is determined by the patrilineal sib affiliation and clans are exogamous but, on the other hand, one also may not marry a female member of his matrilineal sib. Further, the influence of the matrilineal sib predominates in matters of proper kinship relationships involved in funerals and mourning, dancing, ceremonials, and singing.[11] Thus the matrilineal sib plays an important part in the life of a Toda.

10. Rivers, *op. cit.*, p. 112.
11. See Emeneau, "Toda Marriage Regulations and Taboos."

Household, Property, and Inheritance

The Toda household revolves not so much about its members as about the stewardship of buffalo and attendant dairying activities. Husband, wife, and children occupy a room of a house or a subdivision of a double house. The Toda name for room and house is the same. Should there be only one room, the family as a whole will occupy it. Among the Todas an average of six persons in an eight feet by ten feet hut was noted nearly a century ago in the first Indian Census, and there is little evidence to indicate any lessening of the density of occupancy. In these small rooms, with their tiny entranceways not more than three feet high, with a smoking fire that has no chimney, the wife must confine her domestic activities to the rear while the men perform dairying operations and prepare milk products in the front. There is no room or hall set apart for bachelors as is often found among nonliterate tribes. In common with many tribes, however, the eldest brother usually assumes the role of head of the household.

Individual ownership extends in general to clothing, ornaments, and household possessions. A woman possesses very little property, mainly her dowry. Even the ornaments given her by a husband must be returned in the event that she is transferred to another husband.

Individuals and families may own ordinary buffalo, but those which are sacred, as well as the sacred dairies and the major villages, are held by clans. The Toda tribe as a whole does not own or hold property, nor is there any individual ownership of land. As herdsmen, the Todas must migrate with the buffalo; consequently the matter of land is, or has been, of little consequence except as it pertains to grazing and to dairy and village sites.

The house remains the most important possession of the family. It is held jointly by the brothers who inhabit it. Should a brother leave the household he has no property right in the house. If the brothers quarrel, the village head often decides that one brother, or more than one brother, shall occupy the house for a certain time, usually a year, and at the end of this period he (or they) shall move to another village, when another brother or brothers shall occupy the house.[12] Houses are never sold. Either they pass on to the male children of the brother(s), or they are deserted.

Inheritance of property is patrilineal, and only male descendants may inherit. The wife and her female offspring have no formally sanctioned method of acquiring property other than by receiving personal gifts or gifts presented as a dowry. If there is a focus to the matter of inheritance among the Todas, it must center upon the buffalo. So many ceremonies and rituals, including sacrifices at funerals, the giving of gifts, baptisms, and in wife exchange, directly involve these animals that money would seem less conceived of as value in itself and more simply in terms of what it can mean for the acquisition of buffalo.

The inheritance of buffalo is a matter of extreme importance to all male Todas. Although individuals may possess ordinary buffalo, in practice the brothers who live together will keep their animals in a herd which is treated as the property of the family. But whenever the occasion arises there are definite rules for the division of buffalo among them.[13] When a man owning a number of buffalo dies, the animals are not necessarily divided among the sons. For the buffalo to be passed on to the sons, the father must not have had his buffalo part of a common family herd. Should the sons inherit they will divide the buffalo equally with the exception that the oldest and youngest son will each receive an extra buffalo. Should there be only two sons, each will inherit equally, but should there be more than two sons and should there be an odd buffalo, it will go to the eldest son. It must be remembered that "sons" in this case refers to the offspring of one mother who has been "given the bow" by the brother, who then becomes their "legal" father.

12. Rivers, *op. cit.*, p. 559.
13. *Ibid.*, p. 506.

Household goods including dairying paraphernalia are equally divided among the sons so long as they live together. Should they separate permanently each brother receives an equal share. Money and male ornaments in such cases are also equally shared. Conversely, debts are inherited, and sons must pay the debts of the deceased father. Should there be no sons, the brothers must settle.

Family Cycle

In an earlier section of the chapter the marriage and quasi-marriage institutions of the Todas were described, and it may be recalled that fraternal polyandry predominates, that wife transfer exists as a secondary marriage form, and that a consort-mistress quasi-marriage form has also been institutionalized. It remains here to sketch the process by which mates are selected, and the roles of the principals involved.[14]

Infant marriages have been the rule among the Todas, and a child is sometimes married at the age of two or three years. Such marriages are arranged by the father of the boy. It is he who seeks a suitable mate for his son, taking care to observe the prevailing marriage regulations and taboos. Having decided upon a prospective daughter-in-law, he first visits the parents, makes the marriage arrangements, stays the night in the village—he will be in the village of another clan due to the rule of clan exogamy—and returns home the next day. A few days later he and the son travel to the village of the intended wife taking with them a loin cloth as a preliminary wedding gift. The boy salutes the father of the child, the mother, and the brothers, kneeling forward to be touched upon the forehead with each of the other's feet. The gift is presented to the girl, and father and son stay the night to return home the next day. Occasionally the girl returns with

14. Following Rivers, *ibid.*, pp. 502-539.

them to live with the family of her future husband, but more likely she will remain at home until she has passed the age of puberty.

Twice a year thereafter until the girl is ten years old the boy will bring her a loin cloth as a gift. After that he brings a cloak, or *putkûli,* the common garb of the Todas. A rather strange ceremony is performed shortly before the girl reaches puberty. A man from the opposite moiety comes to the girl's house during the daytime, lies down beside her, and covers both the girl and himself with a cloak. They remain there for a few minutes. Two weeks later a virile young man of any division or clan except that of the girl comes to the village for one night and has intercourse with the girl. This must take place before puberty, and, as it seemed to Rivers, "there were few things regarded as more disgraceful than that this ceremony should be delayed till after this period. It might be a subject of reproach and abuse for the remainder of the woman's life."[15]

A year or two after the defloration ceremony the girl joins her husband at his village. She is brought there by a group consisting of the husband, his parents, and a relative from the same clan. Before departing from the girl's village, however, they are given a feast by the family of the girl. After the feast the young husband puts five rupees into the girl's mantle, and the "wedding party" then departs. Other than the feast and the bride gift there is no ceremony. Either the boy or the girl has the option of vetoing the marriage at this time. If they choose to do so, fines are levied, one buffalo if the boy refuses and five to ten buffalo if the girl refuses. Under ordinary circumstances, however, the marriage goes ahead as planned, and the girl returns with her husband, taking with her her personal possessions and such dowry gifts as her parents and brothers choose to give her.

Such, then, has been the typical process of mate selection among the Todas. Wife transfer and the consort-mistress

15. *Ibid.,* p. 506.

arrangement have already been described. It remains only to
add that not all Todas are married in childhood. Should a
boy reach the age of fifteen or sixteen without having been
betrothed, he may initiate proceedings without intervention
by the father. Inasmuch as there is always a shortage of wives,
these young men as well as the widowers may have to be content with a child-wife.

Motherhood

When an expectant mother reaches the fifth month of
pregnancy a "village we leave, hand we burn" ceremony is
performed. She must retire to a small mud-and-sticks hut outside the village. There her husbands assist her in performing
a rather elaborate ritual whose imagery is drawn from the
Toda buffalo complex. With due respect to proper ceremony,
a meal of cereal is cooked and eaten. Then the woman makes
a small roll of threads, puts it into the fire, and burns herself
with the roll, twice on each hand. When the ceremony is over
the woman goes into the hut and remains in seclusion for
nearly a month.

Soon after, the "giving the bow" ceremony establishing
legal fatherhood, described previously, is performed. Now that
the anticipated child has an assigned father, the mother may
live as usual with the husbands and have her child delivered
in the home. During delivery the woman kneels with her head
on the husband's chest. He holds her head and a woman experienced in such matters assists with the delivery. There is no
formal ceremony attending the birth, but prayers are said to
facilitate a difficult delivery.

During the period when female infanticide was practiced
by the Todas a substantial proportion of the female babies
were smothered and buried without ceremony immediately
after birth. Also, if twins were born one was killed even
though both were boys. Today the practice has been discontin-
ued; even so, a preponderance of males still exists in the tribe.

The biological function of childbirth is associated by the

Toda with ideas of impurity. A few days after the birth mother and child retire to the same seclusion hut that was used in the hand burning ceremony. A variety of rites which initiate a ritual cleansing, again drawn substantively from the buffalo complex, are performed by husband and wife. Again she remains in the hut for a period of about a month, depending on the order of the child born and on the phase of the moon.

Childhood

Life for the Toda child begins in the intimacy of the seclusion hut. For three months afterwards its face is covered from all persons except the mother. One might expect that this intimacy, plus the fact that the mother will nurse the child for the next two years, would provide the basis for a strong psychogenic attachment between mother and child. It would also seem, on the surface of the matter, that the placidity of the even-tempered Toda might have as its foundation the security of a drawn-out period of mother-child intimacy, more so in light of the fact that Toda children are born in a family on the average of one every three years. Three to four children per wife constitutes the average number of offspring. After the passing of a three months' period during which the child's face has been covered, an uncovering ceremony, differing with the sexes, is performed. If a boy, the child will be taken to the front of the dairy and his head will be touched to the threshold. Next he will be taken to where the buffalo are standing, his face will be turned to the sun, and, for the first time, uncovered. If the child is a girl, she will be taken to the place where women receive buttermilk from the dairyman and there the mother will uncover her face. In either event the primacy of the buffalo in Toda culture is again reflected in the ceremonies.

The next important ceremony is the naming of the child. The father shaves the middle of the child's head as a preliminary step. Then a boy child is taken before his maternal uncle who names him and promises him a calf. If the baby is a girl, she is named by a female relative of the father; however no calf is promised her. The sexes receive different names, commonly derived from such things as prayer words, gods, hills, villages, dairies, buffalo pens, dairy vessels, and stones.[16] Once named the child is given its first prepared food, usually a gruel made of rice or millet and milk.

A carefree childhood is generally the lot of Toda children. Parents tend to be indulgent, exhibiting great fondness for their offspring. Even though only one brother might be the legal father, all brothers view the children affectionately and feel equal responsibility for their well-being. Playing games takes up a major portion of the children's time. They build artificial buffalo pens and fireplaces for sport, much as American children build tree houses, huts, or shacks of their own. A favorite child's toy is a small imitation buffalo horn. Although playthings, these horns carry a certain deeper significance inasmuch as they are burned with the bodies of males at cremation funerals. Youths practice a rather dangerous sport—hanging on to the horns and around the necks of buffalo. It might be noted that nearly all games in one way or another likewise reflect the cultural emphasis on buffalo stewardship. Rivers could find only one game, probably borrowed, which could be considered an exception.

There is, however, no organized sport among the Todas. Villages, clans, or moieties never engage in sport competition as entities. The chief sporting interest of the adults is watching the children engage in games which imitate the more serious occupations of their elders. In some cases the games so arising are useful in providing the younger members of the community with practice in feats they will later in life be called upon to perform.[17]

The adolescent male Toda finds himself already participating in the adult world. Likely he has been betrothed since

16. Murdock, *op. cit.*, p. 119.
17. Rivers, *op. cit.*, p. 599.

childhood. As soon as he could be of assistance he would have been taken to the grazing grounds to learn the herdsman's duties, and he would also have been initiated into some of the dairying rituals and routines. Should an older brother have already brought a wife into the family, he would have had marital privileges extended to him as soon as he was physically able to accept them.

The girl having reached adolescence would long have mastered the few domestic arts practiced by the Toda women, viz., pounding grain, fetching water, sweeping, cleaning, mending, and embroidering—the last the only domestic "fine art" of the women. Almost certainly by adolescence she would have been married to if not living with a husband. In all probability she would have experienced a variety of sexual contacts—virginity has no defined significance in Toda culture. From adolescence to motherhood the distance for the Toda female is relatively short.

Adulthood: Male

The round of life of the Toda male is unhurried, rhythmic, and, by our standards, relatively uneventful. Stewardship of the buffalo as a cultural focus so organizes the daily activities of the Toda that there appears justification in the viewpoint often expressed by the Todas that the buffalo are the substance and the man the shadow. In the morning the animals are unpenned, driven to grazing areas, grazed, driven back to their pens, and milked. Each day the milk of the previous evening is churned and processed into *ghi*. With the change from the wet to the dry season the buffalo herds may of necessity need to be driven to better pastures. Accommodatingly the Toda family moves with them. Or, as an alternative arrangement, one brother will follow the buffalo while another stays behind to head the household. In a month the itinerant returns, and the roles are exchanged. The routine of the occupation dominates the routine of the sexual union. Prosperity in one brings plenitude in the other.

The Toda cosmology sets forth no great body of spirits to be propitiated heavily, nor are there malignant and uncontrollable forces before which impotent man must cower. Rather Toda religion has eroded into a congeries of formalized and stylized rituals singularly devoid of mythical or spiritual substance. Yet it is these which bridge the gap of cultural and personal discontinuities. The hour, day, year, the changes, cycles, and crises—all are enveloped in formalized ritual or secularized routine. Feasts, ceremonies, holidays, special observances, visiting neighbors, or just sitting and reflecting, the Toda has time for them all. The Toda male walks erect. He lives in a viable world, attending to the buffalo as a matter of dedication, attended by woman as a matter of course, served by neighboring tribes as a matter of right by virtue of superior status.

Adulthood: Female

A much more subservient and subordinate role is played in the Toda society by the female. Inasmuch as the ceremonial of the dairy has a predominant place in the lives and thoughts of the people, the exclusion of women from any share in this ceremonial has produced an almost insuperable status differential. Moreover, such biological functions as menstruation and childbearing have had associated with them ideas of impurity—even extending to the seclusion hut the same uncleanliness imputed to a corpse. The women are further made aware of their inferior status by the fact that they may not cook food in which milk or milk products are used. The preparation of food, incidentally, is a function of the female sex in a preponderant number of societies, nonliterate and modern. And it is the woman who bows her head to receive the foot in the conventional salutation. Finally, not only must she avoid the sacred dairies and stay out of the front portion of the hut where the husband churns the buttermilk, but the Toda woman must walk only on certain paths, taking special pain to avoid those traversed by the buffalo.

The patrilocal rule becomes a pivot around which many relationships favorable to the male revolve. The bride moves to the house and village of her husband and his clan. There the patrilineal sib emphasis makes it impossible for her to participate in a variety of activities such as property holding, dairying, herding, family decisions, the naming of males, matters pertaining to migration, building, divining, sorcery, and to a considerable extent the privilege of staying mated to the same person or group.

By American standards the positive side could hardly be called luminous. Nevertheless there are specified functions for the Toda woman, and, in view of the operation of the matrilineal sib, she always carries a modicum of kinship status. In a kinship system which has always had less than a thousand persons in its range of application, no female who marries and has offspring can, in terms of the system, be inconsequential. A kinship term of reference is extended her from birth through great-grandmotherhood.

The mundane household activities of the Toda woman have already been indicated; pounding grain, sweeping, cleaning, and sewing make up the majority. Once such tasks have been accomplished, the woman has considerable leisure and personal freedom. There being no way legitimately for the Toda female to compete with the male, one basis for marital tension is eliminated. Toda women reflect an attitude of equanimity and good will. Although they are in an obviously subordinate role, it does not seem to depress them. They are not without a sense of vanity, for much of their leisure time is spent in curling and greasing their abundant black hair. They cherish ornaments and, of the two sexes, only they tattoo themselves—on neck, chest, and shoulders.

Ethnographers seem agreed that the social and personal relations between the sexes are on the whole amiable and pleasant. Not that there are no quarrels, for petty household arguments take place among the Todas the same as in most families everywhere. Both sexes are known for the frankness of their remarks, yet after many months of investigation

Rivers could report that he had never seen nor heard anything to indicate that women are treated harshly or contemptuously. The imbalance of the sexes has assured marital unions for virtually all Toda women. Moreover, in view of the many institutionalized forms of marriage and quasi-marriage and the looseness of the sex mores generally, it is evident that few if any Toda women have gone through life deprived of either variety or number of sexual contacts.

Old Age

Age-grading operates in most nonliterate societies to allocate prestige according to age. Among the Todas this is generally the case, although the status of the male is more likely to advance than is that of the female. As the Toda grows older, his personal fortune is likely to increase. Economic resources permitting, he will be in a position as a mature man by buying off his brothers' "share" to indulge in the luxury of a wife of his own, or he may add a wife to the family. Again he may divorce his wife to marry another woman; or, again perfectly legitimately, he may exchange wives with another Toda. Should he be widowed, he may without restriction marry any eligible Toda woman or girl, regardless of age.

With his sons to assist him and care for him in his later maturity, the old Toda is in a sense insured against many of the hazards that befall the aged in other parts of the world. If he falls ill, he will be cared for by members of the family; should he fall into debt, his sons will assume his obligations; and should he die, he is further assured of an elaborate funeral in which buffalo will be sacrificed to be of use to him in the afterlife.

At some point the aging Toda will turn over his buffalo to a son, usually the eldest. In default of brothers to the old Toda to serve as household head, the son will assume that role. Although the elder Todas who have passed down their property and authority have no specially designated status, they are nevertheless guaranteed shelter, sustenance, and respect for the rest of their lives. At the funeral of Laxam, a young female Toda, in the chanting of all the sins she could possibly have committed two of those especially designated were: "sleeping on a bed and letting one's father-in-law sleep on the ground," and "sitting on the veranda and driving one's mother-in-law from it."[18]

When a Toda father or mother dies, the brothers and children and the rest of the clan arrange a rather spectacular cremation funeral as a preliminary to which, as indicated, a number of buffalo will be sacrificed. Also as an indication of respect, although there is no appreciable ancestor cult, the members of the family will henceforth remember the day of the week on which the death took place. Such a day is given a special term in the language of the Toda.

One avenue of status that is open to the aging Toda is service on the clan or supreme tribal council. To attain a seat in either is not only to enhance one's status but also to attain the power that accrues to a position of political power. Among council members it is also the case that the oldest wield the most influence.

The net result seems to be that fewer of the handicaps and hazards experienced by the old in our society are the lot of their Toda counterparts. The Toda family, as with the Hindu families in the larger Indian society, is extended with several generations living together as a unit, and is buttressed by an age-grading system that channels an equitable amount of status to its senior members. Although the average life span is not great, again in contrast to our own society the males live as long as females, if not longer.

Disjunctions

The "broken" family in the conventional sense of the word is an unlikelihood for the Todas inasmuch as the mar-

18. de Golish, *op. cit.*, p. 18.

riage group or household normally contains sufficient members to absorb and provide a relatively complete family life for any one member who has lost a wife, husband, or parent. Widows are assured their bench, and it is not unknown for a Toda with his own wife to send her back to her family in order that he might marry the wife of a deceased brother. The principle behind this, the *levirate,* is not commonly practiced among the Todas simply because under polyandry a wife may lose a husband but will still remain in the marriage group as a wife to his brother(s).

There are few orphans found among the Todas. But if a child is left an orphan, it is looked after by the people of its clan. It is always clearly recognized that the child retains the father's property and belongs to the clan of its father.[19] Curiously, the Todas do not practice adoption.

Suicide occurs very infrequently among the Todas. Much more frequent is the threat of suicide. Under proper conditions of exasperation the Toda may threaten to strangle himself, "My neck tying, I will die," or that he will poison himself, "Opium taking, I will die."[20]

More common among the acts that are disjunctive or disruptive to the ongoing society is divorce. Two grounds are possible: one that the wife is incompetent mentally and the other that she will not work. Should a woman prove barren, the usual recourse of the husband is not to divorce her but to take a share in a second wife. The Todas have no concept of adultery; intercourse between a wife and another man is not regarded as a reason for divorce, but rather as a perfectly natural occurrence.[21] The divorce proceedings are simple. The husband merely sends his wife back to her family. She can take with her only her dowry. The husband, on the other hand, must pay a fine, usually a buffalo, to the wife's people. There seems to be no conception of property use in the

19. Rivers, *op. cit.,* p. 549.
20. *Ibid.,* p. 555.
21. *Ibid.,* p. 556.

females, who by our standards are moved about as chattel. The fine the husband pays for the divorce is identical to what he would have paid if he had been betrothed as a child and had refused to marry the girl when she reached a marriageable age.

Family Controls

Conceivably the family as a unit of social organization may play a passive or active role in the generation, refinement, and the application of social controls. In many nonliterate, folk, and peasant societies the family in fact may be much less of an independent or semi-independent, autonomous or semiautonomous entity, as we view the family in modern Western civilization. For the Todas the family remains a yet unperfected, only partially formed institution. For at least a thousand years the distinctive residence unit of the tribe has been the clan. In assessing the various controls, external and internal, formal and informal, rational and irrational, it must be remembered that the Toda family is a social institution *in becoming*.

Many recognized forms of social control do not exist in this primitive Indian tribe. There are no wars, nor threats of wars, nor is there intratribal strife. The Todas have two weapons, the club and the bow and arrow. Both are used for ceremonial purposes, much as are the swords of fraternal lodge members in America. They have no well-formed ancestral cult on which their energies or loyalties must be expended. Nor have they written laws or rules, codified and bound in volumes of statutes, decisions, and rulings. Further they are without courts. There is little continuity in the dealings and the judgments of the councils; on the whole cases are dealt with *ad hoc*, the council members informed to some extent by a body of customs and traditions.

One key to Todas' social control lies in the terms ritual and ceremonial. These forms of collective action so envelop and suffuse tribal society that it would seem the institutions of family, clan, and moiety exist simply as instrumentalities to stage and perform them. Many of the rites and ceremonies which originally served an observable or demonstrable function are now simply repeated for their own sake, devoid of the meaning that brought them into existence. If asked why he shaves a band around his child's head, the Toda father would doubtless say, "Because he is a child, and a child's head is always shaved thus." Without some deeper explanation such actions may be said to be the product of irrational controls.

If the Toda family does not feel the impingement of such external forces as state, church, corporate association, army, spirits of ancestors, etc., it is nevertheless an agency for the expression of tribal, clan, and even village folkways. Although there are few external *rational* controls impinging on the Toda family, there are many *traditional* controls and a variety of *nonrational,* ceremonial acts which rigidly channel action.

The tradition-bound controls that form a framework for family interaction take the form of rules or prescriptions. The most significant aggregation of these rules, rules which have some logical coherence, is found in the Toda kinship system. Since the structure of this system has already been outlined, we shall here be content to ennumerate some of the specific kinship taboos as they directly affect marriage and the Toda family. The general rule is that no one marries outside his moiety, nor inside his clan, nor with anyone in either his patrilineal or matrilineal sib. A variety of taboos reflect the application of this rule to a specific social relationship. Inasmuch as sexual intercourse with a clan member or a sib member of the opposite sex is prohibited, it follows that most other taboos are to be considered as avoidances to sexual incitement.[22] Such taboos in effect state who shall avoid whom in order that the temptations of sex may not arise. Avoidance taboos begin at puberty for the boy and girl. They apply to relations of parents and young children, between parents and

22. Emeneau, "Toda Marriage Regulations and Taboos," p. 108.

adult children, between father-in-law and daughter-in-law, and between mother-in-law and son-in-law.

Many other taboos channel and restrict personal and social contact: who may sing together, dance together, perform mourning ceremonials in each other's presence, and even recite poems together. Although husbands and wives may in their own discussions use frank or what is considered indecent language, the same words are taboo with reference to clan and sib relations. Reference, whether direct or by circumlocution, is forbidden to sexual intercourse, menstruation, the private parts, including by extension to nipple, navel, the armpit, and pubic hair, to the excreta, or breaking wind.[23] This by no means exhausts the list of tabooed words or subjects. With the operation of both clan and dual sib in providing a range for these taboos, the effect on social relationships is interesting. At any large gathering the discussions must necessarily be constricted linguistically because of the likelihood of violation of the language taboos. On the other hand husband and wife have the greatest freedom in the language of their intercourse, infinitely more so than, for example, the husband with his sister. The result can be seen in the ease of interpersonal relations of husband and wife, on the one hand, and the willingness to take the formal, sometimes meaningless, cut-and-dried language of the ceremonial which in effect has been "taboo-tested" in large gatherings, on the other.

The listing of taboos extant in a primitive tribe is an interesting but almost unending task. Analysis of a related grouping usually indicates a rationale—a set of fundamental beliefs in terms of which the taboos lose much of their husk of irrationality. For the Todas some of the more basic beliefs are the sacredness of buffalo, the dominance of the male, the impurity of the corpse, the impurity of biological functions, especially female, the anathema of incest, and mysteriousness (vaguely felt) or, in some sense, mystical power of women. From these and possibly others the welter of taboos springs.

23. *Ibid.,* p. 109.

Todas seek guidance or ask supplication in prayers to the deities, clan and tribal. There is no totemism, except that the buffalo in a sense is a grand totem for the tribe. No other animals figure in what religious ideology the Todas have remaining. By and large the prayers center around dairying, buffalo, and things related to the buffalo complex. They are for the most part said by dairy priests and individuals performing dairying operations. When misfortune befalls the Toda he seeks an explanation from a diviner—there are a handful of those to whom are attributed powers of divination. Misfortunes are divined to be either the fault of the sufferer or of a sorcerer. In the latter case the sorcerer must be propitiated.

The discussion of controls has dwelt mainly on those which impinge upon the Todas. Those which emanate from the family itself are relatively few. The engendering of consensus based on free give-and-take among family members is impossible in light of the pressure of custom, convention, and taboo. The Toda family is in no position to generate its own controls out of "do it yourself" rituals and ceremonies. Clans, through their clan councils, decide on the propriety of and necessity for the major ceremonials. And the presence of three generations under one roof makes almost impossible the intimacy of an independent nuclear family. Toda family relations upon analysis tend for the most part to consist of a multitude of observances of the rules of kinship and attendant taboos.

Family Functions

From the foregoing it is clear that the Toda family is a significant although by no means full-fashioned institution. The whole social structure of the tribe has been erected around two images: man as a steward of the sacred buffalo and man as an infinitely libidinous being. From the standpoint of the Todas the polyandrous marriage and the composite family function admirably in the service of each image. The Toda buffalo is a superior beast to its lowland counterpart, the Indian water buffalo. Only half-domesticated, migratory, it needs the hill herdsman, not the dairy farmer, to minister to its needs. The Toda family can provide personnel for herding and personnel for dairying. The nuclear basis of all families, husband-wife-children, need never be disrupted by the contingencies of occupation. If one father (husband) leaves, another is present. When all are present, extra-wife sexual outlets are readily available and seldom avoided. Male and female Todas share a sex freedom uncommon in the annals of ethnography, unthinkable to the Western mind.

Child marriage reduces the contingencies of spouse-hunting and lowers intensity of competition for husbands and wives which in many societies builds to a fever pitch through adolescence into young adulthood. The age at which marriages are consummated between husband and wife is no earlier than may be found in some of our own states. Polyandry prevents the tragedy of the virgin widow doomed to her weeds (a common enough sight in Hindu India). Toda women, despite the high incidence of sexual contacts, do not seem overburdened with childbearing nor saddled with an impossible set of household duties and social obligations. Few societies provide the leisure and freedom accorded the Toda woman.

The sexual adventuresomeness of the Toda male, if Kinsey can be believed, has its roots in the biology, not the culture, of man. It is given the greatest possible expression in Toda culture, and there is no residue of guilt to follow its wake.

For her part the Toda woman need never feel that due to marriage she has been prematurely shelved, doomed to a routine of cooking, cleaning, and child care. Grandmothers come young in Todaland. A forty- to fifty-year-old grandmother in the household makes for infinitely less work and strain on the mother. And, so much the better, the husbands do most of the cooking.

The composite family has the advantages of number, advanced division of labor, and versatility. The security it provides is, of course, legend. Yet the married males and a wife, not a congress of kinfolk, make up its nucleus. The child has an intimate relation with its mother, and yet is exposed to the multiple contacts and wide range of roles that only an extended family can offer. No child need find himself unprepared occupationally. The exercise of choice may be slight, for job and wife, yet few Todas have fallen victim to the urban tropism that has filled to the bursting point the major cities of India.

The other side of the coin, the dysfunctions, need be noted. Toda society, even in the hills of India, is today an anachronism. In the face of modern world political, economic, social, and moral movements it has only the formula of physical and cultural withdrawal to offer. Its uniqueness has been its downfall. The excessive formality of its ceremonials and the use of money to compete for or buy a newer, prettier, or more exciting wife, the inability to set up or even properly receive health services in face of the threatened decimation by syphilis, and the deterioration of its religious ideology into ceremonial formalism, may be charged against the tribe and its institutions.

The Toda family represents the most classic instance of polyandry in operation. It can survive only through the intervention or guardianship of a larger, outside society—one which could be tolerant of female infanticide and which would insulate the Todas from any economic activities other than the traditional herding and dairying. The British could assure only the latter, the Indian government neither. Restudy of the Toda family should of necessity focus on an institution in a process of change, of becoming.

REFERENCES

Breeks, James Wilkinson, *An Account of the Primitive Tribes and Monuments of the Nilgiris.* London: India Museum, 1873.

Das, B. N., "The Toda in Changing Times," *The Rotarian* (May, 1957), pp. 32-34.

Emeneau, Murray B., "Toda Marriage Regulations and Taboos," *American Anthropologist,* XXXIX (1937), pp. 103-112.

———, "Toda Culture Thirty-five Years After: An Acculturation Study," *Annals of the Bhandarkar Oriental Research Institute,* XIX (1938), pp. 101-121.

———, "Language and Social Forms: A Study of Toda Kinship Terms and Dual Descent," in Hallowell, A. I. et al., *Language Culture and Personality.* Menasha, Wisconsin: Sapir Memorial Publication Fund, 1941, pp. 158-179.

de Golish, Vitold, *Primitive India,* trans. by Nadine Peppard. London: George G. Harrap & Co., 1954.

Kapadia, Kanailal M., *Marriage and Family in India.* London: Oxford University Press, Indian Branch, 1958.

Karve, Irawati, *Kinship Organization in India.* Poona, India: Deccan College Monograph Series, 1953.

King, W. Ross, "The Aboriginal Tribes of the Nilgiri Hills," *Journal of Anthropology,* No. 1 (1870), pp. 18-51.

Mandelbaum, David G., "Culture Change Among the Nilgiri Tribes," *American Anthropologist,* XLIII (1941), pp. 19-26.

Marshall, William E., *A Phrenologist Amongst the Todas.* London: Longmans, Green and Co., 1873.

Murdock, George Peter, "The Todas of Southern India," in *Our Primitive Contemporaries.* New York: The Macmillan Company, 1934, pp. 107-134.

Peter, Prince of Greece and Denmark, *A Study of Polyandry.* The Hague: Mouton & Co., 1963, Part 2, Chapter III.

Rivers, W. H. R., *The Todas.* London and New York: The Macmillan Company, Ltd., 1906.

3 The Matrilineal Hopi Family

Deep in the desert region of northern Arizona on three adjoining mesas live the Hopi Indians. Today they number some 4,000 people, a remnant of the 20,000 the Spanish found at the time of the conquest. Isolated as they are, these people have passed on the same traditions and the same genetic material generation after generation until today they are homogeneous culturally and physically. We will consider the Hopi of mid-twentieth century, but couch our description in the present tense.

The three mesas on which the Hopi have built their twelve villages in turn rise from a vast semidesert plateau, itself 6,000 feet above sea level. Into the stony mass of the mesa seeps the rare moisture of the area to emerge again as springs at the base of its southern escarpments.

It is near these springs with their life-giving waters that the Hopi have built their villages, for without water even these industrious agriculturists could not maintain their precarious existence. And it is a precarious existence which they eke out in a land where the annual few inches of rain falls in torrential summer downpours, furrowing the arid earth with brief torrents which may flood the fields and sweep away the crops rather than provide the occasional moisture they need. In some years there may be no rain at all, and in others that which falls is not sufficient to bring the plants to maturity.

These are not the only threats posed by a menacing environment. Killing frosts may cut short the brief growing season, fierce sandladen winds may cut the growing plants to ribbons, or rodents may steal food, none of which can be spared. Little wonder that the Hopi attempt to ward off these dangers in their ceremonials and in the storing of food for one to three years ahead. If the ceremonials fail or the springs run dry, many will starve, and the threat of famine hangs heavy over their heads even in the green years.

Hopi crops are planted at the bases of the mesas. The principal crop is maize of a hardy variety designed to withstand the onslaughts of weather, insects, and rodents. Most of the maize is planted in flat fields, where it is irrigated by flood waters sweeping down from higher ground. Some is planted, with beans, on sand dunes where high moisture content allows it to grow without irrigation. Orchards (of peaches, apricots, pears, and apples) and vegetable gardens are planted near the base of the cliffs where moisture seeps through or springs flow.

The Hopi villages, which are built on top of the mesas, consist of one or more large, terraced, multiple-room dwellings built of mud, sticks, and stones. Living rooms are on the upper floor; rooms for the storage of produce are on the lower. For purposes of defense there are a few openings.

In these dark rooms the family lives surrounded by its simple possessions. In one corner may be a fireplace of mud whose smoke ascends through a wicker hood and a chimney of bottomless pots. In another corner are the water jars. Along one wall are three graded *metates* for grinding maize into flour. About the floor are strewn a few blankets or skins upon which the family sleeps.

Add to this picture a few open spaces swept by the desert winds and baked by the desert sun in the cold thin air, and a few stocky, broad-faced, brown-skinned people, and the setting is complete.

Family Structure

Marriage and Family Organization

Monogamy to the exclusion of all other forms is the characteristic marriage institution of the Hopi. Husband, wife, and children make up the nuclear group which becomes a unit in the larger extended family. Inasmuch as rules of matrilineal descent and matrilocal residence are observed, the Hopi household is distinguished, according to one authority, by ". . . the fact that a mature woman, her daughters, and occasionally her granddaughters, occupy a common residence through life and bring up their children under the same roof."[1] This description may obscure somewhat the role of the nuclear family, to be discussed later. On the other hand, we should not overlook the fact that the most significant nonresidential kinship unit is a group of blood relatives traced through the female line, which owns most of the property including the home, which owns and operates the ceremonials, and which is the basis of kin groupings larger than the family. In our terminology this grouping is called the matri-sib.[2]

The matri-sibs carry with them other features, two of which may be mentioned here. Each has its totemic counterpart: bear, lizard, eagle, or other animal. And all matri-sibs are gathered into a handful of constellations or superorders which we call phratries. The phratry is exogamic; thus marriage cannot take place between matri-sibmates within the same phratry, and, as we shall see, the phratry constitutes an important ceremonial unit of the Hopi.

Terminology and Kinship Orientation

The family and household are the Hopi institutions in which the individual forms those associations and learns those patterns of reciprocal behavior which become the prototypes of most of his later associations and behavior in the society at large.

1. Mischa Titiev, *Old Oraibi* (1944), pp. 45-46. By permission of Harvard University Press.
2. The term "clan" is used by many writers to describe this unit. Since there are no clear-cut residential groups organized by blood lines and integrated into operating political and social units among the Hopi, the use of "sib" seems more appropriate.

The kinship terminology reflects this fact. One calls one's own mother, her sisters, and all women of her generation in the matri-sib by the single term "mother." One's mother's brother and all males of his generation in the matri-sib are called "mother's brother." Mother's or father's father and all males of their generation in the matri-sib are called "grandfather." Mother's or father's mother and any old women of their generation in the matri-sib are called "grandmother." All men and women of one's own generation and matri-sib are called "brother" and "sister." All men and women in one's father's generation and matri-sib are "father's brother" and "father's sister." All children of men in one's own matri-sib are "brother's child." All children of women of one's own matri-sib are "sister's child."

As noted, each matri-sib is part of a larger exogamous unit, the phratry, and kinship terms and obligations are extended to cover one's own phratry and the phratry of one's father. The same terminology and behavior are likewise extended to the phratry of one's ceremonial father, and, if one has been cured of a serious illness, to the phratry of the medicine man who cured him. The result is that one finds himself related to about one half of the members of his village. Naturally, not all of these connections are of equal importance. Titiev has listed them in descending order of importance as follows: *INCEST*

1. Limited family, consisting of own parents, brothers, and sisters.
2. Mother's sisters and their children.
3. Other members of own household.
4. Other members of own clan.
5. Father's household.
6. Other members of own phratry.
7. Other members of father's clan-phratry.
8. Ceremonial father's clan-phratry.
9. Doctor father's clan-phratry.[3]

Marriage is actually or theoretically forbidden within the first seven categories but permitted within the last two.

3. Titiev, *op. cit.,* p. 13. By permission of Harvard University Press.

The reciprocal behavior which goes with these kin relations determines many of the attitudes and activities of the Hopi. A brief description of several of these patterns will throw light on the family life of the Hopi as well as on the way in which the familial pattern itself is projected into society as a whole.

1) Husband-Wife

The most important factor in this pattern is the relative position of the husband and wife in the household. The husband is a guest in his wife's household, his closest connections being with his mother's household. The wife, on the other hand, remains in the house in which she has been reared, and in the event of a family quarrel is backed by a solid wall of kin. Perhaps as a result of this difference in position the Hopi husband will often act toward his wife with seeming formality if not brusqueness. In general, however, the bond between husband and wife is variable and depends largely on the characters of the individuals concerned.

2) Father-Son

There is a much closer connection between father and son here than one might expect in a matrilineal society. The sexual division of labor tends to strengthen this bond, for the boy receives from his father much of his instruction in herding, farming, and weaving. Also, jural authority is divided with the boy's uncle, thus permitting easier relations between father and son. In childhood years the bond is less intimate but even then the father makes toys for the child. After the Kachina initiation, described below, and until marriage, the bond is very close and is characterized by mutual consideration for each other's welfare. When a man dies, his son buries him and inherits, directly, much of his father's property. This close tie between father and son does not extend to classificatory fathers; they are, however, treated with friendliness and react in turn by bestowing gifts and attention on their "sons." In general one might say that the bond between real son and father derives its character less from any ideal pattern to be applied to all "fathers" than from a natural affection which is to be expected where contact and cooperation are close and intimate and where the exercise of authority and the disciplining of the son does not rest solely with the male parent.

3) Mother's Brother-Sister's Son

This is the reciprocal relation which should most influence a boy's life according to the classic idea of a matrilineal society. Actually the real father takes over much of the role one might expect the mother's brother to play. The mother's brother is the disciplinarian, and his authority is drawn from his position as the male member of the mother's generation who is in one's own sib and lineage. He carefully supervises the boy's upbringing so that the boy may some day be a reliable worker, and in doing so he often resorts to drastic means, putting the nephew through a series of trials and deprivations. At the boy's marriage he is the chief person consulted in the choice of a mate, and often after the marriage he instructs the couple in their future duties as man and wife. This is not to say that the bond between uncle and nephew is a harsh one. Often great affection is shown on both sides; it is certainly not reduced by the consideration that it is from his maternal uncle that the boy expects to inherit ceremonial and sib offices.

4) Mother-Daughter

This reciprocal relation is one of the closest and warmest to be found in Hopi society, for the ties which bind mother and daughter persist throughout life. The mother teaches the daughter all the things she will need to know as a full-fledged member of society—how to grind corn, cook, take care of children, make baskets and pottery, and how to behave toward strangers, relatives, and mates. In addition to the functional relationship there is a great deal of love and respect shown between mother and daughter.

5) Father-Daughter

The father actually has few duties to perform for his daughter and vice versa. The bond between them is primarily one of affection, but even this is not so warm as that between mother and daughter.

6) Brother-Sister

This is a very close reciprocal relation and one that contains a great deal of affection. There are no taboos on association between them, and they play together until the sexual division of labor separates them. Even after this there is close cooperation between brothers and sisters, and after marriage they become to each other's children "mother's brother" and "father's sister" respectively.

These six reciprocal relations are only a few of the many that the Hopi observe, yet they tend to draw, in miniature, a picture of the many bonds the Hopi individual has and to show the nature of these bonds in governing almost the whole of his behavior. They also illustrate the fact that, although his matrilineal relations in the household play a considerable role in the individual's experience and education, the nuclear family—mother, father, and children—are also a close-knit group sharing obligations, privileges, and affections.

The Family Cycle

Mate Selection

Courtship among the Hopi is informal. A girl who has undergone the important rites of adolescence, usually performed between the ages of sixteen and twenty, is ready to receive suitors, although she will probably not marry until she is seventeen or older. Boys of twelve or thirteen are also ready for courtship, for they begin at this time to sleep in the men's ceremonial house, the *kiva*, instead of at home, and thus have the opportunity for nocturnal assignations.

The stage is set, then, for the custom of *dumaiya*, in the observance of which the boys, partly disguised, pay visits by night to girls of their choice. They usually spend the night, but leave before daybreak to avoid detection by the girls' parents. If, however, a couple is exposed, no serious punishment follows. The parents are well aware of such visits, and, although they do not give them their open sanction, they allow them if the boy is a proper marriage prospect. Indeed, a girl of marriageable age usually has several lovers. Eventually she is likely to find herself pregnant. In this event she names the favorite among her lovers as her choice, and a match is arranged between the families and households involved. As a result, of course, no boy will visit by night a girl he is unwilling to marry.

There are several other occasions on which the choice of a mate may be made. In former days it was customary to give an informal picnic on the day following an important ritual. In preparation for this occasion the girls prepared *somiviki*, or "maiden's cake," to supplement the rabbits and other small animals provided by the boys. If a girl had decided on a youth as a future mate, she would extend an invitation to him to accompany her to the picnic and would present him with a loaf of *qömi*, a bread made of sweet cornmeal, in lieu of *somiviki*. Since such a gift was tantamount to an engagement, boys accepted invitations to picnics only from girls they were willing to marry. The picnics also served as occasions on which nocturnal assignations could be arranged.

Qömi might also be presented to a youth during the bean dance ceremony in the *kiva*. On this occasion it was customary for unmarried girls to hand out *somiviki* to the performers as each passed from the *kiva* on conclusion of the dance; sometimes a loaf of *qömi* was substituted for *somiviki* and had to be accepted for fear of offending the giver. Such a proposal was not accepted as binding however, since the loaf could be discarded or given to the father of the Kachinas. In this event the girl would soon learn that her proposal had been rejected.

Qömi might also be offered during the spring festival, in which girls exchanged *somiviki* for green plants picked by the boys. Here, as in the bean dance, the loaf had to be accepted at least temporarily, but such an acceptance was, again, not necessarily binding.

The form of courtship most frequently described for the Hopi, however, is that in which, when the girls grind corn during the night in a chamber separate from the parents' sleeping room, prospective suitors come to engage in small talk with them and perhaps to propose marriage or even to arrange for a nocturnal assignation.

Certainly, in view of this information and in spite of statements to the contrary, which have been made by many authors, the Hopi do not seem to place a high value on virginity and apparently do not consider it a requisite for marriage.

However, the prospective bride and groom must observe several restrictions if they are to make a marriage sanctioned by society. The principal prohibition is against marriage within the nuclear family, extending to the members of one's phratry. This rule applies not only to one's own phratry, but also to that of one's father, although in the latter instance the taboo is not so strict. In addition it is considered improper for a girl or boy to marry someone previously married. The violator of this taboo is punished, according to Hopi belief, by being forced to carry a heavily loaded basket on the journey to the underworld after death. Finally, the prospective bride and groom are expected to be temperamentally congenial. Outside of these restrictions there is great freedom of choice, and marriage for love is certainly not unknown.

Once the decision to marry is made by the young couple, the boy goes in the evening after supper to the girl's house and there states his intentions to her parents. If he is acceptable, he is told to go home and tell his parents about it. The girl then grinds cornmeal or makes bread, and carries it to the house of her prospective groom. At this time the mother of the boy may refuse the bread or meal, in which case the match is usually broken off. If, however, the food is accepted, it is given by the mother to her brothers and to her husband's clansmen, and the wedding plans go forward.

After this event the girl returns home to grind more meal with the help of her kinswomen, while the boy fetches water and chops wood for his mother. The girl is preparing for her formal bridal visit to the boy's home, and he is completing his last chores for his mother.

In the evening after these chores are completed, the bride dresses in her manta beads and her wedding blanket. Accompanied by the boy, who carries the meal she has ground, she walks barefoot to his house. There she presents the meal to her prospective mother-in-law and settles down for a temporary three-day stay before the wedding. During this period the young couple may see each other, but they must observe sexual continence.

On each of the three days preceding the marriage the bride rises early and grinds cornmeal for her mother-in-law. During this period she is partially restricted in her behavior as she has been and will be during other crisis periods in her life, e.g., at puberty or confinement. She eats, however, with other members of the family, takes part in the conversations, and is not subject to such taboos as being forbidden to eat salt or meat or having to scratch herself with a stick.

At some time during the three-day period the groom's house is visited, or "attacked," by his paternal aunts, who break in on the bride and shower her with invective and often with mud. They accuse her of laziness, inefficiency, and stupidity. The boy's mother and her clanswomen protect the girl and insist that the accusations are unfounded. In spite of appearances all this is carried off in a good-humored way, and finally the aunts leave, having stolen the wood their nephew had brought his mother. The wood is used to bake *piki*, which is given to the mother, and thus all damages are paid for.

On the morning of the fourth day the marriage is consummated. On this occasion the girl's relatives wash the boy's hair and bathe him, while the boy's relatives do the same for the girl. At Old Oraibi[4] the heads of the newlyweds are merely washed together in a basin and their hair is twined together as a symbol of their union. As soon as their hair is dry the couple follow a path of cornmeal sprinkled by the boy's mother to the eastern edge of the mesa, where prayers are made to the sun.

The couple may now sleep together as man and wife, but they remain at the boy's mother's house until the girl's wedding garments are complete. These garments are woven by the groom, his male relatives, and any men in the village who wish to participate. On occasions when various parts of the work are finished the groom's family holds a feast to pay the workers, the necessary food for the feast being supplied by his relatives. The garments themselves consist of a large belt, two all-white wedding robes, a white wedding robe with red stripes at top and bottom, white buckskin leggings and moccasins, a string for tying the hair, and a reed mat in which to wrap the entire outfit.

After the job is completed—a matter of about two weeks—the bride dresses in her new clothes and returns home, where she is received by her mother and her female relatives. She is accompanied on this journey by her husband's relatives, who make a final exchange of gifts with her mother's household. During the evening the groom appears at his mother-in-law's home and spends the night. The next day he fetches wood for her and from then on is a permanent resident in her house—unless a divorce sends him packing.

During the winter and indeed until the following July, the bride may not attend a dance. At the *Niman* dance in

<hr/>

4. Titiev, *op. cit.*, p. 137.

July, however, she finally attends a ceremonial. Her apperance at this time is supposed to ensure rain and a happy married life. Perhaps, however, the wish to show off her wedding robes is as powerful a motive. After this appearance the robes are put away until that time when they will serve as a shroud, since these garments will be necessary for the trip through the underworld.

Nearly all Hopi marry, for without marriage it is difficult to play a full adult role in the society. This fact perhaps emphasizes the role of the conjugal group as a real functioning unit. Indeed, in recent years more and more of these marriage groups are setting up households for themselves, and the old matrilineal household is in danger of disappearing entirely. As long, however, as the extended household exists, the conjugal family can form, break through divorce, and reform without disturbing the household overmuch.

Birth and Infancy

From the moment of birth the newly born Hopi is a member of his mother's sib. His reciprocal relations with his father's relatives are, however, emphasized at this time by a series of rites which end on the twentieth day after birth. Birth takes place in the maternal household with the husband and the wife's relatives in attendance. Immediately after birth the cord is tied to a stirring stick if the infant is a girl, or to a bow if a boy, and is placed in the rafters; thus the Hopi is prepared, symbolically, for the adult role he is to play.

The infant is then "cleaned" with ashes and yucca suds and wrapped in a blanket. During the next twenty-four hours he is bound securely to a cradle, which is a flat board with a wicker head guard. A small pad of folded cloth is placed under the head as a pillow and a roll of cloth under the neck to keep the child from becoming "bull-necked." From this time until somewhere between the ages of three and six months the infant remains on the cradle board except when being cleaned or bathed. He nurses and sleeps on the board, but this restriction does not seem detrimental to him; rather,

it probably contributes to the infant's feeling of security and also conditions him to the expectation of restrictions which though not recognized at first as socially imposed, gradually as the child grows older become a part of the great social web which, while holding him fast within its reciprocal system, gives him a sense of security and well being in an exceedingly precarious environment.[5]

The twentieth day after birth the child's female paternal relatives come to his house. Each woman gives the child a bath and a name, a total, sometimes, of eight or ten. At daybreak his mother and maternal grandmother present the child to the sun, the great father deity of the Hopi.

During the first year the infant is carefully attended by his mother and female relatives. He sleeps with his mother and is nursed or otherwise soothed whenever he cries. After he is released from the cradle board he may be taken from the house from time to time by his mother or a female sibling, slung on her back in a shawl. The child is seldom weaned before he is a year old—more likely after he is two years old. In general, weaning is not abrupt and does not seem to affect the personality of the child in any serious way.

If the child becomes ill, a medicine man is called. He sings songs, sprinkles corn meal, makes use of herbs and clays, and in general practices the traditional medicinal techniques. Infant mortality is high, and much of the illness among infants seems to be digestive. This is not surprising since after the child is weaned he is allowed to eat practically what he wants—tortillas soaked in coffee, green corn, melons, chile, and fruit which is often half-ripe. The medicine man, then, is frequently consulted. If the child is cured of a really serious illness, he becomes a member of the sib of the medicine man who cured him and so extends the network of reciprocal relationships which determine so much of his behavior.

5. Laura Thompson and Alice Joseph, *The Hopi Way* (1945), p. 51. By permission of the University of Chicago Press.

Childhood

Shortly after the child is a year old he is expected to begin to walk and talk. Training in cleanliness also begins at this time, but it does not seem too severe. The child is simply told to go out of doors if he wishes to relieve himself. By the young child this command is taken literally, and he goes just outside the door (older children go to a corner of the plaza; adults leave the village entirely). If the child does not obey he is spanked.

Later the child is expected to inform his mother if he wishes to eliminate during the night, and by the age of two years he is expected to have stopped wetting the bed. If bed-wetting continues, girls are punished by being made to wash their bed clothes. Boys are invariably treated more drastically, disciplinary action being placed in the hands of the maternal uncle. Clad only in a blanket, the boy is carried to the house of a woman of the Corn-Water sib accompanied by other boys of the bed-wetter's sib. The boys sing special songs and the woman throws cold water on all, innocent as well as guilty. There is no teasing or ridicule, however, during the ceremony. This drastic punishment for the boys may indicate that enuresis is more common among boys than among girls, or perhaps that boys are disciplined more severely than girls.

Scolding is the most common type of punishment, and children may be scolded for such offenses as lying, quarreling, showing disrespect for old people, and, indeed, all minor forms of misdemeanors. Ridicule, teasing, and withholding favors are also utilized as punitive techniques. Some corporal punishment is inflicted on the naughty child by its mother or father, or, more often, the mother's brother. This type of punishment is meted out primarily for laziness but may be inflicted for stealing, disobedience, stubbornness, or hurting other children. As mentioned before, the mother's brother is the principal disciplinarian and may, in addition to the punishments listed above, pour cold water on the child, roll him in the snow, or hold him over a green cedar smudge.

In general, however, discipline for children is permissive. Children learn primarily by imitation, and such reward and punishment as is given is in the hands of all the relatives, but especially the mother's brother, who is aided by Kachinas.

The Kachinas are ancestral spirits who accompanied the Hopi on their early wanderings. Today they live in the San Francisco Mountains, returning only during the ceremonial season to participate in the religious life of the tribe. They are impersonated, of course, by elaborately masked men, whom the Hopi children suppose to be the gods themselves, and whom even the adults suppose to have the supernatural powers of the spirits they represent.

A traditional way of punishing children is to frighten them by calling in dreadful Kachinas who are "cannibals" and who threaten to eat bad children. This type of punishment actually accomplishes its purpose of disciplining the child without alienating children and parents, since the latter act as defenders of the children. They hold the door against the "cannibal" Kachinas and induce them to accept other food in lieu of the naughty children.

In general, the period of learning, in childhood, is characterized by a great deal of freedom, and such punishment as is practiced does not have the effect of making the child feel that he has been abandoned or that he is dislodged from his position in his parents' affections. Indeed the Kachina punishment actually makes the children love and depend upon their parents all the more. At the same time these shocks, which seem to the child to come from the external, natural, or supernatural world, condition him early to fear his environment and to depend on the family for protection and security against this world. Psychological tests administered by Laura Thompson and her assistants indicated that among the Hopi children fear is primarily of the supernatural and that many anxieties arise without obvious reason in the night when the child is alone. Thus "fear—the deepest sensation of displeasure—is mainly projected into the supernatural," and, if Hopi beliefs and training methods have succeeded in imbuing the children with great fear, they have apparently also succeeded in concentrating and directing the fear into the supernatural sphere, a fact which implicitly will accentuate (on the other side) the security represented by the mother's lap, the familiar house, the laws and rules, and finally the group itself.[6]

This is not to say that the child is not subject to many restrictions. He is not allowed to go near the edge of the cliff which may border the town, or fire, or the hatchways which lead into the *kivas*. He is not supposed to tease, fight, or injure anyone. He is taught respect for other people's property. He is not allowed to talk back to adults or to watch other people eating. Finally, he may not play at certain games—to play at being sick, for example, might bring on actual illness.

In addition to these restrictions the child has some duties. Although the boy has few duties until he is six years of age, after this he begins to accompany his father in his round of daily activities, performing those small services for which he is suited. He guards the fields and orchards against animal pests; he runs errands and chops wood. He helps to pick and carry fruit and helps with the harvest. He is in addition expected to participate in a number of activities calculated to increase his strength and vigor. For instance, each morning before sunrise he may have to run to some distant spring, bathe in the icy waters, and return to his home before the village is stirring.

The girl's work follows closely the patterns set up by older women, especially her mother. She helps with the housework, carries water, grinds and cooks corn, and takes care of the younger children. Indeed after the age of twelve the girl's play days are over, and she is expected to remain at home and play a full part in the everyday life of the Hopi women.

When the day's work is done, the child can play; and in play he has the run of the village. There are three types of play groups: (1) young girls who act as nursemaids to younger siblings during play hours; (2) boys from four to eight years of

6. Thompson and Joseph, *op. cit.*, p. 105. By permission of the University of Chicago Press.

age, old enough to escape supervision by older sisters but not old enough to work in the fields; (3) and older boys who play in the late afternoon and evening after the day's work is done. In general it can be said that Hopi play imitates the activities of adults. The girls play house. Their make-believe houses are peopled by dolls made of sticks or different parts of the forefeet of calves. Around the house are placed make-believe gardens, fields, and orchards. In these play houses the girls carry on, in miniature, the traditional activities of the Hopi women. They make small pots and grind corn. The boys build imitation corrals in which peach seeds play the part of sheep. They also construct little fields. They do not, however, play house, since traditionally the men have nothing to do with housework. The boys may also imitate other male activities, such as horseback riding and rabbit hunting. Both boys and girls play at ceremonial activity, imitating the dancing, drum beating, and other antics of Hopi adults.

Some Hopi play is not of an imitative sort. The children play at seesaw, have snow battles, roll hoops, and keep pets, which they treat rather cruelly. Many of the games, too, are of a seasonal sort and can be played only on appropriate occasions. These games include shinny, the top game, the stick-throwing game, archery, rabbit hunting, the dart-throwing game, and parchesi.

With the exception of age and sex restrictions already mentioned the Hopi child may play with whom he chooses.

In summary, then, the Hopi child is, in Laura Thompson's words:

... Highly intelligent in a balanced, unchildish way; hard-working and industrious, thrifty and careful of his property, but not necessarily concerned about it; sober, reticent concerning matters of personal intimacy. Family-and-group bound in his moral standards, particularly with regard to the thoughtful and kind consideration of others, and in most of his openly admitted emotions. Happy ... about aspects of death and sickness, and at the same time avoiding sorrow in its greatest and unmanageable impact. Sad and angered by aggression from other members of the group and by discipline with its far-reaching consequences. Strictly condemning all individual efforts to rise above the group through fighting or bullying;

aware of his own abilities but not admitting and not openly desiring outstanding personal achievement which would separate him from the group. Deeply afraid of the supernatural which also seems to have a strong, even a determining influence on his moral conscience and to be a fundamental incentive for good behavior.[7]

Adolescence

As the Hopi boy approaches adolescence his economic responsibilities increase. He now accompanies his father or grandfather to the fields or grazing areas. By the age of fourteen he is expected to have mastered most agricultural skills and to be able to take charge of his own herd and his mother's fields.[8] In winter he accompanies his elders into the *kiva* where the men's handicrafts, including weaving and moccasin making, are taught him. Here also he is expected to learn tribal lore and master the rituals of his sib and of the wider Hopi society.

At the time of transition from childhood to adolescence every Hopi, male or female, must be initiated in the Kachina cult. He learns at this time that the Kachinas are masked men, although this knowledge in no way destroys his faith.

One of the principal parts of the initiation ceremony is a whipping. Masked males ("Whipper Kachinas") do the actual whipping with switches which they obtain from the "Mother of the Kachinas." The youths are supported during the ordeal by a ceremonial "father" or "aunt," depending upon the sex of the initiate. This entire ceremony can be interpreted as symbolic of the complementary functions of maternal and paternal kin in guiding the child. The Hopi mother, symbolized by the "Mother of the Kachina," and her brother, symbolized by the "Whipper Kachinas," are the disciplinarians; the father and his sister, symbolized by the ceremonial "father" and "aunt," are the child's supporters. In this way the recip-

7. *Ibid.*, p. 107. By permission of the University of Chicago Press.
8. *Ibid.*, p. 57.

rocal relations within the household and between households are symbolized in one of the most important of the Hopi ceremonials.

Adulthood

Another example of the symbolic function of the family and household in the ceremonial life of the Hopi is seen in the important *rite de passage* from adolescence to adulthood for the male. This ritual, performed in connection with the annual "New Fire" ceremony, emphasizes the death and rebirth motif on a cosmic scale. The youth "dies," goes to the underworld, and is reborn. He receives a new name and is "reared" to full manhood by his ceremonial fathers. After this he participates fully in the adult male life of the community.

Among adult Hopi the division of labor between the sexes is rather clearly defined and well-balanced. The land for the fields and gardens is owned by the matrilineal household, as are the seeds for planting. Furthermore the crops are worked by the members of the household, the men taking care of the maize fields and the women caring for the gardens.

This division of labor in the household is extended even further. The men care for and own the flocks of sheep and cattle; they weave the clothing and make moccasins, Kachina dolls, and silver jewelry. The women care for the house and perform the manifold tasks involved in such care; they also make baskets and pottery.

It would seem, in the light of this description, that the nuclear family has little part in economic activity. It must be realized, however, that it is precisely this group which cooperates most closely within the household group. Real fathers and sons, for example, work together in the fields and care for the flocks. Moreover it is from his father that a son receives most of his instruction in those techniques which he must learn if he is to participate in the economic life of the village.

It must not be supposed that economic cooperation is

entirely a function of the family and household. All of the men in the village cooperate in caring for the flocks. For instance, two men will watch all the flocks for a few days, then will be replaced by two others, and so on until everyone has taken his turn.

As the adult continues his journey through life he can expect to gain or lose prestige in various ways. To grow older is not to gain prestige automatically. Prestige is correlated with social responsibility and participation in the family and ceremonial groups, and comes when one assumes completely the role outlined for one by the Hopi way—"concentration through an effort of will, on living the good, the peaceful, the happy life, as defined by the Hopi ideal."[9]

Old Age

The transition from adulthood to old age is accompanied by no *rites de passage*. Gradually as the individual becomes too old and feeble to play a full adult role he drops his responsibilities or passes them on to a successor especially chosen and trained. His impending death is accepted, and although he continues to work at whatever tasks he can perform, he drops out of the active life of the community. He has completed a long and useful life.

After he dies he is quickly buried, for the Hopi hate and fear anything connected with death. The hair of the dead man is washed by his father's sister, if living, and his body is buried in a flexed position, covered with a shroud. The Hopi believe that the soul lingers above the grave for three days and on the fourth day begins the long journey to the underworld.

Disjunctions

The incidence of divorce has been rather high among the Hopi, possibly one out of three marriages ending in divorce—

9. *Ibid.*, p. 64.

nearly comparable to the rate for other Americans today. Titiev reports an even distribution of divorce among the various sibs and phraties, noting that "loose marriage ties and frequent adultery are long-standing Hopi traits."[10] One basis of the "loose marriage ties" is the lack of authority of the husband in the matrilineal family.

The mechanics of divorce are very simple. The husband merely goes home to his mother's house. The initiative, however, may be taken by either wife or husband. The wife seeking to terminate her marriage places the husband's belongings outside the door of the dwelling. The children remain with their mother and are cared for and educated by the household group in the absence of a real father.

Family Controls

To the Hopi the universe of man, animals, plants, supernatural things, and natural phenomena functions as an ordered, interrelated system whose essential principle is reciprocity. It is a unified system operating according to principles known only to themselves. The whole is set in motion and controlled through man's activities and volition, for although there are nonhuman elements which operate mechanically in the universe, without man's will, expressed in ritual and psychical acts and states, the universe would cease to function.

The underworld of the dead and the upperworld of the living stand in vital conjunction with a reciprocal and complementary relationship existing between the living and the dead. The spirits of the dead are for the most part benign and helpful. For example they may take the shape of clouds and bring life-giving rain to Hopiland.

The thoroughgoing ceremonialism of the Hopi with the traditional dances, festivals, and rituals, of which the well-popularized snake dance is but one, give meaning and coherence to Hopi behavior, institutions, and culture.

10. Titiev, *op. cit.*, p. 41.

Hopi symbols expressed in art and artifact articulate a system of implicit concepts, attitudes, and values which are meaningful, consistent, and harmonious.[11] Seen as a body of norms or ethical prescriptions this system has appropriately been termed the "Hopi way."[12]

The subjective or personal side of the Hopi way as reflected in personality and character of the individual emphasizes cooperation, unselfishness, modesty, and nonaggressiveness. The Hopi is expected to cultivate the "good heart," and not to feel anger, sadness, or worry, but to be tranquil and of good will.[13]

It should not be assumed that the integrated world view of the Hopi and its reflection in Hopi character automatically produces a culture unruffled by dissension or deviant behavior. Hopi argue, quarrel, show some anxiety, and often stray from the public norms of the tribe. But insofar as individuals are involved, the controls are usually adequate to the task. There are no competing religious doctrines or secular ideologies to challenge the Hopi way. When a village becomes divided over an issue—a rare occurrence—the solution is for the discontented to establish a separate community elsewhere on the mesa.

The Hopi family is an agency of social control acting in part for the larger kinship unit, the matri-sib. The latter, as noted, is part of the phratry system, yet the locus of strength resides with the matri-sib. The emphasis on matrilineality is balanced to some degree by the leadership males exert in ceremonies and their male-centered activities within the *kiva*.

The generation of social cohesion among the Hopi is produced primarily by ceremonial activities. By participating, with "good heart," the members, their emotions excited by the color, rhythm, and sensuousness of the rites with their

11. Laura Thompson, *Culture in Crisis: A Study of the Hopi Indians* (1950), p. 135.
12. Thompson and Joseph, *op. cit.*, pp. 40 ff.
13. *Ibid*, p. 41.

dramatic overtones, develop a deepening sense of the meaningfulness and importance of their religio-ethical beliefs. And
to the extent that such meaningfulness is achieved, the Hopi
balance by internalization—the development of conscience—
and "inner control" the norms and prescriptions that make up
tribal doctrine.

Functions of the Hopi Family

In many ways the Hopi family reinforces or correlates its
activities with other forms of social organization; conversely,
as in the case of the Kachinas, the religious or spiritual world
is directly invoked to reinforce family discipline and training.
But in most day-to-day interaction the parents, wife's brother,
and other kindred, through reward and punishment, through
ordering and forbidding, perform the educative and orienta-
tional functions.

The nuclear family provides a regularized sexual outlet
for its members. Sexual matters are considerably less tabooed
among the Hopi than among other groups and societies, our
own included. Yet the external marriage controls are not
rigid or inflexible. The relative ease with which marriages are
terminated suggests that sexual satisfaction and companionship may comprise the major functions of the Hopi nuclear
family, while child care, sustenance, protection, and some
aspects of discipline may be shared with or relinquished to
the household and matri-sib.

Close ties, nevertheless, exist between father and son and
mother and daughter. The role of the uncle as disciplinarian
and the reward-punishment functions of the Kachinas.relieve
the parents of some of the strain occasioned in the socialization of children and permit bonds of comradeship and affection to develop. The functions of the nuclear family, then,
are for the most part shared, shared in such manner as to dis-
tribute responsibility through the primary marriage units: the
household, kindred, and matri-sib.

REFERENCES

Beaglehole, E. and P., *Hopi of the Second Mesa*. American Anthropologist, *Memoirs*, No. 44, 1935.

Dennis, Wayne, *The Hopi Child*. New York: Appleton-Century-Crofts, Inc., 1940.

Thompson, Laura, *Culture in Crisis: A Study of the Hopi Indians*. New York: Harper, 1950.

————, and Joseph, Alice, *The Hopi Way*. Chicago: University of Chicago Press, 1945.

Titiev, Mischa, *Old Oraibi*. Papers of the Peabody Museum of American Archaeology and Ethnology. Cambridge: Harvard University Press, Volume XXII, No. 1, 1944.

4 The Polygynous Baganda Family

The Baganda consist of over one million members of a subdivision of the Negroid Bantu-speaking peoples of central Africa. Their country, Uganda, some 91,000 square miles in size, and a former British state protectorate, in 1962 became a federal parliamentary state and a member of the Commonwealth of Nations. By the new Uganda Constitution of 16 June, 1967, Uganda was declared a Republic without constituent kingdoms.[1]

Uganda is bordered on the southwest by Lake Victoria and cut across the center by the equator. What would otherwise be an equatorial climate is modified by the altitude of over 4,000 feet above sea level for most of the country. Consequently the climate is mild, with temperatures seldom going above 85°F. during the day and dropping sometimes below 60°F. at night.

The characteristic physical features of the province include grassy rolling hills, swampy lowlands, marshes, seas of grasses, tropical and temperate forests, mountains, swift-flowing streams, and spectacular waterfalls. For the most part the Baganda, though they have few cities, live in a rather high state of human density. Of the 25,000 square miles that make up the area lived in by the Baganda over 8,000 are water covered. The habitable areas average about sixty persons per square mile.

The Baganda are predominantly agriculturists, living mainly on starchy and heavy bulk foods supplemented by fish and occasionally wild game. Bananas or plantains are the major source of food and furnish raw materials for many use-

1. Audrey I. Richards, *The Multicultural States of East Africa* (1969), p. 52.

ful purposes. Cattle, sheep, goats, and fowl are the domestic animals raised by the Baganda, ownership of cattle being associated with social status. Other distinctive characteristics of Baganda society have been: a political organization beginning with village or neighborhood subchiefs and continuing through higher-placed chiefs and administrators, ending with the king and royal family; a strong clan system but the absence of distinct clan communities; the almost universally shared, fairly high standard of living; Baganda personal cleanliness and general orderliness about household affairs; the trim thatch-roofed, beehive-shaped dwellings; a sense of superiority to other native groups; the lack of a written language compensated for in part by a complex system of communication through drums; and a rather complex social organization characterized by three social classes, commoners or freemen, chiefs, and the nobility. Until the advent of British domination shortly before the turn of the century, slavery was common among the Baganda, especially female and child slaves captured in warfare. Thus slaves were to be found in nearly all Baganda households.

Inasmuch as the intent of this chapter is to present another type of family system clearly different from our own, the focus will be on Baganda society of several generations ago when marriage, family, and more extensive social institutions were relatively unaffected by contact with Western culture. The use of the "historical present" in the description is to be noted; we are speaking of the Baganda as they were at the end of the nineteenth century, not as they are past the middle of the twentieth century.

Family Structure

The Marriage Institution of Polygyny

Polygyny, the type of marriage in which the husband has plural wives, is not only the preferred but the dominant form of marriage for the Baganda. The king has hundreds of wives, chiefs, dozens, and commoners, two or three. Since wives are expensive, the commoner must work hard to acquire them. However, as will be explained later, each wife becomes a source of income and constitutes an economic investment. Polygyny is permissively sororal; the husband may acquire as wives the sisters of his spouse or even the widows of his brothers.

Obviously, for polygyny to be widespread, the society in question must have a preponderance of females. Such for centuries has been the case among the Baganda, where male infanticide is practiced in the families of chiefs, rebellious princes are slaughtered, executions are wanton, priests sacrifice an incredible number of victims, and where nearly continuous warfare with neighboring kingdoms produces heavy male losses. Thus, speaking at the turn of the century, females exceed males in the Baganda population by a ratio of about three to one.[2]

Family and Kinship

The nuclear family, consisting of father, mother, and offspring, forms the smallest unit of the Baganda kinship system. Inasmuch as marriages are polygynous the family proper consists of several nuclear units held in association by a common father. To such a composite family there are usually added other relatives of the father: younger unmarried sisters, widowed sisters dedicated to tending the graves of their dead husbands, aged parents, and children of the father's clan who have been sent to him to be brought up. In this expanded household will also be found, among the more well-to-do families, servants, female slaves, and their children, all living within a compound comprised of individual huts for the wives, a cookhouse, and other outbuildings.

Although the type of family here presented is large in numbers it should not be confused with the "joint" family, with its

2. George P. Murdock, *Our Primitive Contemporaries* (1934), p. 540.

several married brothers and their families living together, or the "extended" family, consisting of a group of married offspring living in one household under a patriarch or matriarch. Though subject to a wide range of kinship controls, the father nevertheless remains the head of each of his nuclear family units and of the household in which they are located.

In view of the prevailing patrilocal rule of residence, the new families tend to be located in the general vicinity of the husband's parents. However, since each nuclear family unit has for its economic foundation a garden of its own, cleared by the husband and cultivated by the wife, Baganda families do not cluster in compact villages or communities. Further, with the existence of a patron-client relationship between the chief and the peasants, the Baganda are relatively free to attach themselves to whichever chief or subchief they choose. The consequence is that patrilocal residence operates more as an orientation than as an arbitrary rule. In practice the sons who marry are content to maintain loyalties to their families of orientation and to their clan, while maintaining independent households the location of which will most likely be decided on grounds of economic expediency.

Like the Todas, the Baganda use the classificatory system of kinship terminology, with all brothers of the father called "father," all sisters of the mother "mother," and all their children "brother and sister." What is technically called the "Iroquois cousin terminology" is employed: in male-speaking terms father's sister's daughters and mother's brother's daughters—cross-cousins—are called by the same terms but terminologically are differentiated from parallel-cousins as well as from sisters. Parallel-cousins, as indicated, are classified with sisters.[3] Contrary to Toda practice, however, cross-cousins may not marry. In fact, as part of the avoidance pattern that extends to what we would call parental in-laws, cross-cousins may not even interact socially. Parallel-cousins, considered as brother and sister, may of course intermingle freely, but by virtue of the

3. George P. Murdock, *Social Structure* (1949), p. 223.

extension of the incest taboo are prohibited from marrying. It follows that the working of such a system has rather distinct consequences for mate selection among the Baganda, inasmuch as those with whom one grows up in a neighborhood or community are likely to be ineligible as potential marriage mates on one or another kinship grounds.

A total of sixty-eight linguistic terms of relationship are used by the Baganda. Some departure from the classificatory scheme is noted in the matter of age-grading as "older brother" is designated, and for some relationships the sex of the person speaking of a relative changes the term of reference. The term "father" or "mother" is never used alone but a possessive pronoun must always be attached, e.g., "my father," "my mother," "his father," and so on.[4]

One of the more significant features of Baganda social structure is the consanguineal kin group or "blood line." Seen simply as a line of descent, traced through male members, the term "patri-sib" applies. By combining the patrilocal rule of residence with consanguineal descent, the Baganda have built a formidable system of clans. In fact, for many centuries the clans—adhering to the rule of exogamy, maintaining if not owning their agricultural estates and religious temples presided over by clan chiefs, subdividing in the face of growing population, and organizing and integrating much of the social life of their members through a wide range of specific rules, observances, and taboos—have remained the largest and probably the most important kinship entity of the Baganda, with the nuclear family, the smallest unit of kinship, playing a somewhat subordinate role.

The members of each clan are further linked: by respect for two animal totems, one of the more important from which the clan derives its name; by an identifying drum beat used on ceremonial occasions; by certain distinguishing personal names; by special observances connected with pregnancy, childbirth, the testing of the child's legitimacy as a clan mem-

4. John Roscoe, *The Baganda* (1911), p. 129.

ber, and the naming of the child; and by certain obligations such as assuming responsibility for pleading a member's cause before a high tribunal, or the paying off of a dead member's debts.[5]

Despite the ubiquity of clan organization, clear-cut clan communities have never fully developed among the Baganda. The primary reason pertains to the operation of the monarchy and the attendant impermanent system of chiefs. All land except the clan estates, upon portions of which members are buried, are held by the king, much as in medieval English feudal society. A large number of estates are held by chiefs of the larger administrative sections of the realm, by princes and other members of the royal family, and by still others who have temporarily at least won favor of the king. The remainder of the land, with the exception of the clan estates, is parceled out to the chiefs appointed by the king. They along with the subchiefs in turn make plots of gardens available to the commoners or peasants who, with their wives, accept the responsibility for putting the land into production, for rendering goods and services to their respective chiefs, and for payment of taxes to the king's collectors.

Chiefs meanwhile hold their posts only so long as they are in the good graces of the king. The office is highly prized, for it carries with it great power and the opportunity for gaining wealth and numerous wives. Yet, at the fancy of the king any chief may be deposed. Plotting against the king is a common charge, and upon the flimsiest of evidence—a dream of the king, information passed on anonymously—a chief may be seized by the king's secret police and thrown into jail. Should the relatives and followers fail to plead his case along with offering expensive presents to the king, the deposed chief is likely to be executed.

Customarily the king is expected to follow the recommendations of the respective clans in appointing chiefs and

5. Lucy P. Mair, "Totemism among the Baganda," *Man: A Monthly Record of Anthropological Science,* 35 (1935), p. 65.

subchiefs to head the clan estates. But he is not absolutely bound to do so, and on occasion may elevate an unnominated, possibly disliked member to the office.

The prevailing relationship of chief to superior is one of servility. The prototype of the "yes man" is exemplified in the actions of the chief in the presence of the king. "Yes" is indicated by throwing oneself down face first on the ground, kicking the legs, waving the arms, and beating the forehead on the ground!

Baganda peasants are freemen in the sense that they are not bound to the soil as were the feudal serfs. Instead, if the chief under whom they serve becomes unpopular, they are likely to leave and go to another. This usage serves to keep the peasant from inordinate exploitation by his chief. It also serves to enhance the mobility of the population, so that the loosely organized neighborhoods or villages of the Baganda are normally characterized by considerable family movement. Where clan organization is weak the mobility is even more pronounced.

Household and Inheritance

The peasant Baganda enjoys one of the highest native standards of living in Africa. Chiefs are disposed to make as much land available to the peasant as he can bring under cultivation. Since it is the wife who actually works and cultivates the gardens, the peasant has good cause to seek additional wives. A good plantain garden, tended by one woman, can support three men.[6]

A variety of buildings—huts for the husband, wives, other relatives, servants, and slaves; a cookhouse; fetish house; and a privy, all enclosed by a high fence made of plaited reeds— make up the Baganda compound. Although a man's physical property might be considerable, when he dies, his power over

6. Murdock, *Our Primitive Contemporaries,* p. 513.

the property ends. The clan assumes control of the inheritance; the wishes of the dead person may or may not be honored.

The heir is chosen by the clan, but members of the branch to which the deceased belonged are given the dominant voice. The eldest son cannot inherit. Widows with children may remarry if they can induce the clan to repay the bride-price to the relatives of the deceased. Young widows become the property of the appointed heir, except for those sent to the king or given as part of the inheritance to other members of the clan. Widows, however, never inherit property. Both the son and grandson of the deceased, who are chosen by the clan to perform the burial rites, have the right to receive a widow. The son of the dead man's sister, in return for performing the rituals which end the mourning, also inherits a widow. The remainder of the property belongs to the heir, who also adopts the deceased person's children, calling them his and making no distinction between them and his own children.[7]

The Family Cycle

Mate Selection

Marriages among the Baganda take place at an early age: girls at thirteen to fourteen, boys at fifteen or sixteen if they have sufficient property. Wives may be inherited or received as a gift or captured in war; however, the usual procedure is to acquire a wife by purchase.

Having satisfied himself that the girl with respect to the kinship rule of marriage is eligible as a mate, the boy initiates proceedings through the girl's brother and her paternal uncle. No formal declaration may be made until a present of a small package of salt is accepted from the boy by the parents of the

7. Roscoe, *op. cit.*, p. 270.

girl and by the girl herself. The girl's father will indicate acceptance of the marriage by keeping the present. Actual marriage arrangements, however, will ordinarily be made by the uncle. By far the most important item of the marriage is the bride-price.

The uncle and brother are brought several gourds of beer by the suitor who swears before some of his own relatives as witnesses he will make a good husband. The uncle asks the girl, "Shall I drink?" and if she replies, "Drink," and he does so, the marriage is ratified and nothing can afterwards cancel the contract save the husband's consent and his acceptance of the return of the bride-price which he had paid for her.[8] The uncle and brother then report to the parents that the marriage has been arranged and legitimated. All that remains is to settle the bride-price.

Members of the clan will arrange terms and conditions. The price usually involves a number of goats or a cow and several thousand cowrie shells—Baganda money—all of which usually total more than any young man or his parents have been able to accumulate. Thus there may well be a period of several months, or even a year, during which the groom is separated from the bride while he gathers the required amount.

The wedding takes place as soon as the bride-price, to be divided among the bride's relatives, is accumulated and paid. During the waiting period the bride is annointed with butter to beautify her skin and fed well to make her plump. The day before the marriage she is washed from head to foot by the bridegroom's sister who critically inspects her for infirmities or diseases.

The bride, veiled in a barkcloth, decked in ornaments, and sobbing over the presumed loss of her freedom, is carried in a procession made up of her brother and a number of her friends. Halfway to her new home they are met by friends of the bridegroom who relieve them of the bride. Only one girl,

8. *Ibid.,* p. 88.

"the one who accompanies," proceeds with the bride, to stay and attend her for a few weeks.

When the bride reaches the husband's home, she refuses to enter until he gives her a few cowrie shells, and, once inside, she refuses to be seated until similarly bribed. Nor does she eat at the subsequent marriage feast or move at bedtime until her husband repeats the gift. This proceeding is thought to be a test of the couple's mutual affection.[9]

On the third night the marriage is consummated. Should the bride not be a virgin, a stigma is put upon the parents who are presumed not to have taken proper care of her. For some time—the richer the husband, the longer the period—up to a month, the bride stays in seclusion. Then the girl who attends her is sent home with a substantial gift and any ornaments the bride may have borrowed to wear when going to the husband. As a token of their satisfaction with the marriage, the wife's relatives return 500 cowrie shells from the bride-price. After the feast to mark her return from seclusion the newly made wife is brought to the bridegroom's mother, given a hoe, and taken to dig in her garden.[10] Having demonstrated her agricultural skills, she may now receive a garden of her own and settle down with her husband to assume normal wifely duties.

The first wife is by far the most important; for those who follow, the ceremonies are seldom so involved, nor the bride-price so high. However, the status of the secondary wives may vary with the degree to which they please the husband. As each emerges from seclusion the husband gives her a special name or title. The title most highly prized is "Little Princess," which, among the Baganda, designates the husband's favorite. A wife who behaves badly can be deprived of her title and another may be promoted to it.

9. *Ibid.*, p. 90.
10. *Ibid.*, p. 93.

Motherhood

Within a few weeks after marriage the Baganda wife is expected to show signs of maternity. Such is the value placed on motherhood that the marriage couple may resort to drugs and charms and eventually visits to medicine men and to temple gods for aid in the matter. Even a favorite wife may not keep her favored position should she be unable to bear children. Inasmuch as there is some confusion in their minds as to the nature of conception, the Baganda take precautions to keep the ghosts of the dead from entering the women and being reborn. Pregnant women are treated by drugs from the medicine man, mostly in the form of liquids to drink before meals. Usually one of the elderly female relatives of the husband will come to look after the prospective mother. The clan itself shows considerable interest and may prescribe avoidances and usages to an expectant mother. Also a variety of taboos constrain the actions of the mother during the period of pregnancy; she may not eat certain kinds of food, any salt except that made from marsh grass, a host of other foods including baked plantains, beans, yams, and meat from the head of a goat, and many other items.

When the time for the wife's confinement approaches, she is relieved of many of her more strenuous duties and places herself in the care of her elderly attendant who, to make the delivery easy, massages her frequently with butter. When the time for birth arrives, the old woman usually summons someone to assist her. The wife gives birth to the child in the garden, hanging onto a plantain tree and supported by one of the women. The other receives the child, lays it on a plantain leaf, cuts the umbilical cord with a sharp reed, and assists the child in starting to breathe by blowing up its nose. A medicine man will be called in only to assist in difficult cases. In such a contingency not only will the wife have to suffer from his primitive obstetrics, but because of the difficulty she is considered to have been guilty of adultery.

If the firstborn of a chief is male, it is considered an omen that the father will die. The midwife in such cases will stran-gle the child and say that it was stillborn. Children born feet first are also strangled on grounds that if allowed to live they would grow up to be thieves and murderers. The afterbirth, considered the baby's twin, is carefully buried, but the umbil-ical cord is carefully washed, preserved, and in later life becomes an important adjunct to certain ceremonies.

The birth of twins, considered a catastrophe in Toda society, is an occasion for great rejoicing among the Baganda, as it presumably indicates the direct intervention of the god Mukasa, but at the same time it necessitates great care in the observance of many special taboos so that the displeasure of the god is not incurred for the clan. A remarkable variety of feasts, gift exchanges, and prescribed rites must follow, and the persons of the parents are henceforth sacred. They must wear special clothing and assume new and special names.

After seven days the woman resumes her normal routines of house and field work, carrying the baby around unless the husband should find a female clan member to take care of it. In any event the child is usually carried for about three months in a barkcloth sling on the mother's back. It can be put down to amuse itself only after the performance of a special ceremony by the husband's mother.

Childhood

Having survived early infancy, the young Baganda faces a rather unroutinized, casual childhood during the course of which only a few *rites de passage* mark his progress toward becoming a grown-up. He will be washed, nursed, fed a banana paste supplement after three months of nursing, and visited occasionally by the husband's relatives, who will pass judgment on the manner in which the child is being reared. When the mother is not carrying it on her back, she will rest the child on her hip. Should the upper teeth come in before the lower, it is considered a sign that the child will mistreat the mother in later life. In the home the child is usually allowed to play on the dirt floor, more or less unattended. Little attention is given to early cleanliness training or to the child's learning to walk. The mother may hug or caress the child and comfort it when hurt or in distress. However, children are never kissed—kissing is not known to the Baganda—and the close intimacy of the mother-child relationship as found in America, for example, is not present. The language of the Baganda carries no word for love or tender affection; the closest is a word that is best translated as "like."[11]

An event of transcending importance in the child's early life is the naming ceremony, inasmuch as it is not until this ceremony is completed that the child's legitimacy is once and forever established. In a gathering at the clan chief's house children of both sexes are brought by the mothers carrying a piece of each child's umbilical cord—carefully kept from the day of birth. The paternal grandmothers drop these into a can containing beer, milk, and water. If they float, the clan chief accepts the children as legitimate, but if any cord sinks, the child to whom it belongs is considered born in adultery and disowned by the clan. A feast follows the ceremony, the umbilical cords meanwhile being returned to the mothers for use in future ceremonies. On the day following, the naming ceremony is performed. The paternal grandfather recites names of dead ancestors of the clan, and when the child laughs it is given the last mentioned name, the soul of the ancestor being considered to have entered its body.[12] For the first time the child's head is now shaved and the locks buried in the same place as was the afterbirth.

Baganda children in all but the families of chiefs and of the nobility do not routinely live with their own parents after they are weaned. Rather, the son of the father's eldest brother makes a lawful decision as to where the child should go. The girls until their own marriage will live in the home of an elder married brother or, if they have none, with a brother of

11. *Ibid.*, p. 61.
12. Murdock, *Our Primitive Contemporaries*, p. 537.

the father. Boys will invariably go to live with the brothers of the father. Living with new parents means no particular change in status; the biological parents do not forget their off-spring and are always present for any ceremonies involving their children.

Baganda boyhood may not be idyllic, but in many ways it is a rather carefree time of their lives. They wear little or no clothing until the age of six or seven years and are subject to very few duties or responsibilities. Every two or three months as a sanitation measure their heads are shaved, and, like all clippings, bits of skin, bone, or any other human fragment of the Baganda, the cuttings are carefully disposed of so that no enemy or wrong-doer might use them in sorcery to harm the owner. At puberty boys and girls become more conscious of their appearance, bathe more frequently, and wear clothing that covers most of the body.

Children are expected to assist in any minor household duties they may be able to perform. However, the more important duties revolve around the father's work, and flocks of goats, sheep, and even cattle may be entrusted to the care of young boys. The work of herding is not too demanding; boys are usually left with ample time for playing a variety of games. At about ten years of age the youths are expected to perform light duties for their relatives and to show some apti-tude for a future occupation. A bright, alert boy may find a place in the household of a chief and by this avenue of oppor-tunity possibly some day become a page to the king. Servility in the face of superior status is so universal among the Baganda as to become almost a character trait of the people. Those Baganda youth not inclined toward skilled industries or servant work usually attach themselves to some clan chief and continue the remainder of their lives as peasants.

Girls, perhaps sooner than boys, are taught a variety of household and agricultural duties. As females with a status immeasurably inferior to males, they are called upon early in life to render services to their superiors. Cooking and cultiva-tion are the two main themes of the girl's occupational indoctrination, since to be a successful manager of the plantain grove or to be an expert cook are regarded by the Baganda as a woman's best accomplishments.[13] The weaving of grasses and reeds into mats, baskets, and fences is also considered an important skill to be learned by both sexes. Girls, in distinction to boys, seldom have time to play games.

Until about the age of twelve the girls are unclothed except for a ring made of woven plantain fiber or lizard skin worn around the waist. According to Baganda belief, this must be done to keep the body from developing disproportionately. At puberty girls wear a piece of barkcloth around the loins. During her first menstruation the girl is fed and cared for in isolation by female relatives. Upon "recovery" the father and foster father jump over their respective wives to celebrate and to assure the fertility of the girl.

Adulthood

The Baganda woman at the time she enters her wifely duties is given a new hoe, water pot, cooking pot, and a basket in which to carry food. Her primary duty as already noted is the cultivation of the family garden allotted her by the husband. A diligent wife who uses her hoe until through wear the handle breaks is usually given a goat by her husband as a present. Quite likely at the same time he also gives her a new hoe! It bears repeating that the value of a wife lies primarily in her ability to be economically and biologically productive. Her work begins at daybreak and continues until past dusk. For the male a few hours' work early in the morning and a few late in the day are considered appropriate to his status as a male, if not a provider.

Wives generally take turns cooking for a month at a time, but it is seldom that they are asked by the husband to eat with him, and then only when he does not have company. Normally the wives have their meals in their own huts. Their household routines consist not only of cooking but of making

13. Roscoe, *op. cit.*, p. 79.

their husband's bed, cleaning out the grass used as a covering for the dirt floor of the house, carrying wood and water, and performing other menial chores around the house or compound. The first wife will have charge of the household fetishes; the second will shave the husband's head and trim his nails.

To realize the highest economic "yield" from the first wife a husband will, if possible, bring into the household not only subsidiary wives but unmarried sisters, other female relatives, and female slaves to share in or take over household menial duties. A wife may also assist her husband in preparing materials for the work he will have to perform, when called upon by his chief, by cutting and cleaning reeds, cutting and weaving grasses into thatch, and the like.

The women enjoy little freedom of movement except within the compound of the family household. Without the consent of their husbands or masters they cannot move about the countryside, and in the capital city no woman is permitted to visit friends or relatives without an escort.

The role of husband in Baganda society varies of course with his economic and political status. Although he cannot own land and must obtain his plots from king or chief, under ordinary circumstances he may obtain as much as he and his wives are able to bring under cultivation. In addition to paying various taxes he is obligated to his chief to render services, mostly in the form of manual labor in building and repairing roads, clearing land, and, importantly, in helping to carry out the warfare which engages the Baganda very frequently. Having secured land, the peasant henceforth acquires the title equivalent of freeman. For the young Baganda starting in as a freeman, a house is the first major structure to be built, once approval has been secured from the family god. Two shrines must first be built on the land, and after offerings are made the actual housebuilding may proceed. The husband will clear the land, cutting down trees, shrubs, and tall grasses which the wife will heap up and burn. All the digging and cultivation will be done by the wife, since a husband who does not permit his wife to cultivate a garden will likely lose her back to her parents. The women dig, plant, sow, care for, and harvest crops, the first fruits of which are offered by the husband to the gods. Her work in the garden will vary according to the particular season, but no matter what the season she will likely begin work at about 6:00 A.M. At about 9:00 she will rest and smoke her first pipe, after which she will continue her work for another hour, cutting and wrapping the food for the day to be taken home at the end of this period.

The husband, in addition to clearing land for agricultural use, will consider as work rightfully his hunting, fishing, herding cattle, butchery, cutting trees and brush and carrying heavy firewood, brewing beer (the universal alcoholic beverage of the Baganda), and making barkcloth. Men also specialize in the arts and crafts, making drums, building long plank-sided canoes, erecting houses, working with leather, working at smithies, and performing carpentry and other handicraft. The finest craftsmen will be found working in the royal industries; chiefs likewise attempt to gather round them a body of competent artisans as well as a labor and warrior force.

In those parts of Uganda where pasturage is good, cattle and goats will be raised. The royal herds contain thousands of cattle, those of the chiefs possibly hundreds, and peasants will each have a cow or two. Herding of cattle constitutes a secondary occupation for the Baganda. With their boys the herdsmen drive the cattle out to pasturage each morning and back at nightfall. Cattle are fed entirely upon grass. Cows belonging to king and chiefs are kept in kraals during the night, but the peasant usually takes his cow into his compound or enclosure. While the herdsman generally does the milking, both he and his wife churn the milk in a large bottle gourd. The cattle are not killed by the peasants for food; if a cow dies of sickness, however, the herdsmen do not hesitate to eat the meat. Where cattle are considered a mark of social superiority there is a tendency to exclude women from any work associated with them.[14]

14. Harold B. Thomas and Robert Scott, *Uganda* (1935), pp. 270-282.

Old age presents no frightening spectacle to a Baganda. Under ordinary conditions of life his economic status will increase so long as his wives can cultivate or administer the cultivation of the gardens. Although the idea of saving is foreign to the Baganda, some riches are accumulated through livestock, mats, barkcloths, furniture, ornaments, and occasionally in saved cowrie shells.

As a Baganda becomes too old for work, he will dispose of his properties—with the exception of the land—and join the family of one of his sons. Even so there will be light activities to keep him busy, and there are light activities for the old female whose wisdom and experience in the world of domestic affairs make her presence worthwhile. The aged are never without a household.

Women outlive their husbands in substantial proportion. Constant warfare, human sacrifices, executions, maiming, and mutilating take their toll. Sickness carries off many of both sexes. At the age of sixty the Baganda is likely gray- or white-haired, grizzled, gaunt, and, more than likely, partly infirm.

Disjunctions

Whatever problems arise from widowhood tend to be defined and handled in terms of clan rather than family solidarity. At the death of a husband the fate of the wives varies according to several conditions. If she is the first wife, her primary duty is to live near and attend the grave of her husband. Under ordinary circumstances she will join the family of the brother living closest to the burial ground. Other wives may be claimed by relatives, but those wives who have none to claim them will become the property of the heir. Should the one who cares for the husband's grave wish to remarry, she must take up the matter with her brother, who will in turn have to refund the bride-price to the deceased's relatives. She then reenters the clan and can remarry in the usual fashion, with the exception that the new husband will have to make an offering at the first husband's grave in order to pacify the spirit. A widower may take a new wife from the clan of his former wife, again paying the usual bride-price.

An almost universal "built in" source of family disjunction concerns the above-mentioned practice of sending children to live with relatives. Primarily the relatives of the father will be the recipients of the children, but the mother's brother who arranged her marriage will have a right to take any of her children unless they are "redeemed" by gifts.[15] Redemption is nearly always practiced even though the gifts are by Baganda terms rather substantial. The mother's brother, incidentally, is the Baganda counterpart of the cruel stepmother.[16] The basis for this is that he has no clan obligations to the child. On the other hand, children sent to a father's brother are considered to have been rescued from the overindulgence of the parents. The new parents, it is held, will bring them up more strictly, and not only treat them fairly, but possibly choose them as heirs in preference to their own children!

The father's parents might at any time ask for and get a grandchild. The parents would never think of refusing such a request, even though it is considered a foregone conclusion that the child taken in by its grandparents will be overindulged. Despite this the rationale for sending out a child is that it is in the interest of the child's own future, and that for the most part he will receive education and opportunities for advancement not available at home.

Family Controls

The Baganda family falls heir to a variety of external controls, some expressions of larger forms of social organization, such as clan and state, others more particularistic and immediate in the culture. Unlike the Todas or Hopi, the Baganda live under the control of a despotic, virtually all-powerful king whose system of administrative government, feudal in

15. Lucy P. Mair, *An African People of the Twentieth Century* (1934), p. 61.
16. *Ibid.*, p. 62.

many respects, bears down heavily upon his subjects. The responsibilities of the Baganda to the clan and king are highly inclusive and constricting, consuming much of their everyday life. The importance of the clan is evident from earlier discussion. Its influence upon the control of the family in such matters as mate selection, bride-price, pregnancy, birth, legitimation of children, naming, disposition of children, inheritance, and funeral behavior suggests the inclusive nature of this social unit.

A wide variety of beliefs, taboos, fears, avoidances, and other usages further acts to control, direct, channel, or restrict Baganda activity. Some, such as totemic belief, clan temple worship, worship of national gods, avoidance of certain categories of nobility, support or express features of the broader social units. But the use of fetishes and amulets, the great stock put in omens, and the recourse to medicine men are in a sense particularistic. They exist in the culture, possibly serving one or a variety of functions, but are not expressive of the larger forms of social organization.

The Baganda live in an animistic world peopled with ghosts of ancestors, spirits of animals, trees, stones, lakes, wells, hills—literally all of nature. Additionally, many of the living are thought to be possessed with spiritual qualities. A thorough investigation into the manner in which the spirit world affects that of the living is beyond the scope of this chapter.

On the other hand, listing a few of the taboos, proscriptions, and avoidances which directly affect Baganda family behavior might prove instructive. The women may assist the man in many endeavors, but should he have cattle or be a herdsman, they may never milk the cows. A variety of taboos must be observed by pregnant women, especially with regard to food and drink. The afterbirth is called the "second child" and is buried carefully; the umbilical cord also has magical properties and must be carefully preserved and prepared for use in ceremonies. Twins as noted are felt to be due to the direct intervention of a benevolent god; death is the work of the sorcerer's art. Also, unfaithfulness of the husband causes sickness in the wife, neglected graves result in angry ancestor ghosts, and the ghost of the maternal aunt is malevolent, although most ancestor ghosts are benign and helpful.

The many proscriptions dealing with sexual behavior upon examination reveal a balance of emphasis on procreative, economic, and sexual aspects of marriage.[17] Sexual urges are reckoned as normal; the guardians of the young, especially girls, are expected to be responsible for their charges' remaining chaste. Virginity is valued; its absence reflects negatively on the girl's parents and clan. In most violations of those aspects of the code dealing with sexual intercourse, amends may be made, or partially made, by payment of compensation to parents or fines to the courts.

Chastity for unmarried youths is not especially required, although they are warned against indulging in sexual intrigues with married women. Adultery with a married woman is so severely frowned upon that the husband whose rights have been infringed upon may kill the offender. The wife guilty of adultery may be beaten, even to death, by the husband; conversely, the spirits of the supernatural, not those physically present, are expected to punish the husband who commits the act.

Despite the plethora of proscriptions and taboos exterior to the family, there are internal conditions which give rise to the building of intrafamily usages through interaction of its members. For example, husband-wife interaction is conditioned by her role in the economy of the family as steward of the family garden as well as manager of the domestic affairs. Despite the clearly subordinate relation of the wife, her position is by no means menial. The first wife in the confines of the compound may with dignity and aplomb express her views and make such demands upon the husband as the situation seems to warrant. If he pays no attention to her the Baganda say with derision "he does not know she is his wife."[18]

Although somewhat obscured by the heavy blanket of

17. Mair, "Native Marriage in Buganda" (1935), pp. 1-17.
18. *Ibid.*

external social controls and forces for compliance, a core of companionship exists between the husband and his wives. The deference shown by the wife and the body of etiquette defining their interpersonal relations emphasize the social front to be publicly maintained—a duplication of the king-subject and the chief-patron relationship. Backstage in the compound, especially when the husband has neither visitors nor relatives present, the interpersonal interaction is easy, the language quite unrestrained. From the outside it might seem that the institutional impress on the family is so all-encompassing as to make virtually every act of husband and wife, if not of child, the playing of a role, the response to a defined situation. From within, the picture must be changed to take into account the intimacy of each other's company, the expression of affection, the creation of companionship, and at least a semblance of control through consensus of the family members.

Family Functions

The polygynous Baganda family, consisting of a number of nuclear family units headed by a single father, is the only recognizable and sanctioned agency of human reproduction among the Baganda. Having children constitutes the major role for the wife. Offspring are sought and infanticide is abhorred, except in certain specifically prescribed conditions in which the continued living of the child threatens the survival of an adult person, family, clan, or nobility. Whereas the Todas kill one or both twins, the Baganda accept their arrival with elation. Families among the Baganda tend to run large—ten children for a wife is not considered abnormal. A well-to-do commoner might well have fifty children, a chief many more. There is no call to limit family size or population; as high as 3 million people have at one time lived in the Baganda kingdom. The soil is fertile, and the growing seasons succeed each other rapidly. Thus, the Baganda never starve, their standard of living is high, and their life expectancy, in comparison with most nonliterate tribes, is high.

Within the household the children receive a casual, unhurried, something less than intense socialization into the adult society. Teen-age parents relinquish their first- and perhaps second-born children to the families of older, more responsible brothers and thus reduce the complications in an early marriage which must inevitably start with the couple in debt and with a garden to manage. The young wife may nevertheless start early to discharge her important childbearing role, without overly jeopardizing her status as steward of the family economy. In a few years, with most debts paid and with the development of some maturity, the young couple are presumably more prepared to assume continuing parental roles.

No studies have been made of the consequences of separation of Baganda children from their parents after weaning. Casual observations of earlier students of Baganda culture seem to indicate little personality damage inflicted on the child. In any event, since the child nurses for two years or more, since it is carried about constantly by the mother, and since the husband's parents show an abiding interest in the infant's welfare, it is reasonable to hypothesize a fairly anxiety-free infancy—until weaning is accomplished. The shock of transfer may be great enough to produce a sense of uncertainty and possibly some individuation. In the large Baganda household the child is not likely to find it necessary to polarize his affectional needs around one or two persons—there are many "significant others" present or in the neighborhood.

Baganda personality or character structure is likely, then, to be somewhat shallow. With the cultural emphasis on etiquette, form, courtesy, and manners there is no cause for the overcommitment of one's personality—with respect to peers, parents, chief, or king. Loyalty to parents does not stand in the way of a son's desire to maximize his economic potential, nor is his allegiance to a chief absolute and unrenounceable. Chiefs are servile but not necessarily loyal. Kings themselves have no guarantee of unyielding fealty from chief or commoner. When a king dies the social structure temporarily dissolves; no simple machinery of succession operates to install a new king. Thus the Baganda must grow up and take his place in a society characterized by folk and mass relationships in which arbitrary exercise of power is counterposed against the rational workings of an elaborate bureaucracy. The consequence is an undercurrent of diffuse anxiety and apprehension, mixed with respect, and the desire to enhance one's status, come what may.

It is evident that the family must share in and often defer to clan interests. Functions such as naming, status-conferring, sponsorship, mate selection (including setting the bride-price), protection, and the providing of a sense of group identity are for the most part performed by the clan or under its auspices.

Still the Baganda family retains its vitality, form, and several basic functions. Children are born, reared by parents or close relatives, fed and sheltered, educated for traditional roles, and given a sense of being wanted and of being necessary. Presently it may be noted that the family system of the Baganda, though altered in many ways, continues to exist as an ongoing social unit, while the clan system has become increasingly weakened and within the century may disappear.

REFERENCES

Mair, Lucy P., *An African People of the Twentieth Century*. London: George Routledge and Sons, 1934.

———, "Totemism among the Baganda," *Man: A Monthly Record of Anthropological Science*, XXXV (1935), pp. 65-67.

Murdock, George Peter, *Our Primitive Contemporaries*. New York: The Macmillan Company, 1934.

———, *Social Structure*. New York: The Macmillan Company, 1949.

Richards, Audrey I., *The Multicultural States of East Africa*. Montreal and London: McGill-Queens Press, 1969.

Roscoe, John, *The Baganda*. London: Macmillan and Company, 1911.

Thomas, Harold B., and Scott, Robert, *Uganda*. London: Oxford University Press, 1935.

5 The Classical Chinese System of Familism

China, one of the world's larger land masses, contains about 4.5 million square miles and exhibits a wide range of climatic conditions. Its people, the Chinese, reflect in their physical appearance the variety of races and ethnic groups which at various periods in the thousands of years of its history have occupied the land. The original Chinese themselves were probably Central Asian tribes who moved to the east to occupy and establish political hegemony over the aboriginals. The governmental centers set up became city-states which in turn were brought within kingdoms. By 1122 B.C. the House of Chou emerged supreme in the center of ancient culture and government.[1] In the dynastic periods which followed, government was hierarchized and centralized, with an imposing bureaucratic structure to give it rational organization. However, the central government's contacts with the people were, for the most part, made indirectly through the extralegal channels of the village and clan heads. The upshot was an interesting administrative combination in which the hierarchy was centralized but the relation between the people and government was decentralized.[2]

Most of China's terrain is rough, mountainous, and dry, the geographic habitat on the whole is undesirable, and most of the population has tended to cluster along the more fertile river-made plains and lowlands along the seaward fringe.[3]

1. Daniel H. Kulp, "Chinese Continuity," *Annals of the American Academy of Political and Social Science,* 152 (1930), pp. 18-29.

2. Marion J. Levy, *The Family Revolution in Modern China* (1949), p. 238.

3. Joseph R. Schwendeman, "Geographic Features of the Habitat of the Chinese Peasant," in Irwin T. Sanders et al., eds., *Societies Around the World* (1953), p. 34.

Erosion, drought, unpredictable rainfall, typhoons, and floods have plagued the Chinese throughout history, bringing uncertainty and hardship into their lives. Man-made disasters in the form of warfare, revolution, and military occupation have added their share of insecurities, along with population surges that have produced areas of extremely high human density.

Despite the grimness of the battle for survival, the measure of continuity in Chinese culture, social organization, mentality, and style of life is astonishing. True, within the present century Chinese civilization has been undergoing revolutionary changes in political, economic, and social institutions and Granet, for one, has also shown that the changes from a clan-centered to a feudalistic, and then to an administratively centralized government under an emperor, were likewise revolutionary in the manner in which the social structure of Chinese society was altered.[4] Nevertheless, for a period of nearly 2,500 years, lasting up to the beginning of the present century, a remarkable social and cultural continuity characterized Chinese social institutions. Among these institutions the family assumed and maintained a typical form: patriarchal, patrilineal, patrilocal, extended, located within the broader social organizational forms of clan and sib, and integrated within a system of ethico-religious beliefs centering around ancestor worship.

It is to this traditional, extended family which persisted over two millennia without significant structural change that we turn now for description and analysis. As a family type it represents a cultural ideal, most likely to be achieved by the officialdom and gentry of China but to be emulated, if possible, by the peasant—the "earnest imitator of the life patterns established by the gentry-scholar class."[5] Again, although we shall be describing the character and workings of a family form that may no longer exist in substantial form in the

4. Marcel Granet, *Chinese Civilization* (1951).
5. Shu-Ching Lee, "China's Traditional Family, Its Characteristics and Disintegration," *American Sociological Review*, 18 (1953), p. 272.

China of today, the use of the "historical present" form of exposition will be employed. The reader should not confuse the "traditional" Chinese family hereinafter described with the "transitional" family as it has been developing in China in the past half century or better. Our goal is not to compare China's families, old and new, but to characterize as fully as possible within the limited space of the present chapter a classic instance of a multifunctional family of great stability.[6]

Family Structure

Marriage Institutions: Monogamy

The dominant marriage institution of the traditional Chinese extended family is monogamy. Marriage, regarded primarily as a social arrangement between two families, emphasizes family rather than individual needs. Thus a husband and wife form a union whose importance in Chinese society revolves not around the affection, intimacy, and personal gratifications of the marriage couple, but upon considerations having to do with the functions of the family as a vehicle for the perpetuation of lineage and for the worship and propitiation of the spirits of departed ancestors. Upon marriage the wife enters the service of her husband and his mother; the husband remains as son in the service of his father, who in turn is in the service of his departed ancestors. In all these basic relationships *respect* is expected to take precedence; of them only the husband-wife relationship allows for some latitude in the matter of affectional response—and then only under the most restricted circumstances.

6. For fairly recent studies of Chinese families in transition see Levy, *op. cit.*, and C. K. Yang, *The Chinese Family in the Communist Revolution* (1959).

Marriage Institutions: Concubinage

Long before the Christian era concubinage, the taking of secondary wives, existed among the Chinese nobility. Often additional wives were sisters of the principal wife, and in such cases kinship complications were less likely to develop than when the secondary spouses were from other families. Within roughly the last 2,000 years, the period we use as the "historical present," concubinage has been prevalent among all groups except the peasants, in whose rural mores only the monogamous union has been acceptable. When the secondary wife resides in the family and shares in the economic cooperation of the household members, as well as in sexual association with the husband, the marriage form may be termed polygynous.[7] Although it is possible for concubines to achieve this status, which amounts to that of a cowife, both in practice and in rationale the concubine is more likely to be found in an inferior and a much more precarious position in the family household than is the principal, first wife.

The rationale for this practice of concubinage is the assurance of male progeny, the presence of whom guarantees perpetuation of the family lineage and eventually the performance of appropriate rituals of ancestor worship. When the first wife fails repeatedly to give birth to a son, the husband may acquire a concubine, but the latter in no socially legitimated way may replace the former. The principal wife retains the status which is ascribed to her at marriage. She cannot be reduced to the status of a concubine, nor can the concubine be raised to the status of a first wife. When the concubine gives birth to a son, often by a social fiction it is considered to be the offspring of the principal wife.

But for many middle- and upper-class Chinese, concubinage represents a social device for satisfaction of the polyerotic tendencies of the male[8] and, among one's male cohorts

7. George P. Murdock, *Social Structure* (1949), p. 26.
8. Francis L. K. Hsu, *Under the Ancestor's Shadow* (1948), p. 106.

at least, as a mode of acquiring prestige. In any event concubines are taken into many families where male progeny already exist, and in such cases the practice suggests that where affectional bonds have weakened, or have failed to develop, concubinage becomes an alternative to divorce. The consequence is that although some aspects of husband-wife relationships are changed, social unity of the family remains intact.[9]

Family and Kinship Organization

The universally exalted family in China is the large, extended family (Chia-Chang) comprised of three or preferably more generations living under the same roof, constituting a household of some twenty, thirty, or more members, presided over by a head, or patriarch. For most of the Chinese, however, such a family remains the ideal. Peasants and workers are likely to have families considerably smaller in size, organized about the nuclear unit of husband, wife, and children. Among the gentry and officialdom, the large family, with patriarch and wife, married sons and their wives, unmarried sons and daughters, grandchildren, and sometimes great-grandchildren, exists both as an ideal and a reality. This also is the form of family most likely to be depicted in Chinese art and literature, song and drama.

The value orientation of the traditional Chinese family tends to follow almost classically the familistic pattern. Attributes of familism, seen as "a form of social organization in which all values are determined by reference to the maintenance, continuity, and functions of the family groups"[10] include: (1) emphasis on the father-son relationship; (2) family pride; (3) encouragement of the large family; (4) the cult of

9. This point is developed by Lin Yutang in his *My Country and My People* (1935), pp. 162-165.
10. Daniel H. Kulp, *Country Life in South China: The Sociology of Familism* (1925), p. 188.

ancestor worship; and (5) common ownership of property by the family.[11] Of these, ancestor worship and filial piety are the most basic and particularly deserve elaboration.

Ancestor worship exists as the dominant emphasis of the religious cosmology of the Chinese. The ancestors are thought to take their place in an ordered spirit world that is the counterpart of the human world left behind. "The spirit world," notes Hsu, "is based upon and functional to the existence of the world of humans, and the human world is in turn supervised and guided by the spirit world . . . In the popular mind the spiritual hierarchy is a part of the social order just as much as the bureaucratic hierarchy is."[12] The close, reciprocal relationship of the two worlds is signalized by the father-son relationship, the vital link in an unending chain between generations, leading upward to ancestor worship and downward to the "sin" of no posterity.[13] The filial relationship thus constitutes the first principle of familism in the social organization of China.[14] In its essence it calls both for reverence and propitiatory activities toward the departed ancestors and respect and obedience to one's living parents. The father-son nexus is most crucial, inasmuch as the family line is perpetuated through it. As expounded in the code of Confucius, the son is to serve and take good care of his parents, to take good care of his physical body because it is given to him by his parents, and to have offspring to continue the name of the family.

The kinship system for the Chinese, as for all societies, expresses and defines the rights and obligations of individuals to each other. In his analysis of the Chinese kinship system, Fêng notes that the systematic recording of kinship terms goes back as far as the *Erh Ya*, a work of the third or second cen-

11. Following Lee, *op. cit.*, pp. 272-273.

12. Francis L. K. Hsu, in Ralph Linton, ed., *Most of the World* (1949), p. 778. By permission of Columbia University Press.

13. Lee, *op. cit.*, p. 273.

14. Cheng Ch'eng-K'un, "Familism the Foundation of Chinese Social Organization," *Social Forces*, 23 (1944), pp. 51-52.

tury B.C. in which the relationships are carefully classified and arranged, and that many encyclopedic works have from then to the present been devoted to the subject.[15] Another important work, and the one most consulted by students of Chinese culture, is a set of ritual works, the *Li*, written some 500 years B.C., which do not deal with kinship *per se* but with the subject of ritual.[16] As a consequence it has become a common practice to identify kinship relations functionally as those persons for whom one wears mourning.

Through the application of the principles of lineal and collateral differentiation and generation stratification, the Chinese kinship system provides a comprehensive matrix within which three groups of kinsmen, paternal relatives, maternal relatives, and the relatives of the wife are located. In anthropological terminology, the Chinese kinship system finds its basis in the exogamous patrilineal sib.[17] With the emphasis on relatives in the male line, the circle of paternal kinsmen will include those within nine generations and five collateral grades, making up a total of twenty-one categories of relatives including lineal ascendants, lineal descendants, brothers and their wives, sisters, uncles and their wives, and cousins and their wives.[18] Such grouping of kinsmen most closely approximates the traditional Chinese conception of "the family," living in one household and constituting an economic unit. Maternal relatives, inasmuch as the patrilocal residence rule is rigidly observed, seldom, if ever, join the household, and only maternal grandparents, uncles, aunts, and first cousins are included in the circle of maternal kinsmen for whom one wears mourning. Relatives of the wife, who complete the kinfolk circle, include parents, grandparents, uncles, sisters, and brothers of the wife.[19]

15. Han-Yi Fêng, *The Chinese Kinship System* (1937), and also "The Chinese Kinship System," *Harvard Journal of Asiatic Studies*, II, No. 2 (July, 1937), pp. 141-275.

16. *Ibid.*, p. 145.

17. *Ibid.*, p. 173.

18. Olga Lang, *Chinese Family and Society* (1946), p. 20.

19. *Ibid.*

In addition to the family and the kin for whom one wears mourning, a third, the sib, is the most external kinship grouping. Two characteristics of the sib, patrilineal descent and exogamy, already noted, have direct influence upon the alignment of relatives. Relatives are divided along sib lines into *sib relatives* and *nonsib relatives*. All sib relatives belonging to the same sib of ego possess the same sib name, and trace their descent to a common ancestor. Paternal relatives descended from females through males or females are nonsib relatives. Maternal and affinal relatives all belong to the same nonsib group.[20] Consequently they do not bear the same sib surname. It is possible, then, in this strictly sib-exogamous group, to marry a person who by our way of thinking would be a "blood" relative, e.g., first cousin, providing he or she were a nonsib relative from the "mother's side" of the family.

As with most societies in which kinship systems are well elaborated and which organize behavior, sib membership has a variety of implications for the roles, expectations, privileges, rights, and duties of the Chinese. The sib not only helps regulate marriage but often forms the basis for village organization —many villages will be made up exclusively of members of the same sib and thus, by our usage, constitute a clan. The sib maintains temples for the worship of ancestors, holds property as an organization, and finances a variety of economic institutions, including pawnshops. Moreover, it cuts across rich and poor families to provide a measure of integration to a well-stratified society, and it exercises broad judicial functions on an extralegal basis.[21] Kulp, who studied intensively village life in South China, concludes his analysis of the sib by referring to its patrilineal, patronymic, exogamous character, adding that it is also inclusive of the village which he studied and "the area of effective social opinion, the determiner of status in the community, and made up of a plurality of subgroups, sex, economic and ancestral alignments."[22]

20. Fêng, *op. cit.*, p. 175.
21. Levy, *op. cit.*, p. 49.
22. Kulp, *Country Life in South China*, p. 145. By permission of Columbia University Press.

Household, Property, and Inheritance

The household proper of the large Chinese family, in addition to the regular members of the family, will include servants, boarders, and possibly relatives staying temporarily with the family. Each household has its head in whom authority and great responsibility are entrusted. He is usually the senior member of the family, so that the principle of filial piety operates in support of his office. He is responsible for the proper conduct of domestic affairs and takes charge of the financial organization and operation of the family, with the right to compel all members to turn in their earnings to a common purse; he manages the properties of the family and he must care for and disburse the funds in a way that will insure the support and maintenance of the whole family.[23]

The importance of the father-son relationship is indicated by the fact that at the death of the "honored head" of the family, his eldest son, not the brother of the deceased nor any of his sons, will assume the headship of the family.[24] Tradition strongly militates against the division of family property, and only if there is no one to take the place of the family head who dies or, much less likely, if all sons decide to establish separate families and are granted permission by the head to do so, will the large family be broken into constituent parts, i.e., smaller households headed by the married brothers. Ordinarily both craft and property pass from generation to generation along lines of the father-son relationship. The skills that make up the family craft are thus transmitted only to male heirs, never to daughters or daughters-in-law. Tangible property is allotted equally among the sons, except that some special privileges are possessed by the eldest in descent; sons of a concubine are recognized as having little claim.[25] So long as her husband is alive the wife has no absolute

23. Sing Ging Su, *The Chinese Family System* (1922), pp. 49-50.
24. *Ibid.*, p. 32.
25. Lee, *op. cit.*, p. 274.

ownership of anything; even her personal effects can be sold by the husband if he wants to brave the gossip and censure of the community. At the death of the husband, however, the widow generally receives a share in the property and goes to live with one of the sons.

The Family Cycle

Mate Selection

The selection of a mate for one of its members represents one of the more responsible and fateful decisions to be made in the traditional Chinese family. Marriages, arranged by the heads of the families, are concluded by marriage contract. Significantly, it is the signatures of the family heads which are required, not those of the marriage couple.[26] The marriage union, one recalls, has its social significance to the Chinese as primarily an instrumentality for the perpetuation of the family line through its male members.

Romantic love is not a concept totally foreign to the Chinese. In ancient feudal China falling in love was not an unusual antecedent to marriage, although parental consent was necessary before the various ceremonies preparatory to marriage could go forward. But for the more than 2,000 years that make up the period in which the traditional large Chinese family under consideration flourished, romantic love has been looked upon as dangerous and definitely inimical to the development of the decorum and deportment proper for married family members in their primary roles of respectful son and subservient daughter-in-law.

Convenience to the families involved provides the basis for mate selection. The will and wishes of the prospective bridegroom and bride are a matter of little moment. Match-

---

26. Lang, *op. cit.*, p. 35. The description of marriage in the traditional Chinese family follows Lang, pp. 35-41.

makers "professional or amateurs, men or women" are indispensable[27] in the arranged marriage. One face-saving consequence of a marriage arranged by a matchmaker is that should the union prove unsuccessful a good portion of the responsibility must rest with this "middleman of marriage."

In the matter of mate selection certain rules of social organization are observed. Since the Chinese sibs are exogamous, two persons with the same surname may not marry unless they are at least five generations removed. While parallel cousins who bear the same surname never marry, those who do not, may. A traditionally preferred type of cross-cousin marriage is between a girl and her father's sister's son. Conversely, because of the traditional attitude that the female has only her mother's blood, the marriage between a boy and his father's sister's daughter is taboo. In brief, not all cross cousins may marry, but one type of cross-cousin marriage is preferred, and not all parallel cousins may marry, but the grounds for the prohibition are more clearly an expression of exogamy.[28]

Matchmaking begins either with a visit by the matchmaker to the girl's parents or a visit to the matchmaker by the parents of a girl looking for a mate for their daughter. The matchmaker is in effect a sort of matrimonial agency; on occasion he may even suggest matches to parents without waiting to be approached. The first step is to arrange for a trial betrothal. The matchmaker secures on cards the eight characters standing for the name, hour, day, month, and year of birth of the boy and girl. These are taken to a fortune teller or diviner to determine if the characteristics harmonize sufficiently to provide an acceptable basis for marriage. The lack of concern over the wishes of the potential marriage partners is indicated by Kulp:

> The potential marriage-mates never see each other during the betrothal negotiations, and their own personal consent is not essential. Usually

27. *Ibid.,* p. 37.
28. Kulp, *Country Life in South China,* pp. 166-168.

they behold each other for the first time on the day of marriage. Selection of mates is thus made on a highly conventionalized basis. Not only do the persons themselves have nothing to do with the selection of primary mates, but even the heads of the economic families play only a secondary and initiatory role. They may agree on an alliance satisfactory to them but if the horoscopes are not favorably divined, the betrothal may not be consummated. Thus is the matter finally taken out of the hands of people entirely and put into the realm of spirit.[29]

The next step, as outlined by Lang, is the sending of betrothal gifts consisting of a wild goose and a roll of silk—the equivalent of our wedding gift. Once the gifts have been accepted (at times sums of money have been included also) the betrothal contract is signed, usually in the ancestral temple, and the agreement is considered legally binding.[30] It should be noted that betrothal usually precedes puberty and that the usual age for the marriage is about sixteen for a boy and fourteen for a girl.

In the selection of a primary mate such matters as wealth, scholarship, position, age (marrying across a generation brings confusion into the system of kinship relations and is highly disfavored among Chinese), personality, temperament, and health are all given judicious consideration by the elders. They pay about as much attention to the wishes of the offspring as adult Americans give in setting up college scholarship funds for their children or in enrolling them in a medical care plan. These are matters for older heads, wiser minds.

For the more wealthy the interim between betrothal and marriage may last three or more years. For the poorer the time is shortened. Among the poorest families whose children are not young at the time of betrothal, marriage takes place with only enough time intervening for the girl to make her wedding dress.[31] The girl's parents provide her with a dowry, the elaborateness of which varies with the economic status of

29. *Ibid.,* p. 171. By permission of Columbia University Press.
30. Lang, *op. cit.,* p. 38.
31. Martin C. Yang, *A Chinese Village: Taitou, Shantung Province* (1945), as quoted in Irwin T. Sanders et al., *op. cit.,* p. 144.

her family. Inasmuch as there is usually an attempt to make the dowry as complete and elaborate as possible "marrying off" a daughter is considered something of an economic burden to the parents.

Until the wedding neither the engaged couple nor their families may see each other, except for necessary meetings. Engagement is not considered as immutable as marriage, but, should the two families have been intimately associated, a broken engagement could be the occasion for considerable embarrassment on both sides.[32]

The wedding date will have been set by the diviner or fortune teller. On this day a red sedan chair borne by four men will be sent by the groom's family to deliver the girl to his family home for the wedding ceremony. The bride, wearing red, her face veiled, will be carried into the sedan by one of her elder brothers or an uncle. Father and mother are left behind as the sedan, followed by two brothers or close relatives, moves slowly through the streets. Though the bride will be hidden behind curtains, the items making up her dowry will be in plain sight for the people of the village or town to admire. The wedding takes place usually in the front court of the groom's family home. The groom, dressed in formal wedding gown of blue and jacket of black, stands with the bride in front of a table. The ceremony is a family affair with the family head performing the marriage rites. The bride remains veiled until the couple and wedding party retire indoors, and then the groom, in what is considered an important moment, removes her veil. Although this may be the first time they have seen each other, their mating has not been a haphazard affair. Much deliberation and wisdom will have gone into the selection. On the basis of a matching of income, status, and prestige of the families to be related by the marriage, with some thought toward the personal compatibility of the principals involved, and with the added skills of matching by the matchmaker and the "intimation of approving divination" of

32. *Ibid.*

the fortune teller, the wedding cannot help but be off to an auspicious start. Significantly missing, from the American point of view, are romantic love and individual choice. In the feast and merrymaking that follow the wedding ceremony, along with the congratulations of the honored guests and the admiring glances and remarks of those who inspect closely all the items of the bride's dowry, their loss may be less sharply felt than one might suppose. The roles of husband and wife in the traditional Chinese family do not, as we shall see, loom up so significant as those bearing on the functioning of the extended family grouping and upon the values that relate it to the realm of departed ancestors.

Birth and Infancy

During the nine months of her pregnancy the mother is spoken of as having "happiness in her body." When the midwife arrives to deliver the baby, the husband, unmarried girls, and children are either sent away or banished to separate rooms and enjoined to keep still while the baby is being born. The birth of a son is always well received, a daughter much less so. Among the gentry where the large family ideal is most perfectly expressed, the sex difference is somewhat less crucial. However, among the peasantry where land holdings and family resources may be too meager to permit the feeding and care of a child, infanticide is the acceptable response. Since females grow up only to leave their families at the age when they could be expected to make a substantial contribution to the family economy, female infanticide far predominates.

The third day following the birth of a child is ceremonially celebrated. The infant, bathed and clothed in a red jacket, is presented to his grandparents. A feast of moderate proportions follows. Food is also distributed to the neighbors who in return bring red cloth-covered baskets containing food thought to be particularly good for the mother. Donors will be rewarded in the future with reciprocal gifts, thus making for an endless series of gift exchanges. Usually the mother of the family making the gift presents the basket, is permitted to see the child, and, as is universally the custom, praises it to the mother.[33]

The Chinese recognize five periods of age, beginning with the period of infancy and ending with later maturity. Each has rather clear-cut status and role differences, cut across by the factor of sex. The subordinate status of females relative to males in the Chinese family has its beginnings in infancy.[34] The son's importance extends to the economic, religious, and ceremonial spheres of family life. Even as an infant he may be expected to receive preferential treatment. As a matter of fact, all Chinese infants are regarded tenderly, and, if the eldest male offspring occupies a special status, the smallest child, boy or girl, is the pet of the family.[35]

For the first two years of its life the child lives a life of comparative freedom, even indulgence. The mother pays close attention to its wants, nurses, looks after its cleanliness needs, and cares for it in case of sickness. The father maintains a certain degree of aloofness from the child, at least in the presence of other persons. Little systematic training or discipline is attempted during these first two years. The child is fed when hungry and subjected to only the mildest cleanliness training. Little insecurity attends the alimentation-elimination dimension of infant experience.

At about age three the child is expected to exercise some control over its natural functions, but the expectation is not reinforced by harsh discipline. More traumatic to the child at this age would be the birth of a new family member. In such event the child is separated from the mother and usually sleeps with the father, who assumes responsibility for helping it dress in the morning and for giving it other incidental per-

33. A detailed description of the ceremonies attending the birth of a child is found in Martin C. Yang, *op. cit.*

34. Levy, *op. cit.*, p. 67. This section on role differentiation by age groups among the Chinese follows Levy's treatment, pp. 63-163.

35. Lang, *op. cit.*, p. 238.

sonal care no longer available from the mother. Servants in the families of the gentry also assist in child care; it is customary, moreover, to bring a wet nurse to very young infants who have been displaced from the mother's breast by a new arrival.

Childhood

By the age of four the child is ready for admission into an age group that extends from this lower level up to fifteen or sixteen years. During this period the children, who through oft-repeated stories told by grandparents already have become acquainted with the value of filial respect, are now subject to an increasingly severe program of discipline and training. Sex differentiation is now signalized by the boy's being sent to live in the adult male section of the house, henceforth to be under the supervision of the father, while the girl remains with the mother. For the girl the next dozen years will be spent in preparation for the role of wife and mother.

Boys are tutored or attend school. Schooling tends to be rigorous, demanding, and given over mostly to rote learning. Teachers have unquestioned authority over the pupils and may punish them severely without fear of parental interference. Training in filial respect and obedience continues apace. The boys are likely to receive many beatings from the schoolmaster and father before moving on to the next age group. Girls in the custody of the mother are spared some of the harsher discipline. Also as a means of lessening the discipline the daughter may be lucky enough to achieve the highly valued female role, "father's favorite."

The earlier part of the child-youth period is often looked back upon by the Chinese of both sexes as the most enjoyable time of their lives. Until they are about ten the sexes play together freely, servants perform most onerous duties except on the lowest economic levels, and the children enjoy considerable freedom.

As the period draws to a close the boy has mastered his

studies, learned to recite from the classics and to perform the brush strokes requisite for character writing. Also, importantly, he will have learned the ceremonial observances now performed by the father but someday to be his own responsibility. The Chinese girl becomes increasingly aware that with marriage she will leave, virtually forever, her family and must be prepared to start in anew as a low-status "outside" member of her husband's family. Her personal freedom will also decrease as she matures. Chinese women, for the most part, are expected to stay within the compound. Men, on the other hand, are free to come and go at will. The practice of footbinding has at least part of its rationale in the attitude that women should not have to walk any great distance. If they must leave the household, they should be carried.

Young Adulthood

The third age period, that of young adulthood, covers roughly the years from seventeen to thirty. The severe discipline of schoolmaster and father gives way to guidance and advice. The young man's studies lead now to the taking of examinations and with their passage to the coveted status of a member of the literati. During this period he will experience sexual relations, usually with servant girls and prostitutes, and will learn gambling and drinking—hithertofore denied him. When it becomes apparent to the parents that these diversions are weakening his family ties, a marriage is arranged. The son and groom-to-be becomes a center of attention until the marriage and then as a husband and full-fledged adult "returns" to the family to assume the serious familial and parental duties.

Girls, although the prospects of playing the daughter-in-law role may be something less than enjoyable, move into this third period with a minimum of personal stress. Premarital intercourse being an extremely serious thing, their opportunities for sexual gratification are likely limited to be clandestine contacts and, infrequently, to affairs with male

servants. The practice of betrothal at puberty or shortly thereafter serves to mitigate the problem of sexual outlet, although
for the more well-to-do marriage occurs at a later age, especially
for males, than for young people in the peasantry.

The daughter-in-law role is the most difficult for young
Chinese women to play. This role takes precedence over that
of wife. Likewise, the husband's subordinate position *vis-à-
vis* the father makes it difficult for the wife to secure his inter-
cession in cases of mistreatment. On the other hand, should
the parents disapprove of the wife, the husband is expected to
divorce her no matter what his personal feelings in the matter
may be.

In her new role the daughter-in-law has more duties and
fewer rights than in her own home. She must display obedience and affection, avoid her father-in-law and brother-in-
law, and spend most of her time in the service of her mother-
in-law. The cruel mother-in-law plays in Chinese fiction and
folklore the role that the wicked stepmother plays in European fairy tales.[36] By having children, especially males, and
by being displaced as the most recent daughter-in-law with the
marriage of another son in the family, she can improve her
status. The threat of suicide, which would cause loss of face
in the in-law family, is also an effective, if "last ditch,"
maneuver to alleviate distress.

The husband, as a full-fledged adult, a "finished person,"
now joins the family as a junior partner to be consulted by
his father, the head, on many matters affecting the family. He
must accept all the responsibilities of a husband plus those
ascribed him by virtue of his order of birth. In the words of
Levy:

> Not only could the married son expect to be consulted, but also he
> could now represent the family. As a . . . married man—a responsible hus-
> band and possibly a father—he could fully represent his family in cere-
> monial and legal functions. If he were the head of his own family, he would

36. *Ibid.*, p. 48.

have to do so, of course, but, even if he did not become its head upon marriage, he became fully qualified to represent it in lieu of the true head if circumstances required it.[37]

With the birth of his first male child the young, married Chinese male gains heavily in prestige, for the means of continuation of the family line are now assured. Additional children, especially boys, are welcomed. At the same time the reserve maintained between married son and father—a relationship almost ingrained from infancy—begins to break down or lessen, and the son finds it easier to deal with this somewhat awesome parental figure.

Maturity and Headship

As he moves into full maturity, the Chinese male can expect to inherit the headship of the family if he is the eldest son; he can also look forward to becoming a grandparent. Should he not become the head of the family, he will, nevertheless, be responsible for the supervision of the upbringing of his grandchildren. Thus he assumes the role of disciplinarian and leader.

A continuation of adulthood takes the Chinese into the edge of later maturity. By now he is unquestionably a man of power, dignity, respect, and authority. He is many times over a grandfather, has married off his daughters, and has his married sons and their growing children in his family along with an aged relative, probably widowed. While he still conducts the important ancestor ceremonials and other revered rituals, he now can feel secure that one or more of his sons can assume these duties at any time. It is a period of little strain and considerable comfort.

The wife, now a grandmother, has numerous daughters-in-law to serve her, yet by now some if not most of them will have been "integrated" into the family and have families of

37. Levy, *op. cit.*, p. 91. By permission of Harvard University Press.

their own. Her responsibilities in the matter have lessened greatly. On the other hand her own mother-in-law has either died or has retired from active participation in family affairs. Her life has by now assumed a pattern not likely to be upset or altered by the contingencies of everyday living. She has come to be, finally, an accepted member of her husband's family—her ability to treat daughters-in-law harshly signalizes the fact. Levy notes that the suicide rate for Chinese women, high as compared to the rate for women in other parts of the world, drops off during this period of full maturity almost to zero.[38]

Old Age

The period of old age for the Chinese begins roughly around the age of fifty-five. Unless they have been unfortunate enough not to have had children, the aged Chinese couple have little to worry about in their declining years. Those in what we today call "later maturity" occupy a secure status, receive formal deference, and are objects of great respect. They do not as a rule exercise the authority which they might command by virtue of their position, reserving their judgment for problems that transcend everyday household matters. Neither the aged husband nor his wife is saddled with the responsibility for the personal behavior of family members or, for that matter, family affairs generally.

The wife finally finds herself relatively free from male domination although she may be dependent upon her sons for care and support. So long as the large family with its numerous generations under one roof stays intact there is security for the aged. The pattern of filial piety and deference toward the aged combine to produce a security which is something more than a simple guarantee to meet economic needs. The mother is, after all, the source of affectional relations for the offspring. Chinese writers and poets, for example, write

38. *Ibid.*, p. 124.

with great warmth and understanding of the mutual love of mother and son.[39] The Chinese mother in her later years has good cause for gratification in her motherhood.

Disjunctions

Family relations in the traditional Chinese family can be upset in a variety of ways, some peculiar to and in part representative of the distinctive culture of Chinese society and others, such as birth and death, common to family groupings everywhere. Some of the former have been discussed and will only be mentioned in passing. For example the birth of a female child tends to pose a problem, specifically, of rearing a family member through the formative years, socializing it, training it in skills of wife and mother, only through marriage to lose it almost completely to another family. As already indicated, female infanticide is one, and to Western ears a singularly harsh, solution.

The role of new wife is most difficult, and though it may be pointed out by analysts removed from the scene that the trial-by-ordeal of the daughter-in-law is necessarily agonizing, inasmuch as old familial and affectional ties must be sundered so that the large family unity will not be threatened by the intrusion of an outsider, this "functional" explanation does nothing to make her travail less onerous. The upshot of the matter is that a new daughter-in-law has to "take it"; if she can't, the consequences in the form of her returning to her own parents or of suicide are productive of even more social and personal disjunctions.

The birth of the second child as indicated means a sudden change in fortune for its predecessor who must perforce give up bed and breast in favor of the new arrival. The consequences of such abrupt change in infant experience have not been analyzed; there remains a sociological presumption, at least, that it has some effect on the personality of the child.

39. Lang, *op. cit.*, p. 29.

Although heterosexual contacts between young Chinese males and females are discouraged and the proper young Chinese maiden is expected to keep at home, the possibilities of romantic attachments, especially between cousins, have always threatened the system of arranged marriages. Some forms of cross-cousin marriages are, of course, permitted, even preferred. But many categories of close kin, especially among those bearing the same surname, are prohibited from marriage. When members of such groups fall in love the consequence can only be frustration and disappointment. In point of fact, though not a primary focus of this work, one of the dynamics making for family change in China seems to have been the growing resentment among Chinese youth to parental control and direction of their personal lives, including choice of mates.[40]

Concubinage has already been described and to some degree analyzed. Considering its manifest rationale—the need to have male descendants through a secondary wife when the primary wife is unable to produce them—it has been fairly well sanctioned in Chinese culture, and theoretically the role of the primary wife is not threatened by the addition of a concubine to the family. Yet opportunities for disjunctions and discord are and probably always have been plentiful. Husbands often acquire concubines as an outlet for sexual desires and as a source of affectional response. Concubines have been known to take advantage of their primacy in the affections of the husband to exercise considerable informal power in the family, even to the point of causing its disruption. Only those wives who have strongly internalized the wife role, defined as subordinate and inferior, can accept concubines without feeling their status threatened by younger, usually better-looking additions to the household.

Divorces of three types are possible in the traditional Chinese family: by either husband or wife, by mutual agreement, and by order of authorities such as family head, clan head, or

40. See Levy, *op. cit.*, pp. 273-350.

through governmental auspices. The basic premise which makes divorce in any form permissible is that it is for the best interests of family unity. The personal feelings of the principals are definitely of secondary importance. Nevertheless in practice it is usually the case that the husband repudiates the wife. Legal grounds for repudiation include wife's disobedience to husband's parents, failure to bear children, commission of adultery, suffering from a repulsive disease, garrulousness, and stealing.[41]

The Chinese wife having no property rights does not have the threat of a division of property to protect her. Her major hope for justice lies in the acceptance in Chinese culture of the "three reasons for not repudiating wives." These as formulated by the ancient sages were that the wife could not be sent away if she had mourned her husband's parents for three years, if her husband's family had become wealthy, and if she had no family to take her in.[42]

On the whole, divorce in the traditional Chinese family is relatively infrequent. Other avenues, most of them favoring the husband, are available. The wife may visit her own family for extended periods of time, she may find occasion to be rather heavily involved in the domestic affairs, and, possibly as a last resort, she may herself initiate the matter of a secondary wife. The husband may, with judgment, intercede on the wife's behalf to his parents, but should they press the matter he would probably repudiate her. The solution to his own personal difficulties in marital adjustment need not involve divorce; he may and usually does find it easier to neglect and avoid his wife, or, simply, to acquire a concubine.

The high birth rate of the Chinese is offset by a high death rate, with the consequence that in most Chinese families death is a familiar, expected event. It is to be accepted fatalistically, yet each death is an occasion for an elaboration of

41. Lang, *op. cit.*, p. 40.
42. *Ibid.*, pp. 40-41.

funeral activity which varies directly with the status of the dead and the economic condition of the family. Death marks the passage of the individual from the mundane to the spirit world. Hsu indicates four goals of a Chinese funeral with reference to the spirit world: (1) expediting the spirit's safe entry into that world; (2) gaining its comfort in that world; (3) expressing sorrowful feelings on the part of the living and their reluctance to let the dead go; (4) making sure that the death has not created conditions for future disaster through circumstances which are beyond his or her control.[43]

As a consequence of factors of age and status grading, the finest and most elaborate funerals are accorded elderly males. Since they are not presumed to be "complete," children are buried almost perfunctorily and with little or no ceremony. For a respected adult Chinese, funerals involve considerable family ritual. A massive coffin will be purchased, if it has not already been built to order in advance, and the body, bedecked appropriately in burial robes, will lie coffined in the home for a month or longer—the longer a family can afford to suspend most household activities to mourn the dead, the more esteem is felt to be exhibited.

The central feature of the funeral is the procession which usually features an elaborately carved catafalque, chanting monks, banners describing virtues of the deceased, mourners in white, the dead person's favorite sedan chair, musicians, beggars, uniformed hired bearers, satin umbrellas carried by friends of the deceased, and objects for burning at the grave —these to be of use to the dead person in afterlife. The body in its heavy coffin is either buried in a clan burial plot or almost anywhere deemed propitious by the geomancer. Continued worship of the dead follows on stipulated days: third, twenty-first, thirty-fifth, forty-ninth, and sixtieth. Mourning observances take place daily in the home for a length of time varying with the kinship and age status of the deceased. Three

43. Hsu, *op. cit.,* p. 154.

great festivals, spring, summer, and autumn, take the families to the burial grounds for special ceremonies. All these great feasts are a restatement of the unity, solidarity, and continuity of the family.[44]

Family Controls

In traditional Chinese society the family and its larger counterpart, the sib, serve as the primary agencies of social control. The content of social control takes several forms, not the least important of which are codes, rules, and laws formulated as early as 4,000 years ago. Many of these have passed from one historical period to another to be expressed virtually unchanged in the "new" family laws. For example the basic principles that "between husband and wife there should be attention to their separate functions, between father and son, affection, and between old and young, a proper order" have appeared in the laws of all dynasties, relatively unchanged from their earlier expression in primitive laws and customs of ancient China.[45]

To these codes and laws must be added the traditions which have come to be expressed in maxims, poems, and folklore. Ancient classical literature contains many normative prescriptions, some of which depict the rules of society as cruel and harsh, but necessary and, in the end, just. Exemplary tales depicting approved behavior, especially that of offspring to parents and of the living to the dead, abound in Chinese tale and legend.

Certain features of the large Chinese family which make it an excellent agency of control may be noted. For one, individual resistance can be absorbed or checked better when there are a number of relatives who make up the family. By contrast the nuclear family has only husband and wife to discipline a child, and in the competition for affection, coali-

44. Robert W. Habenstein and William M. Lamers, *Funeral Customs the World Over* (1960), p. 27.
45. Su, *op. cit.*, pp. 21-25.

tions may form in such manner as to vitiate or destroy the family as a social unit. The possibilities of such disruption taking place in the traditional extended family are, of course, much less. Another way of saying this is that the socialization process is distributed among a wider range of persons; they represent to the child a set of "significant others." Long before he develops a conception of society a Chinese child can see himself through the eyes of a group of close relatives—a group by the way who have a socially legitimated right to assist in the proper unbringing of the Chinese child.

Approval of family and sib are of the utmost significance to any Chinese, so much so that the concept of "gaining face" or "losing face" has gained universal currency in describing one form of social motivation. Family disgrace is abhorred. To be outcast from one's family is perhaps the most excruciating thing that can happen to a Chinese, and it is certainly to be avoided at all costs. To the Chinese such broader forms of organization as institutionalized religion or government are of small note. The government is not felt to represent them, the people, but is looked upon as a potential predator—the "tiger."[46] Officials of the central government seldom deal directly with the people. The effective governmental unit, extralegal but recognized and dealt with by central governmental administrators, is usually a local self-governing unit, known in many regions as the "public family." The function of such a unit, headed by the elders, heads of families, and scholars, is to look out for the public affairs of the community: problems of irrigation, self-defense, mediation in personal disputes, mutual aid, burial of the dead, recreation, and religious activities.[47] In the clan communities where all residents bear the same sib surname, it is not erroneous to think of the effective social controls in their entirety as an emanation of nuclear and extended family relations.

So salient are the family controls that it is worthwhile to

46. Robert Redfield, in his introduction to Hsiao-tung Fei's *China's Gentry* (1953), p. 9.
47. *Ibid.*, p. 81.

review some of the features that give rise to them. Ancestor worship is based on the principle that the spirits of dead ancestors hover about looking after the welfare of their descendants. It is vital that they be assured of their proper respect; thus the worship of ancestors in the ancestral temples and the feasts and observances (public and in the homes) are of the utmost importance. The respect of the father to his ancestors is duplicated by the filial piety of his own offspring. In the words of Lee:

> Observance of the cardinal virtues, filial piety and obedience, is exhorted in the name of the ancestors, rewarded by the inheritance of the patrimony, and reinforced by the family traditions and rules which sanction punishment of any offender. It is the binding force of this virtue and of its far-reaching effects that has reduced juvenile delinquency to a minimum in the Chinese family; and it is also this aspect of life which leads an able American observer to remark: "Of almost no moral law in any civilization can it be more confidently said that it is not honored in the breach. In fact it has become so deeply ingrained, so firmly interwoven in the unconscious, as to constitute almost a biological principle."[48]

The system of mourning, conceived on the basis of kinship and extending to five degrees of intensity, reinforces family controls. In the large traditional family it would be likely that at all times during a family member's life he would be observing mourning in some form of intensity for some dead relatives. The highest expression of grief would of course be reserved for the primary relatives.

The upshot of the various features of Chinese family organization is a sense of collective responsibility. Each member feels responsible for the security and good name of the family as a whole; each thinks twice before he acts.

Family Functions

Enough has been said by now to indicate the central role of the traditional family in Chinese society; it is no exaggeration to say that the whole Chinese social structure is built

---

48. Lee, *op. cit.*, p. 278. By permission of the American Sociological Association.

upon the basis of the principle of extended family organization. On the side of the individuals involved, the traditional
family teaches them the necessity of cooperation, courtesy,
patience, and self-control in family relationship, inculcating
in their minds the supreme importance of working for the
honor and glorification of the family name, and it arouses
in them family consciousness, not national consciousness.[49]

As an institution the traditional Chinese family serves a
wide range of functions. Economically it serves as a unit of
production for the peasants and as a unit of distribution of
wealth to the gentry. In the case of the latter, family wealth
will be managed by one person, but be put into the service of
all. In either case, peasantry or gentry, there will be a large
degree of isolation of the family in the economic realm; the
former tills the soil of his farm, owned or rented, and is
limited in contacts to neighbors and villagers usually of the
same surname, while the latter remains as isolated from the
marketplace as is possible. In the scale of Chinese values commercial activities rank relatively low; the Chinese gentry in
most cases delegate those which are unavoidable to one
family manager.

Administratively the household plays an important role,
serving as the basic unit in the machine of the state. The individuals within are responsible to the family head who in turn
reports necessary information to the central government. It
should be remembered that most administrative and governmental matters are handled by such extralegal groups as the
clan and the local self-help organizations.

The religious life of the Chinese is woven into the fabric
of family organization. Essentially animistic and particularistic, it does not lend itself to church or sect organization. For
the most part religious expression is carried on in the context
of ancestor worship and practiced in the home and in the
ancestral temples.

As an educational institution the traditional Chinese family serves to indoctrinate the incoming generation rather

49. Ch'eng-K'un, *op. cit.*, p. 50.

thoroughly into the values and norms of the society. Within the family most of the indoctrination is carried on as part of the socialization process. Ethical behavior is defined in literally hundreds of maxims, adages, and admonitions, and inculcated in an "ordering and forbidding" manner which becomes reinforced by sharper sanctions as children grow older. Formal education outside the family provides no surcease from discipline. The tutor or headmaster assumes the stern parental role and plays it spiritedly! Advanced education and scholarship are most highly valued by the Chinese: wisdom, sagacity, knowledge—these are the marks of the "complete man."

Family solidarity and individual security are the end products of a social system which gives each member at any age and generation a well-defined set of role expectations and an identity. Each family may be seen, then, as a constellation of relationships, many of them, such as that of father-son, intense and vital to the family's continued existence as a link in a chain that begins with the descendants as yet unborn and ends with one's dead ancestors. A second source of solidarity arises in the affective or emotional gratifications that characterize or come to characterize some of the family interrelationships. These in the main are found in the nuclear family in the relations of husband-wife and parents-children. Although the Chinese place a high value on composure and poise and much expression is formalized, as in lavish funerals and weddings, the love of parents for their children and for each other is not inhibited to the point of extinction. Romantic love, considered a threat to family order, crops up again and again in the classical literature of the Chinese. The fact that the married couple have their own rooms, suites, or household areas makes intimate association a physical possibility, and it should be noted that while overt expressions of affection between husband and wife are disapproved there is also the expectation that those who wed as virtual strangers will develop personal bonds in the course of married life. When such bonds do not develop, the husband has recourse to concubines for love and affection. The wife, whose relations with the mother-in-law would already have made her existence in the family a trying one, has little by way of affective gratification except that which could be developed between herself and her children.

As a recreational agency the traditional Chinese family supplies numerous situations and personnel in which, and toward which, expressiveness could be released. Each family has its own storyteller, usually the grandmother, and children and grown-ups alike are fond of folk tales, sagas, and legends, many of which carry exemplary or cautionary burdens. Itinerant performers, opera groups, and companies of players are often hired by families of the gentry for the entertainment of their members and selected friends. Painting and calligraphy carry prestige and are generally tied into the religious and ethical dimensions of the society. Family scholars include such skills in their intellectual training. Yet the pervasive formalism of Chinese family life, and the stringent controls over demeanor, and conduct, as well as the value placed on leisure —especially for male adults—make for such constraint that some seek relief in extrafamilial activities such as gambling, opium smoking, and visits to houses of prostitution. All the latter activities have long been institutionalized in China. Their presence suggests that with respect to avenues of expression and the search for new experiences and variety in life, the traditional Chinese family falls short of the mark.

But, in sum, it would be difficult elsewhere to find an institutionalized form of family life serving procreative, maintenance, status- and role-giving, protective, and educative functions so adequately, an institution which can readily expand to include new members or contract without strain in the loss of its old. As a social unit such family articulates with sib and clan. Its self-sufficiency and unity make it highly functional to a society in which the individual is less important than the kinship group of which he is a member, the living less important than the dead, the young than the old, and the central government less important than the village or clan community.

REFERENCES

Ch'eng-K'un, Cheng, "Familism the Foundation of Chinese Social Organization," *Social Forces*, XXIII, No. 1 (October 1944), pp. 50-64.

Fei, Hsiao-Tung, *China's Gentry.* Chicago: University of Chicago Press, 1953.

Fêng, Han-Yi, *The Chinese Kinship System.* Philadelphia: University of Pennsylvania, 1937.

Granet, Marcel, *Chinese Civilization.* New York: Barnes and Noble, 1951.

Habenstein, Robert W., and Lamers, William M., *Funeral Customs the World Over.* Milwaukee: Bulfin Printers, 1960.

Hsu, Francis L. K., *Under the Ancestor's Shadow.* New York: Columbia University Press, 1948.

———, "China," in Ralph Linton, ed., *Most of the World.* New York: Columbia University Press, 1949, pp. 731-813.

Kulp, Daniel H., *Country Life in South China: The Sociology of Familism.* New York: Columbia University Press, 1925.

———, "Chinese Continuity," *Annals of the American Academy of Political and Social Science*, CLII (1930), pp. 18-29.

Lang, Olga, *Chinese Family and Society.* New Haven: Yale University Press, 1946.

Lee, Shu-Ching, "China's Traditional Family, Its Characteristics and Disintegration," *American Sociological Review*, XVIII (June 1953), pp. 272-280.

Levy, Marion J., *The Family Revolution in Modern China.* Cambridge: Harvard University Press, 1949.

Murdock, George P., *Social Structure.* New York: Macmillan Co., 1949.

Schwendeman, Joseph R., "Geographic Features of the Habitat of the Chinese Peasant," in Irwin T. Sanders, et al., eds., *Societies Around the World.* New York: Dryden Press, 1953.

Su, Sing Ging, *The Chinese Family System.* New York: Columbia University Press, 1922.

Yang, C. K., *The Chinese Family in the Communist Revolution.* Cambridge: Massachusetts Institute of Technology, 1959.

Yang, Martin C., *A Chinese Village: Taitou, Shantung Province.* New York: Columbia University Press, 1945.

Yutang, Lin, *My Country and My People.* New York: Reynal and Hitchcock, 1939.

6 The Minimum Family of the Kibbutz

A kibbutz is an agricultural collective settlement characterized by common ownership of property and communally organized production, consumption, and care of children. Economically, the *kibbutz* operates as a self-sustaining unit and as one household. The family, meanwhile, ceases to be an autonomous group from the point of view of the division of labor.[1] Until recently all *kibbutz* settlements were located in Israel although the principles upon which they are founded are distinct enough to legitimate the use of the term to designate a *type* of collectivity.[2] While the first *kibbutz* was founded in 1909 on the banks of the River Jordan near the Sea of Galilee, the impetus to establish such settlements came after World War I. Today their number approaches 250; however, their 80,000 members constitute less than four percent of the total Jewish population of Israel.

1. Yonina Talmon-Garber, "The Family in Israel," *Marriage and Family Living,* 16 (1954), p. 347. The basic studies upon which the present chapter draws heavily are those by Melford E. Spiro: *Kibbutz: Venture in Utopia* (1956), and *Children of the Kibbutz* (1958). For a general picture of *kibbutz* society by a member of one, Murray Weingarten's *Life in a Kibbutz* (1955) is recommended; and for the historical and cultural backdrop against which the *kibbutz* movement may be viewed, see Mark Zborowski and Elizabeth Herzog, *Life Is with People* (1952). For a personal account of the development of the first *kibbutz,* see Joseph Baratz, *A Village by the Jordan: The Story of Degania* (1954). See also footnote 36 below.

2. One nonJewish *kibbutz* was established in southern France. See "The Mysterious Kibbutz," *Time,* 77 (Jan. 6, 1961), p. 48. A follow-up article by *Time* some eleven years later points to the industrialization of many *kibbutzim,* the expansion of material goods and well-being, the presence of paid nonmembers in productive enterprises, and the variety of modifications in social practices, all of which have made for structural and organizational changes. See "Change on the Kibbutz," *Time,* 88 (Nov. 6, 1972), pp. 78-80.

In his case analysis of one type of *kibbutz* society Spiro found a body of moral values or postulates common to the structure of *kibbutz* communal organization. Before identifying these it should be recalled that historically the movement represents a form of group protest by young Jewish intellectuals, mainly European, against the folkways and mores of the traditional Jewish village community (*shtetl*) of eastern Europe and the ghetto culture of the cities. Democracy, socialism, and full social and political equality with all mankind were embraced as general ethical and political ideals. More specifically, the postulates of the *kibbutz* movement include: (1) the placement of a very high value on labor—labor as a calling, with physical labor enjoying the highest prestige; (2) communal ownership of all property used or produced by the community itself; (3) social and economic equality within the *kibbutz*, the latter determined according to the venerable socialist maxim, "From each according to his ability; to each according to his need"; (4) the principle of individual liberty and the limitation of personal power; and (5) the transcending importance of the group.[3]

As a self-sustaining economic entity the *kibbutz* in its typical mid-twentieth century form will most likely, though not always, devote itself to agricultural pursuits. All able-bodied adults, regardless of sex, are expected to engage in tasks felt necessary to the operation of the collective. Husband and wife work at independent jobs alloted by a central committee, and the routine of daily tasks is supervised by a work coordinator—an elected official of the *kibbutz*. The main meals of the day are eaten in a communal dining hall which serves also as a community recreation center and, importantly, as a central meeting hall. Literally the *kibbutz* attempts to assume complete

---

3. These are elaborated in Spiro's *Kibbutz: Venture in Utopia,* pp. 10-37. Another analysis of basic *kibbutz* ideology is found in Stanley Diamond's "Kibbutz and Shtetl: the History of an Idea," *Social Problems,* 5 (Fall, 1957), pp. 71-99.

responsibility for satisfying all the needs of its members.[4]

The primary goal or at least necessity of any *kibbutz* in its infancy is the provision of adequate housing. Education for the children and medical care for all members rank high as *kibbutz* values, and, whereas the institutionalization of health services follows a pattern not uncommon to welfare-oriented societies, the education and socialization of the children are distinctly innovational.

Children are cared for in nurseries and special schools. Except for infants, children are apart from their parents for all but a few hours a day, living in their own quarters and attending schools staffed by trained nurse-teachers and, for the older children, teachers. This separation from parents continues through all the age groups or layers until graduation from high school, at which time the youths enter the *kibbutz* as members and are assigned their own quarters. Parental interaction with children is restricted severely as to hours, but the intimacy and affection of the contacts are not cross-cut by requirements for disciplining and otherwise socializing the child.

In addition to assuming responsibility for housing, medical, educational, and socializing services the *kibbutz* takes care of such matters as providing showerhouses, laundries, tailoring services, cultural and artistic experiences, and vacations with a modest amount of spending money for its members.

Inasmuch as there has been variation both in social organization and in emphasis on specific social arrangements it is necessary to specify that one particular subtype of the *kibbutz* will serve as the focus for the remainder of the chapter. This type represents the more revolutionary, Marxist-oriented, highly collectivized form of *kibbutz* organization. In 1960 there were seventy-three such settlements, with a total population of 27,500 (14,000 members and candidates) combined into a general federation (*Hakibbutz Haartzi*) which in turn affiliated with the revolutionary Socialist United Workers Party

4. Weingarten, *op. cit.*, p. 52.

in Israel (*Mapam*).[5] It was one of these which was earlier chosen by Spiro and his wife for intensive case study. A further limitation to the chapter must be indicated. Descriptions and generalizations that follow should be understood to apply most saliently to the *kibbutz* life and times at mid-century. The "historical present" will again be used as a matter of convenience in exposition. To restate two essential qualifications, our use of the term *kibbutz* should be understood to designate specifically one rather uncompromising form of the several varieties extant in Israel, and the location in time will be that of mid-century. Some attempt will be made at the end of the chapter to describe and assess the changes taking place since the State of Israel was founded in 1948.

Family Structure

The Marriage Institution in the Revolutionary Socialist-Type Kibbutz

Marriage of *kibbutz* members in so many respects differs from marriage as conventionally conceived that there has been some doubt as to whether the term has applicability. As indicated by Spiro:

> From the very beginning the terms "marriage," "husband," "wife," were abandoned because of their invidious connotations. A man and a woman do not get "married"; they become a "pair" (*zug*). A woman does not acquire a "husband," she acquires a "young man" (*bachur*) or a "companion" (*chaver*). By the same token, a man acquires not a "wife" but a "young woman" (*bachura*) or a "companion" (*chavera*).[6]

Nevertheless, while heterosexual attachments are generally agreed to be the personal matter of the persons involved, most young couples do fall in love and enter into an enduring inti-

5. *The Israel Yearbook 1960*, pp. 193-194; 274; 277-278. Nonmembers are mostly new immigrants who are sheltered and oriented to the new ways of the welfare state but who will not become located permanently in *kibbutzim*.

6. Spiro, *Kibbutz: Venture in Utopia*, p. 113. By permission of Harvard University Press.

mate relationship. Having decided to become a "couple" they petition for a room to share together and settle down to a monogamous attachment. In the earlier years of the *kibbutz* movement it was felt necessary to delay having children, at least until the collective could adequately provide for their physical and educational needs. Yet expectation of children has always been a strong motivational influence; in a utopian-oriented group it could hardly be expected to be otherwise. Moreover, the "couples" eventually go through a formal marriage ceremony according to the laws of the state, usually around the time of the birth of the first child, as children born out of wedlock have no legal rights according to state law.[7]

Family Type and Kinship

An institutional "couple" relationship sanctioned also by state law and ceremony, focused sharply on maximation of love, affection, and emotional security, but one in which the socialization of the child and economic cooperation between the spouses are minimized, in sum, characterizes *kibbutz* marriage. The nuclear family subsequently formed becomes the affectional agency through which the physiological and psychological needs of the members are to a great extent assured. Were it not for the performance of these latter functions, it might be argued that the rational organization of *kibbutz* collectives had resulted in the complete elimination of the nuclear or conjugal family form.[8]

7. Melford E. Spiro, "Is the Family Universal? The Israeli Case," *American Anthropologist*, 56, No. 5 (1954), Part I, pp. 839-846. Reprinted with addendum in Norman W. Bell and Ezra F. Vogel, *A Modern Introduction to the Family* (1960), p. 67.

8. The point of view that the *kibbutz* had dispensed with the family has been advanced by those holding to the definition of the family as necessarily a socializing agency in which the husband and wife share in an economic division of labor. The minimizing of socialization and the absence of economic cooperation in the *kibbutz* "couples" seemed adequate justification for the conclusion. For those who put primary emphasis on the sustained, affective component of the relationship, however, the terms "marriage" and "family" are seen to apply to *kibbutz* couples.

If it is relatively simple to identify the small group consisting of the couple and their child or children, at least during the after-work hours, much more difficulty attends the task of identifying any more inclusive, extended form of kinship organization in the *kibbutz*. For historical reasons this is partly explainable by the fact that most *kibbutzim* were founded by a young generation whose members were not likely to have brought their parents with them to the rather forbidding frontier land of the Jordan. During Hitlerian times many lost their parents through extermination. By mid-century, offspring of the original settlers had emerged as a distinct group with a special designation, *sabras*. But for the pioneers there was little transplantation of the *shtetl* forms, and certainly no reestablishment of a functioning face-to-face or near face-to-face extended family grouping consisting of primary relations gathered under one roof or inside a community, held together by rules of residence, authority, lineage, and other customary forms of social grading and allotment of roles.

Moreover, the ideological values of the founders of the *kibbutzim* ran counter to the continuation or reestablishment of traditional Jewish forms of family organization. The socioeconomic theories of Karl Marx were joined with the psychological formulations of Sigmund Freud! All vestiges of the patriarchate were to be removed—the solution to the Oedipus complex. Likewise to be eliminated was the traditional subordinate, submissive role of the mother. Without such functional bases as were present and operative in the traditional Jewish culture, the extended family *kinship* group operated and still operates in the *kibbutz* mainly to designate those to whom love and affection might most uninhibitedly be expressed. Of course the "blood line" is not so attenuated as to be lost completely to members of the *kibbutz*. Relatives on the outside are not forgotten; on the contrary, one of the most important decisions for many middle-aged members whose parents or close relatives live in America, Europe, Africa, or in oriental countries, is whether or not to make a trip, bound usually to take several weeks or a month, "to see the old folks while they are still alive." The decision, it should be noted, will necessarily be made in the general meeting of the group and will be more on the order of a community than an individual decision. In fact, what might seem to us as normal matters of family choice or of individual concern—occupational choices, decisions as to type and conditions of residence, the kinds of meals prepared, household furnishings, vacations, and even the decisions involving family planning— are either totally or partially decided by the community. Thus, in effect, the *kibbutz* as a whole acts as a "great family" for all its members.

Descriptive and analytical categories of anthropology employed in earlier chapters must be used with caution in explaining the nature and operation of *kibbutz* social organization. Perhaps it is better to note the traditional forms of organized Jewish life which have been erased or attenuated as a result of the rationally planned social arrangements of the founders of the *kibbutzim*. The patriarchal family system, the patrilineal sib, and patrilocality, long identified with the traditional *shtetl* society, were, along with many other traditional social forms, consciously dispensed with as unnecessary or inimical to the development of a new way of life. If the traditions and customs of Jewish culture, their roots extending back some three millennia, were not erased by fiat of the *kibbutz* pioneers, they were at least for a generation suspended in favor of a consciously and purposefully organized set of communal usages which from time to time could be changed or modified by consensus of the members. For example the patrilocal rule of residence traditionally associated with *shtetl* social organization gives way in the *kibbutz* to the choice of residence as a matter involving special conditions such as the availability of housing, size of the *kibbutz*, and the ideological commitment to furthering the growth of the movement through establishment of new *kibbutzim*. Not only are new collectives to be desired, but the older settlements were by common consent limited in their number of members—at mid-century to about 200 members—and it was often necessary for the new generation of *sabras* to seek another or set out to establish a new *kibbutz.*

The Family Cycle

Mate Selection

In the type of *kibbutz* under consideration the children have lived most of their lives in groups, or age-layers, apart from their parents. Inasmuch as the sexes are not separated, there are few restrictions as to heterosexual contacts. Children of the *kibbutz* eat, sleep, shower, play, and go to school together. It is not until the young reach high school that they begin to show any signs of romantic heterosexual attachment. Even so, at the high school level there is very little group preoccupation with matters of sex. For one thing, pointed out by Spiro, "The host of sexual stimuli that evoke sexual fantasies in adolescents in our society—pictures, billboards, magazines, movies—are not found in the *kibbutz;* so too, such artificial techniques as cosmetics and perfume for arousing sexual desire are taboo."[9] It is his further contention that the normal sex drives of the adolescents are effectively sublimated in the intensive program of classes, work, and extracurricular activities.

Dating as a dalliance period in which paired couples explore personalities, focus or diffuse sexuality, and learn the ropes of interpersonal interaction, is not generally found in the *kibbutz.* Rather the *kevutza,* or specific age group, tends to act as the sociability group par excellence. Group dating in the American sense is not practiced, for the *kevutza* is not a temporary protective device for adolescents who are too inse-

9. Spiro, *Children of the Kibbutz,* p. 127. By permission of Harvard University Press.

cure to pair off heterosexually but wish to associate under somewhat less individualized conditions. Rather, the *kevutza* is the entity felt by its members to be the *sine qua non* of their existence, challenged perhaps only by the competition of parental love. Significantly, it is during the high school period that the youth begin to look forward with less anticipation to the evening visit with their parents than do the latter to visits with their offspring.

The collective orientation of *kibbutz* youth toward matters of sex reflects a mixture of realistic understanding of the anatomy and functions of sex taught them in school and a somewhat puritanical orientation toward its expression, both symbolically and physically. Thus the obscene tale or dirty joke is absent from the discourse of *kibbutz* youth, and there is the generally shared feeling that romantic attachments can only divert one's energies from intellectual and social activities.[10] Once a person has graduated from high school, he becomes a member of the *kibbutz* with attendant privileges and responsibilities. At this point he leaves the dormitory life behind, is assigned a single room, and joins the adult society. His sex life, henceforth, becomes a personal matter, and he may enter into sexual affairs experimentally with no sense of community restraint. Falling in love becomes an appropriate development at this period, and when a pair decides to get married or become a "couple," as noted above, they apply to the housing committee for a common room. Insofar as the *kibbutz* community is concerned, the granting of a room to the couple constitutes legitimation of the marriage, and no further ceremony is expected. As already indicated, sometime before or at about the time of the birth of the first child there will be a marriage ceremony in accordance with state law.[11]

10. Spiro, *Kibbutz: Venture in Utopia*, pp. 112-113.
11. It should again be kept in mind that these statements refer to only one type of *kibbutz* but that they do not necessarily hold for this type at the present moment. In many, if not in a majority of, cases in and out of *kibbutzim* the wedding has become an important religious and social as well as a legal ceremony.

Age mates of the same *kibbutz,* who, having lived together communally some eighteen years, tend to look to the opposite sex in a sibling or brother-sister fashion and as a consequence develop a form of exogamy that often takes them out of their own *kibbutz* for a marriage mate. However their identification with the *kibbutz* movement in general leads most to seek mates from members of other *kibbutzim,* a type of endogamy unrelated to considerations of kinship but functional to the continuance of social cohesion and the strengthening of the *kibbutz* ideology.

Choice of a marriage partner then, nearly always takes the young member outside his own *kevutza* and usually outside his own *kibbutz.* Marriage, though deferred in the earliest days of *kibbutz* settlement, takes place at a fairly early age for the *sabras,* mostly between the ages of twenty-one and twenty-five. This is considerably younger than for the country as as whole.[12]

Childbirth and Childhood

Children are wanted, loved, and treasured by the adult society of the *kibbutz.* As the uncertainties and harshness of living conditions in the early settlements have subsided, the decision to have children has increasingly become an individual matter. Family size, in the past more or less by common agreement held to two children, has shown a tendency to increase. *Sabras* look forward to larger families than did their parents, but they too plan their families.

Pregnancy and childbirth are looked upon so much as natural occurrences in the *kibbutz* that no great excitement is engendered by such events. The majority of women in the *kibbutz* enjoy healthy pregnancies with few difficulties and

12. Average age at marriage in *kibbutzim* in 1949 was 26.5 for males and 23.5 for females as compared with 30.7 and 25.1 for the whole country. See Talmon-Garber, *op. cit.,* p. 349. Of course not all marriages in the *kibbutzim* at mid-century were among *sabras.* Others, newcomers from the outside especially, push up the average.

little complaint.[13] Until her eighth month the woman will continue working at her assigned tasks; after this her hours of work will be reduced, and she may be assigned to lighter tasks. She will probably have supplemented her diet starting about the sixth month, but otherwise little concern is shown. On the whole, then, the attitude toward pregnancy is rational, even casual.

Birth of the child is effected with a minimum of assistance. The mother delivers her child in a hospital, usually "naturally," i.e., unless there are complications, without anesthetic. The *kibbutz* woman is supposed to exhibit great control and to bear her children without outcry. Child and mother spend less than a week in the hospital. During this period the most important event is the naming of the child by the parents. Names are usually chosen from the Bible or from nature, although during the Nazi persecutions infants were named for friends or relatives who were killed in Europe.[14]

When the mother and child return to the *kibbutz*, the mother spends a week in her room convalescing; the baby, however, is taken into the Infants' House where, except for nursing visits from the mother, he is given entirely to the care of the nursery personnel. The child is weaned slowly, the process beginning at the third and ending at the ninth month. As the mother visits the nursery less often for nursing, she adds to the time spent at work. When the weaning is nearly completed, the mother will have been able to resume full-time work at her regularly assigned tasks.

The first year of the child's life, then, is spent in a nursery, designed and usually well-equipped to accommodate infants under one year of age. The nurses, *metaplot,* one head nurse and several assistants, are female members of the *kibbutz* who have been trained at a center set up by the federation with which the *kibbutz* is allied. For the first six months the infants must stay at the nursery at all times. Mothers come to

13. Spiro, *Children of the Kibbutz,* p. 101.
14. *Ibid.,* p. 102.

the nursery during the day and both parents may visit after working hours. For most couples the hours spent playing with their children are frankly considered the most gratifying in their day-to-day *kibbutz* life. An index of the strength of this feeling is seen in the inclination of *kibbutz* members to start work almost at sunrise in order to have more afternoon time to spend with the children. Thus, while the nurses are responsible for supplying most of the child's needs, parents, the mothers especially, do have several hours a day to spend in sustained contact with their offspring. It bears repeating that the interaction of parents and child will almost completely be given over to expressions of affection, but will not involve disciplining or other attempts to train or socialize him. At the age of six months the child may be brought to the home of the parents to visit for an hour. Henceforth for the rest of his youth the child will regard the visit to the parents' room as an important, perhaps the important, event of the day.

After a year in the Infants' House, the child is moved to a Toddlers' House where, as one of eight children, he finds different nurses, peers, and physical environment. The socialization process is accentuated; the child now learns to play with others, to feed and dress himself, and to respond gradually to toilet training. Child care is characteristically warm, affectionate, and permissive; physical restraints in clothing, in arrangement and construction of the rooms, and in the handling of children are minimized. Spiro notes:

> If a baby experiences frustration, it is primarily because his individual needs cannot always be satisfied in a system based on routine. Differences in need are often great, not only because each infant has his own rhythms, but because there is an age difference of one year separating the youngest from the oldest; and yet they are all expected to conform to the same schedule.[15]

Between the ages of two and three the children of the Toddlers' House come under the care of a specially trained nursery teacher, *gannenet,* who henceforth takes charge of their social and intellectual development. Some two years

15. *Ibid.,* p. 108. By permission of Harvard University Press.

later they will join with another group of toddlers to form a *kevutza*. Until they reach high school, the members of this group will eat, sleep, play, and attend class together in their own classrooms. The sustained contact of peer group members tends to produce both a sense of identity with and at the same time a dependency upon the group. Socialization into a group-oriented society is apparently one of the significant achievements of an educational system which is integrated with other everyday aspects of life. During the kindergarten period, life becomes routinized, with little variation in life experiences for either sex. They sleep in the same room and use the same showers and toilets.[16] After the evening meal, they are permitted to visit their parents for approximately two hours, following which they receive a shower and are put to bed by their nurse.

During the pre-high school years the nurses and nurse teachers tend to take on the character of "significant others." Spiro details the functions of these parental surrogates:

> They care for almost all his physical desires and needs—they feed, bathe, and clothe him, and nurse him when he is ill. They rear him and, hence, care for many of his social needs. Most of the child's knowledge of his physical environment, his skills, and his knowledge of his own (*kibbutz*) culture including its value, behavior patterns, and techniques are taught him by these women. Finally, since they are for him psychologically significant persons, they are of great importance for his emotional development.[17]

Parents, nurse-teachers, and the *kevutza*, then, make up the groups in which, or in reference to which, the children of the *kibbutz* receive their most significant personal and social experiences. In their attempt to foster individual growth, creative self-expression, and personal freedom while at the same time socializing the child into a group orientation, if not dependency, *kibbutz* members have attempted to create children's communities in which education is related to the reality of the child's immediate experience. School, as distin-

16. Spiro, *Kibbutz: Venture in Utopia*, pp. 132-133.
17. *Ibid.*, p. 133. By permission of Harvard University Press.

guished from kindergarten, brings the children into the larger
dormitory-school, where, although each *kevutza* remains intact,
the total school population, or *cheveran,* becomes the effective
society for the school children. The school becomes a "children's village" and serves as the framework for an autonomous
organization which directs social and cultural activities and
discusses and decides on questions of behavior, discipline, and
cooperation in almost all spheres of school life.[18]

Although the age groups under twelve are supervised and
guided by adults, the children from the sixth or seventh
grades on increasingly assume responsibility for their own
direction. Classroom instruction centers around the group-
project method, with the students exercising considerable
influence in defining, shaping, and developing the projects
undertaken. External discipline as a means of socialization
and control of students is avoided. Sympathetic understanding and a considerable amount of patience along with teaching skills are requisite for the teacher.[19] With adolescence the
children join the youth movement, and their group becomes
a branch of the country-wide movement which belongs to
their own particular *kibbutz* sector. The youth movement
takes up a large part of the free time of the youngsters.[20]

Entry into high school marks another significant juncture
in the educational process for youth in the *kibbutz.* The children move to a different location; their *kevutza* is dissolved
into one of several larger groups made up of children from
various *kibbutzim*; their main teacher, who will probably stay
with the group until its graduation, is likely now to be a
male. Students will now spend part of the day in the fields
working at tasks assigned them by adults under whose supervision they are placed, and, in time the student will usually
learn most phases of the *kibbutz* economy. In high school

18. Moshe Smilansky, et al., eds., *Child and Youth Welfare in Israel*
(1960), p. 109.
19. *Ibid.,* p. 102.
20. *Ibid.,* p. 109.

rather broad powers are granted the students. Committees take responsibility for most nonacademic matters, including discipline. Upon graduation the students will automatically serve two years in the army, following which time they may petition for membership in the *kibbutz*. Few if any are rejected; practically all, despite two or more years contact with non*kibbutz* society, elect to return to the *kibbutz*. In the *kibbutz* studied by Spiro no child failed to announce his candidacy for membership.[21]

Adulthood

The seriousness of the venture into the agricultural utopias has had reflection in the conception of the adult roles of *kibbutz* members. Marriage, an individual matter, was of secondary importance to those groups whose personnel had to expend maximum effort in the establishment and development of the collective. The married couple would often attempt to deny, or at any rate "play down," their relationship. Sexual relations in the early stages of *kibbutz* development were not, for adults, limited by public opinion or mores to married persons, and considerable experimentation took place.

Traditional Jewish marriage, looked upon as bourgeois and hypocritical by the early founders of the *kibbutz,* was replaced by a nonexploitative companionship, love-oriented relationship. Yet the focus of energies was to be the settlement and its establishment in an inhospitable environment; its development and growth was the harbinger of a new society of agricultural socialists.

For the first generation of *kibbutzniks,* then, marriage was a second order of *kibbutz* business. Husband and wife roles were indistinct. In face of the injunction to devote all energies and attention to the community, to call attention to the marriage relationship was to divert attention from the crucial

---

21. Spiro, *Kibbutz: Venture in Utopia,* p. 139.

job at hand. Thus their work roles were assigned them, they ate their major meals in a communal dining hall, and most often personal services were supplied them by established agencies. Children, as already indicated, were provided for in nearly all respects by the community. In short, familial roles have been reduced both in number and in importance in the *kibbutz* as the community has absorbed many of the functions of the family found in the traditional Jewish *shtetl.* The subordination of the family to the larger group is epitomized in the story of the *kibbutz* child who asked his father: "Who told you to make a boy?" and was given the answer, "Your mother." He rejected this as a fable and gave his own theory: "It must have been on the daily work sheet."[22]

Equality of the sexes is scrupulously observed, and no status differential is reflected in one's being a male or female parent. There is no formal "head of the family," nor is there intrinsically any difference in value of the work performed by the sexes. On both counts, however, there is some deviation from the ideal: children are more likely to look to the father as a hero figure, both in terms of the importance of his work and his role in the defense of the *kibbutz* against marauders.[23] Women likewise find themselves more likely working in communal kitchens, laundries, clothing storehouses, and nurseries than in driving tractors, performing heavy manual labor, or, for that matter, administrating *kibbutz* business affairs. This condition of affairs should be stressed as a tendency; exceptions are more than infrequent. Yet, there is no doubt that some of the less interesting work over a period of time has devolved upon the females and, as will be noted later, has become a source of disjunction in the social organization of the *kibbutz.* In other fields of *kibbutz* activities women have found opportunity for development of skills. As Weingarten notes:

22. Repeated from Elizabeth E. Irvine's "Observations on the Aims and Methods of Childrearing in Communal Settlements in Israel," *Human Relations,* 5 (1952), p. 255.

23. *Ibid.,* p. 267.

To a degree unparalleled in the outside world, where women, unless they are wealthy, are unable to participate in community affairs because of household and child care responsibilities (American women's organizations, for example, are made up mostly of middle-class rather than working women and to a large extent of women whose children have already grown up), women in the *kibbutz* take an active part in all *kibbutz* affairs, in politics, both in and out of the *kibbutz,* and in the life of the movement as a whole.[24]

Old Age

The founding of *kibbutz* collectives by young adults has tended to make for a community population structure at mid-century "shortchanged" in adults who have reached later maturity. Those in the fifty- to sixty-year age bracket represent for the most part seasoned *chevarim,* founders or builders of the settlement. As an age-layer they represent one of the most powerful and important groups in the *kibbutz.* There are no indications that old age will represent a period of economic or social deprivation, isolation, or diminished status for *kibbutz* members. Political power may well flow downward to younger age-layers, yet there are other compensations for the aged. In a welfare-oriented society their economic needs will be taken care of when it becomes no longer feasible for them to work. Equally if not more importantly they will not, as is often the case in America, suffer from isolation. The grandparent role, always important in Jewish life, has not been rationalized out of existence in the planned society of the *kibbutz.* Rather, the contacts between parents and children, so vital when the children were young, but likely to become less frequent as the offspring reach high school age, are reintensified with the appearance of grandchildren. Inasmuch as the indulgence pattern of the parents resembles closely that which traditionally was reserved for grandparents, it can be argued that *vis-à-vis* children and grandchildren the adult member of the *kibbutz* need undergo no significant redefi-

24. Weingarten, *op. cit.,* pp. 137-138. By permission of Reconstructionist Press.

nition of role. To be a parent is to be something less than a grandparent, but to be a grandparent is to be something not much beyond being a parent. Perhaps the most significant gratification for the old is to find the young electing to stay within the *kibbutz,* dedicated to working within its collectively oriented framework and to the furtherance of the goals of the movement.

Disjunctions

Most members of the *kibbutz* marry, and most of these find spouses within *kibbutz* settlements. There are relatively few unattached *kibbutzniks,* few enough so as not to constitute a social problem. More serious are divorce and the leaving of the community for the non*kibbutz* life. The divorce rate for all *kibbutzim* is 3.54 per year per thousand persons, while in the non*kibbutz* cooperative settlements the rate is 2.16.[25] The frequency of divorce has diminished considerably, however, since the early years of the *kibbutz* movement, when in the absence of a state there were no legal problems and for the most part divorces meant only the parting of childless couples. *Sabras* on the other hand show as much intolerance toward divorce as their parents show tolerance in accepting the practice.

The decision to leave the *kibbutz* is disjunctive both for the individual and for the community. Individuals who leave cannot help but feel some sense of failure or inadequacy, no matter how strong their rationalizations. For those who enter from the outside and leave after a brief stay, the problem is less acute than for those who after many years of effort have come to the conclusion that they cannot continue. To the collective, each departure threatens the cohesion of the whole —thus the concentration of effort on the socialization process for the young. The older the *kibbutz,* the smaller the number of people who leave, and the greatest turnover is found in the

25. Talmon-Garber, *op. cit.,* pp. 347-349.

newly established colony made up of young people, as yet mostly unmarried and unsettled.[26]

Controls, Functions, and Dysfunctions

The *kibbutz* society, founded on radically different principles of social organization, presents almost a classic case of external group control over its members achieved at the cost of losing the institutional services of the family as an agency of social control. In direct contrast to the traditional Chinese family, for example, that of the *kibbutz* is marked by an absence of familism.

Consequently ancestor veneration, the sense of identity established through lineage, parent-child relationships based on filial piety and dutiful obligation, preferential marriage, status conferring by family, family glory and family tradition, succession to or inheritance of family crafts and occupations, and the determination of values by reference to the maintenance, continuity, and functions of the family are either highly attenuated or absent in *kibbutz* communal organization. The development of familism in the family groupings within the *kibbutz*, it can be held, would serve to weaken the primary group characteristics of the community as a whole. Put starkly, familism constitutes a threat to the classic form of *kibbutz* social organization.[27]

Infant care, socialization, and education of the children of the *kibbutz* reflect the determination of *kibbutz* adults to erase familism or family-centeredness and at the same time permit parents and children to maximize their human potential or need for love and affection. The results of such planned socialization are not easy to determine or evaluate, and such studies as have been made do not, because of the variety of *kibbutz* modes of social organization, add up to simple comprehensive generalizations. With this in mind, it

26. Weingarten, *op. cit.,* p. 159.
27. This point is elaborated by Talmon-Garber, *op. cit.,* p. 348.

might be profitable first to examine some of the aspects or by-products of socialization in the *kibbutz* which have been characterized as detrimental to personality formation and possibly dysfunctional to *kibbutz* social organization.

It has already been observed that the parents, nurses, and nurse-teachers divide the loyalties and affections of the child. Children, for example, may inadvertently call a nurse "mother." The limited contact with the parents has been linked with a degree of insecurity among *kibbutz* children higher than prevails among those "home bred."[28] Since nurses must take care of a group of children, such problems as toilet training must be dealt with in a group fashion, and to some extent the individual needs of the child cannot receive the fullest attention.[29] Some selective neglect seems inevitable, both in the Infants' House and the Toddlers' House. Thumbsucking, enuresis, high incidence of unmitigated aggression, jealousy, insecurity, and at a later period a lack of individuality and an inability to accept authority from any other source than from the peer group have been noted as characteristic of *kibbutz* children. However, such findings as a lower level of ego development of *kibbutz* infants as compared to their non*kibbutz* peers and retardation of interpersonal responsiveness have been pointed out as relatively absent among ten-year-olds reared in the *kibbutz*.[30] The problems of personality development which seem acute when infants are the focus of investigation apparently lose much of their cruciality as the infant matures. "Intermittent" mothering, in other words, does not seem to have the long-lasting deleterious effects claimed or feared by students of the *kibbutz*.[31]

Bringing under analysis the *kibbutznik* of high school

28. Irvine, *op. cit.*, p. 269.

29. David Rapaport, "The Study of Kibbutz Education and its Bearing on the Theory of Development," *American Journal of Orthopsychiatry*, 28 (July, 1958), p. 593.

30. A. I. Rabin, "Infants and Children Under Conditions of 'Intermittent' Mothering in the *Kibbutz*," *American Journal of Orthopsychiatry*, 28 (July, 1958), p. 593.

31. *Ibid.*, p. 583.

age, Spiro points out in nonevaluative fashion the high degree of sexual repression among fellow *sabras* who, because of a self-developed exogamy, must perforce seek marriage partners outside the group. Further, their conservatism in matters of sex has led to what might be called *sabra* "puritanism"; likewise many *sabras* eagerly accept marriage as an occasion for religious and social ceremonies with the festivities and gift exchanges as an integral part of the wedding.[32] The role of the woman is being critically reexamined by the *sabras*; many females are unconvinced that equality of the sexes has been achieved. More serious is the characterization of *sabras* as hostile to immigrants, self-exalted, discontented, bored with Jewish culture, inflexibly assimilationist, insecure with the insecurity expressed in an insistence on the superiority of Israel.[33] Diamond formulates many of Spiro's observations into a characterization of the *sabras* as a *created personality type*, a rare phenomenon in human history.[34] The family can no longer serve as a mediating agency between society and child; rather, interposed between child and parent are other institutional arrangements involved in the socialization process. The net result is both a *sabra* perspective on society and a distinctive *sabra* personality type. Such personality type does not lend itself to integration with ascending generations and to the development of a system of kinship reciprocities. Reared in a peer-group world of his own, and sheltered in many ways from the parental generation, the *sabra* as a personality type stands impervious to integration in social forms other than those beginning and ending with his peer group. Consequently, argues Diamond, there is no true folk society or extended family character to the *kibbutz* community, inasmuch as integration of *sabras* and other groups into a solidary social whole is impossible.[35]

32. Spiro, *Children of the Kibbutz*, p. 349.
33. Spiro, "The *Sabras* and Zionism: A Study in Personality and Ideology," *Social Problems,* 5 (Fall, 1957), pp. 100-110.
34. Diamond, *op. cit.,* pp. 88-92.
35. *Ibid.,* pp. 89-90.

Recent Familistic Trends

Since mid-century, more particularly within the last fifteen years, the position of the family within the *kibbutz* has been strengthened.[36] Survival as a nation, and Israel became such in 1948, no longer presents a primary motivational theme; the collectives, still vital enough to the continued existence and growth of Israeli society, must now see their role as servitors, not saviors of Israel. External, mostly large-scale complex organizations—associations of collectives, embracing political parties, federations, centers, unions, marketing boards, development corporations, ministries, the army, settlement agencies, the Civil Service, and the like—directly or tangentially are interposed between individual *kibbutz* and the "society." Complex organizational entities, in short, make it difficult for the *kibbutzim* to exist as independent economic and social entities. As decision-making shifts to higher organizational levels and falls into the hands of a professionalizing managerial class, it becomes harder for the individual *kibbutznik* to maintain a clear conception of role and sense of purpose within the community. One reaction is to turn toward smaller social units within which he may "find himself."

Within the *kibbutz* pressures for reestablishment of familism or family-centeredness are noticeable. Housekeeping, commensal, and sociability functions increasingly devolve to or are arrogated by the family unit. With a rising level of living new standards of consumption reflecting taste, individuality, and resistance to communalized dress, eating, furnishing, and use of leisure time are appearing.

As new generations emerge and the majority of *kibbutz* youth stay with the collective, intergenerational ties prolifer-

36. This concluding section relies heavily on recent studies by the recently deceased Yonina Talmon-Garber, the Hebrew University, Jerusalem. Her structural-functional approach sets her apart somewhat from earlier sociological, anthropological, and psychological students of the *kibbutz*. Yet the recency and depth of her work makes her the leading authority on the sociology of the *kibbutz*.

ate and gain strength. The continuing decrease in age at marriage has the effect over time of increasing the pool of relatives and assuring more complete ascending generations. Kinship ties extend not only through the generations but now are spread out across collateral and affinal kin. However, the process is selective, based on particularistic rather than systematic and corporate grounds. The birth rate shows a steady increase; divorce rates conversely are lower. As family structure regenerates perhaps the most important development is the increased responsibility parents take for the socialization of the children.

In the occupational sphere the emphasis on performance of occupational role remains strong; nevertheless there is a decided tendency toward occupational role differentiation. Husbands are increasingly engaged in productive field and more lately factory work, while wives are more likely to be found performing service tasks within the *kibbutz*. Differentiation between the sexes is enhanced by the return toward feminism as reflected in dress, adornment, and beauty care. Sexual freedom for both sexes remains fixed in principle, but informal pressures tend to define sexual relations as permissible only for those who are married. Marriage, now conventionalized, is considered the first step toward acceptance of more of the responsibilities that have traditionally been assigned to parents. Family stability and marital fidelity are increasingly part of the *kibbutz* normative system.

Family authority is expressed in what Talmon-Garber calls "regional" divisions, with the wife tending to make the practical day-to-day household related decisions, the husband to speak for matters of wider principle that reflect community norms. Neither sex has a clear-cut, socially legitimated balance of authority.

In summary, we see a fairly steady evolvement toward a companionship family supported by familistic values. Resistance to the change is most pronounced, and the changes are consequently slower in developing, in the more revolutionary *kibbutz* settlements. Many departures from the rigid collectivistic pattern have no doubt come about with the disappearance or lessening of the political, economic, and demographic contingencies that led to their creation. The ideological polarization that gave rise to the revolutionary type of *kibbutz* described earlier remains a factor, but probably only a limiting factor in forming and maintaining social and economic arrangements in collectives.

Rational considerations involving the best utilization of human, natural, and technological resources, a penchant for working things out practically, and the current disposition to seek affective and sociability gratifications within smaller units than the *kibbutz* itself can provide are some of the subjective factors involved in the transformation. To these the organizational, bureaucratic pressures of larger social entities within a self-consciously expanding, rapidly industrializing, society must be added. The net effect is a set of changes broad enough in scope to make the mid-century revolutionary *kibbutz* and the attendant *sabra* personality type of its youth yesterday's cultural case-types in the natural history of a rapidly developing new society.

REFERENCES

Baratz, Joseph, *A Village by the Jordan: The Story of Degania.* London: The Harvill Press, 1954.

"Change on the Kibbutz," *Time*, 88 (Nov. 6, 1972), pp. 78-80.

Diamond, Stanley, "Kibbutz and Shtetl: the History of an Idea," *Social Problems*, V (Fall, 1957), pp. 71-99.

Irvine, Elizabeth E., "Observations on the Aims and Methods of Childrearing in Communal Settlements in Israel," *Human Relations*, V (1952), pp. 247-275.

The Israel Yearbook 1960. Israel: Israel Yearbook Publications, Ltd.

"The Mysterious Kibbutz," *Time*, 77 (Jan. 6, 1961), pp. 48-49.

Rabin, A. I., "Infants and Children Under Conditions of 'Intermittent' Mothering in the Kibbutz," *American Journal of Orthopsychiatry*, XXVIII, No. 3 (July, 1958), pp. 577-586.

Rapaport, David, "The Study of Kibbutz Education and its Bearing on the Theory of Development," *American Journal of Orthopsychiatry*, XXVIII, No. 3 (July, 1958), pp. 587-597.

Smilansky, Moshe, et al., eds., *Child and Youth Welfare in Israel.* Jerusalem: The Henrietta Szold Inst. of Child and Youth Welfare, 1960.

Spiro, Melford E., *Kibbutz: Venture in Utopia.* Cambridge: Harvard University Press, 1956.

———, "The *Sabras* and Zionism: A Study in Personality and Ideology," *Social Problems*, V, No. 2 (Fall, 1957), pp. 100-110.

———, *Children of the Kibbutz.* Cambridge: Harvard Univ. Press, 1958.

———, "Is the Family Universal? The Israeli Case," *American Anthropologist*, LVI, No. 5 (Oct., 1954), Part I, pp. 839-846. Reprinted with addendum in Norman W. Bell and Ezra F. Vogel, *A Modern Introduction to the Family.* Glencoe, Ill.: The Free Press, 1960, Chapter V, pp. 64-75.

Talmon-Garber, Yonina, "The Family in Israel," *Marriage and Family Living*, XVI (1954), pp. 343-349.

———, "Sex Role Differentiation in an Equalitarian Society," in Thomas Lasswell, John Burma, and Sidney Aronson, eds., *Life in Society.* Chicago: Scott, Foresman, 1965, pp. 144-154.

———, "The Family in a Revolutionary Movement—The Case of the Kibbutz in Israel," in Meyer Nimkoff, ed., *Comparative Family Systems,* Boston: Houghton Mifflin Company, 1965, pp. 259-286.

———, and Cohen, E., "Collective Settlements in the Negev," in Joseph Ben-David, ed., *Agricultural Planning in the Village Community in Israel.* Paris: UNESCO, 1964, pp. 58-95.

Weingarten, Murray, *Life in a Kibbutz.* New York: The Reconstructionist Press, 1955.

Zborowski, Mark, and Herzog, Elizabeth, *Life is With People.* New York: International Universities Press, 1952.

Part Two

7 The Patriarchal Family of the Ancient Hebrews[1]

In the preceding chapters we have been dealing with the family systems of cultures very unlike our own and apparently without influence upon ours. Except for the Chinese and the *kibbutz*, these cultures are appropriately designated nonliterate because they do not include writing. With the same exception each of them represents the way of life of a rather small group (tribe, nation, people) relatively isolated from other peoples. We turn now to the family complex in some cultures that resemble our own in certain respects and that have certainly influenced the development of our system. These cultures have attained a literature; our knowledge of them is derived from documents and artifacts preserved sometimes for centuries. Most of the groups represented in this and succeeding chapters are larger than those of the nonliterates. However, in early times the numbers, the breadth of the culture base, and some aspects of the family system among the Hebrews, Romans, and Anglo-Saxons were similar to those of the nonliterates already described.

From the ancient Hebrews, we in twentieth-century North America have received a heritage transmitted largely through the Old Testament. With specific reference to the family this heritage includes the traditions of male dominance, respect

1. This account is based primarily on the Old Testament, especially the books of Genesis, Exodus, Leviticus, Numbers, Deuteronomy, and Ruth. Use is also made of the Babylonian Talmud and several secondary sources.

for women of one's own group and class, the command to "honor thy father and thy mother," pride in a patrilineal family tree, a double standard of sex morals, and some definitions and rules pertaining to incest and sexual perversions. Of course these culture traits have not come down to us unchanged, nor can we attribute them exclusively to the ancient Hebrews. Nevertheless there is a continuity which cannot be ignored and which helps to account for some aspects of the family patterns of contemporary North America.

It is important to remember that the materials at our disposal concerning the ancient Hebrews pertain to several rather different stages of cultural development. In the earliest times of which we have record, the Jews were nomadic desert groups living in tents, driving their sheep about in search of pasture and water. The patriarchal chiefs practiced polygyny, held slaves, sacrificed animals to their tribal god, Jehovah, and met the demands of justice through the *lex talionis*, "an eye for an eye and a tooth for a tooth," with responsibility shared by a whole sib. This was a kinship group of persons related through the male line plus their wives.[2] The Old Testament stories of Abraham and Lot are representative of this stage.

About the middle of the twelfth century B.C. they began to take possession of Canaan, to settle in villages, and to become farmers. They raised barley, wheat, beans, olives, figs, and grapes, along with other fruits and vegetables. Some of them continued to live in tents, some occupied one-room cabins of sun-dried brick or uncut stone, and a few had more elaborate houses of cut stone and timber, with several rooms. The humbler homes were shared with domestic animals and had very little furniture. The better homes contained beds, tables, oil lamps, earthen jars, skins for holding liquids, and pegs on which to hang clothing and other articles.

---

2. These kinsmen constituted a patrilineal sib. They and their wives constituted a clan, a group involving both consanguinity and residence as basic principles.

Settled abodes and the raising of crops gave rise to new conceptions of property in land, purchase, sale, mortgage, inheritance, redemption, trespass, and theft. Hence there developed new laws and legal machinery. The so-called Deuteronomic code appeared during this period, probably in the seventh century B.C. Tribal life gradually gave way. The Jews became a nation with a king, a capital, and a temple at Jerusalem. Social classes developed with a military and courtly aristocracy at the top and with a miscellany of landless freemen, servants, and debtors at the bottom.

In the tenth century B.C. the kingdom was divided as a result of rebellion. In the eighth century the kingdom of Israel was conquered by the Assyrians. In the sixth century the kingdom of Judah was overthrown by the Babylonians, and a large number of its people were carried away into exile for nearly fifty years. After this there was a partial restoration, but from then on Judah was under the domination of some foreign power—Persia, Egypt, Syria, Greece, or Rome.

During the exile and thereafter the Jews were in close contact with other peoples. They felt themselves hard pressed and developed regulations, ceremonies, traditions, and aspirations which served to maintain a measure of group integrity. Though sharing political rule and economic activities with the larger society, they solidified themselves around family and synagogue, stressing their idealized customs and institutions. Finally, for the purposes of this narrative, came the Roman conquest and the scattering of the Jews through the Mediterranean world in the first century A.D., the so-called Diaspora.

Our principal sources of information about the ancient Hebrews are the Old Testament and the Talmud. In using these ancient works we encounter problems not presented in the study of contemporary preliterate cultures. The latter are reported to us through monographs written by first-hand observers who are trained anthropologists, but the Old Testament and the Talmud are very different from scientific monographs. What we now possess has been transmitted over many centuries, first in the form of written manuscripts and only in more recent years in printed form. Both collections have been translated and suffer all the losses which inevitably are incurred in transcribing a document from one language into another. Furthermore neither the Old Testament nor the Talmud was written all at once. Each is made up of numerous accretions spread over a very long period of time. Hence for their interpretation we must depend on the analyses of critical students of the available texts. In these ancient compendia there is a mixture of elements that are almost sure to confuse the amateur. There are folktales assembled in written documents after perhaps centuries of transmission by word of mouth. There are legal codes and statements of what is supposed to be done by men and women. There are exhortations by reformers and prophets, sometimes recalling people to mores from which they have drifted, sometimes projecting new ideals of conduct. There are poems whose relation to everyday living is difficult to determine. There are genealogies and narratives whose historical accuracy can probably be accepted as very high. Along with the task of differentiating and interrelating these varied materials we must wrestle with the problem of discovering what we can about the lives of the masses, for histories of the Jews, as of other peoples, portray chiefly the experiences of prominent men. The folkways of common people are often left in obscurity. It is noteworthy, too, that records of antiquity are almost exclusively the works of men. Much is said about women, but little by them. Hence we who are not specialists in Hebrew literature, law, and custom must proceed with caution.

Family Structure

Throughout historic times the ancient Hebrew family may be legitimately described as patriarchal and polygynous. By the term patriarchal we mean that great power was vested in the male head of each household. This was especially marked during the period of nomadic pastoral life, and under the circumstances then obtaining was probably quite necessary to survival. However, the traditions and customs of the patriarchy continued after settled agriculture had developed. Polygyny was the accepted thing, at least for chieftains and kings, although the sex ratio was probably never so low as to provide more than one wife for most of the men. At any rate, polygyny was recognized in Hebrew law, though not without some restrictions. After the exile there were protests against it offered by various prophets. Nevertheless it appears that plural marriages continued even into the Middle Ages. In addition there was the practice of concubinage. The stories of Sarah, Leah, and Rachel are familiar. Having no offspring of their own, they gave their personal maids as concubines to their husbands and claimed the sons of these maids as their own. Concubines and their offspring were treated as full-fledged members of the household, though their status was inferior to that of legal wives and their children.

Normally descent was patrilineal in the historic periods. But there is evidence of a different system having existed in the dim and distant past. In the thirty-sixth chapter of Genesis we find "the generations of Esau" listed in the female line. Normally inheritance was by sons, with a double portion to the oldest. In other words there was a modified form of primogeniture. In the nomadic stage the headship of the household seems usually to have gone to the patriarch's oldest son. However, the oldest was sometimes passed over. Thus Jacob passed over three sons—Reuben, Simeon, and Levi—to give the headship to Judah. It is hard to say whether any significance should be attached to the fact that these four were all sons of Jacob's first wife, Leah. The case of Jacob and Esau suggests similarly the right of the patriarch to designate his heir. Certain other privileges apparently belonged to the firstborn son of a man. One of these was a blessing often bestowed by the father in his advanced years.

The provision for the estate of a man who had no sons is set forth in Numbers 27:8-11:

And thou shalt speak unto the children of Israel, saying,

If a man die, and have no son, then ye shall cause his inheritance to pass unto his daughter.

And if he have no daughter, then ye shall give his inheritance unto his brethren.

And if he have no brethren, then ye shall give his inheritance unto his father's brethren.

And if his father have no brethren, then ye shall give his inheritance unto his kinsman that is next to him of his family, and he shall possess it: and it shall be unto the children of Israel a statute of judgment, as the Lord commanded Moses.

In the Babylonian Talmud we read that a man might "by verbal will" divide his estate among his children as he pleased, provided he did not use the word inheritance. In the same tract (*Baba Bathra*) a man is forbidden to disinherit a son in favor of a daughter, or a daughter in favor of a stranger. Also, "if one dies and leaves sons and daughters, if the inheritance is of great worth then the sons inherit and the daughters must be supported from it; and if a moderate one the daughters must be supported and the sons go a-begging."

The son of a concubine might be driven out of the house without any inheritance, as in the case of Ishmael, son of Abraham and Hagar. On the other hand, it appears that the son of a concubine might be made the heir if there were no son by a wife. Thus, before the birth of Isaac, Abraham complained that Eliezer, who was evidently his son by a concubine, was in line for the inheritance of his estate. In the case of Sheshan who had no sons but only daughters, one of the latter was married to a servant, Jarha, who thus became to all intents and purposes a son, though it might be argued that he merely bridged the gap between Sheshan and the grandson-to-be.

Several scholars have propounded the theory that in an earlier period the Hebrew family was matrilineal rather than patrilineal in type. As evidence of this they call attention to the naming of children by their mother rather than by their father. Considering the several documents on which the Hexateuch is based, it appears that in the earliest times the naming was almost entirely by mothers. Proceeding to subsequent manuscripts in chronological order, we find a decline in mother-naming and a marked increase in father-naming. Another bit of evidence is the matrilocal residence of certain of the patriarchs. Thus Jacob, Moses, and Samson lived with their respective fathers-in-law for extended periods of time. Gideon had a concubine who lived with her own people, and Amasa's father was an Ishmaelite who came to live with his mother. Attention is called to the statement that Rebekah ran to tell "her mother's house" that Abraham's servant had come. Gifts were offered to her mother and her brother, but she went to live in the camp of her husband's father. After Jacob had lived twenty years with his father-in-law, Laban, he had to steal away, and was allowed to absent himself permanently only after pursuit and protest and a contract to deal properly with Laban's daughters, who were Jacob's wives. In spite of all this evidence pointing toward a possible matrilocal system in earlier times, the periods concerning which we are best informed display a definitely patriarchal, patrilocal, and patrilineal type of family.

The Family in the Social System

The basic unit of ancient Hebrew society was the household (beth). It often included several marriage groups, for which, interestingly, we find no Hebrew name. In the nomadic stage the household included the patriarch, his wives and concubines, their small children, grown sons with their wives and children, slaves, bond servants, and sometimes strangers who had placed themselves under the patriarch's protection. All these lived together in the same camp, occupying numerous tents. The patriarch exercised great authority over his household, but apparently this did not extend to matters of life and death over wives, except in case of adultery. It appears that there was such power over children in the earliest period, although this was later diminished. A man might sell his daughter to a fellow Hebrew, though not to a foreigner. Also a man's children might be claimed by his creditors. In this situation they were not only under their father's power, but were part of his assets. If a man "bought" a Hebrew servant he must release him after six years of servitude. He was forbidden to beat his servants to death. If he injured them very seriously he must let them go free. A child who struck or cursed his parents was to be stoned but evidently not by the father. At least in the period of living in towns a disobedient son was to be stoned by the citizens after complaint by the father.

A number of related households constituted a clan (*mishpahah*); a number of related clans constituted a tribe (*shebet*); the twelve tribes constituted the nation (*am*). All of these were regarded as extensions of the family and the whole people was united by a sense of kinship.

We have observed that the conjugal family group was completely swallowed up in the household and had almost no independent existence, but this must not obscure the evidence of strong husband-wife and parent-child attachments. Households sometimes grew to very great size, but occasionally the numbers became too great, or the flocks were too large for the available pasturage, and such a household was divided. So we have the story of Abraham and Lot, who amicably agreed to travel in separate directions in order that there might be a sufficient living for both parts of the previously united group. A similar division was arranged by Jacob and Esau.

The Family Cycle

Marital Selection

In sharp contrast to our system, marriage among the ancient Hebrews was not the culmination of "free choice" and romantic love on the part of a boy and girl. It was most frequently arranged by their fathers and in early times closely resembled wife purchase, if indeed it was not exactly that.

The purchase price (*mohar*) might take several different forms. Jacob's fourteen years of service to Laban for his wives Leah and Rachel is, of course, well known. In other cases the bride-price appears to have been in military service or in goods. Wife purchase of early times seems gradually to have given way to the offering of gifts and finally to the formality of the bridegroom placing a coin in the bride's hand.

As indicated above, the essential requirement for marriage was usually an agreement by fathers of the young man and young woman. It appears, however, that the wishes of the young folks themselves were not wholly ignored; witness Jacob's love for Rachel and Michal's love for David. In a later period the consent of the two immediate parties to a marriage was required along with that of their parents. Eventually they did not have to have their parents' consent if they were of age, but respect for parents doubtless meant that marriages were seldom contracted against the latter's will. By Talmudic law the legal age was twelve for girls and thirteen for boys. A father might betroth his daughter before puberty, but at that age she might refuse to go through with the contract, whereupon it became null and void.

Betrothal was counted as the beginning of marriage even though the union might not be consummated until much later. Betrothal involved agreement between fathers of the young man and young woman; in later periods agreement was between the young persons themselves. In early times a purchase price was often paid or elaborate gifts were presented to the girl's family. Later there was a ceremonial giving of money (*kaseph*) or the drawing up of a written document (*kiddushin*). In later times both cases required the presence of two witnesses. In addition, there was sometimes a benediction by a priest or a male relative of the girl.

After betrothal the girl might be taken immediately to her husband's house for celebration of the nuptials. In early times this was usual. In later centuries it was frequently delayed. Likewise, in early times the wedding involved almost no ceremony at all, greatest importance being attached to the betrothal. As the two events were more and more separated, the betrothal declined in importance and the wedding gained. In later times the principal features of a wedding were the procession and the feast. The bridegroom, accompanied by friends, went to the home of the bride where she awaited him with some of her companions. The whole party then proceeded to the house of his parents. En route songs were sung and if it were evening the procession was lighted by torches. At the home of the groom's father a banquet was held, after which friends conducted the pair to the bridal chamber. Benedictions were said by the groom, or by the priest, or by one of the required witnesses. Throughout all these centuries betrothal and wedding were essentially domestic ceremonials requiring no participation by priest or magistrate.

The motives underlying marriage appear to have been on the part of the man the enjoyment of sex and the having of children, and on the part of the woman, security and social status. However, any such statement as this must be regarded as an undue simplification of the real facts. At all times the economic aspect of marriage was important. In later centuries both dower and dowry were required. The dower was property set aside for the wife in case of divorce or the husband's death. The dowry was a gift from the girl's father, usually in the form of personal property, sometimes including slaves.

During the nomadic period there was apparently some intermarriage with other desert tribes. However, this must have meant for the woman almost complete and perhaps final severance from her original kinship group. Whether for this or for other reasons, there was strong pressure for endogamy. During the invasion and conquest of Canaan there were strict rules against marriage covenants between Jews and the peoples already in the Promised Land. (Exodus 34:12-16) However, popular sentiment did not always support the rule. Living in close proximity to other ethnic groups, young Hebrew men seem to have found Canaanite women attractive and frequently married them. This led in turn to adoption of "strange" customs and the worship of "heathen" gods. Naturally reformers rose up to protest against such disloyalty and apostasy. The efforts to "restore" strict Jewish endogamy continued during the exile and after the restoration. There was even a determination "to put away all the (foreign) wives and such as are born of them." (Ezra 10:3)

Status and Roles of the Sexes

From what has already been said it is apparent that women were definitely subordinate. On the other hand they seem to have been generally respected and loved. In early times a woman was always in the power of some man—her father, her brother, her husband, or her father-in-law. But a widowed mother living with her son, or a divorcée, was relatively free. In one sense woman was treated as property, but she was valuable property and was as a rule well cared for. She was not isolated, as among the Mohammedans and the Athenians, but had considerable freedom and influence. This is indicated by the well-known stories of Sarah, Rebekah, Deborah, Jael, Abigail, and Jezebel. Not only were Jewish women at least indirectly influential; what is equally important, they were sometimes the devoted and loved companions of their husbands. Thus we read that "Abimelech, King of the Philistines, looked out a window, and saw, and behold, Isaac was sporting with Rebekah his wife." (Genesis 26:8) In Deuteronomy 24:5 we find the interesting instruction that "when a man hath taken a new wife, he shall not go out to war, neither shall he be charged with any business; but he shall be free at home one year, and shall cheer up his wife which he hath taken."

As to division of labor, men's work usually included tending the flocks, tilling the soil, performing religious ceremonies, and carrying on political activities and war. Women did spinning, weaving, made clothing, prepared food in accordance with ritual law, organized and conducted the housework, and sometimes sold the products of household industry.

We have little notion of how their status and their roles

might have been described by the Jewish women themselves. We can only guess that for the most part they probably accepted their position and carried on the expected activities with a minimum of complaint or evasion. On the other hand, so long as we are speculating, we may wonder if there were not some dominant wives and hen-pecked husbands, especially after the development of town life. But enough of guesswork. We really do not know much about the acceptance and rejection of traditional roles and status, about conjugal affection and respect, nor about changes in these relationships from one period to another of Hebrew history.

Growing Up in the Ancient Hebrew Family

"Lo, children are a heritage of Jehovah; and the fruit of the womb is his reward. As arrows in the hand of a mighty man, so are the children of youth. Happy is the man that hath his quiver full of them." (Psalm 127:3-5) Here is a poetical expression of desire for children and delight in their coming. Sons in particular were wanted to carry on the family line, to inherit and preserve estates when these existed, and to become workers and warriors. Daughters too had an economic value. But over and above these materialistic considerations it seems clear that children were desired for their own sake. Hence, there was often, if not generally, rejoicing at the birth of a child.

The delivery itself was attended by women of the household and sometimes by a midwife. The mother apparently did not go to bed, as with us, but commonly sat on a stool or stood in a crouching position. The experience would have been very hard for a modern woman and was probably not easy for the ancient Hebrew mother. After the cutting of the umbilical cord the infant was washed, rubbed with salt, and wrapped in "swaddling clothes" or cloth bands. Nothing is recorded about a cradle, and it appears that the baby was carried at the breast or laid on a bed or on the floor, depending on the economic status of the family. Ordinarily the child was named at once, in early times by the mother, but later most often by the father. The mother then had to abstain from touching any sacred object for forty days after the birth of a son and eighty days after the birth of a daughter. Then she regained ceremonial cleanness by formal sacrifice.

Babies were usually nursed by their mothers, although on the higher social levels they had the attention of servants and sometimes received nourishment from wet nurses. The period of lactation was much longer than with us, often extending to two or three years. During this time the mother was not supposed to have intercourse with her husband. Hence each child normally had a period of three or four years without the appearance of a younger rival sibling. What this meant in the way of emotional security is hard to tell. At least it protected the mother against becoming weakened from frequent child-bearings.

It is clear that babies were carried in the arms, while older children were taken on the shoulder or astride the hip. Also they sat on the laps of adults and were played with. When they were a little older they played various games and began to help their elders—gathering fuel, carrying water, watching sheep, and the like.

In early times there was no formal education. Children learned by observing, listening to parental instructions, and actually doing things in and about the home. In this fashion boys of the nomadic period learned to tend the sheep and to fight, while their sisters learned to prepare food and make clothing. In addition oldest sons were trained to perform religious ceremonies. As a matter of fact religious festivals were the occasion and the means of transmitting folklore, moral codes, religious beliefs, and a sense of identification with family, tribe, and nation.

After the settlement in Canaan boys were taught farming, house building, pottery making, and other acts that go with agriculture and village life. Girls too had more elaborate programs of housework to master. Both apparently learned something of singing and dancing. A few—probably not girls— learned to read and write. Real schools came rather late, perhaps not until after the Exile, and never reached a large number of children. But for all there was supposed to be thorough home instruction in manners, morals, and religion.

From Proverbs and especially from the apocryphal book Ecclesiasticus we gather that children were expected to be irresponsible, foolish, and rebellious. Hence their wills must be broken—a point of view repeated with scriptural authority in Elizabethan England and Colonial America. "A horse not broken becometh headstrong; a child left to himself becometh wilful. Bow down his neck while he is young, and beat him on the sides while he is a child, lest he wax stubborn and be disobedient unto thee." (Ecclesiasticus 30:8, 12)

The virtues which were emphasized included honoring the parents, respecting the aged, avoidance of boasting and gluttony, simplicity, hospitality, truthfulness, and implicit obedience. Here was "character education" sternly inculcated. Through much of their history life was hard for the ancient Hebrews. They were prepared for it by strict discipline tempered, however, with affection. The product of such upbringing cannot be easily characterized, but at least the Jews were then, as later, hardy, persistent, demanding, loyal, and affectionate.

By the time the daughters were married and gone from the parental household, the sons had married and brought their wives to live with their parents or nearby. Thus there were often, if not usually, three generations sharing the domestic menage with the corresponding privileges and responsibilities. As old age approached the patriarch engaged in less work, but apparently kept his authority. Both he and his wife were usually respected and cherished. There was no question of what to do with old folks, as so often arises with us.

Death and Divorce

We have now sketched briefly the expected life cycle of an ancient Hebrew family. But sometimes the cycle was broken by death or divorce. There were widows, divorcées, orphans, and occasionally other detached persons. However, as in the preliterate cultures which we have examined, we find among the ancient Hebrews almost no place for unmarried adults. Everyone was expected to marry and practically everyone did. If a home were broken by death there was definite provision for the survivors. A widower might already have another wife or concubine, and if not he could presumably obtain one. A widow too might remarry, but if childless she was sometimes expected to marry her deceased husband's brother and by him have a son who would be regarded as the descendant and heir of the dead man. This is the custom called *levirate*. A widow might live in the home of a grown son and enjoy considerable freedom. Failing a male kinsman of her dead husband who could and would provide for her, she might return to her father's house, as in Tamar's case. If impoverished, she was commended to public sympathy and permitted to glean in field and vineyard.

A divorcée was relatively free. If innocent of grave fault she apparently lost little, if any, social standing. In later times she gained control of her dowry and was permitted to marry a man of her choice, but she could never remarry her former husband.

Orphans and half-orphans obviously continued as members of the household in early times and were taken in by near relatives in later periods. Should there be no near kinsmen, they were to receive special consideration from benevolent Hebrews, and in still later times might be made "wards of the congregation." Without formal organizations or procedures being established, it was nevertheless ordered that kindness be shown to the blind and various other persons with physical handicaps, as well as "sojourners." An impoverished brother was to be received and supported as a sojourner.

Family Controls

As we have already seen, authority, especially in the early nomadic period, was vested in the patriarch, usually the oldest living male in a household. But he was not entirely free to rule in an arbitrary manner. He was restrained by the customs and traditions of his people, especially by the unwritten laws which had the sanction of religion. "Thus saith the Lord" must have been a powerful restraining and guiding influence. Later there were various public officials from "elders of the city" to the king. These officials passed on questions relating to the virginity of a betrothed maiden, premarital sex relations in general, adultery, the levirate, and inheritance. But so far as we can discover, the arrangement of marriage and divorce were primarily matters to be settled by the family itself and not by the community or state during the periods in which we are particularly interested.

As examples of the mores and laws which governed family life "from the outside," we shall refer to several rules pertaining to marriage, concubinage, the levirate, divorce, and sexual behavior.

Marriage and Concubinage

The Hebrews, like all other peoples, had laws prohibiting marriage between persons within certain degrees of kinship and affinity. In earliest times stress was laid on the mother's line. Thus a man might marry his half-sister if they had different mothers, but not if they had the same mother. In those early days the prohibition included mother's sister, mother, and daughter. Later regulations extended the ban to paternal half-sister, stepmother, mother-in-law, and daughter-in-law. The levitical code barred, in addition to the preceding, marriage of a man with any wife of his father, his father's sister, father's brother's wife, daughter's daughter, son's wife or daughter, brother's wife (without levirate duty, to be described later) and wife's sister (during the lifetime of the wife). This rather elaborate definition of relationships considered incestual is set forth in the eighteenth chapter of Leviticus and has been cited by modern lawmakers in support of their legislation. If the reader is surprised that all this has been stated in terms of action by the man, he must remember that in such matters the initiative belonged to the male sex. Hence it was quite natural that Hebrew law should impose these prohibitions directly on the man and only indirectly on the woman.

The taking of secondary wives and concubines, not always clearly distinguished, was regulated in a number of ways. The following passage (Exodus 21:7-11) evidently regulates the purchase of a secondary wife.

And if a man sell his daughter to be a maidservant, she shall not go out as the menservants do.

If she please not her master, who hath betrothed her to himself, then shall he let her be redeemed: to sell her unto a strange nation he shall have no power, seeing he hath dealt deceitfully with her.

And if he have betrothed her unto his son, he shall deal with her after the manner of daughters.

If he take him another wife: her food. her raiment, and her duty of marriage, shall he not diminish.

And if he do not these three unto her, then shall she go out free without money.

Sometimes during a war or a raid women were captured and taken by the victors as secondary wives or concubines. Thus we read in Deuteronomy 21:10-14:

When thou goest forth to war against thine enemies, and the Lord thy God hath delivered them into thine hands, and thou hast taken them captive.

And seest among the captives a beautiful woman, and hast a desire unto her, that thou wouldest have her to thy wife;

Then thou shalt bring her home to thine house; and she shall shave her head, and pare her nails;

And she shall put the raiment of her captivity from off her, and shall remain in thine house, and bewail her father and her mother a full month: and after that thou shalt go in unto her, and be her husband, and she shall be thy wife.

And it shall be, if thou have no delight in her, then thou shalt let her go whither she will; but thou shalt not sell her at all for money, thou shalt not make merchandise of her, because thou hast humbled her.

Divorce

As to divorce, the following passage (Deuteronomy 21:1-4) evidently covers marriages of the highest order.

When a man hath taken a wife, and married her, and it come to pass that she find no favour in his eyes, because he hath found some uncleanness in her: then let him write her a bill of divorcement, and give it in her hand, and send her out of his house.

And when she is departed out of his house, she may go and be another man's wife.

And if the latter husband hate her, and write her a bill of divorcement, and giveth it in her hand, and sendeth her out of his house; or if the latter husband die, which took her to be his wife;

Her former husband, which sent her away, may not take her again to be his wife, after that she is defiled; for that is abomination before the Lord: and thou shalt not cause the land to sin, which the Lord thy God giveth thee for an inheritance.

We have previously noted the prohibition of divorce in cases where a man falsely accused his bride of not being a virgin, and those of "forced" marriage.

Levirate

To put pressure on the brother of a man who died without a male heir, in case he should be unwilling to become the father of a child to be regarded as his dead brother's son, there was a definite though humiliating procedure through which he might be exempted. This was called *chalitza*. The regulation pertaining to this is set forth in Deuteronomy 25:5-10:

If brethren dwell together, and one of them die, and have no child, the wife of the dead shall not marry without unto a stranger: her husband's brother shall go in unto her, and take her to him to wife, and perform the duty of an husband's brother unto her.

And it shall be, that the first-born which she beareth shall succeed in the name of his brother which is dead, that his name be not put out of Israel.

And if the man like not to take his brother's wife, then let his brother's wife go up to the gate unto the elders, and say, My husband's brother refuseth to raise up unto his brother a name in Israel, he will not perform the duty of my husband's brother.

Then the elders of his city shall call him, and speak unto him: and if he stand to it, and say, I like not to take her;

Then shall his brother's wife come in to him in the presence of the elders, and loose his shoe from off his foot, and spit in his face, and shall answer and say, So shall it be done unto that man that will not build up his brother's house.

And his name shall be called in Israel, The House of him that hath his shoe loosed.

The opening phrase of the foregoing passage "if brethren dwell together," suggests that the situation to which the levirate applied was one in which the patriarch was still alive, but one of his sons living in the household died leaving a widow with no child. The story of Ruth suggests that, failing a brother-in-law, other kinsmen in order were looked to as those who might perform this function.

The Sex Code

In general the sexual code of the ancient Hebrews was stern and harsh. It enforced a double standard requiring fidelity of women but not of men, usually punishing women more severely than men. However, in case of adultery the death penalty was to be inflicted on both offenders if the woman were married. To test the guilt or innocence of an accused wife an ordeal was specified. She must swear before a priest and drink some holy water. If guilty it was expected that her body would swell and her thigh would rot away. If innocent no harm would come to her and she would bear a child. (Numbers 5:11-28) In case of sex relations with a betrothed girl, the death penalty was prescribed for a man, not because of his injury to the girl, but because he had violated another man's rights. If the affair had taken place "in the field" no penalty was imposed upon the girl because it was assumed that she could not have secured help. But if it happened in town she too was to be stoned to death "because she cried not being in the city." If a husband accused his bride of not being a virgin, his parents were supposed to take "the tokens of her virginity" to the elders of the city. If they adjudged her innocent her husband could not divorce her at any time, but if they found her guilty she was to be stoned to death. If a betrothed girl who was a bondmaid had intercourse with some man, both were to be punished but neither was to be put to death. Presumably this was on the ground that she was not as important as a free woman. The man was required to bring a ram to the priest as a trespass offering. Nothing further is said about what should be done to the girl. In the case of sex relations between a man and a woman neither married nor betrothed, the man was required to make a payment to her father—fifty shekels is specified in one passage—and he must make the girl his wife if her father consented.

Prostitution was probably very rare in the early period and was mildly forbidden after the development of town life. Indeed, a harlot might live in a Hebrew community without any special condemnation. (Joshua 6:25) However, if the prostitute were attached to some heathen cult, perhaps to a temple, then the prohibition was stern.

Sodomy, a form of homosexual relations, and "bestiality," or intercourse with an animal, were strictly forbidden and to be punished by death. Coitus interruptus was condemned, at least by implication. All these regulations and the penalties for violation might seem to be expressions of a kind of puritanism. But it would probably be more accurate to regard them as related to the notion of sex as a divine gift to perpetuate family, tribe, and nation and as such to be enjoyed but not wasted.

The rules of incest have been stated in an earlier section of this chapter. The penalty for violation of these rules was death by stoning, burning, or choking.

Modesty required the wearing of rather full clothing by both sexes. It was, moreover, ordered that everyone must wear the clothes of his own sex. The incident will be recalled in which Noah got drunk and lay in his tent without any clothing. One of his sons happened upon him and ran to call his brothers who took a garment and walked backward toward their father, whom they dared not look at until he was again covered.

Generalizing about the "external" controls of sex and family life we may say that the regulations were founded on these principles: (1) Sexual relations with foreigners represented disloyalty to the Hebrew nation and heresy against its religion. (2) Irregular sexual behavior by or with a woman was an invasion of the property rights of her father or husband. (3) Other sexual irregularity, such as intercourse during menstruation or soon after childbirth, sodomy, and sex relations with animals, was likely to bring on some supernatural penalty. Marriage, concubinage, and the levirate were in part means of perpetuating, not only a family line, but the Chosen People.

Family Functions

In conclusion let us remind ourselves that the Hebrew family, for most purposes, was not the small conjugal group, but the household or even larger kinship group. Marriage was not unimportant, but the wedded couple was absorbed in the consanguine family of three generations and many collateral relatives.

The ancient Hebrew family in the sense of household had a most inclusive array of functions. Through it children were produced and reared "that a man's house might not die out of Israel." It was an almost self-sufficient economic unit. The head of the household was a religious functionary who conducted various ceremonies and supervised the ritual cleanliness and dietary laws. In early times he had charge of *teraphim,* or sacred images. The household was an educational institution wherein the elders were the teachers who gave practical and religious instruction to the youth. It was a protective agency, caring for handicapped members and taking in impoverished "brothers" as well as "sojourners." In a sense the household determined right and wrong, made laws, and administered justice. It would have been possible for life to go on almost without any other social group or institution.

As nomadic life gave way to living in towns, the nuclear family became more often a separate unit. As concubinage was reduced, procreation became more definitely a function of the conjugal group. Also child rearing and economic provision or maintenance were more identified with the small nuclear family. On the other hand, religious ceremonies were to a large degree transferred to the synagogue and the temple. Hence we see that among the ancient Hebrews there was not a fixed array of functions permanently identified with either the nuclear or the extended family.

REFERENCES

Cross, Earle B., *The Hebrew Family: A Study in Historical Sociology*. Chicago: University of Chicago Press, 1927.

Epstein, Louis M., *Marriage Laws in the Bible and the Talmud*. Cambridge: Harvard University Press, 1942.

Feldman, W. M., *The Jewish Child, Its History, Folklore, Biology and Sociology*. London: Bailliere, Tindall and Cox, 1917.

Hastings, James, ed., *Dictionary of the Bible*. New York: Charles Scribner's Sons, 1909.

Jewish Encyclopedia. New York: Funk and Wagnalls Company, 1901-1906.

Kennett, R. H., *Ancient Hebrew Social Life and Custom*. London: Oxford University Press, 1933.

Mace, David R., *Hebrew Marriage*. New York: Philosophical Library, 1953.

The New Jewish Encyclopedia, David Bridger, ed., in association with Samuel Wolk. New York: Behrman House, 1962.

Smith, W. Robertson, *Kinship and Marriage in Early Arabia*. London: A. & C. Black, 1903.

Soares, T. G., *The Social Institutions and Ideals of the Bible*. New York: Abingdon Press, 1915.

Swift, F. H., *Education in Ancient Israel from Earliest Times to 70 A.D.* Chicago: Open Court Publishing Company, 1919.

Talmud, new edition of the Babylonian Talmud. Original text edited, corrected, formulated, and translated into English by Michael L. Ridkinson. Boston: The Talmud Society, 1918.

8 *The Ancient Romans—Continuity and Change*

The second source of influence on the modern American family is, for the purposes of this study, Ancient Rome. The Roman family in early times was like that of the ancient Hebrews in being primarily a household or kinship group dominated by a male head, yet by no means lacking in marital and parental affection. The two peoples differed sharply in that the early Romans were strictly monogamous, never approving polygyny or concubinage. In both cultures important changes occurred. Among the Jews these were associated with the destruction of their nation, among the Romans with successful wars of conquest and accumulated wealth.

Of course there was no sudden change in customs, traditions, and mores in either Judaea or Rome, but there are many reasons for considering the Punic Wars as a turning point in the history of the Roman family—long absences of men serving in the army, growth of the capital city, rise of a leisure class, and importation of slaves. These and other changes in the structure of Roman society meant inevitably changes in family life. Many of the innovations were regarded as vicious and degenerate, both by Roman satirists and later by Christian apostles. Hence it may be held that early Christian standards of family life drew heavily on the patriarchal tradition represented by the Jews and the Romans, but they also constituted a reaction against the innovations and the disorganization evident especially in the upper classes of Imperial Rome.

THE ROMAN FAMILY BEFORE THE PUNIC WARS

Family Structure

In the period before the Punic Wars the Roman family was patrilineal, patrilocal, and patriarchal in character. Dominance of the *pater familias* was not identical with that of the head of a Hebrew family, but it was no less thoroughgoing.

The Roman *familia*, or household, included all those persons subject to the authority of the same *pater familias*. These might be wife, unmarried daughters, sons and adopted sons, whether married or not, their wives, sons and unmarried daughters, and even remoter descendants, but always counted in the male line. In later centuries *familia* included slaves and clients. Such a household usually broke up only on the death of its head. When this occurred there might be as many new *familiae* as there were persons directly subject to the *patria potestas*. We have already noted that individuals might be detached from the household by marriage, adoption, or emancipation without destroying the group as a whole.

The Roman *gens*, which we have called clan in the description of other cultures, meant a group of households tracing their descent through males from a common ancestor. Membership in the Roman *gens* was indicated by the *nomen*, usually the second of three names that a citizen commonly possessed. Certain *gentes* were supposed to be descended from *patres* who in the days of the kings constituted the senate. Others had a later origin. The *gens* seems to have been much more than a listing of kinsmen, as frequently is the case in our culture. It was a group that provided guardians for minor children, the insane, and spendthrifts; it took over property left by members who died without any heirs; it conducted certain religious services and sometimes had a common burial plot; it even passed resolutions which were binding on its members.

The Roman system of computing kinship, with English instead of Latin terms, is charted on page 177. This scheme of counting degrees of kinship was used for many centuries in Christian Europe, even after the decline of the Roman Empire. Those persons were called *agnati* whose descent was traced through males to a common ancestor (real or fictitious) in whose *potestas* they would be if he were alive. In addition, *agnatio,* the relationship established by such common descent, was made to include the wife and the adopted son of any man belonging to the group. The term *cognati* was applied to all blood relations regardless of line or *potestas*. In general, *cognati* within the sixth degree were not supposed to marry, but those within the fourth degree were said to have the right to kiss. *Cognati* might exchange presents and hold family reunions, but they did not constitute an organic body, as the *agnati* constituted the *gens*. Persons connected by marriage only were called *adfines*. There were no formal degrees of *adfinitas* ("affinity" of kinship by marriage) as there were of *cognatio* (blood relationship), although there were distinctive names for grades of kinship which we must label with clumsy compound terms. (Compare, for example, *avunculus* with maternal uncle, *atavus* with great-great-grandfather, *nurus* with daughter-in-law.) Perhaps these terms symbolize the difference in the stress laid on family ties by the Romans and by ourselves.

As in ancient Judaea, there was no place in early Roman society for detached persons. Everyone was supposed to belong to a household and to be under the control of its *pater familias*. When the latter died, each of the adult males under his direct control might become the head of a new household, inheriting a share of the estate. Sometimes estates were kept intact instead of being divided. This was managed by agreement of the heirs or in later years by provisions in the father's will. Minor children who were left orphans or half-orphans and unmarried grown daughters were commonly placed under a guardian (*tutor*) selected by their *gens*. In later times, when daughters sometimes inherited property,

ROMAN SYSTEM OF COMPUTING DEGREES OF KINSHIP

(One degree for each act of procreation)
With English Kinship Terms*

Great-great grandfather
Great-great grandmother (4)

Great grandfather
Great grandmother (3)

Grandfather
Grandmother (2)

Father
Mother (1)

SELF (0)

Son
Daughter (1)

Grandson
Granddaughter (2)

Great grandson
Great granddaughter (3)

Great-great grandson
Great-great granddaughter (4)

Great-great uncle (5)
Great-great aunt

x (6)

Great uncle (4)
Great aunt

Uncle
Aunt (3)

First-cousin (5)
once removed

First-cousin (4)

Second-cousin (6)

second-cousin (6)

Third-cousin (8)

Second-cousin (7)
once removed

First-cousin (5)
once removed

Brother
Sister (2)

Nephew
Niece (3)

Grandnephew
Grandniece (4)

Third-cousin (9)
once removed

x (8)

x (6)

* Based on Harold W. Johnston, *Private Life of the Romans* (1932), p. 39. By permission of Scott, Foresman and Company.

they were not permitted to marry without consent of the *gens,* nor could their share of the family lands be alienated from the *gens.* If there were no immediate heirs, property was supposed to be divided among the nearest *agnati* (relatives descended from a common ancestor through the male line).

In all this we see again that early Roman society was organized in kinship groups—household and *gens*—which were apparently stable and not often broken up. However, individuals could be detached from these groups. In fact, when a girl married she usually became a member of her husband's *familia* and *gens.* A boy or man might be emancipated or adopted.

Family Cycle

Marital Selection

In general, marital selection at Rome was of the sort we have now come to regard as "normal" in many cultures, namely, arrangement by the fathers of the young couple. As among the Greeks, Hebrews, and others, romance had little to do with the approach to marriage. Roman fathers chose wives for their sons and gave their daughters in marriage without necessary consideration of their children's wishes. If the young people knew and were fond of each other, certainly that was no obstacle, but neither was it essential. When the Roman law spoke of consensus (consent of both parties), it meant agreement of the fathers, not of the bride and bridegroom. However, the *patres* were not entirely free. Law and the mores required that both parties to a marriage be physically mature, unmarried, and not too closely related.

Formal betrothal, though not required by law, was considered good form. In the *sponsalia* (betrothal) the girl was promised by her *pater familias* or *tutor* to the *pater familias* of her husband-to-be. Only in case either of them were an independent person (*sui juris*) was the pledge made by or to the actual party to the engagement. There was sometimes a ceremony in the *atrium* of the girl's home, certain formulae were repeated, gifts were exchanged, perhaps the man gave the girl a ring to wear on the third finger of her left hand, and finally came congratulations, refreshments, and a "social hour." In case there were later dissatisfaction with the engagement, it was most likely to be canceled by the girl's *pater familias*. In case the boy's family wanted to break the engagement, they could not recover any of the presents. How regularly betrothal was followed by a wedding and how often engagements were broken we do not know, but we may suppose that in this early period such agreements were usually kept. We may also suppose that the formalities mentioned were observed in patrician rather than in plebeian homes.

Marriages were of two general kinds. If bride and bridegroom were both Roman citizens, their marriage was called *justae nuptiae* or *matrimonium justum* (regular marriage). The children would be citizens and possessed of all civil rights. If one of the mates was a Roman citizen and the other belonged to a group with *jus conubii* (privilege of marrying Romans) but without citizenship, the marriage was still called *matrimonium justum,* but the children acquired the civil status of the father. Marriage contracted between man and woman of different rank, e.g., a patrician and a plebeian, was legal and the children were legitimate, but they took the civil status of the parent of lower degree. Such a marriage was called *injustae nuptiae* or *matrimonium injustum*. The *jus conubii* was gradually extended, first to plebeians in 442 B.C., then to inhabitants of various Italian cities, and long after the Punic Wars to exslaves or freedmen.

For the solemnization of a marriage no legal forms were necessary in the sense of a license to be procured from a magistrate or ceremonies to be performed by persons authorized by the state. The only real essential was *consensus,* that is, agreement of both parties if they were *sui juris,* but usually of their *patres familias.* The acts considered most important in a wedding ceremony were the joining of hands in the presence of witnesses, escorting the bride to her husband's house, and, in later times, the signing of a marriage contract. Great pains were taken to select a lucky day. Auspices were taken and the results reported before the rest of the ceremonies proceeded. On the eve of her wedding day the bride dedicated to the *lares,* or family gods of her father's house, her girlhood garments and ornaments. The next morning she was dressed for the wedding by her mother. She wore a long, one-piece tunic fastened around the waist with a woolen band tied in the "knot of Hercules," which only the husband was privileged to untie. Over the tunic she wore a brightly colored veil. Finally there was a special coiffure and a wreath of flowers. The ceremony might take one of several forms. The one most commonly used by patricians in early times was called *confarreatio.* In the girl's home the bride and bridegroom were brought together by a once-married matron living with her husband in undisturbed wedlock. They joined hands in the presence of ten witnesses, after which the bride repeated the words "Quando tu Gaius, ego Gaia" (Wherever you are Gaius, I am Gaia). Then the bride and groom sat side by side on stools covered with the skin of a sheep killed for the sacrifice. An offering was made to Jupiter of a cake of spelt (*far*), from which the ceremony got its name. Then the cake was eaten by the bride and groom, and a prayer was offered to Juno and some other deities. Following this the couple was congratulated, and the main ceremony was over.

Another type of ceremony was called *coemptio.* This was a fictitious sale of the girl made in the presence of five witnesses or less. A single coin was laid in some scales which had to be held ceremoniously. Then followed the joining of hands and words of consent as in the ceremony called *confarreatio.* Afterwards a prayer was recited, perhaps a sacrifice was offered, and then came congratulations.

Still a third form of ceremony associated with *matrimonium justum* was called *usus*. We have very little information about its details, though it appears that hands were clasped, words of consent spoken, and congratulations offered. If the wife then remained in her husband's house, not absenting herself as much as three nights in succession for a year, she came under his authority. It seems that *usus* was the form most frequently employed by plebeians, though they also used *coemptio*. All three, however, probably involved subjection of the wife to her husband's control (*conventio in manum*).

After the principal ceremony the bridegroom, with a show of force, tore the bride from her mother's arms and set forth in a public procession to his own house. Accompanied by torch-bearers and flute players they passed through the streets amidst singing and feasting. On the way the bride offered one coin to the gods of the crossroads, gave one to the bridegroom as a symbol of her dowry, and gave him another as a gift to his household gods. The groom scattered nuts through the crowd. When the procession reached the groom's house, the bride wound bands of wool about the doorposts, after which she was carefully lifted over the threshold. Only invited guests accompanied them into the house, the rest of the crowd then dispersing. In the *atrium* the husband offered his wife fire and water. With a torch she lit a fire on the hearth and then recited a prayer. Finally she was placed by the attending matrons on the marriage bed, which stood in the *atrium*.

It seems to have been a matter of some importance for the Roman bride to bring her husband a dowry (*dos*). This was usually provided by her *pater familias* and became the property of her husband or of his *pater familias*.

That the customs involved in mate selection and marriage were similar in all times and on all social levels is quite certainly not true. For people of modest means they must have been much simpler than those described. For slaves there was probably little or no formality.

Child Rearing

As among the ancient Hebrews, children were desired, and boys were especially wanted in order to continue the family line, its religious ritual, and its property.

The first important event in the postnatal career, of a patrician child at least, was the determination of whether it was to be accepted as a member of the family. It was customary to lay the newborn baby at the father's feet. If he took it in his arms, he thereby acknowledged it as his own and admitted it to the rights and privileges of membership in the family. Should he refuse to do this, the child would become an outcast and would probably be exposed by the roadside. In that case it might perish or it might be taken away and reared by someone who wanted a foster child or a slave. It appears that such exposure was less frequent than in Greece. It also appears that the sale of children, which was permitted by law, rarely occurred in fact.

On the ninth day, called *Dies Lustricus*, the child was given its individual name (*praenomen*), and various domestic rituals were performed. This was a festive occasion with congratulations and gifts from friends and relatives. A string of beads was placed around the baby's neck, partly as a magical protection and partly as a means of identification. Often there was also hung around the child's neck a locket which was worn until the end of childhood. In earliest times single names were apparently the rule. But along with them were also found double names. Somewhat later, though still long before the Punic Wars, freemen often had three names. First came the *praenomen*, which, like our first name, indicated the individual. Next was the *nomen* which indicated the *gens*, and third was the *cognomen*, which indicated the *familia*. This order was not always followed, and occasionally additional names were given. There were never over thirty *praenomena* in use, hence of necessity they appeared over and over again. Fathers of patrician families were at some pains to avoid *praenomena* used by members of their *gens* whose social standing was inferior. Some of the plebeian branches of large families used no *cognomen*. Women less frequently had three names. Commonly, instead of a *praenomen*, a woman was called *maxima* or *minor, secunda* or *tertia*. It should be noted that this is the first culture we have described in which family names appear somewhat in the manner that is familiar to contemporary Americans.

In those early centuries Roman babies were usually nursed by their mothers. However, the care of the child was often shared by slaves who washed and dressed it, told it stories, sang to it, and rocked it in a cradle. For playthings Roman children had dolls, blocks, carts, hoops, stilts, and other articles which would be familiar to many an American child. They had pets, too—dogs and birds, especially. They played games of many kinds.

Training of the children was conducted by both parents in person. Special stress was laid upon moral development, reverence for the gods, respect of law, obedience to authority, and self-reliance. Most of this education was informal and came from steady association with the parents. In early days children not only sat at the table with their elders but helped to serve the meals. For the more formal part of their education Roman boys and girls were apparently taught the elements of reading, writing, and arithmetic by their mothers. Girls received almost all of their education from the mother, while boys at the age of seven became their fathers' companions. If the father were a farmer, his son helped in the fields. If he were a man of affairs living in the capitol city, the son would join him in receiving guests and visiting the Forum and would otherwise acquaint himself with business and government. Sometimes a father would be too busy to give his son much attention and would turn him over to a slave, who not infrequently was a more competent teacher than the father. Sometimes a number of other men would send their sons to be taught by the same slave. But in general the training of Roman children was the responsibility of their parents.

There was no special ceremony to mark the passing of girls into womanhood. But for boys there was an important celebration. Usually on the seventeenth of March nearest his seventeenth birthday, the boy formally laid aside his boyhood toga and put on the garb of a man. A sacrifice was offered, and there was a procession to the Forum. Every effort was put forth to make this an impressive occasion. If it was on the feast day called *Liberalia*, the Forum was sure to be crowded, an offering was made in the temple of Liber, and the day ended with a feast at the father's house.

Again the records and narratives which have come down to us appear to describe the growing up and the ceremonies experienced by the sons of patricians. How differently things went for the children of plebeians, those recently freed, and those still in slavery we can only surmise. But in any case, growing up in early Roman society seems to have been fairly serious business, relieved, however, by affectionate ties within the family and a considerable degree of security.

Breaking Family Ties

However, family ties were sometimes broken deliberately. As we have seen, when a girl married she usually joined her husband's *familia*. Even a boy might leave his parental home and control through emancipation or adoption. Emancipation involved a ceremony consisting of a fictitious sale whereby a son was set free from the *patria potestas* and detached completely from his family. Adoption involved the formal transfer of a person from one household to another. The Romans adopted not only small boys, but even grown men, the purpose of the adopting group being to assure itself of a successor to a previously heirless head, and of the adopted person to gain security and status.

The conjugal family or marriage group, like the household and *gens* in which it was embedded, also seems to have been very stable before the Punic Wars. The first Roman divorce of which we have definite information occurred about 300 B.C.,[1] but there seems to have been earlier provision in the law.

As among the early Hebrews, it was only men who could take the initiative to terminate an unsatisfactory marriage. However, in contrast to a Hebrew husband, a Roman was restricted in a number of ways. If the marriage had been celebrated with the formal ceremony called *confarreatio*, it could be dissolved only with considerable difficulty and a corresponding ceremony of *difarreatio*. If a man were contemplating the dismissal of his wife, he was required by law to assemble a council of his own and her male relatives, unless he caught her in adultery, in which case his hands were free and he might punish her even with death. The grounds for divorce were, in addition to adultery, making poison, drinking wine, and possibly counterfeiting house keys. Toward the end of this period less serious grounds were used as a basis of divorce. One man dismissed his wife with the charge that she had appeared in the streets without a veil, and another complained that his wife had gone to the public games without informing him. Also divorce was essentially a private matter, and the right to it was a privilege of the husband or his father; nevertheless, if he got rid of his wife on other than recognized grounds, he might be severely reproved by the Censor as well as by his kinsmen and the general public. A *pater familias* could not only divorce his own wife but could arrange the divorce of his son with or without the latter's consent.

Family Controls

Theoretically the Roman father had absolute power over his children and his sons' children. He decided whether the

1. James Donaldson, *Woman: Her Position and Influence in Ancient Greece and Rome, and Among the Early Christians* (1907), pp. 116-117.

newborn babe was to be reared or not, he punished miscon-
duct often by severe penalties, he alone could acquire and
exchange property, he could claim the earnings of his offspring, and he alone could proceed against anyone who
injured or abducted them. In a sense the members of the family were his chattels. But this theoretically absolute power
was restricted in practice, at first by custom and later by law.
Very early the right to expose or kill a child was limited,
although the father continued to decide whether or not a child
should be admitted to his household. Custom also put a check
on arbitrary and cruel punishments. It obliged the *pater
familias* to call a council of relatives whenever he contem-
plated inflicting severe penalties on a child, and public sentiment probably forced him to accept its verdict. In regard to
the ownership of property the father was not so much an individual titleholder as a trustee for the family as a whole.
Finally, he was a kind of priest responsible for sacrifices to the
gods, offerings to the spirits of departed ancestors, and family
worship in general. His power, *patria potestas*, might be
extinguished in several ways—obviously by death, but also by
loss of citizenship. The marriage of his daughter usually
removed her from the family and transferred her to the
authority of her husband. The emancipation or adoption of
a child freed it from the father's power.

Earlier we observed that within the family the *pater
familias* had authority to arrange marriages and divorces but
always subject to certain mores and laws. Thus he was
required to see that bride and groom were physically mature,
unmarried, and not too close of kin. He was restricted in the
matter of divorce by the necessity of calling a council of his
own and his wife's relatives, if his marriage had involved the
ceremony called *confarreatio*.

The sex mores of the early Romans constituted a stern
code which seems to have been rather generally lived up to.
But if a wife were caught in adultery she might be killed at
once, and the unchastity of a betrothed girl might be punished in the same way. Concubinage was disapproved. Appar-

ently, however, by the third century B.C. Romans had a double standard, for Cato is quoted as saying, "If you were to catch your wife in adultery, you would kill her with impunity without trial; but if she were to catch you, she would not dare to lay a finger upon you."[2]

Before the Punic Wars family controls were chiefly internal, though not entirely so. Moreover, they seem to have been pretty effective through most of this period. Along with these controls there seems commonly to have been a sense of unity and solidarity comparable to that of the early Hebrew family. This bound together not only husband and wife, parents and children, but very frequently a three-generation household under *patria potestas*. As among the Hebrews, a wife might be technically subject to her husband's rule, but she was in fact his companion and partner, and respected and loved as a person.

THE ROMAN FAMILY AFTER THE PUNIC WARS

In the second and third centuries B.C. there were three long wars with Carthage which took Roman men away from home for years at a time. During those years of war women inevitably assumed many responsibilities and found some freedom from the usual control of their husbands and fathers. These probably were the opening wedges for the "emancipation" of women and the establishment of a more equalitarian pattern of family life. No doubt the wartime experiences of men in the army and of women left behind contributed also to a breakdown of the old code of sex mores. Besides, the family system was inevitably affected by the changing economic situation in Rome. Wealth poured in from tribute levied on conquered peoples. There was an increase of idle rich at one end of the scale and of slaves and landless freemen at the

2. Willystine Goodsell, *A History of Marriage and the Family* p. 126, (1934).

other. When the Republic finally gave way to the Empire, extravagance, conspicuous consumption, and domestic intrigue had become notorious, at least in the upper classes.

During the Punic Wars the sex ratio appears to have changed from one of male to one of female predominance. Whether this new ratio continued and whether it contributed significantly to the rising number of unmarried adults we do not know. But by the opening of the Christian era there was a considerable number of bachelors as well as of unmarried women. With increasing frequency women who did marry remained legally members of their fathers' families although actually living with their husbands. Therewith the power of the husbands was greatly reduced, while wives became more independent. Although we have no statistics on the subject, there is no doubt that divorce became more frequent. In general, marriage and the family became less important and less stable. Even the *atrium* reflected the declining significance of the family, for family gods were often tucked away, the hearth was sometimes removed, and meals were taken in various parts of the house.

Growing Instability of the Family Structure

Enough has already been presented to demonstrate that there were significant changes in attitudes and practices affecting marriage and the family. Of course we are not justified in identifying change with deterioration. But in this period we can safely say that there was an increase in family disorganization and instability.

To begin with, some marriages were contracted without the former expectation of an enduring union. Although our information on this point is very limited, it is alleged by some historians that upper-class Romans occasionally entered upon what might be called companionate marriages; that is, husband and wife agreed openly or tacitly to continue their marriage only so long as it suited them.

It is certain that after the Punic Wars divorce became easier and more frequent. Some prominent Romans divorced their wives on the grounds of mere suspicion, or were really actuated by desires to marry younger or wealthier women or to secure political advantages. Apparently women also found it possible to secure divorces. How frequent divorce really became we cannot tell. It is likely that the true facts have been much exaggerated. In any case, much publicity has been given to the divorces of socially prominent persons, just as happens in contemporary America. It appears that Ovid and the younger Pliny each married three times, Cleopatra and Antony four times, Sulla and Pompeii five times. Juvenal tells about a woman who had eight husbands in five years, and Martial tells of another who had ten husbands. However, there is no good reason to suppose that this was representative of the common people.

Economic Changes

The custom of a dowry (*dos*) provided by the wife's family continued from early times. But instead of being the unquestioned property of the husband or his *pater familias*, it was the husband's to use only while the marriage lasted. If the marriage were broken by death or divorce, the dowry normally went to the wife, her father, or her heirs, depending on a number of circumstances. If, however, a divorce should be caused by some fault of the wife, her husband might retain part of the *dos*. In the later imperial period another sort of matrimonial property was developed. It was called "gift for the sake of marriage" (*donatio propter nuptias*). It was presented by the husband, but it remained his property both during and after the marriage unless there should be a divorce in which he was held to be at fault. In that case all or part of the *donatio propter nuptias* might be claimed by the injured wife. Both the *dos* and the *donatio* appear to have contributed to the financial stability of the family, but the arrangements just mentioned indicate that enough marriages were expected to end in divorce to necessitate some definite provision for disposing of this property.

There were other departures from customs and laws of the past which had to do with the title to property and its inheritance, especially in the case of women. As we noted in our review of the earlier period, property was commonly thought of as belonging to the family as a whole, but it was usually administered by the *pater familias*. In the later period we find increasing emphasis on individual ownership and disposition of property.

Fathers who had means frequently left large sums in trust for their daughters. Husbands sometimes willed property to their widows. Thus arose a class of wealthy women. This seemed such an anomaly to some Romans that they tried to check it. Therefore, a law of 169 B.C. forbade a citizen owning property worth more than 100,000 asses to make a woman his heir. Under other laws the woman who remained a member of her father's family, instead of being transferred to her husband's, had only a limited right of inheritance from her husband if he died intestate. In this case she received no consideration until her husband's relatives as remote as second cousins had received a share.

Changing Status of Women

All these changes in customary practices and in attempts at legal control depict radical changes in the status and roles of the sexes. Women were said to be following "male pursuits." They were described as attending military maneuvers, playing politics, studying philosophy, and joining new religious movements.

With the gradual disappearance of marriage with *manus*, with the accumulation of independent wealth in the hands of women, and with their participation in many activities outside the home, the relative status of the sexes changed from one of complete masculine dominance to one of near equalitarianism. This change was greatly resented by some conservative Roman men who gave vent to their feelings in statements both picturesque and exaggerated. Thus the elder Cato is quoted as saying, "All men rule over women, we Romans rule over all men, and our wives rule over us."[3] It is possible however, that middle- or lower-class women still carried on the household tasks much as in the past, and that the independence of upper-class women manifested itself very little on lower socio-economic levels.

Changing Sex Mores

Along with all this went changes in the sex mores as they are more narrowly defined. In fact, many lurid details have been told about the corruption of Roman morals under the Empire. It has been reported that concubinage and prostitution grew "by leaps and bounds," that abortion and infanticide became common, and that adultery was all but universal. Apparently it is true that upper-class women attended the theater and the circus and witnessed licentious dances. At banquets women as well as men reclined while they sometimes drank to excess or were entertained by ribald songs and plays. Occasionally a Roman lady would run away with a gladiator. Upper-class women often displayed themselves in the streets and wore clothing that attracted attention to their physical charms. Clearly there was enough of this sort of thing to stir some moralists to express themselves vigorously. Thus Juvenal in his sixth satire was presumably urging a certain man to refrain from marriage on the grounds of women's faithlessness, intrigues, orgies, and extravagances. He said, "Chastity has long since left the earth . . . No woman is content with a single lover nowadays." Nevertheless the penalties for adultery continued to be severe, although they may not have been so regularly imposed. Not only an adulterous wife, but her husband also, was deemed guilty of crime. If sixty days after her

3. *Ibid.*, p. 135.

offense was known neither her husband nor her father started legal action against a woman, any interested citizen might prosecute. If she were found guilty she was supposed to lose one half of her dowry, one third of her other property, and to suffer banishment to a desert island. In certain cases the father of a woman might kill both her and her lover. The husband had similar privileges, but he might instead claim compensation from the offending man and hold him until he paid. If a man were guilty of adultery he might be condemned to lose one half of his property, to restore all of his wife's dowry, and to suffer banishment.

Family Cycle

Apparently the ancient custom continued whereby fathers arranged the marriages of their children. But with the growth of the metropolis they often resorted to matchmakers who made this a regular business. In such cases a betrothal was a contract, but not a personal relationship. Seneca is quoted as saying, "Any animal or slave, or every article of clothes or dish is tested before purchase, but never the bride by her groom. Any vices she may have of passion, stupidity, misshapedness, or evil breath one learnt only after marriage."[4] We stated that a betrothal was a contract, but apparently it created no legal right such as that on which breach of promise suits are based in our culture today. If the contract specified that a financial penalty might be imposed in case of breach, such a provision was considered disgraceful. However, if anyone entered into an engagement while betrothed to another, he was deemed infamous. Moreover, if the engagement were broken, either party might reclaim whatever presents he or she had given the other. Now it is hard to know just what

4. Ludwig Friedländer, *Roman Life and Manners under the Early Empire* (1908-13), Vol. 1, p. 234. By permission of E. P. Dutton and Company, Inc.

inferences should be drawn from these data, but we are probably safe in believing that a good many betrothals were broken off and that young men and women enjoyed more freedom of choice than in earlier times.

Gradually marriage without *manus* became customary. The three formal ceremonies which had accompanied *matrimonium justum* gradually disappeared. The contracting of marriage continued to be a private affair, for it required no participation by any civil officer or religious functionary. In many cases the old-fashioned family council was convened in order to obtain its consent, but emphasis came to be placed more and more on the consent of the bride and groom themselves. It is apparent that this did not eliminate bargaining, nor did it always make for a stable marriage, for instead of considering such basic matters as affection, health, personal habits, and continuance of the family line, the young couple was often concerned with political and economic advantages of a temporary nature. When the particular purpose had been achieved, either or both might secure a divorce and seek new marital ventures.

Evidently many people were ceasing to regard marriage as a sacred obligation to family and state. Not only did they contract and dissolve marriages more lightly than in the past, increasing numbers did not marry at all. The early Romans, like the Hebrews and like most nonliterate peoples, had practically no place for unmarried adults. But the growth of Rome into a great city, the piling up of wealth, at least in the hands of certain classes, and the consequent possibility of maintaining oneself comfortably and respectably outside of marriage changed matters. Undoubtedly some men and some women, too, sought freedom from family cares. It has been alleged that Roman men abstained from marriage because of resentment against the growing independence of ambitious women. This sounds, however, very much like rationalization. Whether the actual numbers of celibates were very great, they at least stirred the government, and various penalties were imposed upon unmarried adults.

All these changes in the sex mores, the relative position of men and women, the frequency of divorce, and the lowered sanctity of family life must have had important repercussions on the thinking, feeling, and behavior of children. But unfortunately we have very little concrete information about this.

It is evident that the authority of a *pater familias* over his children and grandchildren gradually diminished. He was still entitled to their earnings or other acquisitions. But his authority to punish was limited to "moderate chastisement," and for serious offenses a son must be turned over to the civil courts instead of to a family council. Quite apart from legal changes restricting paternal control, there appears to have been a shifting away from stern discipline toward moderation and even indulgence. Thus we read of children being spoiled and growing up to be "idlers and wastrels." No doubt this occurred, but again we lack specific accounts.

Many upper-class mothers turned the care of their small children over to nursemaids and slaves, who fed them, supervised their play, told them fairy tales, and gave miscellaneous instruction. The girls learned to spin, weave, make clothes, and perform various household tasks. Some of them were also taught music and dancing and how to develop good posture. Their brothers were either tutored at home or sent to school where they studied grammar, rhetoric, and literature, along with sports of various kinds. There is, however, good reason to believe that the majority of Roman children were still educated informally through observing and helping their elders. At least there must have been a wide discrepancy between the lives of children on different socio-economic levels. But unfortunately our information is very sketchy. Most of what has come down to us pertains to those in the higher strata. Even in their case we are told about the general conditions of their upbringing rather than about the children themselves. Ancient Rome had no nursery schools, child guidance clinics, or juvenile courts to record the actual behavior of youngsters of any social class.

Family Controls

From the foregoing it is evident that the old controls over family life not only were slipping from the *pater familias*, but they were not being effectively transferred to religious or civil authorities. Some of the efforts to replace "internal" family controls with "external" controls have already been noted. A few others will be mentioned here.

As early as 131 B.C. one of the Censors recommended the adoption of a law compelling everybody to marry, observing that "if it were possible to have no wives at all, everybody would gladly escape that annoyance, but since nature had so ordained that it was not possible to live agreeably with them, nor to live at all without them, regard must be had rather to permanent welfare than to transitory pleasure."[5] Actual legislation came later, extending privileges to men and women in accordance with number of their children, and imposing penalties on bachelors. The *lex julia et papia pappaea* in 9 A.D. made unmarried women between the ages of twenty and fifty and unmarried men between twenty-five and sixty ineligible to receive estates or legacies, except from near relatives, unless they married within a short time. Whether such laws had any important effects we do not know. But at least they are indirect evidence of a decline in the importance earlier attached to marriage and family life.

In the attempt to reduce the number of divorces, Augustus required "the active party" to execute a written document (*repudium*) in the presence of seven witnesses, all full Roman citizens. This apparently remained the law for some 500 years, though how effective it was we cannot tell.

Family Functions

Until the Punic Wars the functions of the Roman *familia*, i.e., household, often of three generations controlled by the

5. James Bryce, *Studies in History and Jurisprudence* (1901), Vol. 2, p. 801.

pater familias, were pretty inclusive. It was at once a religious, educational, economic, and legal institution. Each family had a system of worship of its own. There were family gods and spirits of deceased ancestors that required attention. The head of a Roman family was bound to offer food and drink to the departed so long as he lived and to provide for the continuance of these acts of affection and piety after his death by perpetuating his family line. It was, therefore, a solemn religious duty to marry and have children. Thus the religious and the procreational functions were entwined. As we have already noted, the greater part of a boy's education took place in the home, and for centuries practically all of the girl's training was given by her mother. Early households were largely self-sufficing. Hard work was a virtue engaged in by all. The property, while held by the *pater familias,* was regarded as belonging to the family as a whole. Finally, the *pater familias* exercised judicial functions. Alone, or in consultation with his kinsmen, he passed on the guilt of members of the family, and in accordance with the decision made he imposed punishment. The Roman family, therefore, was in many respects the most important institution in that culture during its early history.

But after the Punic Wars it appears that the Roman *familia* lost some of its importance, at least in the upper classes. Most obviously it lost ground as an agency of social control. It was less often the center of religious ceremonials and training. It sometimes ceased to be an economic unit. Education of the young was more often carried on by tutors, who were sometimes slaves, and some upper-class children were sent to school. But we suspect that for common people the family underwent less change, that for them it continued to be the arena for a rather inclusive array of activities and services—procreation, child rearing, maintenance, and perhaps religion, and social control.

REFERENCES

Bryce, James, "Marriage and Divorce under Roman and English Law," *Studies in History and Jurisprudence.* Oxford: Clarendon Press, 1901, Volume II, Chapter XVI.

Carcopino, Jerome, "Marriage, Woman, and the Family," *Daily Life in Ancient Rome.* New Haven: Yale University Press, 1940, Chapter IV.

Donaldson, James, "Ancient Rome," *Woman: Her Position and Influence in Ancient Greece and Rome, and Among the Early Christians,* London: Longmans, Green, and Company, 1907, Book II.

Friedländer, Ludwig, *Roman Life and Manners under the Early Empire,* translation of the seventh German edition. New York: E. P. Dutton, 1908-1913. See especially Volume I, Chapter V, "The Position of Women."

Goodsell, Willystine, *A History of Marriage and the Family.* New York: The Macmillan Company, 1934, Chapter IV.

Johnston, Harold W., *The Private Life of the Romans.* Chicago: Scott, Foresman and Company, 1903 and 1932 (revised edition by Mary Johnston).

Juvenal, *Satires.* See any convenient translation, especially of Satires II, VI, and XIV.

Leffingwell, Georgia W., *Social and Private Life at Rome in the Time of Plautus and Terrance.* New York: Columbia University, 1918.

McDaniel, Walton B., *Roman Private Life and its Survivals.* Boston: Marshall Jones Company, 1924.

Ovid, *The Art of Love.* See any convenient translation.

Pliny, the Younger, *Letters.* See any convenient translation, especially of Book I, letter 14; Book II, letters 4, 20; Book III, letter 16; Book IV, letters 2, 10, 19; Book V, letter 16; Book VI, letter 4; Book VII, letter 5.

Roby, Henry J., *Roman Private Law in the Times of Cicero and of the Antonines.* Cambridge: Cambridge University Press, 1902.

Rogers, H. L., and Harley, T. R., *Roman Home Life and Religion.* Oxford: Clarendon Press, 1923.

9 The Legacy of the Early Christian Family

Unlike the other peoples we have studied, the early Christians were not a distinctive ethnic group or a separate nationality. They were a religious sect. In the beginning they were few in number, low in socio-economic status, members of a conquered people. This means that on the whole their institutions, folkways, and mores were those current among the common people of Palestine nineteen centuries ago. As the religion spread its adherents came to include middle- and upper-class folk, Greeks, Romans, and many others. At the same time beliefs and practices underwent modification through the gradual assimilation of varied elements and the changed status of the group.

In the first century domestic mores were not distinctively Christian, but Jewish, Greek, Roman, and so on. In spite of the "universal" rule of Rome there was great diversity of family life and of moral codes. Hence when the Church began to assemble its doctrines and lay down regulations for human conduct conflicts inevitably arose. Ultimately there developed a fairly homogenous set of rules for sex, marriage, child rearing, and so on, but it is quite certain that there never was a time when Christians everywhere lived in accord with identical mores.

For about three centuries most of the Christians were poor and despised; part of the time a determined effort was made to destroy their sect. Under Roman law any new cult had dubious status, if it were not actually forbidden. The proscription of images by Jews and Christians caused both to be regarded as atheists. The emotional character of much Christian worship led to charges of sexual irregularity. Refusal of military service and failure to attend public spectacles and to honor the emperor's birthdays brought accusations of being unpatriotic. Christians in the early Roman Empire were about as unpopular as communists in twentieth-century North America. They were subjected to all manner of humiliating experiences and not infrequently to mob violence. The Emperors Decius, Valerian, and Diocletian sought avowedly to eradicate the whole movement. Because of this hostility on the part of respectable and powerful elements it was natural that the Christian codes should condemn many practices of their social "betters" and urge conduct of an opposite character. Thus there were reactions against easy divorce, "emancipation" of women, and sexual freedom. But it would be incorrect to attribute the "puritanical" codes of the early Church Fathers entirely to antagonism between the lowly Christians and the dominant groups of the Mediterranean world. Undoubtedly the Christian subordination of women was in part a reversion to the earlier Hebrew, Greek, and Roman mores. The Christian efforts to suppress all expression of sex, along with other worldly pleasures, were associated with teachings which pitted the "spirit" against the "flesh." This dualism, emphasized especially by Paul, was common to numerous religious systems of the East. Probably the expected Second Coming of Christ contributed further to a low regard for sex, for marriage, and for family life. If this world were shortly to end and men were to be transported either to eternal glory or to eternal punishment, what was the use of marrying and begetting children? Should not every effort be directed toward preparation for the Day of Judgment? Thus it appears that the basic hostility between a new sect and "the world" combined with certain cultural heritages and the doctrine of chiliasm (that the world would soon come to an end) to set the stage for a new set of domestic mores which may be called Christian.

Our principal sources of information about family life among the early Christians are the New Testament, writings of the Church Fathers, imperial edicts, and various histories of the first few centuries of the present era. Unfortunately for our purpose, these tell us little about the ways in which people actually selected their mates, divided their household duties, reared their children, transmitted their property, and otherwise lived as members of family groups. They tell us for the most part how *leaders* of the Church *thought* family life *ought* to be conducted, and they exhibit certain viewpoints with such consistency as to suggest their widespread acceptance. In using the sources at our disposal we must constantly be on the alert to detect and to make allowance for the interpretations of later editors who must frequently have sought to use historical accounts for the support of their sides of religious controversies. But we shall note repeated emphasis upon certain notions of sex, the status of women, and divorce, which—however representative or unrepresentative of early Christianity—have unquestionably had great influence in subsequent centuries.

Family Structure

Questionable Status of Marriage

There is little doubt that the early Christians accorded marriage and family life a lower status than was assigned by any other people we have studied. In almost every culture the family is a basic institution honored in the mores and desired by individuals. Among the early Christians marriage was probably desired by most individuals, but was belittled in their formal teachings. Thus in his first Epistle to the Corinthians Paul said: "To avoid fornication, let every man have his own wife, and let every woman have her own husband . . . For I would that all men were even as I myself [a bachelor] . . . I say therefore to the unmarried and widows, It is good for them if they abide even as I. But if they cannot contain, let them marry; for it is better to marry than to burn."[1] Thus marriage is tolerated only to avoid a greater evil.

1. I Corinthians 7:7-9.

At all events it may be assumed that young people among the early Christians did get married and rear families. Their marriages were almost certainly monogamous and probably were broken less often by divorce than by death. In the second chapter of the Gospel of John we read of Jesus attending a wedding at Cana, and Paul, in his letter to the church at Ephesus, advised wives to obey their husbands and husbands to love their wives. At the end of an extended exhortation Paul said, "For this cause shall a man leave his father and mother, and shall cleave unto his wife; and the two shall become one flesh." (Eph. 5:31) Perhaps we could paraphrase the apparent contradiction thus: it would be better if people did not become involved in family relations, but since they will do this, let them be orderly about it and give the world an example of obedience, fidelity, and devotion.

But the confusion did not quickly end. Truly a long road had to be traveled before marriage became a sacrament of the Church. Yet from the beginning, even among Christians, the urge to mate could not be denied. Hence a variety of rationalizations appeared. Some held rigidly to the proposition "that marriage was immoral, that the flesh was corrupt, that those who sowed to the flesh must reap corruption, and that in the kingdom of God on earth, as in heaven, there is neither marrying nor giving in marriage."[2] But most of the Church Fathers avoided open condemnation of marriage. While they held with Methodius that "virginity is something supernaturally great, wonderful, and glorious, . . . [the] best and noblest manner of life,"[3] they recognized that there must be families to produce virgins for the service of the Church; moreover, according to the Gospels, Christ himself seemed to give his sanction to marriage. Hence we find in Tertullian the compromise of regarding celibacy as a higher state than matrimony, "not as if we

2. James Donaldson, *Woman: Her Position and Influence in Ancient Greece and Rome and Among the Early Christians* (1907), p. 169. By permission of Longmans, Green and Company, Inc.

3. Methodius, *The Banquet of the Ten Virgins,* Discourse I, Chapter i, *Ante-Nicene Fathers,* Vol. 6, p. 310.

superseded a bad thing by a good, but only a good thing by a better. For we do not reject marriage, but simply refrain from it."[4] Virginity, then, was a state of special purity, particularly pleasing to Christ. It meant not only avoidance of immorality, but protection against absorption in the joys and care of family life. "The unmarried woman cares for the things of the Lord, that she may be holy both in body and spirit; but she that is married cares for the things of the world, how she may please her husband."[5] Thus wrote Jerome in one of his letters. Elsewhere in the same letter he spoke of "the disadvantages of marriage, such as pregnancy, a crying baby, the tortures of jealousy, the cares of household management, and the cutting short by death of all its fancied blessings."[6]

Thus while the Roman emperors were penalizing men and women who failed to establish families, the Church Fathers were praising those who avoided matrimony. Bachelors and maids occupied higher positions than did husbands and wives. Not only was great merit attached to abstention from marriage and from sexual intercourse, but special prestige belonged to those who pledged themselves to lifelong celibacy. In no other culture have we found anything like this.

We noted above that Paul advised men to *love* their wives and women to *obey* their husbands. This suggests that male dominance was taken for granted.

Male Dominance

Perhaps reacting against the emancipation of upper-class women at Rome, just as they reacted against the licentiousness of many persons in high places, the early Church Fathers insisted on an inferior status for their women. Perhaps this was a harking back to the subordination of earlier times in Judaea,

4. Tertullian, *Against Marcion*, Book I, Chapter 29, *Ante-Nicene Fathers,* Vol. 3, p. 294.

5. Jerome, Letter XXII, Wright Edition, p. 101. By permission of Harvard University Press.

6. *Ibid.,* p. 57.

Greece, and Rome. In any case there is little doubt about their attitude. The classic statement of early Christian doctrine is found in Paul's first letter to the Corinthians:

> But I would have you know, that the head of every man is Christ; and the head of the woman is the man; and the head of Christ is God. Every man praying or prophesying, having his head covered, dishonoreth his head. But every woman praying or prophesying with her head unveiled dishonoreth her head; for it is one and the same thing as if she were shaven. For if a woman is not veiled, let her also be shorn: but if it is a shame to a woman to be shorn or shaven, let her be veiled. For a man indeed ought not to have his head veiled, forasmuch as he is the image and glory of God: but the woman is the glory of the man. For the man is not of the woman; but the woman of the man: for neither was the man created for the woman but the woman for the man: for this cause ought the woman to have a sign of authority on her head . . .
>
> As in all the churches of the saints, let the women keep silence in the churches: for it is not permitted unto them to speak; but let them be in subjection, as also saith the law. And if they would learn anything, let them ask their own husbands at home: for it is shameful for a woman to speak in the church.[7]

One of the most severe statements appears in Tertullian's essay, *On the Apparel of Women:* "You are the devil's gateway: You are the unsealer of that forbidden tree: You are the first deserter of the divine law: You are she who persuaded him whom the devil was not valiant enough to attack. You destroyed so easily God's image, man. On account of your desert—that is, death—even the Son of God had to die."[8]

Chrysostom is quoted as declaring the fair sex to be a "necessary evil, a natural temptation, a desirable calamity, a domestic peril, a deadly fascination and a painted ill."[9]

In the *Apostolic Constitutions* we find occasionally a milder note: "Ye wives, be subject to your own husbands, and have them in esteem, and serve them with fear and love . . .

---

7. I Corinthians 11:3-10; 14:33-35.

8. Tertullian, *On the Apparel of Women,* Book I, Chapter I, *Ante-Nicene Fathers,* Vol. 4, p. 14.

9. Ralph de Pomerai, *Marriage: Past, Present and Future* (1930), p. 137.

In like manner, ye husbands, love your own wives as your own members, as partners in life, and fellow-helpers for the procreation of children. . . ."[10]

In *The Instructor,* Clement sounded a note of equalitarianism: "For if the God of both is one, the master of both is also one; one church, one temperance, one modesty; their food is common, marriage an equal yoke; respiration, sight, hearing, knowledge, hope, obedience have all alike. And those whose life is common, have common graces and a common salvation; common to them are love and training."[11]

Jerome, writing to Oceanus in 399 A.D., held that men and women are equal in respect to divorce and sex mores:

> A command that is given to men applies logically also to women. It cannot be that an adulterous wife should be put away and an unfaithful husband retained . . . Among the Romans men's unchastity goes unchecked; seduction and adultery are condemned, but free permission is given to lust to range the brothels and to have slave girls, as though it were a person's rank and not the sensual pleasure that constituted the offense. With us what is unlawful for women is equally unlawful for men, and as both sexes serve God they are bound by the same conditions.[12]

The actual roles to be played by women in the Christian family were indicated by Paul in his epistle to Titus: ". . . to be sober, to love their husbands, to love their children, to be discreet, chaste, keepers at home, good, obedient to their own husbands . . ."[13]

They were set forth in more detail by Clement in *The Instructor:*

> Nor are women to be deprived of bodily exercise. But they are not to be encouraged to engage in wrestling or running, but are to exercise themselves in spinning, and weaving, and superintending the cooking if necessary. And they are with their own hand to fetch from the store what we

10. *Apostolic Constitutions,* Book VI, Sec. V, paragraph xxix, *Ante-Nicene Fathers,* Vol. 7, p. 463.
11. Clement, *The Instructor,* Chapter 4, *Ante-Nicene Fathers,* Vol. 2, p. 211.
12. Jerome, Letter LXXVII, Wright Edition, p. 315. By permission of Harvard University Press.
13. Titus 2:4-5.

require. And it is no disgrace for them to apply themselves to the mill. Nor is it a reproach to a wife—housekeeper and helpmate—to occupy herself in cooking, so that it may be palatable to her husband. And if she shake up the couch, reach drink to her husband when thirsty, set food on the table as neatly as possible, and so give herself exercise tending to sound health, the Instructor will approve of a woman like this.[14]

From passages such as those just cited we seem justified in assuming the subordination of woman, but without harshness. The actual status of an early Christian wife was probably not very different from that of a Hebrew or Roman matron of earlier periods.

Another inference we make is that in this group the extended family was considered even less important than the nuclear family. Kinship, descent, and the rights and obligations of relatives outside the nucelar family are barely mentioned in the New Testament or the Patristic writings. One passage in particular emphasizes the importance of "spiritual kinship" rather than biological. "For whosoever shall do the will of God, the same is my brother, and sister, and mother." (Mark 3:35)

The Family Cycle

Marital Selection

We have noted that under the declining *patria potestas* Roman marriage came to rest essentially on the free consent of the contracting parties. Presumably this was the basis on which most early Christian families were established. However, parental control did not wholly disappear, "for even on earth children do not rightfully and lawfully wed without their father's consent."[15] Also the Church itself early sought to exercise some control over marriage. In the first century

14. Clement, *The Instructor*, Book III, Chapter 10, *Ante-Nicene Fathers*, Vol. 2, p. 283.
15. Tertullian, *To His Wife*, Book II, Chapter 8, *Ante-Nicene Fathers*, Vol. 4, p. 48.

Ignatius wote to Polycarp, "It becomes both men and women who marry to form their union with the approval of the bishop, that their marriage may be according to the Lord, and not after their own lust."[16] Much later the Church established sweeping regulations concerning persons forbidden to marry. The prohibited categories included: (1) consanguinity, blood kinship within the seventh degree; (2) affinity, relatives of a husband or wife within the seventh degree; and (3) spiritual affinity, godfathers and godmothers at baptism and sponsors at confirmation. But these rules seem not to have taken definite shape until the sixth century.

In addition to its efforts to control the degrees of kinship within which marriage was prohibited, the Church also developed some rules of endogamy. Thus the Council of Elvira, in 305 A.D., ruled that "unless heretics allow themselves to be converted to the Catholic Church, daughters of Catholics shall not be given to them in marriage; neither shall they be given to Jews nor heretics, for there can be no social intercourse of believers with infidels. If parents violate this interdict, they shall be excommunicated for five years."[17] Concerning the same matter Tertullian wrote, ". . . It is certain that believers contracting marriage with Gentiles are guilty of fornication, and are to be excluded from all communication with the brotherhood."[18] He went on to mention some of the possible conflicts between a Christian wife and a nonChristian husband —curiously nothing was said about a Christian husband and a nonChristian wife. The "Gentile" husband might arrange a feast on a Christian fast day; he might object to his wife's charities, her attendance on all-night religious services, her visiting Christians in prison, her going "to meet any one of the

16. Epistle of Ignatius to Polycarp, Chapter 5, *Ante-Nicene Fathers*, Vol. 1, p. 95.

17. Quoted in James S. Slotkin, "Jewish Intermarriage in Chicago," unpublished Ph.D dissertation, Department of Anthropology, University of Chicago (1940), p. 41, from Concilium Elibertanum, Sacrorum Conciliorum Collectio (Vol. 2, Cols. 1-56), can. 16.

18. Tertullian, *To His Wife, Ante-Nicene Fathers*, Vol. 4, p. 45.

brethren to exchange the kiss," or her hospitality to a visiting Christian. Besides, there was the danger of his insisting that she take part in "heathenish" rites and revels. But if a woman were converted after her wedding, she was bidden to persevere in the marriage. Betrothal was presumably a free agreement entered into by a man and woman, sometimes with parental consent. It might be broken without legal penalty. The wedding apparently followed the pattern in vogue at a given time and place and in a given social class. The first Christian innovation appears to have been the adding of a priestly benediction. After a time it became customary for newlyweds to attend religious services in the church and partake of the sacrament. These were the ordinary services and only later were special phrases introduced taking cognizance of the marriage just solemnized. It was several centuries before the Church adopted a formal liturgy for the wedding ceremony.

The fourth Council of Carthage in 398 A.D. ruled that a newly married couple should spend the first night "in a state of virginity out of reverence for the benediction." Subsequent enactments extended this period of abstinence to three nights, but later the rigors of the canon were mitigated, permitting intercourse on the wedding night provided a fee were paid to the proper ecclesiastical authority.

Ultimately, as we know, the Church prescribed definite forms and laid down precise rules concerning the procedure to be followed in betrothal and wedding. But in the first few centuries these were apparently not matters of great concern to the Fathers. In part this was in keeping with their general attitudes toward sex and marriage. In part it may be regarded as a continuation of the Hebrew tradition and the Roman law, in accordance with which marriage was essentially a private or family matter.

Children in the Background

Amazingly little was written about children during the first three centuries of the Christian Church. Doubtless those who had offspring loved them and cared for them. But their rare mention indicates that children did not play a very important role in early Christian society. This apparent indifference is in great contrast to the ardent desire of the ancient Hebrews, Greeks, and Romans for heirs, but it is in keeping with the general belittling of family life by Christian writers. Not only did Christians ask with Tertullian, "Why should we be eager to bear children?" but if they had offspring they seemed to prefer girls to boys. Thus Jerome praised wedlock and marriage "because they produce many virgins."[19]

Children for their part were theoretically bound more to the Church than to their families. Again and again the Patristic writers referred to the promptness with which John and James left their father, Zebedee, to follow Jesus; also they recalled that when one of the disciples wanted to attend to the burial of his father, Jesus forbade him, saying, "Let the dead bury their dead."[20] Jerome said in one of his letters, "Great is the reward for forgetting a parent."[21] Although little importance was attached to childbearing and to affection between parents and children, new life was to be protected. Repeatedly the Church Fathers condemned abortion, infanticide, exposure, and sale of offspring. However, the Christian Emperor Constantine authorized parents in great destitution to sell their children, and, as a matter of fact, children were exposed and sold for many centuries in western Eupore.

Training and education of boys and girls was to be centered about religious doctrines, warning against the ways of the world, and imposing stern discipline. In the *Apostolic Constitutions* fathers were instructed to "educate your children in the Lord . . . teach them such trades as are agreeable and suitable to the Word . . . be not afraid to reprove them and to teach them wisdom with severity . . . bring them under with

19. Jerome, Letter XXII, Wright Edition, p. 95. By permission of Harvard University Press.
20. Matthew 8:22.
21. Jerome, Letter LIV, Wright Edition, p. 233.

cutting stripes."[22] One of the most interesting documents we have found pertaining to the rearing and education of children is the letter which Jerome wrote to Laeta, a well-to-do woman, in 403 A.D. How representative it may be we do not know, nor can we say how common were the practices referred to therein. But for whatever they may be worth, we present the following excerpts:

Let boys with their wanton frolics be kept far from Paula: let even her maids and attendants hold aloof from association with the worldly, lest they render their evil knowledge worse by teaching it to her. Have a set of letters made for her, of boxwood or of ivory and tell her their names. Let her play with them, making play a road to learning . . . When she begins with uncertain hand to use the pen, either let another hand be put over hers to guide her baby fingers, or else have the letters marked on the tablet so that her writing may follow their outlines and keep to their limits without straying away. Offer her prizes for spelling, tempting her with such trifling gifts as please young children. Let her have companions too in her lessons, so that she may seek to rival them and be stimulated by any praise they win. You must not scold her if she is somewhat slow; praise is the best sharpener of wits . . .

For teacher you must choose a man of approved years, life and learning . . . And so you must take care not to let women's silly coaxing get your daughter into the way of cutting her words short, or of disporting herself in gold brocade and fine purple . . . When she sees her grandfather [not a Christian], she must leap into his arms, hang on his neck, and sing "Alleluia" whether he likes it or not. Let her grandmother snatch her away, let her recognize her father with a smile, let her endear herself to all, so that the whole family may rejoice that they have such a rosebud among them . . .

Her very dress and outward appearance should remind her of Him to whom she is promised. Do not pierce her ears, or paint with white lead and rouge the cheeks that are consecrated to Christ. Do not load her neck with pearls and gold, do not weigh down her head with jewels, do not dye her hair red and thereby presage for her the fires of hell.

She should not take her food in public, that is, at her parents' guest-table; for she may there see dishes that she will crave for . . . Until they have reached their full strength, however, strict abstinence is dangerous for young children: so till then, if needs must, let her visit the baths, and take a little wine for the stomach's sake, and have the support of a meat diet, lest her feet fail before the race begins . . .

22. *Apostolic Constitutions,* Book IV. Sec. II, paragraph xi, *Ante-Nicene Fathers,* Vol. 7, pp. 435-436.

Let her every day repeat to you a portion of the scriptures as her fixed task. A good number of verses she should learn by heart in the Greek, but knowledge of the Latin should follow close after . . . You must be her teacher, to you her childish ignorance must look for a model. Let her never see anything in you or her father which she would do wrong to imitate . . . Let no youth or curled dandy ogle her. Let our little virgin never stir a finger's breadth from her mother when she attends a vigil or an all-night service . . . Let her choose as companion not a spruce, handsome girl, able to warble sweet songs in liquid notes, but one grave and pale, carelessly dressed and inclined to melancholy. Set before her as a pattern some aged virgin of approved faith, character, and chastity . . .

Let her learn also to make wool, to hold the distaff, to put the basket in her lap, to turn the spindle, to shape the thread with her thumb . . . Let her have clothes which keep out the cold, not expose the limbs they pretend to cover. Let her food be vegetables and wheaten bread and occasionally a little fish . . . let her meals always leave her hungry and able at once to begin reading or praying or singing the psalms . . .

If you ever visit the country, do not leave your daughter behind at Rome . . . Let her not be present at slaves' weddings, nor take part in noisy household games. I know some people have laid down the rule that a Christian virgin should not bathe along with eunuchs or with married women, inasmuch as eunuchs are still men at heart, and women big with child are a revolting sight. For myself I disapprove altogether of baths in the case of a full-grown virgin. She ought to blush at herself and be unable to look at her own nakedness . . .[23]

We have no personality studies of children in early Christian families, but we may hazard a few guesses about the possible effects of growing up under circumstances like those described in this chapter. The persecutions must have produced a strong sense of insecurity which was compensated for, in varying degrees, by religious doctrines of a future life. The scorn of lowly Christians by good Romans may very well have promoted feelings of inferiority. The warnings against too close association with worldly people were quite likely frustrating to many a boy and girl. How often teachings of the Church inhibited the development and expression of affection between parents and children we do not know. But there must have been some mental conflict involving the matter of loyalty

23. Jerome, Letter CVII, Wright Edition, pp. 347-367. By permission of Harvard University Press.

to Church and to family, and the natural desire to be like other boys and girls and to associate with them. The imaginative picture we have of children in early Christian families is not one of happy youngsters. Yet, who knows, maybe the things we would find very restricting were taken by them as a matter of course.

Perhaps the same comment should be made about adolescents in relation to the teachings about sex and marriage. It must have been hard to accept the doctrine that the attraction of male and female for one another is evil and that sex is only vile. One may well suspect the existence of terrific conflicts and guilt feelings among youths and young adults.

But whatever may have been true of those who lived in the first few centuries of the Christian era, the teachings of the Church Fathers have come down to us and have undoubtedly had a great, though unmeasured, influence on the people of our own time.

Virgins and Widows

During the era of persecutions there must have been many nuclear families broken by death and imprisonment. Since they were sometimes, perhaps usually, detached from kinship groups, the Church took over some responsibility for widows, orphans, and others in special need. Very early deacons, virgins, and widows were given responsibility for various social services.

Deacons were appointed by the original disciples in Jerusalem. (Acts 6:1-6) "Virgins" were girls and women who were not only unmarried and chaste, but who in addition had taken a vow to be the "bride of Christ." Virgins in this sense were assigned to the duties of visiting Christians in prison, caring for the sick, and administering other forms of relief. Very high status was assigned to these "virgins" and almost as high to "widows."

Next to virgins the highest status was held by widows. As in the case of virgins, we note two uses of the term: women whose husbands were dead and such women who were pledged to refrain from second marriages. Some of the latter were employed by the Church for religious and charitable work. For these duties older women were preferred. Thus Paul wrote to Timothy:

> Let not a widow be taken into the number under three-score years old, having been the wife of one man, well reported of for good works; if she have brought up children, if she have lodged strangers, if she have washed the saints' feet, if she have relieved the afflicted, if she have diligently followed every good work. But the younger widows refuse: for when they have begun to wax wanton against Christ, they will marry; having damnation, because they have cast off their first faith. And withal they learn to be idle, wandering about from house to house; and not only idle, but tattlers also and busybodies, speaking things which they ought not. I will therefore that the younger women marry, bear children, guide the house. give none occasion to the adversary to speak reproachfully.[24]

Paul evidently thought remarriage a lesser evil for young widows, but some of the Church Fathers condemned it without qualification. Athenagoras said, "A second marriage is only a specious adultery."[25] In the *Apostolic Constitutions* we read: "Once marrying according to the law is righteous, as being according to the will of God; but second marriages, after the promise, are wicked, not on account of the marriage itself, but because of the falsehood. Third marriages are indications of incontinency. But such marriages as are beyond the third are manifest fornication, and unquestionable uncleanness."[26]

Jerome put the case against remarriage on a more practical basis:

> Young widows, of whom some are already turned aside after Satan, when they have begun to wax wanton against Christ, in their lustful moments are wont to say: "My little estate is wasting every day, the property I have inherited is being scattered, my footman has spoken insultingly to me, my maid pays no attention to my orders. Who will appear for me in court? Who will be responsible for my land-tax? Who will educate my little chil-

---

24. I Timothy 5:9-15.
25. Athenagoras, *A Plea for the Christians*, Chapter 33, *Ante-Nicene Fathers*, Vol. 2, p. 146.
26. *Apostolic Constitutions*, Book III, Sec. I, Paragraph i, *Ante-Nicene Fathers*, Vol. 7, p. 426.

dren and bring up my houseslaves?" Shame on them! They bring forward as a reason for marriage the very thing which should in itself render marriage impossible. A mother sets over her children not a stepfather but an enemy, not a parent but a tyrant. Inflamed by lustfulness she forgets her own offspring, and in the midst of the little ones who know nothing of their sad fate the lately weeping widow arrays herself freshly as a bride. Why these pretexts of property and arrogant servants? Confess your vileness. No woman marries with the idea of not sleeping with a husband. If you are not spurred on by lust, surely it is the height of madness to prostitute yourself like a harlot merely to increase your wealth, and for a paltry and passing gain to pollute that precious chastity which might endure forever. If you have children, why do you want to marry? If you have none, why do you not fear the barrenness you have already known? Why do you put an uncertain gain before a certain loss of modesty? A marriage settlement is made in your favour today, but soon you will be induced to make your will. Your husband will feign illness, and will do for you what he wants you to do for him: but he means to go on living, and you are destined for an early grave. Or if it should happen that you have sons by your second husband, domestic warfare and intestine feuds will be the result. You will not be allowed to love your own children or to look kindly on those to whom you gave birth. You will hand them their food secretly; for he will be jealous of your dead husband, and unless you hate your sons he will think you still in love with their father. If he, for his part, has issue by a former wife, when he brings you into his house, then, even though you have a heart of gold, you will be the cruel stepmother, against whom every comedy, every mime-writer, and every dealer in rhetorical commonplaces raises his voice. If your stepson falls sick or has a headache, you will be maligned as a poisoner. If you refuse him food, you will be cruel; if you give it, you will be said to have bewitched him. What benefit, I pray you, can a second marriage confer sufficient to compensate for these disadvantages?[27]

That people were discouraged from marrying does not mean that they did not live in families. Indeed, until the establishment of monasteries and other "institutions" we may reasonably assume that most unmarried adults and widows, as well as small children, lived in family groups. A passage from the *Apostolic Constitutions* indicates that orphans were expected to be taken into established households. But to make sure that "the brethren" did not overlook them, nor others whose homes were broken, they were made a special responsibility of the bishops.

27. Jerome, Letter LIV, Wright Edition, pp. 255-259. By permission of Harvard University Press.

Broken Homes

When any Christian becomes an orphan, whether it be a young man or a maid, it is good that some one of the brethren who is without a child should take the young man, and esteem him in the place of a son; and he that has a son about the same age, and that is marriageable, should marry the maid to him: for they which do so perform a great work and become fathers to the orphans, and shall receive the reward of this charity from the Lord God.

Do you, therefore, O bishops, be solicitous about their maintenance, being in nothing wanting to them; exhibiting to the orphans the care of parents; to the widows the care of husbands; to those of suitable age, marriage; to the artificer, work; to the unable, commiseration; to the strangers, an house; to the hungry, food; to the thirsty, drink; to the naked, clothing; to the sick, visitation; to the prisoners, assistance. Besides these, have a greater care of the orphans, that nothing may be wanting to them; and that as to the maiden, till she arrives at the age of marriage, and ye give her in marriage to a brother; to the young man assistance, that he may learn a trade, and may be maintained by the advantage arising from it; that so, when he is dextrous in the management of it, he may thereby be enabled to buy himself the tools of his trade, that so he may no longer burden any of the brethren . . .[28]

Evidently families were occasionally broken by divorce. Sometimes the underlying conflict arose out of religious differences, as when one spouse was a Christian, the other not. In keeping with their Hebrew and Roman traditions the early Christians seem at first to have regarded divorce as an affair of the persons or families immediately involved. Hence we would not be surprised that the early Fathers adopted no well-defined position with reference to the disruption of marital relations, were it not for the fact that divorce had become frequent, casual and notorious, at least among upper-class Romans. In curious contrast with its later stern opposition to divorce, the Church's attitude during the first four centuries was wavering and uncertain. There was much controversy over the matter. The Gospel of Matthew indicates that Jesus approved the divorcing of an adulterous wife.[29] But no corre-

28. *Apostolic Constitutions,* Book IV, Sec. I, paragraphs i-ii, *Ante-Nicene Fathers,* Vol. 7, p. 427.
29. Matthew 5:31-32.

sponding rule is laid down explicitly for an adulterous husband. All of the first three Gospels forbid the remarriage of divorced men and women alike. In his first Epistle to the Corinthians, Paul took a somewhat equivocal position:

> And unto the married I command, yet not I, but the Lord, Let not the wife depart from her husband: but and if she depart, let her remain unmarried, or be reconciled to her husband: and let not the husband put away his wife. But to the rest speak I, not the Lord: If any brother hath a wife that believeth not, and she be pleased to dwell with him, let him not put her away. And the woman which hath an husband that believeth not, and if he be pleased to dwell with her, let her not leave him. For the unbelieving husband is sanctified by the wife, and the unbelieving wife is sanctified by the husband: else were your children unclean; but now are they holy. But if the unbelieving depart, let him depart. A brother or a sister is not under bondage in such cases: but God hath called us to peace. For what knowest thou, O wife, whether thou shalt save thy husband? Or how knowest thou, O man, whether thou shalt save thy wife?[30]

Family Controls

Church Slow to Regulate Divorce

From the foregoing it is apparent that the "internal" controls through patriarch, maternal uncle, groups of kinsmen, and the like, were giving way to "external" controls through officials of the Church. However, ecclesiastical rules and machinery for their enforcement developed slowly. Thus the Church Fathers debated the issue of divorce for about three centuries. Hermas, about 140 A.D., held that divorce might be permitted on the grounds of idolatry, apostasy, covetousness, and fornication. Origen, in the first part of the third century, said that a woman might be divorced if she were guilty of a crime equal to or greater than fornication. Jerome, about 400 A.D., agreed with Hermas as to the legitimate grounds for divorce, as did his contemporaries, Ambrose and Epiphanius. Chrysostom changed his mind a great deal, but in the end held that marriage might

30. I Corinthians 7:10-16.

be dissolved absolutely on account of adultery. Augustine also shifted from one position to another. In the early part of his career he held that for "unlawful lusts . . . a man may without crime put away his wife and a wife her husband."[31]

The Council of Elvira in 306 A.D. declared that if a woman put away her husband, even though he were guilty, and married another man, she should be excommunicated. Only in case of mortal illness would she be permitted to take Communion until after her first husband's death. If she left her husband without cause and entered into another marriage, she was denied Communion, even on the death bed. The Council of Arles, in 314 A.D., pronounced the general principle of the indissolubility of marriage but made concessions to the practical difficulty of enforcing such a rule. A husband who put away a guilty wife was to be "advised" rather than forbidden to marry again during her lifetime. Finally, at the Council of Carthage, in 407 A.D., the Church definitely laid down the strict doctrine of indissolubility.

The changing position with reference to divorce is further displayed in the legislation of the early Christian emperors. Thus in 331 A.D. Constantine ruled that so-called trifling causes should no longer be an adequate basis for legal divorce at the will of one party. A wife might repudiate her husband only if he were a murderer, poisoner, or violator of sepulchres. A man might put away his wife only if she were guilty of poisoning, procuring, or adultery. At another time Constantine permitted a wife to divorce her husband if he had been absent in the army for four years without sending her word. In 363 A.D. Julian repealed the divorce law of Constantine. In 439 Theodosius II tried to restore the law of the early Empire. But after ten years of leniency he issued another and much more stringent law. In addition to the causes included by Constantine, Theodosius permitted a woman to secure a divorce if her husband had plotted against the government or were guilty of

31. Augustine, *Concerning the Sermon on the Mount*, Book I, Chapter 16.

fraud, robbery, cruelty to his wife, or intimacy with prostitutes. He allowed a man to put away his wife on similar grounds, and also for spending the night away from home, or for visiting the theater, circus, or other public place against his will. Justinian in the sixth century revoked the ancient privilege of divorce by mutual consent unless the husband was impotent, the husband had been for five years in foreign captivity, or either the husband or wife wished to enter a monastic order. Thus the matter was pushed back and forth, the Church more and more opposing divorce, the state wavering, but ultimately conforming to the rule of the Church.

A Stern Sex Code

We have already observed similar "feeling of the way" with reference to marriage and child rearing. As to sex the general position of the Church was pretty consistent—sex was vile—but the sanctions were not so clear. The Church Fathers condemned not only fornication, adultery, pederasty, masturbation, and bestiality, but also contraception, abortion, the reading of "lascivious" books, singing "wanton" songs, dancing "suggestive" dances, bathing in mixed company, wearing "improper" clothing, and attending the theater. A sterner code would be hard to envisage. Several of the Church Fathers, notably Origen, actually practiced self-mutilation, becoming eunuchs for the sake of their religion.

Among the early Christians the kiss was a frequent form of salutation. No doubt it was in many cases a dignified, ritualistic act, but naturally it sometimes had another significance. This led to warnings such as that of Athenagoras: "If any one kiss a second time because it has given him pleasure, [he sins]. Therefore the kiss, or rather the salutation, should be given with the greatest care, since, if there be mixed with it the least defilement of thought, it excludes us from eternal life."[32]

32. Athenagoras, *Plea for the Christians.* Chapter 32, *Ante-Nicene Fathers,* Vol. 2, p. 146.

Tertullian's essay *On the Apparel of Women* insists that women should avoid showiness and ostentation in dress, ornaments, hair dress—no precious stones, no gold and silver, no bright colors. Beauty is not to be feared, but it is to be shunned as unnecessary and vainglorious. Christian women do not go out to public gatherings as do the "Gentiles." Hence they have no need for fine clothes and ornaments. "To Christian modesty it is not enough to *be* so, but to *seem* so too."[33] Jerome, writing to a mother and daughter living in Gaul, gave this revealing statement of Christian modesty:

> Your very robe, coarse and sombre though it may be, betrays your unexpressed desires, if it be without crease, if it be trailed upon the ground to make you seem taller, if your vest be slit on purpose to let something be seen within, hiding that which is unsightly and disclosing that which is fair. As you walk along, your shiny black shoes by their creaking give an invitation to young men. Your breasts are confined in strips of linen, and your chest is imprisoned close by a tight girdle. Your hair comes down over your forehead or over your ears. Your shawl sometimes drops, so as to leave your white shoulders bare, and then, as though unwilling to be seen, it hastily hides what it intentionally revealed. And when in public it hides the fact in a pretence of modesty, with a harlot's skill it shows only those features which give men when shown more pleasure.[34]

Thus the Church Fathers lashed out against all expressions of sex. But as a matter of fact, we know very little about the sex life of the rank and file. We have before us only the stories of certain prominent individuals and the formal teachings of outstanding leaders. But, regardless of what Christian people actually did in the first four centuries, these narratives and these doctrines have survived to influence the Western World even in the twentieth century.

33. Tertullian. *On the Apparel of Women, Ante-Nicene Fathers,* Vol. 4, pp. 14-25.
34. Jerome, Letter CXVII, Wright Edition, pp. 387-389. By permission of Harvard University Press.

REFERENCES

Augustinus, Aurelius, St. (Bishop of Hippo), also **Augustine,** *Concerning the Sermon on the Mount.* New York: The Christian Literature Company, 1888.

de Pomerai, Ralph, *Marriage: Past, Present and Future.* London: Constable and Co., Ltd., 1930.

Donaldson, James, "Early Christianity," *Woman: Her Position and Influence in Ancient Greece and Rome, and Among the Early Christians.* London and New York: Longmans, Green and Company, 1907, Book III.

Goodsell, Willystine, "The Influence of Christianity upon Marriage and the Family in the Roman Empire," *A History of Marriage and the Family.* New York: The Macmillan Company, 1934, Chapter V.

Howard, George E., *A History of Matrimonial Institutions.* Chicago: University of Chicago Press, 1904. See especially Volume I, pp. 291-297; Volume II, pp. 11-38.

Jerome, *Select Letters of St. Jerome,* translated and edited by F. A. Wright. New York: G. P. Putnam's Sons, 1933.

New Testament. See especially the letters of Paul to the Corinthians, Timothy, and Titus.

Roberts, Alexander, and **Donaldson, James,** eds., *The Ante-Nicene Fathers.* Buffalo: The Christian Literature Company, 1886. See especially:

The Apostolic Constitutions (Volume VII);
Athenagoras, *A Plea for the Christians* (Volume II);
Clement, *The Instructor* (Volume II);
Clement, *Stromata* (Volume II);
Ignatius, *Epistle to Polycarp* (Volume I);
Methodius, *The Banquet of the Ten Virgins* (Volume VI);
Tertullian, *On the Apparel of Women* (Volume IV);
    Letter to His Wife (Volume IV);
    Against Marcion (Volume III).

Slotkin, James S., "Jewish Intermarriage in Chicago." Unpublished Ph.D. dissertation, University of Chicago, Department of Anthropology, 1940.

10 The Anglo-Saxon Family—
Folkways in Transition

From the preceding chapters it is clear that our domestic folkways and mores have some of their roots in classical antiquity. This does not mean that we continue precisely the patterns of marital selection, child training, kinship organization, or other aspects of family life as found among the ancients. It merely means that in accounting for the family complex of our own culture we cannot ignore those of the Hebrews, Romans, and early Christians. If we may be permitted to oversimplify and to trace our history backwards, we have something like this. Our ideas and practices are influenced by the New Testament and other writings of the Church Fathers. These in turn were partly a reaction against some things that were happening in Roman society. Finally, family life in Imperial Rome may be pictured as a rejection of early Roman mores, while the family code of the early Christians, most of whom were Jews, constituted a radical departure from the family system of the Hebrews.

But we did not inherit our domestic folkways and mores directly from the ancient world. The customs, traditions, and laws of the Hebrews, Romans, and Christians were confronted by those of the Celtic, Scandinavian, and Germanic peoples of northwestern Europe. One meeting ground of these divergent cultures was England. Hence we find it important to learn what we can about the family life of the Anglo-Saxons before they had much contact with the peoples and institutions of the Mediterranean world.

Perhaps it would have been desirable to go back still farther and precede the study of Anglo-Saxon family life with an examination of that in some Germanic tribe prior to its settlement in Britain. But unfortunately we do not have access to the necessary data. We have scattered bits of information about the Westphalian Saxons, Frisians, Danes, and others, and we have broad generalizations of dubious validity about the "Germans" as a whole, but we do not have a full account of the family system in any particular tribe. Hence we turn directly to the domestic folkways and mores of what is called Anglo-Saxon England, in which there were Germanic and Scandinavian elements sometimes mingled with remnants of Roman-Celtic culture of the towns and later with features introduced by Christian missionaries.

The sources of our information include laws of undoubted authenticity, charters that are genuine and others that are probably forgeries, ecclesiastical rulings which represent what the Church wanted the people to do, chronicles and histories, many of which have been discredited as to detail but which seem to reveal dominant attitudes and customs, and epic poems like *Beowulf*. To the best of our ability we shall describe family life in England from the time of Aethelbert, King of Kent in the sixth century, to the time of Cnut, Danish King of England in the eleventh.

But first let us have a brief look at the background of Anglo-Saxon England. It appears that before 1000 B.C. Britain was inhabited by short, stocky people, who lived in scattered villages under tribal chieftains. During the next thousand years the island was occupied by Celtic tribes. In physical appearance these people offered some contrast to their predecessors, being a mixed type, but what little we know of the two cultures suggests that they were much alike. From the invasion by Julius Caesar in 55 B.C. to the withdrawal of the last Roman legion in 407 A.D., there was an infiltration of Roman culture, but it seems to have left little lasting impression on England. In the middle of the fifth century the Jutes settled in Kent. From about 450 to about 550 Angles and Saxons occupied Sussex, Essex, Wessex, East Anglia, and Northumbria, taking few prisoners, driving the surviving Britons into Wales, Cornwall, and Strathclyde, destroying towns, and apparently wiping out Roman culture and Christianity. But Christianity was revived by missionaries who came from Ireland and from Rome (Augustine in 597). In the ninth century came the Danish invasions and in the eleventh the Norman conquest. When, therefore, we employ the term Anglo-Saxon, we are using the name of a dominant group to stand for the whole population and the changing culture of England over a period of time which takes in about 500 years.

The Anglo-Saxons have been called "the backwoodsmen of Europe." Before migrating to England they lived in regions too remote to be much influenced by the Romans, as were the tribes of the Rhineland. But it is supposed that they were much like the Germans described by Caesar and Tacitus, fierce, adventurous, cruel, famed as warriors, hunters, and drinkers.

Each tribe was in theory at least a group of kinsmen. Its chief was chosen in an assembly (*mote*). In time of war the power of a chief (*king*) often increased greatly; conquered lands were given to his favorites (*eorls*), for whom lesser men (*ceorls*) often had to work. At first these tribal kingdoms were small isolated realms and groups. Occasionally some king more powerful than his neighbors would gain the upper hand and extend his rule over tribes previously independent. From 600 to 850 England was torn by struggle for supremacy between three relatively great Saxon kingdoms.

From our standpoint the culture was crude, perhaps on a level with that of the Hopi. The bulk of the people lived in huts of "wattle and daub" or mud and straw, without windows or chimneys, and with dirt floors. The well-to-do had houses of logs or rough-hewn timbers. These dwellings were grouped in settlements of varying sizes. The term *tun* was applied indiscriminately to a large village containing a group of freemen, to the *vill* of a king or *eorl*, or to the farm of a humble *ceorl*. It looked like a fort with a ditch, a stockade of earth and pickets, a yard, and a collection of small buildings. If it were a *vill*, there was a hall (*heal*) where the householder, his retainers, and his guests feasted at long tables and slept on the straw-covered floor. Separate, but often connected, were small buildings (*bur* or "bower") which served as bedchambers and living rooms for women and children. Other buildings were kitchens and storehouses. Such was the home (*ham*) of a great man. As we go down in the social scale buildings become smaller and fewer, until in the lowest grades we find small huts crowded together in squalid conditions.

Family Structure

Dominance of the Sib

In Anglo-Saxon literature we find little mention of the conjugal or nuclear family. The group most often referred to was the body of kinsmen (*maegth*), which we call a sib. Since kinship was reckoned in both lines, there was dual descent. When there was a strong chieftain "his friends and relations obeyed him with gladness,"[1] and "in joy passed their time and in prosperous wise." (*Beowulf*, 99-100.) Loyalty to the group was a major virtue; "in a right-minded man nought can ere set aside the claims of his kin." (*Beowulf*, 2600-2601.) Obviously the sib (*maegth*) was very important among the Anglo-Saxons, but apparently it was less powerful than in early Judaea, Greece, and Rome. It differed furthermore from the sibs of classical antiquity in that kinship was counted definitely in both the paternal and the maternal lines and that some responsibility was fixed on both sets of relatives. While a husband assumed great authority over his wife, it was her relatives that offered guarantees of her good conduct. According to one authority, if a man were found guilty of murder his paternal kinsmen must pay two thirds of the victim's *wer-gild* (compensation) and the maternal kinsmen must pay one third.[2] Under a law of King Alfred (ruled 871-900)

1. *Beowulf*, Hall translation, lines 65-66. Numbers that follow are of lines in the same edition.
2. Willystine Goodsell, *A History of Marriage and the Family* (1934), p. 193.

a murderer with no paternal relatives must be helped by his maternal relatives.

In early times there seem to have been a good many inter-sib feuds which not only rested on the tradition of group responsibility but also must have contributed greatly to group solidarity. Such feuds were often passed down from generation to generation until one side or both would be seriously weakened or they would "for tribute make terms." (*Beowulf,* 156.) At first vengeance might be wreaked on any kinsman of the offender, but gradually by law and doubtless by other pressures this practice was restricted. A law of King Edmund (ruled 940-946) represented an effort to limit such feuds.

If anyone henceforth slay any man, that he himself bear the *faehthe* [feud]; unless, with the aid of his friends, and within twelve months, he compensate it with the full *wer,* be he born as he may be. But if the kindred forsake him, then I will that all the kindred be *unfah* [free from hostility] except the perpetrator; if afterwards they do not give him either food or *mund* [protection] . . .[3]

That the idea of sib responsibility did not die easily is shown by a law of King Ethelred (ruled 978-1016) which held that if a murder had been "committed within a *burh,* let the inhabitants of the *burh* themselves go, and get the murderers, living or dead, or their nearest kindred, head for head." [4] In general the mores of this period were bound up with the assumption that everyone belonged to a localized kinship group or clan, to which he was answerable and which in turn had considerable responsibility for him. A sib might expel a member who became an intolerable nuisance, or an individual might eliminate himself. But such a detached individual was treated as an outlaw, whom everyone was permitted if not bound to kill. Strangers had to give a satisfactory account of themselves or be treated as "treacherous spies." (*Beowulf,* 253.) Not only was everyone thought of as belonging to a

3. Thorpe, *Ancient Laws and Institutes of England* (1840), Vol. 1, p. 249.

4. *Ibid.,* p. 287.

localized kinship group; he was also expected in due time to marry and have children, thus continuing and increasing the strength of the clan. But with the coming of Christianity there was provided a possible escape from family and sib through life in a religious institution. In convents were found girls arbitrarily placed by their fathers, maidens who used this as an escape from unwanted husbands selected by their fathers, and widows and women from otherwise broken homes. It is conceivable that these refugees from unhappy family situations may have been more numerous than those who chose institutional life for reasons more directly associated with religion. However, no figures are available. Men and boys in similar circumstances were found in monasteries. Thus the Christian religion furnished an escape from family life and actively urged practice of celibacy. It is held by some historians that religious orders were open chiefly to members of the upper classes and that relatively few of the common people gained admission. But this is another point on which figures are lacking.

Inheritance

Another aspect of Anglo-Saxon life which displayed the relationship between conjugal and consanguine groups, or nuclear and extended families, was the inheritance of property. Although kinship was counted in both the patrilineal and the matrilineal lines, a child inherited his rank, or social and legal status, from his father. In general property was passed through the male line, but there was no legal obstacle to the inheritance even of land by a daughter or a widow.

Usually at the time of betrothal a man specified what provision he would make for his wife in case he predeceased her. Sometimes a widow's rights were prescribed by law. Thus a law of King Aethelbert ruled, "If she bear a live child, let her have half the property, if the husband die first." Under King Edmund it was held that a bridegroom should declare what he would grant his wife "if she live longer than he. If it be so agreed, then it is right that she be entitled to half the property, and to all, if they have children in common, except she again choose a husband."[5] Whether these royal edicts merely gave expression to common practice, or whether they were a replacement of earlier control of such matters by the kinship groups, we cannot be sure, although the latter interpretation seems the more plausible.

In the latter part of the Anglo-Saxon period it appears that the making of wills was common, at least for people of means. This practice, whereby an individual might decide for himself what should be done with his property, suggests that the *maegth* was losing some of its earlier power. By means of these legal instruments property might be left to a wife, a husband, children, a charitable or ecclesiastical institution, or be otherwise disposed of. Husband and wife sometimes made a will together. In one will a man and his wife agreed that "whichever of them live the longer succeed to the land and all the property." Another will, dated 958, reads, "And I give the land at Illey to my younger daughter, for her day; and after her day to Berthnoth [her husband] for his day if he live longer than she. If they have children then I give it to them . . . And I give the land at Cotham to Berthnoth and my younger daughter for their day."[6] Thus we have indications of both separate and community property bequeathed either for life or without restriction.

In contrast to this growing independence of the individual and the nuclear family, the system of land tenure called *gavelkind*, found chiefly in Kent, represented the persistence of strength in the kinship group. Under this system the real estate of a man who died intestate, as most men did, was divided equally among all the sons, or among brothers or other collateral heirs on failure of direct or nearer heirs. If

5. *Ibid.*, pp. 23, 255.

6. Florence G. Buckstaff, "Married Women's Property in Anglo-Saxon and Anglo-Norman Law," *Annals of the American Academy of Political and Social Science*, 4 (1893), pp. 248, 249. By permission of the editor.

wife and children survived, personal property was divided into three parts: one for the widow, one for the children, and one for the dead—presumably for his collateral relatives.

The importance of the sib was manifest in other ways, as when paternal kinsmen assumed guardianship of fatherless children or when relatives on either side prevented a father from disposing of an unwanted infant if milk or honey had touched its lips.

Thus in many ways the kinship group of the Anglo-Saxons was much like that of the ancient Hebrews and that of the early Romans. The nuclear family in all three cultures was relatively subordinate and was an integral part of the larger, more powerful sib. Some historians refer to all three systems as "patriarchal." A recent writer uses the term "trustee family system," thus emphasizing the fact that the sib was the important, continuing entity, while the individual and the nuclear family were its temporary representatives or "trustees."[7] However, the evidence at our disposal leads us to believe that the nuclear family of the Anglo-Saxon had somewhat more independence than did that of the early Romans or Hebrews.

Status and Roles of the Sexes

Traditions concerning the relative status of men and women among the Anglo-Saxons are, unfortunately for us, conflicting. Thus one historian says, "Woman was to them almost a sacred thing . . . the Anglo-Saxons honoured them both in public and in home."[8] A less sentimental, though perhaps no more accurate statement is this:

In contradiction to the generally received opinion, it may be said, that the Anglo-Saxon women were, at one time, sold by their fathers and always beaten by their husbands; that they were menial servants even when of

7. Carle C. Zimmerman, *Family and Civilization* (1947), pp. 128 ff.
8. Cyril E. Robinson, *England, A History of British Progress* (1928), p. 17. By permission of Thomas Y. Crowell Company.

royal rank; that they were habitually subject to coarse personal insult; and that they were never addressed, even in poetry, in the language of passion or respect.[9]

Still another writer first glorifies the position of woman and then insists that her place is in the home.

. . . She was the attentive housewife, the tender companion, the comforter and consoler of her husband and family, the virtuous and noble matron. Home was her especial place; for we are told in a poem in the Exeter Book [11th century] that "It beseems a damsel to be at her board [table]; a rambling woman scatters words, she is often charged with faults, a man thinks of her with contempt, oft her cheek smites."[10]

Being "at her board" meant being busy with cooking, brewing, making clothing "from the sheep's backs to her family's backs," making soap and candles, washing, tending the children, and working in the fields. Men engaged in farm work, hunting, fighting, and making weapons.

The early Anglo-Saxon woman, like her early Roman sister, was always under the guardianship of some man: father, brother, husband, or other kinsman. In early times her marriage was arranged; only gradually did she acquire the right to veto her father's choice. For a long time she received no part of the *wergild* for a slain kinsman. But little by little her status improved. By the time of King Alfred the *weotuma* or bride-price was paid to her instead of to her father. Sometimes she shared her husband's estate and she had definite claims on it in case of his death. She also might receive by gift or inheritance both real and personal property. Moreover, we are told that "the wife's property was not answerable for the debts of her husband nor his for hers."[11] However, this seems questionable, since it is scarcely in harmony with the rest of the Anglo-Saxon system. Other evidence of the changing status of women appears in the later practice of sitting at table with the men instead of serving them as depicted in *Beowulf,* attending the *witenagemot* and other assemblies,

9. John Thrupp, *The Anglo-Saxon Home* (1862), p. 21.
10. Thomas Wright, *The Homes of Other Days* (1871), pp. 65-66.
11. Buckstaff, *op. cit.,* p. 249.

suing and being sued in courts of justice, carrying the house keys, and having a storeroom, chest and cupboard of their own under lock and key. How many women attained these privileges we do not know—probably a small minority—but in any case they were not lasting achievements.

The Family Cycle

Marital Selection

The sources at our disposal indicate that mate selection took a number of forms in Anglo-Saxon England. In some historical works we find marriage by capture discussed as though at one time it had been very common, if not predominant. Certainly there were raids and wars in the course of which women prisoners were made the mates of their captors. No doubt some of them were accepted in the victorious tribe as wives, but we may be sure that others bore an inferior status and a more casual relation to the men who carried them off. The frequent prohibition of concubinage in Anglo-Saxon law is one bit of evidence supporting this inference. Moreover, while women were captured from other tribes, most marriages must have been between members of the same tribe. Hence we must reject the notion that capture was ever the general basis of marriage.

For the hypothesis of marriage by purchase there is more evidence. Thus in the laws of Aethelbert, King of Kent (ruled A.D. 560-616), we read:

If a man buy a maiden with cattle, let the bargain stand, if it be without guile, but if there be guile, let him bring her home again, and let his property be restored to him.[12]

If a man carry off a maiden by force, let him pay L. shillings to the owner, and afterwards buy the object of his will of the owner. If she be betrothed to another man in money, let him make *bot* with XX. shillings.[13]

12. Thorpe, *op. cit.*, Vol. 1, p. 23.
13. *Ibid.*, p. 25.

If a freeman lie with a freeman's wife, let him pay for it with his *wer-geld,* and provide another wife with his own money, and bring her to the other.[14]

Such passages leave us in doubt as to whether the bride-price was usually determined by bargaining or by custom. There is also some question as to whether this was a real contract of sale, making the woman a chattel. Howard regards the transaction as a transfer of authority rather than of property and holds the distinction to be important. Yet he grants that "when the powers of the husband are so great as they were among our ancestors, there can be little difference in popular conception between possession of the *mund* and ownership of the woman."[15] Another possible interpretation is that the "bride-price" was a fund out of which the woman's kinsmen might care for her in case of need or meet the responsibility for misdeeds of which she might be charged. Also it is possible to regard it as a recognition of her worth and importance. However, it seems clear that the deal was made by the would-be bridegroom and the girl's father without necessary regard for the girl's wishes. It also appears that a man might betroth his daughter when she was no more than seven years old. But Archbishop Theodore in the seventh century held that after a girl was sixteen or seventeen she could not be married off against her will.

Between the fifth and the tenth century English women gradually obtained the right of disposing of themselves in marriage. At first both state and church required the daughter to accept without question or comment whomsoever her father pleased. She obtained, however, at a very early period in England [and also in Rome and on the continent] the right of making an objection to a suitor for some grave and specific cause, as insanity, leprosy, or crime; but of the validity of this objection her father was sole judge. The church and the state, however, insisted with a constantly increas-

14. *Ibid.,* p. 11.
15. George E. Howard, *A History of Matrimonial Institutions* (1904), Vol. 1, p. 261. By permission of the University of Chicago Press.

ing earnestness that it was a father's duty to weigh these objections fairly; and after an early period if he did not do so the right of judging passed from him to his family or the public tribunals.[16]

Finally a law of King Cnut (ruled 1017-1035) seemed to give women the right to make their own decisions concerning marriage, or at least to impose a veto. "And let no one compel either woman or maiden to him whom she herself mislikes, nor for money sell her; unless he is willing to give anything voluntarily."[17] Thorpe holds that people usually read too much into this law:

. . . A change of this important nature was not likely to be announced in a short clause such as the present text; and the sale of the female ward was at the time permitted by every code of Europe. The better opinion, therefore, seems to be, that the purport of this law was to prevent the guardian from forcing his ward into an unwilling union, and demanding more than the *mund* established by law, unless indeed the future husband might choose to give more.[18]

As we have seen, every culture prohibits the marriage of kinsmen of certain degrees. What were forbidden degrees among the early Anglo-Saxons we do not know, but by the eleventh century the rules of the Church had become law in England. A law of King Cnut ordered

. . . that no Christian man every marry in his own family within the relationship of vi. persons: nor with the relict of his kinsman who was so near of kin; nor with the relative of the wife whom he had previously had; nor with his godmother, nor with a hallowed nun, nor with one divorced . . .[19]

Ritual and Economics of Marriage

In contrast with some peoples we have studied, the Anglo-Saxons did not have much domestic ritual. But in connection with betrothal and nuptials they developed some rather elab-

16. John Thrupp, *The Anglo-Saxon Home* (1862), pp. 25-26.
17. Thorpe, *op. cit.*, Vol. 1, p. 417.
18. *Ibid.*, p. 416, fn.
19. *Ibid.*, p. 365.

orate fiscal arrangements. A law attributed to King Edmund indicates what was considered proper procedure for a betrothal in the tenth century:

1. If a man desire to betroth a maiden or a woman, and it so be agreeable to her and her friends, then is it right that the bridegroom, according to the law of God, and according to the customs of the world, first promise, and give a *wed* [surety] to those who are her *foresprecas* [representatives], that he desire her in such wise that he will keep her, according to God's law, as a husband shall his wife: and let his friends guarantee that.

2. After that, it is to be known to whom the *foster-lean* [drink-money] belongs: let the bridegroom again give a *wed* for this; and let his friends guarantee it.

3. Then, after that, let the bridegroom declare what he will grant her in case she choose his will, and what he will grant her, if she live longer than he.

4. If it be so agreed, then it is right that she be entitled to half the property, and to all, if they have children in common, except she again choose a husband.

5. Let him confirm all that which he was promised with a *wed;* and let his friends guarantee that.

6. If they then are agreed in every thing, then let the kinsmen take it in hand, and betroth their kinswoman to wife, and to a righteous life, to him who desired her, and let him take possession of the *borh* [down payment] who has control of the *wed.*

7. But if a man desire to lead her out of the land, into another thane's land, then it will be advisable for her that her friends have an agreement that no wrong shall be done to her; and if she commit a fault, that they may be nearest in the *bot* [have primary responsibility], if she have not wherewith she can make *bot*.[20]

Obviously this was not an "original" Anglo-Saxon procedure; it developed gradually through a series of stages. In earlier times betrothal was apparently a completed contract in which payment was made in full and the bride was delivered. Later the transfer of the woman was postponed, thus separating *beweddung* (betrothal) and *gifta* (nuptials). Still later payment of the bride-price was also deferred until the nuptials, only a nominal sum being turned over at the betrothal. This was a sort of down payment or surety that the

20. *Ibid.*, pp. 255-257.

deal would be completed. Along with the fiscal arrangements there was at various times and places "hand-fasting," or the giving of a ring, or a kiss, or some combination of these.

As the *gifta*, or what we would call the wedding, was more and more distinguished from the *beweddung*, or formal engagement, *gifta* came to include a number of customs. In early times the transfer of authority from the bride's father to her husband probably took place at the former's home. Later it sometimes occurred at the home of the bridegroom's parents or on the porch of a church. In early times the transfer of authority and announcement of consent to take each other as husband and wife were the essential parts of the marriage ceremony. Under the influence of the Church a benediction was added and eventually made compulsory. This benediction was sometimes pronounced under a *care-cloth* held at each corner by a tall man. If the bride were single and of good character she might be given a wreath by the priest. Other gifts were presented by kinsmen of the couple. A less pleasing feature of the occasion was crude horseplay freely indulged in by youths of the vicinity. There was commonly a wedding feast which might last three or more days marked by gluttony and drunkenness. On the evening of the first day, if the principals were people of consequence, a procession headed by the clergy led the couple with music to the nuptial couch. The priest blessed the bed, the bride and bridegroom drank from the marriage cup, and the guests returned to their feasting.

Sometime between the seventh and the tenth centuries there developed a custom according to which the bridegroom might offer his bride a morning-gift on the morning after the wedding. In so doing, he acknowledged that he was satisfied with his bargain. On receipt of the morning-gift the bride rose and dressed her hair in the style used by married women. Once this ceremony was performed the woman could not be returned to her parents; the marriage was fully established. At first the morning-gift was optional; later it become compulsory. At first it was commonly a trivial present; later it became more valuable. The third paragraph of the law of King Edmund, quoted above, is interpreted to mean that the amount of the morning-gift as well as of the *weotuma* (bride-price) must be stipulated in the betrothal. Eventually the two seem to have merged with the Norman dower, which, like the Roman *donatio,* was a provision for the wife in case of her husband's death.

In early times *beweddung* and *gifta* were "private" affairs, arrangements made between a young man and the father of a young woman. They were regulated by mores, of course, but without the intervention of priest or magistrate. Gradually the Church interjected its rules and its functionaries into these ceremonies until it gained a large measure of control over marriage.

Children

We have rather little information about children, their care and training, their play and work. But some things we do know. As among the Hebrews, Greeks, and Romans, the Anglo-Saxon father had a great deal of power over his new-born child. He it was who decided whether the child should be accepted into the family or disposed of. If the baby were sickly, malformed, or unusually timid, the father might have it killed or exposed. Timidity was sometimes tested by placing the infant on a sloping roof or tree branch; if it laughed or crowed, the child was considered worthy of life and a place in the family; if it cried, the opposite decision might be made. Evidently exposed children were often rescued and reared by strangers, as in classical antiquity. With this in mind and also anticipating the possibility of wanting to recover the child, a token was sometimes left with the baby for later identification. Children were also sold into slavery under pressure of extreme poverty or as part of a penalty for the father's wrong-doing. Furthermore, a man might place his son in a monastery or his daughter in a convent without any attention to the child's desire in the matter, and release was not to be had even upon the attainment of majority. The clergy early sought to place some restrictions on parental authority. Theodore, Archbishop of Canterbury in the seventh century, ruled that a man might not sell his son into slavery after the age of seven, nor his daughter into marriage after the age of sixteen or seventeen. But neither Archbishop Theodore nor any other ecclesiastic of this period seems to have ruled against forcing girls to enter and remain in convents against their will. Perhaps this was because endowments often accompanied such admissions to religious institutions.

As in our own time, a father was responsible for the acts of his children, but unlike the practices of our day, children shared the legal responsibility for their father's misdoing. This responsibility was restricted by a law of Ine, King of Wessex (ruled 688-725):

> If any one steal so that his wife and his children know it not, let him pay LX. shillings as *wite*. But if he steal with the knowledge of all his household, let them all go into slavery. A boy of X. years may be privy to a theft.[21]

In the tenth century "the bishops and the reeves" of London ordained that anyone over the age of twelve who stole anything worth more than twelve pence should be put to death. But this ordinance was disallowed by King Aethelstan, who decreed that no one under the age of fifteen should be hung for theft. From these and similar acts we gather that Anglo-Saxon boys attained a sort of majority between the ages of ten and fifteen—varying with time and place—and that girls acquired an even more attenuated majority between ten and seventeen.

Education was mostly informal and dealt with matters of everyday life: housekeeping, farming, hunting, fighting, morals, and religion. Most boys and girls appear to have received this training at home. But the sons of kings and *eorls* were sometimes placed in other households. Beowulf tells of having had this experience:

21. *Ibid.,* p. 107.

I was seven years old when my generous lord, the gracious friend of the people, brought me from my father's house. He reared and protected me, that good King Hrethel; nourishment and fair gifts he gave me; the duties of kinship he did not forget. Not a whit less mindful of me, a youth in his courts, was he than he was of his own sons, Herebeald and Haetcyn and my beloved Hygelac.[22]

On another occasion Beowulf recommended to Hrothgar that he send his eldest son away to receive training for his future responsibilities, expressing the general principle in these words: "Far places are best for that youth who would excel in manly virtues."[23]

Monastic schools provided formal education for a small number, but these schools were generally destroyed or abandoned during the Danish invasion. It was said of King Alfred that through "the wicked negligence of his parents and nurses" he had not learned to read by the age of twelve. However, he must have had some appreciation of formal education, because after beating off the Danes he set to work reviving schools. He urged that all sons of freemen be sent to school and that the better students stay on to study Latin, to which were later added church history, theology, and psalm singing. But through most of the Anglo-Saxon period the curriculum was very limited; books were scarce, and most instruction was given by word of mouth—dictating, repeating, catechizing.

Going to a monastic school, being placed in a convent, and living in a strange household were ways of being separated temporarily or permanently from one's parental home and sib. Interestingly, we do not read about orphanages in this period.

In case their father died, children were expected to remain in the care of their mother, but paternal kinsmen assumed guardianship of their property. A law of King Ine provided thus for the half-orphan of a *ceorl:*

22. *Beowulf*, lines 2428-2434, translated for this chapter by W. Roy Mackenzie.
23. *Ibid.*, lines 1838-1839.

If a *ceorl* and his wife have a child between them, and the *ceorl* die, let the mother have her child and feed it: let VI. shillings be given her for its fostering; a cow in summer, an ox in winter. Let the kindred take care of the *frumstol* [dwelling-house] until it be of age.[24]

An illegitimate child was not an acknowledged member of his father's sib. He had no rights of inheritance. On the other hand, if he were killed the right to collect *wer-gild* was restricted. King Ine ruled that "he who clandestinely begets a child, and conceals it, shall not have the *wer* for its death; but his lord and the king."[25] If the parents of an illegitimate child subsequently married, their action cleared up his status. Thrupp says that "when the bride and bridegroom had already a family, the children knelt between them at the marriage service under the *care-cloth,* and were supposed thereby to obtain the benefit of the nuptial benediction."[26]

Broken Homes

It appears that in early times a dissatisfied husband had the right to return his wife and thus terminate their marriage. But by the seventh century he was required to assign some ground for his action. We have already cited a law of King Aethelbert in accordance with which a man who had been deceived in the marriage contract might send his wife back to her family. This was one sort of annulment. Another sort was implied in a law of King Edmund enjoining careful examination of degrees of kinship, "lest that be afterwards divided, which before was wrongly joined."[27] The influence of the Church, as might be supposed, was brought to bear against divorce, but that compromise was necessary is indicated in some of the bishops' manuals called *Paenitentiales.* Thus we read in the nineteenth Paenitentiale of Archbishop Theodore:

24. Thorpe, *op. cit.,* Vol. 1, p. 127.
25. *Ibid.,* p. 121.
26. Thrupp, *op. cit.,* p. 61.
27. Thorpe, *op. cit.,* Vol. 1, p. 257.

If any layman dismiss his own wife and take the wife of another, let him do penance eight years . . . Whoever dismisses his own wife and takes another woman in marriage, not however the wife of another man, but a single woman or virgin, let him do penance seven years.

A man and woman being joined in matrimony, if he wishes to dismiss her and she objects, or if she wishes to dismiss him, if he is infirm, or if she is infirm, let them not be separated, except with the consent of both . . .

If a woman separate from her husband, despising him and being unwilling to return and be reconciled to him; after five years and with the consent of the bishop he may take another wife.

If anyone's wife be led into captivity by force and cannot be ransomed, after seven years he may take another. If she has been taken captive and her husband hopes to recover her, let him wait five years. Likewise the woman, if the situation be reversed. If in the meantime the man has taken another wife and the first wife later returns, let him receive her and dismiss the second woman. Likewise the wife, if the situation be reversed.[28]

This document was clearly based on the expectation of separation and remarriage. Note particularly in the second quoted paragraph that there was at least indirect acceptance of divorce by mutual consent. Other *Paenitentiales* permitted a woman to divorce her husband if he were imprisoned for crime. They allowed one spouse to dismiss the other if the first was converted while the second remained heathen, or, in case of both being Christians, if the second gave up the faith. In these ecclesiastical pronouncements we find a position taken which was undoubtedly a compromise between the wishes of the Church and the practices of the people.

From the foregoing it is plain that divorced persons were permitted to remarry, albeit with some restrictions. Naturally the same privilege was open to those whose marriage was broken by death. But curiously, from our standpoint, they were hedged about by similar regulations. We have seen that a widow sacrificed part of her estate if she remarried. Archbishop Theodore in the *Paenitentiale* just quoted made a distinction between the cases of widows and widowers.

28. *Ibid.*, Vol. 2, pp. 18-19.

If any man's wife be dead, he has the right to take another after one month. If the man is dead, the woman may take another husband after one year; but if, after one month, she is desired by some man, no crime of fornication is committed.[29]

In the eleventh century King Cnut added the authority of the State to that of the Church in the effort to delay the remarriage of widows. But while the clergy seemed eager to prevent all second marriages, the King forbade the precipitate taking of vows of permanent widowhood:

> And let every widow continue husbandless a twelve-month; let her then choose what she herself will; and if she, within the space of a year, choose a husband, then let her forfeit her *morgen-gyfu* [morning-gift] and all the posessions which she had through the first husband; and let the nearest kinsmen take the land and the possessions that she had before . . . And though she be taken forcibly, let her forfeit the possessions, unless she be willing to go home again from the man, and never again be his. And let not a widow take the veil too precipitately . . .[30]

Family Controls

It is probable that in early times marriage, divorce, sexual behavior, child rearing, and the like were controlled by the *maegth* or sib in accordance with well-established customs and traditions. But during the period which concerns us here, the sixth to the eleventh centuries, there were more and more formal laws and procedures administered by kings and their subordinates or by bishops and other ecclesiastical authorities. We have more information about the "external" than about the "internal" controls.

The laws pertaining to sex fit naturally into the system we have been describing. Extramarital and premarital intercourse was forbidden, but the penalty for violation varied with the status of the parties to the act. In general the offending man had to pay the guardian or master of the woman for

29. *Ibid.*, Vol. 2, p. 13.
30. *Ibid.*, Vol. 1, p. 417.

injury presumed to have been suffered by the other man. The following excerpts from Anglo-Saxon laws illustrate these points.

If a man lie with the king's maiden, let him pay a *bot* [compensation] of L. shillings. If she be a grinding slave, let him pay a *bot* of XXV. shillings. The third class XII. shillings . . . If a man lie with an *eorl's birele* [cup-bearer], let him make *bot* with XII. shillings . . . If a man lie with a *ceorl's birele*, let him make *bot* with VI. shillings. (Aethelbert)[31]

If a man carry off a maiden by force, let him pay L. shillings to the owner, and afterwards buy the object of his will of the owner. If she be betrothed to another man in money, let him make *bot* with XX. shillings. If she become *gaengang* [pregnant], XXXV. shillings and XV. shillings to the king (Aethelbert)[32]

If a man kill a woman with her child, while the child is in her, let him pay from the woman her full *wer-gild*, and pay for the child half a *wer-gild*, according to the wer of the father's kin . . . (Alfred)

If a man lie with the wife of a twelve-*hynde* man, let him make *bot* to the husband with one hundred and twenty shillings. To a six-*hynde* man, let him make *bot* with one hundred shillings. To a *ceorlish* man, let him make *bot* with forty shillings. (Alfred)[33]

If, during her husband's life, a woman lie with another man, and it become public, let her afterwards be for a worldly shame as regards herself, and let her lawful husband have all that she possessed; and let her then forfeit both nose and ears; and if it be a prosecution, and the *lad* [purgation or ordeal] fail, let the bishop use his power, and doom severely. (Cnut)

If a married man lie with his own maid-servant, let him forfeit her, and make *bot* for himself to God and to man; and he who has a lawful wife, and also a concubine, let no priest administer to him any of those rites which ought to be administered to a Christian man . . . (Cnut)[34]

It is interesting to observe that most of the legal penalties were imposed on the men who violated the sexual code. One wonders whether the unwritten mores were in essential agreement with the written laws or whether, as in our time, they imposed more severe penalties of disgrace on women than on men.

We have already noted some legal provision for widows, halforphans, and illegitimate children. It appears that in part

31. Thorpe, *op. cit.*, Vol. 1, p. 7.
32. *Ibid.*, p. 25.
33. *Ibid.*, pp. 67, 69.
34. *Ibid.*, p. 407.

these laws reinforced old traditions, but it is certain that in part they were new, especially those that were imposed by the Church. In the next chapter, which deals with family life in Medieval England, we shall get a more vivid picture of conflict between ancient customs, civil law, and ecclesiastical requirements.

Family Functions

In early times the functions of the Anglo-Saxon family were rather inclusive. The consanguine family or *maegth* exercised considerable control over its members and assumed considerable responsibility for them. As a group the kinsmen paid or collected *wer-gild*, carried on feuds, divided the property of deceased members, assumed guardianship over orphans, and helped each other in time of distress. The nuclear family, or marriage group, was the primary unit for making a living and rearing children. The household was definitely the center of production—raising crops and livestock, preparing food, making clothes, tools and implements. Here too most children learned the arts of farming, hunting, homemaking, and related crafts; they received instruction in morals and in the traditions of their people.

Because the marriage group was an integral part of the sib and the sib had its place in the tribe, the kinship system determined to a large degree the status of each individual. So, to sum it up, the functions of the conjugal or nuclear family were procreation, child rearing, and economic sustenance. The functions of the larger kinship group or *maegth* were chiefly in the realms of social control and mutual aid. All this was very much like the social structure and its functioning among the ancient Hebrews and the early Romans. However, the ancient Hebrew household sometimes included several nuclear families of the same generation—each consisting of a part-time husband, wife, and children. Among Hebrews, Romans, and Anglo-Saxons there were many three-generation households, functioning as single units for economic maintenance and child rearing. Among all three power and prestige seem to

have been attached to the sib rather than to the nuclear family.
But among upper-class Romans of the late Republic and the
Empire and among Christians of the first two or three centuries
the sib counted for much less, and even the nuclear family
meant less to its members than had been true in an earlier
time. The late Roman elite participated in politics, business,
sports, and other activities apart from the family; they often
sent their children out to school. The early Christians gave
first loyalty and service to the Church. But among the Anglo-
Saxons both sib and nuclear family were important social
units, each with important functions for its members and for
the larger society.

REFERENCES

Beowulf, a metrical translation into Modern English by John R.
Clark Hall. Cambridge: University Press, 1926.

Buckstaff, Florence G., "Married Women's Property in Anglo-
Saxon and Anglo-Norman Law," *Annals of the American Academy of
Political and Social Science,* IV (1893), pp. 233-264.

Hodgkin, R. H., *A History of the Anglo-Saxons.* Oxford: Clarendon Press, 1935, 2 volumes.

Howard, George E., *A History of Matrimonial Institutions.*
Chicago: University of Chicago Press, 1904, 3 volumes. Chapter VI,
"Old English Wife-Purchase Yields to Free Marriage"; Chapter VII,
"Rise of Ecclesiastical Marriage."

Robinson, Cyril E., *A History of British Progress.* New York:
Thomas Y. Crowell Company, 1928.

Thorpe, B., ed., *Ancient Laws and Institutes of England.* London:
Commissioners on the Public Records of the Kingdom, 1840, 2 volumes.

Thrupp, John, *The Anglo-Saxon Home: A History of the Domestic Institutions and Customs of England from the Fifth to the Eleventh
Century.* London: Longman, Green, Longman, and Roberts, 1862.

Wright, Thomas, *The Homes of Other Days: A History of Domestic Manners and Sentiments in England from the Earliest Known
Period to Modern Times.* London: Trubner and Company, 1871.

Zimmerman Carle C., *Family and Civilization.* New York:
Harper and Brothers, 1947.

11 The Medieval English Family—Values in Conflict

If we were to undertake a complete history of the family in Western civilization, we would have to include Germany, Scandinavia, the Latin countries, and others. But our concern now is with those cultures or cultural stages which have strongly influenced the dominant family system of contemporary United States. While many peoples besides the English have contributed to the making of our social system, the general pattern and many specific traits were largely English products. Hence, instead of turning to the continent of Europe, we proceed from the Anglo-Saxons to the Medieval English of the eleventh to the fifteenth centuries, or from the Norman Conquest to the Reformation. Now in dividing our study of family systems in England into three periods—Anglo-Saxon, Medieval, and Modern—we do not want to leave the impression that there was uniformity throughout any of these periods or that English family life underwent sudden transformations with the coming of William the Conqueror and the divorces of Henry VIII. We assume, on the contrary, that changes were always going on, usually slowly, but sometimes more rapidly, and that these can be most easily identified by taking soundings, as it were, at convenient intervals.

In the period under study in the present chapter we find, therefore, both continuities and innovations. Among the former were the semipatriarchal traditions of the Anglo-Saxons with male dominance, arranged marriages, and strong emphasis on the economic aspects of marriage and family life. In fact there developed under feudalism a very elaborate set of laws pertaining to the ownership and inheritance of property. This was bound up with the kinship system, but the sib, which meant a great deal to the Anglo-Saxons, declined in importance. However it was not the nuclear group which replaced the sib as the basic social unit, but a rather inclusive type of household. The Church, which had already begun to impose its regulations on marital affairs, extended its control during the Middle Ages.

In all of the foregoing we see clear evidence of gradual transition and modification of old patterns of family living. But the Normans brought one innovation that seemed to be a complete break with old customs and traditions—chivalry, with its code of romantic love and the glorification of women. This new culture complex might have been a serious threat to the whole established system of family life, but, for reasons which we shall see later, its immediate effects were probably very limited.

Family Structure

The Family as an Economic Institution

As in most of the cultures we have examined, the household in medieval England was an important economic unit. In rural areas its members worked together, raising crops, attending to the livestock, in fact, producing most of the articles they consumed. In towns the household of the craftsman or merchant included not only his own close of kin, but also servants, apprentices, and journeymen, all of whom worked together at the common trade or business.

Marriage itself was a matter of bargaining, as we shall see later in this chapter. Special concern was expressed over the size of dowry or dower, the ownership of property, and the payment of debts. One might almost say that the major objective in establishing a new nuclear family was the economic protection or advancement of an extended family.

Whatever property was owned was largely, if not entirely, under the control of the male head of the household. Women's property rights as defined in law were more restricted than in Anglo-Saxon times. If a woman acquired any real estate before or during marriage, it came under the complete control of her husband. The dower, which was intended to provide for her in case of widowhood, was also completely in the power of her husband. If he sold it over her protest, she could not recover it after his death. At marriage a woman's dowry and other personal property became her husband's. Theoretically he could even sell or give away her clothing, jewelry, linen, or any other chattels. He was the one to bring suit for any debts owed to her. On the other hand, he was liable for any debts incurred or wrongs committed by her before as well as during marriage. A wife could not make a contract on her own behalf, but only as her husband's agent, and this was practically restricted to the procuring of food and similar necessities. Hence it must have been difficult to secure proper maintenance from an unwilling husband. The whole matter was summed up in the reign of King John: "It is adjudged that the wife has nothing of her own while her husband lives, and can make no purchase with money of her own."[1] This suggests the old formula that "husband and wife are one person, and that person is the husband." But Pollock and Maitland deny the validity of this conception, quoting Bracton to the effect that "they are *quasi* one person . . . for the thing is the wife's own and the husband is guardian as being the head of the wife."[2]

The laws of inheritance likewise operated to keep family estates intact and under control of the head of the house. The feudal system definitely favored males and particularly eldest sons. Women were not wholly excluded, but they were clearly subordinated. By the end of the thirteenth century the common law of inheritance had taken approximately the form it

1. Frederick Pollock and Frederic W. Maitland, *The History of English Law Before the Time of Edward I* (1911), Vol. 2, p. 432. By permission of Cambridge University Press.

2. *Ibid.*, p. 406.

was to retain for six hundred years. In general this excluded spouses and ascendants and it postponed the claims of collateral relatives until there was a lack of direct descendants. In words of the jurists, if a man left an "heir of his body," no other person would inherit his real estate. Among his heirs precedence was determined by the following six rules:

Note— *Oct 4/73*

(1) A living descendant excludes his or her own descendants. (2) A dead descendant is represented by his or her own descendant. (3) Males exclude females of equal degree. (4) Among males of equal degree only the eldest inherits. (5) Females of equal degree inherit together as co-heiresses. (6) The rule that a dead descendant is represented by his or her own descendants overrides the preference for the male sex, so that a granddaughter by a dead eldest son will exclude a younger son.[3]

Failing direct heirs, the choice of collateral relatives proceeded thus: members of the first *parentela* took precedence,

- age - oldest son   - male side line
- maleness   direct side
*   inheritance*

PATRILINEAL INHERITANCE

*Parentelae as Used in Establishing Potential Inheritance**

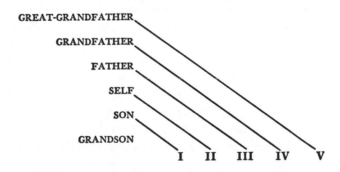

*After Pollock and Maitland, *The History of English Law*, Vol. 2, p. 297. By permission of Cambridge University Press.

3. *Ibid.*, p. 260. By permission of Cambridge University Press.

then members of the second, and so on. Now a *parentela*, as shown in the accompanying chart, is simply all those who are direct descendants of a given individual. Within each *parentela* the basic six rules applied. This would seem to be a workable system, provided genealogies were accessible and accurate, as was doubtless true of most families in a stable, rural population. But there was another complication, for everyone had two parents, four grandparents, and so on. When a male line was broken and direct heirs were lacking, there was a possibility of conflict. The rule applied here was that the heir must be related not only to the deceased but also to the person who last acquired the estate otherwise than by inheritance, that is, presumably by purchase.

From all these rules we can see that women and younger sons were usually excluded from the inheritance of real estate. Glanvill said in the twelfth century: "If any one has a son and heir, and besides him a daughter or daughters, the son succeeds to the whole . . . because in general it is true that a woman never takes part in an inheritance with a male, unless a special exception to this exist in some particular city by the ancient custom of that city."[4] Primogeniture was a natural development under feudalism. An important fief involved office as well as property, and the former was hardly divisible. At the other end of the socio-economic scale the holdings of a villein were so small and so precarious that division of them also was unacceptable. However, an exception to the system just described was found in Kent. There, according to the custom of *gavelkind*, land might be held jointly by a group of brothers or other heirs, or it might be divided among them. When a small tenement was partitioned it meant the breakup of a joint-family. Also it sometimes left each marriage group with a holding too small to provide a living. What then happened we are not sure, except that real hardship ensued.

What happened to the widow, daughters, and younger

4. Quoted by Florence G. Buckstaff in *Annals of the American Academy of Political and Social Science*, 4 (1893), p. 254.

sons of the deceased? The widow had life use of one third of her husband's real estate—but not including the main dwelling house—and one third of his personal property, also for her own lifetime without the privilege of transmission to her heirs. In the eleventh century the one third was computed on the basis of property owned when a marriage was contracted. By the thirteenth century this was changed, or permitted to be changed, to one third of a man's possessions at the time of his death. Strictly speaking, a widow did not inherit anything, but had the benefit of her dower. Daughters and younger sons might receive up to one third of their father's personal property, if so specified in his will. They were really more dependent upon the system of dowries and dowers. That is, instead of legacies, a father made wedding gifts to his children.

The Medieval Household

All this meant that there was a mingling of Anglo-Saxon and Norman traits which eventually brought about important changes in English family life. However, there is no reason to suppose that there was a sudden, drastic change in English family life after the Norman Conquest. On the contrary, it is more reasonable to suppose that most husbands and wives, parents and children, marriage groups and kinship groups carried on about as they had before. Bargaining and paternal arrangements of matches did not yield abruptly to romantic love as a basis for matrimony. Children were not quickly emancipated from parental control, nor did the responsibility of relatives for one another's conduct and welfare suddenly diminish. For the masses there was only a gradual transition.

Among the villagers social change proceeded most slowly. Many rural households continued to include a large number of persons. In what is sometimes called a stem-family there might be the *husbond,* housewife, their children, the *husbond's* widowed mother or aged and infirm father, his unmarried brothers and sisters, and servants both married and unmarried. The _husbond_ was responsible for the support of all members of this group; he directed their work; on demand he might have to produce them in court and even answer for damages they had done. Such a household was associated with "impartible inheritance," i.e., undivided estates or tenements. But in Kent and in some other parts of England, where "partible inheritance" was the rule, several brothers might inherit and jointly occupy and manage a holding. Under these circumstances several marriage groups constituted that which has been called a joint-family. Sometimes the tenement was divided among the brothers and the joint-family broke up as an economic unit. But the stem-family was much more common in medieval England than was the joint-family; hence there was usually continuity of family and landholding over long periods of time.

Among townsfolk the kinship group dropped into the background, its place in the social structure being partly taken by the gild. But the separate marriage group, as we know it, did not put in an early appearance. The urban family was no private unit. There lived and worked together in the same quarters the master with his wife and children, some of his unmarried or widowed kinsfolk, domestic servants, apprentices, and journeymen. These commonly ate at the same table, worked in the same rooms, slept in the same dormitory, joined in family prayers, and took part in the same amusements. This household was at once more inclusive than a modern city family, and more limited than a medieval rural kinship group.

Likewise the nobleman's menage included a group of servants and retainers much larger than his immediate family, but smaller than a so-called clan—more correctly, sib. Both in town and in castle the household was based less on kinship than on function. One's place in the group depended more on the services he rendered than on his blood relationships. However, we must be careful not to exaggerate the amount of shifting from kinship to contact, and from inherited status to a nexus of economic and military ties. Basic social structures have a way of changing slowly, and there is no evidence that this was a period of rapid and dramatic metamorphoses.

Unmarried adults were probably less numerous than in our day and more numerous than in Anglo-Saxon times. Large numbers, especially women from the upper classes, found places in religious houses. Daughters of villeins were more likely to secure employment at agricultural labor or domestic service. Some of them apparently succeeded to their fathers' "tenements" and rendered the same services for them that sons would have performed. One author maintains that there was a low sex ratio (excess of females) and hence a considerable number of spinsters.[5] During this period, in which most women had very limited rights before the law, unmarried women "of full age" were "fully competent persons" for all the purposes of private law; they could even sue and be sued.

Presumably most aged, crippled, blind, feebleminded, and other handicapped persons were cared for by kinsmen, but in the towns religious orders, gilds, wealthy individuals, and sometimes municipal governments established institutions called hospitals. These were really almshouses rather than medical institutions, since they housed miscellaneous collections of miserable persons who had somehow become detached from their kinship groups. While one of the principal motives behind these institutions was undoubtedly the religious merit of almsgiving—salvation of the donor's soul—their establishment is at least circumstantial evidence of the partial disintegration of some kinship groups. The statutes of laborers adopted in the fourteenth century provide additional indirect evidence on this point.[6]

Chivalry

The outstanding innovation which followed the Norman Conquest was a cultural borrowing from the Continent called chivalry. It has been variously defined as "tenure by military

5. Eileen Power, "The Position of Women," in C. G. Crump and E. F. Jacobs, eds., *The Legacy of the Middle Ages* (1926), pp. 410-411.

6. Stuart A. Queen, *Social Work in the Light of History* (1922), pp. 168-169.

service," "a combination of war, religion, and gallantry," and "the whole knightly system of the later middle ages, with its peculiar religious, moral, and social codes and customs."[7] We may properly regard it as a culture complex which overlapped but was not identical with feudalism. It included the folkways and mores of the social class made up of knights and ladies. It contained a literary element contributed by poets, singers, and others. All this is generally believed to have developed first in southern France, whence it spread to other parts of Europe and, in the seventh century, to England.

Knights of the early Norman period are described as purely feudal personages, holding land on conditions of rendering military service, owing certain other services and dues to their lords. Evidently they were not loved by the rest of the population. They were feared and their activities were resented by the common people, the clergy, and the king. Plain folks regarded them as privileged bandits; the clergy found them greedy and aggressive; the king discovered that they were inefficient soldiers and constant troublemakers. These eleventh- and twelfth-century knights were not suddenly transformed into Christian gentlemen, but gradually changes took place in their character. The influence of the Church and the experiences of the Crusades, coupled with the growing amenities of manor house and castle, helped to tame these militant, feudal barbarians. Consequently, their reputation, as it was passed on to later centuries, credited them with remarkable qualities. They were supposed to possess the military virtues of courage and loyalty, the religious virtues of faith, piety, and obedience, the "social" virtues of courtesy, compassion for the weak and oppressed, generosity, and self-sacrifice. No doubt these qualities were actually found in varying degrees and combinations in individual knights. But their courage was associated with love of adventure and the glorification of war. Their religion was apt to be a mere formality. Their courtesy was for ladies of the castles, not for

7. E. Prestage, ed., *Chivalry* (1928), p. 2.

women of the cottages. Their faithfulness, veracity, and chastity were often notably absent. As we shall see, lovemaking became for them a major sport, and this often meant making love to another man's wife, deceiving her husband, and changing mistresses despite the swearing of eternal fidelity to each.

There developed during this period a literature which defined the code of chivalry and glorified the conduct of "true" knights. Most of the earliest romances were in French. Later some of these were translated and adapted. Thus Chaucer translated the *Romance of the Rose*. In this the hero gives himself to the service of the god of love, saying:

> My lyf, my deth, is in your honde,
> I may not laste out of you bonde.

"He must leave villainy and avoid speaking evil and words of ribaldry and he is enjoined to be the first to salute whom he meets; to serve and praise all women; to defend their good names and endeavor to please them that they may be well disposed toward him. He is warned against pride:

> For pryde is founde, in every part,
> Contrarie unto Loves Art.

"He should dress well, be merry and joyful as possible, accomplished in riding, arms, singing, playing on instruments, dancing, and in making songs and complaints for his lady's sake so she would pity his pain. He was counseled to be generous in giving and spending . . . and above all else is stressed the importance of constancy."[8]

In Chaucer's *Compleynt of Venus* are described some of the trials of a medieval lover. We are told that 'it is fitting that love should pay dearly for what love gives; lovers must

8. Katherine F. Kramer, "A Contrast of the Ideals of Love in Medieval and Elizabethan Literature," The Ohio State University, unpublished Master's thesis (1929), p. 9.

wake when they should sleep, fast when they should eat, weep instead of laugh, complain instead of sing, cast down their visages and often change color, complain in their sleep and dream at the dance, 'al the revers of any glad feeling.' "[9]

In general, the lovers of these medieval stories were not spouses. In the *Morte d'Arthur*, compiled about 1470 by Sir Arthur Malory, we see the typical adulteries—for example, that of Lancelot with Guinevere. But in the earlier story of Geraint and Enid the lovers were married. In John Gower's *Confessio Amantis*, written about 1390, the love of paramours was condemned as a source of trouble.

In the later Middle Ages there were numerous "courtesy books" which set forth didactically or in story form the rules of etiquette to be followed by knights. One such was the *Book of the Order of Chivalry*, written in Spanish in the thirteenth century and translated into English in the fifteenth. In the sixteenth century appeared a work of this kind called *The Court of Love*.

As already stated, the pattern of chivalry was a cultural borrowing from France. Yet it took root in England and came to represent the ideals at least of the upper classes. To some extent the literature from the eleventh to the fourteenth century constituted a foreign influence on English mores of sex and marriage, to some extent it reflected the actual customs and codes of English knights and ladies and to some extent, as in every literature, it was an escape from the routine of everyday living into a dream world of adventure and romance. We have no means of knowing how much weight to attach to each of these aspects. But we are disposed to regard chivalry as a challenge to the ecclesiastical attitude toward sex and a threat to marital stability. At the same time it glorified romantic love which, several centuries later, was to become the approved and expected gateway to marriage.

9. *Ibid.*, p. 26.

The Family Cycle

Marital Selection

Courtly love, which was played up in the literature of
chivalry, had little to do with marital selection in any social
class. Marriages were usually arranged by parents, overlords,
and patrons on a basis that to us smacks more strongly of
commercialism than of romance. We read, for example, of
William Molynes, who had the option of purchasing a piece
of real estate. But he was short of funds and in danger of losing the property unless he acted promptly. So he made an
agreement with a London merchant that his son should
marry the merchant's daughter as soon as they became of age.
In return William Molynes was to obtain the money needed
to buy the piece of land.[10] In the Paston Letters discussion of
prospective marriages included little or no concern for the
affections or happiness of the intended bride and groom. The
writers spoke of "dealing," "inspecting evidences," and making sure that the property "stands clear."

However, we would be guilty of misrepresentation if we
described these marital agreements as entirely mercenary in
character. The feudal lord was concerned that his lands be
held by men capable of bearing arms and rendering other
services required by the system. Even humble parents were
eager for their daughters to have dowries that would attract
suitable husbands, and it was important that the sons secure
wives who would bring goods or lands useful in establishing
the new conjugal family on an acceptable basis. Also it was
considered essential that a husband provide a dower for his
wife in case he should leave her a widow. All this had more
to do with security than with avarice and, while personal
attraction had little place in marital selection, exploitation
was probably not general. Outright buying and selling of

10. H. S. Bennett, *The Pastons and Their England* (1922), p. 28.

spouses had certainly disappeared. But impoverished knights sometimes married the daughters of well-to-do townsmen, trading title and social position for a rich dowry. Also noblemen sometimes profited financially when arranging marriages for their female wards. In some cases the objective was a "wedding of fiefs" or estates, in which "the woman went with the land." Thus matrimony and economics were closely interrelated.

This matrimonial bargaining sometimes involved children of very tender ages, and the practice was long continued; for Coke, writing about 1600, said that a nine-year-old widow should have her dower, "of what age soever her husband be, albeit he were but four years old."[11] Before the end of the Middle Ages a child of seven was held to be capable of making a marriage agreement. Such a marriage could be annulled while either of the parties was below the age at which it could be consummated, the presumptive age of consummation being fourteen for boys and twelve for girls.

Over against these coldly calculated arrangements we must set occasional love matches. Thus Margery Paston loved and married her brother's chief bailiff despite violent opposition from her kinsmen, and young John Paston wooed Margery Brews with little interference except from parental wrangling over financial details.[12] But cases like these seem to have been the exception rather than the rule.

Once a preference was expressed by a young person, or more commonly by his father or guardian, it was important to see that forbidden degrees had been avoided and that prescribed ceremonial was carried out. Marital selection in medieval England was a matter of clever bargaining and formal routines, in contrast to the romantic adventure it has become in modern England and America.

11. Quoted by Pollock and Maitland, *op. cit.*, Vol. 2, p. 391. Cambridge University Press.
12. Bennett, *op. cit.*, p. 46.

Relations of Men and Women

In the preceding sections we have described chiefly the institutional aspects of marriage and family organization in medieval England. We have reviewed the formalities which were involved in contracting a marriage. We have noted the emphasis on economic aspects of the family. We have found evidence of conflict between the Anglo-Saxon tradition, the canon law, and the code of chivalry. But we have been unable to offer more than fleeting glimpses of the actual feelings and behavior of men and women toward each other.

We have not been aided much by the tradition of courtly love, for it pertained exclusively to the feudal nobility. Moreover, not even the knights and ladies occupied consistent positions in relation to each other. Along with glorification of romance went legal subordination of wives and daughters. Courtly love was formalized, extramarital, and upper class.

The Church, too, offered inconsistent ideologies. Woman was at once the wife of Adam and the mother of Christ. In the first role she was a temptress, an "instrument of the devil," and grossly inferior to man. In the second she was pure and undefiled, an advocate and mediator for sinning mortals. Thus were chivalric and ascetic elements mixed, leaving the English lady "oscillating between a pit and a pedestal."

Among the townsfolk and peasants there was theoretical subjection, but actually a considerable degree of "rough and ready equality." These "hard-working and reasonably docile wives" shared work and responsibility with their husbands, rearing children, managing households, even carrying on agriculture, trades, and crafts.

When we come to sex, in the limited meaning of the term, we have the lively tales of knights and ladies, the stern condemnation of the Church, and practically no information about the actual behavior of ordinary husbands and wives.

In general the position of the Church was that all sexual desire was evil and that passionate love was to be condemned. Even between husband and wife such impulses were regarded

women - nasty
- inferior
but have to be taken care of.

as sinful. *Omnis ardentior amator propriae uxoris adulter est,* wrote Peter the Lombard in the twelfth century. Of course the sexual act itself, when performed by husband and wife, was "excused" by the desire for offspring, but any other satisfaction derived from *copula carnalis* was wicked. Hence the use of contraceptives was obviously evil, because they could have no other purpose than to facilitate the enjoyment of sex without helping to perpetuate the species. Churchmen quoted St. Thomas Aquinas: "In so far as the generation of offspring is impeded, it is a vice against nature which happens in every carnal act from which generation cannot follow."[13] Violation of the sexual code in any respect was a religious offense to be dealt with by ecclesiastical courts rather than an ordinary crime to be handled by civil courts.

Over against these ecclesiastical views was the ideology of chivalry, in which love was all important, surpassing marriage and procreation. But on one point religious teachings, the code of chivalry, and popular mores agreed: marriage was a duty rather than a pleasure. Marriages should be properly planned for the good of the order, due consideration being given to property, social status, and procreation. But chivalry not only accepted marriage without love, it went on to exalt love without marriage. Now it is interesting to observe some differences between medieval courtly love and the relations with *hetaerae* in ancient Athens. The Athenian gentleman entered into wedlock as a matter of duty, but found sexual pleasure and feminine companionship outside the family. His wife, however, was supposed to remain faithful to him that the legitimacy of offspring might be unquestioned. Under chivalry both husband and wife had opportunities for love-making outside the drab relationship of marriage. In fact one might almost say that chivalry reversed the Athenian scheme, giving wives the special privilege of entertaining unmarried knights and singers. The general position was that love should

13. Quoted by Norman E. Himes, *Medical History of Contraception* (1936), p. 167. By permission of Williams and Wilkins Company.

be a free gift, especially a lady's love. The very fact that in marriage she was compelled to accept sexual union destroyed the real value of this experience and threatened her dignity. Even if it were her lover whom she married, she thereby extinguished love. Hence she might well let her father or lord select a husband and devote her attention to the choice of a lover.

We cannot help wondering—and we cannot possibly discover—what proportion of men and women lived according to the code of chivalry, what proportion followed the teachings of the Church, how many found sexual satisfaction in marriage, and how many suffered mental conflicts because of diverse ideologies and practices. Our guesses—and, unhappily, that is all we can offer at this point—are that the pattern of chivalry was followed by a small minority, that the Church's doctrines of sex influenced the masses superficially, that only a few were troubled by conflicting ideas and sentiments, and that the great majority mated in a matter-of-fact way.

As to the other phases of married life we are similarly lacking in information. We know that some men beat their wives with staves or fists, while others displayed tender solicitude. In general we get the impression that most spouses were satisfied with their mates and the pattern of their relationships. After all, as has been pointed out repeatedly, marriage was a duty, not a pleasure; mates were "properly" selected by parents; male dominance was perfectly "natural."

Children

If the family life of adults was uninspiring, that of children must have been depressing. At least that is the impression drawn from the literature that has come down to us.

The number of births in a medieval English family was often large, but infant mortality also was high, so that only three or four out of a dozen or fifteen were likely to reach maturity. This situation has been described as a "melancholy procession of cradles and coffins." In the twentieth century this might have produced strong sentimental attachments between the surviving children and their parents. But in the Middle Ages we suspect that this was taken pretty much for granted and that it did little to cement parent-child relations. Undoubtedly there was affection between mothers and infants. But as the complete dependence and the intimacy of baby-hood tapered off and were replaced by the noisy, mischievous play of later childhood, the repressive code of that era must have come between the youngsters and their mothers. Toward their fathers, children were taught to behave with such formal-ity and awe that the familiarity we often experience in the twentieth century was unthinkable in the Middle Ages.

For the masses of simple country folk life was hard; chil-dren had to help with the work and share the meager priv-ileges of their parents. In the towns boys were commonly apprenticed at an early age to live, work, and learn a trade in a stranger's house. Sons and daughters of the nobility, too, were frequently sent away to be trained in the homes of others. In keeping with the economic motivation behind many arranged marriages the effort was frequently made to place a son or daughter in the household of some nobleman or rich patron, with the hope of eventually promoting a profitable match. So common was this practice of placing-out that there was sometimes gossip about a boy or girl not placed in a foster home. An Italian visitor to England in the late fifteenth cen-tury was strongly impressed by the custom of separating chil-dren from their parents. Perhaps his statement is an exaggera-tion of the facts and perhaps his inferences are not entirely warranted. But at all events they represent the observations of an outsider at the end of the Middle Ages:

The want of affection in the English is strongly manifested toward their children; for after having kept them at home till they arrive at the age of 7 or 9 years at the utmost, they put them out, both males and females, to hard service in the houses of other people, binding them generally for another 7 or 9 years. And these are called apprentices, and during that time they perform all the most menial offices; and few are born who are exempted from this fate, for every one, however rich he may be, sends away his children into the houses of others, whilst he, in return, receives those of strangers into his own. And on inquiring their reason for this severity, they answered that they did it in order that their children might learn better manners. But I, for my part, believe that they do it because they like to enjoy all their comforts themselves, and that they are better served by strangers than they would be by their own children . . . If the English sent their children away from home to learn virtue and good manners, and took them back again when their apprenticeship was over, they might, perhaps be excused; but they never return, for the girls are settled by their patrons, and the boys make the best marriages they can, and, assisted by their patrons, not by their fathers, they also open a house and strive diligently by this means to make some fortune for themselves.[14]

It is reasonable to suppose that, under such conditions as we have described, discipline was severe. How much distinction was made between treatment of one's own children who happen to remain at home and apprentices or pages or maids we do not know. Probably all were expected to render instant obedience and servile respect. "The didactic books of manners and morals which became popular during the fifteenth century enjoin children to rise early, wash and dress and then seek out their parents to kneel and humbly ask their blessing."[15] The reference to parents makes us wonder whether the rules were only for younger children still at home or also for older children living with masters and patrons.

The education of a future knight commonly involved spending about seven years as a page in the castle of his father's feudal lord. During this time he was instructed by the women in menial duties of various kinds and in "the rudiments of love." At the age of fourteen he usually became a squire and was taught the care of arms and horses, hunting, music, poetry, and such games as chess and backgammon. Meanwhile his sister studied some manual of etiquette,

14. Charlotte A. Sneyd, translator, *A Relation, or Rather a True Account, of the Island of England, about the Year 1500* (1847), pp. 24-26.

15. Willystine Goodsell, *A History of Marriage and the Family* (1934), p. 243.

learned to sew and embroider, and perhaps acquired some skill as a nurse. The future artisan or merchant was apprenticed at an early age and spent long hours in shop or counting house, serving his master and learning a trade or business. But the great majority of children lived with their parents in simple, rural homes. Their education consisted largely in learning by doing, in helping and imitating their parents in house, and field, and pasture.

Thus they were prepared to renew the cycle by founding families of their own. The eldest son, or another, if designated as heir, worked very closely with his father and sometimes took charge of the "tenement" or "estate" upon the father's retirement. In such case the elders were likely to occupy a room at one end of the house, while they ate with the rest of the household and engaged in such activities as their strength permitted.

Family Controls

We have seen that among the Anglo-Saxons, as among the Hebrews, Romans, and many other peoples, marriage was usually contracted on the basis of "collective bargaining" between kinship groups or their respective heads. In like manner, divorce, sexual behavior, child rearing, and other family matters were pretty much under control of the *maegth* or sib. During the period we have called Anglo-Saxon these controls were being worn away by state and church, but there were many compromises with the old customs. However, after the Norman Conquest, the sib yielded more and more to pressures from the feudal system and the Church. In their zeal to convert and direct the peoples of northern Europe, leaders of the Church, like those of other effective revolutionary groups, sensed a need to overthrow the strong family and sib organizations, which were appropriately viewed as bulwarks of the old regime. Specifically into England there came with William the Conqueror Norman churchmen trained in Roman and canon law. These newcomers replaced many of the native bishops. They also implemented the Church's determination to gain control over the sex life of the laity as well as of the clergy. They laid down rules concerning marriage and divorce, forbidden degrees, legitimacy, second marriages, sex relations, and the like. Since some of these regulations were strange to the people of England and some were even in conflict with their customs, there ensued a period of doubt and confusion.

First of all, there appears to have been considerable confusion as to the degrees of kinship and affinity within which marriage was prohibited. Certain rulings were to the effect that spouses must not be nearer than the seventh degree, but in 1215 Pope Innocent III specified the fourth degree. Affinity was sometimes interpreted in an extreme fashion. It might include the kinsmen of one's spouse to the fourth or seventh degree, and the spouses of the spouse's kinsmen to the same degree. Similar complications were encountered in regard to spiritual affinity—godfather and goddaughter, and their kinsmen to the seventh or fourth degree. Moreover, there were various ways of computing the degrees of kinship and affinity. One might count the acts of generation between the persons. On this basis father and daughter represented the first degree, brother and sister the second, uncle and niece the third, first-cousins the fourth degree, and so on. A different method was to rank persons from the standpoint of their common ancestor. On this basis his children were kinsmen of the first degree, his grandchildren of the second, and so on. "It was long before the Church established a uniform fashion of interpreting her own prohibitions, the so-called 'canonical computation.' "[16]

There was also confusion as to the amount and kind of ceremonial essential to a legally binding marriage. But the Church sought to impose regulations which would bring order out of chaos and, incidentally, increase its own power. Thus a

16. Pollock and Maitland, *op. cit.*, Vol. 2, p. 386. By permission of Cambridge University Press.

"constitution" of the late eleventh century ordained that without a priest's benediction "the marriage shall not be deemed legitimate, but as fornication."[17] Archbishop Walter in 1200 required the publication of banns three times in church and public solemnization "in face of the church." Some of the problems involved and the position of the Church in the twelfth century were set forth in the famous ruling of Pope Alexander III in his letter to the Bishop of Norwich.

> We understand from your letter that a certain man and woman at the command of their lord mutually received each other, no priest being present, and no such ceremony being performed as the English church is wont to employ, and then that before any physicial union, another man solemnly married the said women and knew her. We answer that if the first man and the woman received each other by mutual consent directed to time present, saying the one to the other, "I receive you as mine," . . . then, albeit there was no such ceremony as aforesaid, and albeit there was no carnal knowledge, the woman ought to be restored to the first man, for after such a consent she could not and ought not to marry another. If, however, there was no such consent by such words as aforesaid, and no sexual union preceded by a consent *de futuro,* then the woman must be left to the second man who subsequently received her and knew her, and she must be absolved from the suit of the first man; and if he has given faith or sworn an oath [to marry the woman], then a penance must be set him for the breach of his faith or of his oath.[18]

From such documents as this we infer that some marriages were entered into practically without any ceremony whatsoever. A man and a woman simply agreed to take each other as husband and wife (not, however, without control by their feudal lords or parents). But there was one troublesome technicality: if they plighted their troth in words of the present tense (*per verba de praesenti*), the agreement was held to be binding even if there were no witnesses. However, if they used the future tense (*per verba de futuro*), it was not binding

17. George E. Howard, *A History of Matrimonial Institutions* (1904), Vol. 1, p. 313. By permission of the University of Chicago Press.

18. Pollock and Maitland, *op. cit.,* Vol. 2, p. 371. By permission of Cambridge University Press.

unless the promise was followed by intercourse (*copula carnalis*). These rules afforded a potential escape from parental and feudal control, opening the way to actual freedom of choice by the persons immediately concerned. They also invited confusion and controversy involving questions of dower, legitimacy, and inheritance.

In its effort to bring the whole matter under control the Church pressed more and more for the participation of a priest in every wedding, declaring marriage to be one of the seven sacraments. Bracton in the thirteenth century held that no woman could claim her dower unless she had been endowed at the church door. The purpose he had in mind was apparently not to insist on a religious rite so much as to secure publicity for the establishment of propery rights. In any case there were two issues at stake: first, whether marriage should be public and subject to regulation; second, whether that regulation should be ecclesistical or civil. In the Middle Ages the Church held the upper hand, but it was unable to enforce it rules on everyone in England. Hence the Church was in a dilemma. It wanted to require a religious ceremony as a basis of binding matrimony. But there were so many marriages without benefit of clergy that the Church hesitated to declare the children of such unions illegitimate. Hence it held that marriages contracted without knowledge of the Church were "illegal but not invalid." This meant that they were penalized but not voided. Such marriages were called "clandestine" and were of three grades: first, those which were absolutely secret and hence could not be proved; second, valid and provable marriages not solemnized by a priest at the church door (*in facie ecclesiae*); third, marriages so solemnized but without preceding publication of the banns.

The Church sought not only to regulate who might contract marriages and how, but also to specify the circumstances under which "putative marriages" might be liquidated. While divorce as we conceive it was definitely forbidden, and hence a valid marriage could rarely be dissolved, the forbidden degrees (*impedimenta dirimentia*) and espousals in the future tense (*verba de futuro*) could be used to secure annulment (*divortium a vinculo matrimonii*). Because of the involved and hazy rules about consanguinity and affinity there must have been a good many persons who innocently married within the forbidden degrees. Others no doubt ignored the prohibitions in order to secure a desired mate. If later marital conflict developed, it was possible for such persons, assuming the necessary wealth and influence, to secure a decision from an ecclesiastical court to the effect that no true marriage had existed. If domestic discord became serious in cases where no *impedimenta* could be demonstrated, the court could pronounce a judicial separation (*divortium a mensa et toro*), ordering the couple to live apart, but not freeing either party to remarry. One other possibility of escape from unwanted matrimony was available to a few. If the marriage had not been consummated, either party might be released by entering a religious order. Thus while the front door of divorce was closed, the back door of annulment and the side doors of judicial separation an religion provided exits for those who knew how to use them. Such a situation must have invited the use of subterfuge and bribery. Indeed it is alleged that annullment became a thriving business. Undoubtedly there was a great deal of compromising, rationalization, and commercialization in the handling of marital conflict. But for obvious reasons legal indirection must have been employed mainly by members of the upper classes. It is doubtful if marriage was often dissolved among the common people.

The general position of the Church was, as we have noted, to prohibit all sexual relations between men and women "unless excused by matrimony." By the end of the thirteenth century the Church had forced recognition of its jurisdiction over fornication and adultery. However, the civil courts actually continued to punish some sex offenses. The ecclesiastical courts employed a kind of forced confession, or self-accusation, that appears to have resembled a procedure employed in Soviet Russia. They also used the medieval procedure called compurgation. If found guilty, a man or woman might be punished in various ways, such as walking barefooted and bareheaded, clad only in a sheet, in a church, market, or other public place, while proclaiming his or her sin. Other penalties were "suspension," i.e., denial of the right to attend church, occasionally excommunication, or making a pilgrimage. A couple might be forced to get married if both parties were single. Under various circumstances these penalties might be commuted by payments of money, a policy which resembled one of early Anglo-Saxon law.

Family Functions

We have seen in this chapter evidence of changing functions in conjugal or nuclear families and in sibs or *maegth*. Perhaps the nuclear family, as distinguished from household and sib, was most significant for younger sons and others who left the parental home to make a fresh start in towns. We refer, of course, to the new nuclear or conjugal group established by their marriage (sometimes called family of procreation), and not to the nuclear family of which they were a part in childhood (sometimes called family of orientation). Being physically detached from kinsmen, they might assume responsibilities and direct their lives with a measure of independence. But it appears that young men who left their rural homes in search of livelihood and adventure often wound up as part of some urban household in the roles of apprentices or journeymen. Otherwise, they might enter the armed forces, the merchant marine, or maybe the Church. In such cases the family was even less significant for them. Its functions were reduced to the vanishing point.

We have noted the transfer of some functions from one social institution to another. For the nuclear family procreation continued to be a major function. But economic maintenance, child rearing, training, and discipline belonged to the household, of which the conjugal family was the nucleus, but which also included unmarried and widowed kinsmen, apprentices, pages, servants, and sometimes others. For the upper classes chivalry identified love more with adultery than with marriage. Status was conferred more often by the feudal system than by kinship group. Social control was largely taken over from the *maegth* by the Church and the feudal system. So we find the Middle Ages in England not at all static and stable, but a period of important changes in the allocation, if we may call it that, of functions previously associated with the family.

REFERENCES

Abram, A., *English Life and Manners in the Later Middle Ages.* New York: E. P. Dutton and Company, 1913, Chapter IV, "The Position of Women"; Chapter X, "Family Life."

Bennett, H. S., *The Pastons and Their England.* Cambridge: Cambridge University Press, 1922.

Buckstaff, Florence G., "Married Women's Property in Anglo-Saxon and Anglo-Norman Law," *Annals of the American Academy of Political and Social Science,* IV (1893), pp. 233-264.

Chaucer, Geoffrey, *Canterbury Tales.* See any convenient translation into modern English.

Dodd, William G., *Courtly Love in Chaucer and Gower.* Boston: Ginn and Company, 1913.

Gairdner, James, ed.. *The Paston Letters, 1422-1509.* London: E. Arber, 1872-1875, 3 volumes.

Goodsell, Willystine, *A History of Marriage and the Family.* New York: Macmillan Company, 1934.

Himes, Norman E., *Medical History of Contraception.* Baltimore: Williams and Wilkins Company, 1936.

Homans, George C., *English Villagers of the Thirteenth Century.* Cambridge: Harvard University Press, 1941, Book II, "Families."

Howard, George E., "Rise of Ecclesiastical Marriage," *A History of Matrimonial Institutions.* Chicago: University of Chicago Press, 1904, 3 volumes, Chapters VII and VIII.

Kramer, Katherine E., "A Contrast of the Ideals of Love in Medieval and Elizabethan Literature," unpublished Master's thesis. The Ohio State University, 1929.

Pollock, Frederick, and Maitland, Frederic William, *The History of English Law Before the Time of Edward I*. Cambridge: Cambridge University Press, 1911, Volume II, Chapter VI, "Inheritance"; Chapter VII, "Family Law."

Power, Eileen, "The Position of Woman." in C. G. Crump and E. F. Jacobs, eds., *The Legacy of the Middle Ages*. Oxford: The Clarendon Press, 1926.

Prestage, Edgar, ed., *Chivalry*. New York: A. A. Knopf, Inc. 1928.

Putnam, Emily James, "The Lady of the Castle," *The Lady*. New York: Sturgis and Walton, 1910, Chapter IV.

Queen, Stuart A., *Social Work in the Light of History*. Philadelphia: J. B. Lippincott Company, 1922.

Sneyd, Charlotte A., translator, *A Relation, or Rather a True Account, of the Island of England about the year 1500*. London: J. B. Nichols and Son, 1847.

12 The Later English Family —Romantic Love and a Power Struggle

Between the late Middle Ages, as described in the preceding chapter, and the early modern period, which we are about to present, there was no sharp break. Gradually feudalism and chivalry gave way, but the class system which dominated England from Henry VIII to Victoria was much like that which preceded. At the top was the nobility. Next came gentlemen who could "live idly and without manual labor." On the third level were burgesses and yeomen. Burgesses were relatively prosperous trades people and master craftsmen who held town offices and served on juries. Yeomen were small land owners and independent farmers. Below them were petty traders, ordinary craftsmen, farm tenants, and day laborers, "folk of the meanest class," who had no share in the government. This stratification grew naturally and gradually out of that of the Middle Ages. But there were other aspects of English life in which greater and more rapid changes occurred. Among the more significant innovations were Humanism, Protestantism, and Colonial Imperialism.

Humanism involved a redirection of intellectual interests from medieval scholasticism to Latin and Greek classics, from theology to "human interest" stories. In time it yielded a growing literature in the vernacular, the language of the common people. With the invention of printing and the expansion of formal schooling the new literature reached increasing numbers of people. Some of the new publications dealt with problems of marriage, divorce, and the training of children. Hence we may assume, first, that people were beginning to think for themselves about such matters instead of leaving them to lawyers and the clergy and, second, that the books and pamphlets stimulated such thinking.

The Protestant Revolt was at first less a matter of ideology, doctrine, and principle in England than in Germany. But even the Anglican Church gradually widened the breach with Rome, and presently the Puritans and other Dissenters developed still more divergent beliefs and practices. The continued presence in England of Catholics, Anglicans, and Dissenters kept religious controversy alive and added to the confusion of preceding centuries concerning marriage and divorce.

During this period the English common law was taking shape. Cases brought before the courts had long been settled without clear precedents or explicit legislation, on the basis of folkways and mores. Gradually there was an accumulation of court decisions and parliamentary statutes, which were eventually systematized by justices and lawyers such as Coke and Blackstone. In the common law men were recognized as the responsible heads of families, administering property, providing support, accountable for torts by members of their families, and making important decisions within the home.

Finally, the sixteenth, seventeenth, and eighteenth were centuries of exploration and colonization, of expanding horizons, of growing commerce, of enlarged economic opportunity, and of empire building. The increased wealth, the development of town life, the growth of London into a great metropolis, and the strengthening of the central government contributed to other cultural changes including the structure of family life. Those who were restless or discouraged over prospects in the place of their birth were no longer bound to the land. They often went to the city or to one of the colonies where they could start life anew. In these new surroundings they were relatively free from the traditional controls of kinsmen and patrons. There was at least a possibility of marriage as an independent adventure and of new conjugal groups developing new patterns of behavior and organization. Word of such happenings was bound to get back to the home community and further stimulate dissatisfaction with a marriage system controlled by kinsmen and patrons, spurring revolt.

Family Structure

Decline of the Sib

On the whole English families continued to display a semipatriarchal character. Men were dominant, but wives were increasingly treated as partners and friends. Here and there protests were made against the superior privileges of men. In the upper classes the formality of chivalry gave way to the formality of Platonic love. In all classes most marriages were arranged, but some were the outgrowth of romantic love. The patriarchal character was most evident in the households of large landowners, where the heads of the families ruled over kinsmen and servants, sometimes numbering 100. But the man of the house also exercised authority in humbler rural homes and in urban households. A master craftsman ruled over his wife and children, his servants, apprentices and journeymen. Everyone in the household was busy—men, women, and children. There were few pampered youths or idle ladies. Children continued to be apprenticed, to be placed out to learn manners, or to grow up at home, depending upon their social class. But slowly increasing numbers attended schools outside their homes.

In keeping with the continued economic emphasis in the English family, laws and customs of inheritance changed very little during the sixteenth, seventeenth, and eighteenth centuries. Male heirs continued to take precedence over female, and oldest sons over their younger brothers. Especially among the landed gentry and nobility the custom of entail, i.e., primogeniture in respect to real estate, provided a stimulus to younger sons. Knowing that the estate would go to their oldest brother, they often prepared themselves for some profession, the civil service, or the army. The heir, on the other hand, lacking any incentive to "get out and hustle," was often said to be "untaught and good for nothing." Hence the natural conservatism of propertied and titled folk was doubtless strengthened. The young men who were forced to make places for themselves found many opportunities in the colonies, in foreign trade, and in governmental offices in London. As to the lower classes, there was so little to inherit that the issue was unimportant. Following the "enclosures" of the fifteenth and eighteenth centuries there were fewer feudal tenants and more landless laborers.

With the breakup of feudal society, the growth of towns, and the increased mobility of the population there were evidently increased numbers of persons detached from their kinsmen. These included "sturdy rogues" and "vagabonds" who might in fact be dispossessed farm tenants, discharged soldiers, minstrels, begging "scholars," petty chapmen or peddlers, undisguised mendicants, and outlaws. The monasteries and "hospitals" to which they had formerly turned in time of need had largely been taken away from the religious orders. Hence the care of "indigents" was held by law to be responsibility first of kinsmen, then of the parish in which they had a legal residence. The Poor Laws from 1597 on made the support of his dependent parents, children, grandparents, and grandchildren obligatory on anyone able to provide for them, thus clearly continuing the tradition of an earlier period. At the same time enactment of these laws was a tacit admission that the ties between kinsmen were weakening.

We have already noted some of the factors that contributed to the decline of the larger kinship groups. Among these were "enclosures" of farm land, separation of tenants from the land, migration to towns and to the colonies, and employment as individuals. Less often than in earlier centuries could sons of tenants expect to succeed their fathers. Landless folks had little to pass on to their children. But those who did have property, personal or real, rural or urban, increasingly disposed of it by wills instead of trusting to custom. Through these and other developments of the early modern period the sib ceased to be significant and the extended family lost some of its importance. The actually functioning unit was the household built around the nuclear family.

Status and Role of Women

As in the Middle Ages, women continued to be legally subordinate to men. However, in actual practice there was a good deal of the "rough and ready" comradeship and partnership mentioned in the preceding chapter. Moreover, as we shall presently note, there were increasing numbers of cases in which romantic love was associated with marriage. The pseudoworship of women which belonged to chivalry gave way to more nearly equalitarian friendship, sometimes referred to as Platonic love. Finally, the seventeenth and eighteenth centuries witnessed formal protests against the subordination of women.

However, masculine dominance did not easily give way to equalitarianism. Writing in 1631, Richard Brathwayte advised women to confine their discourse to "household affairs and other private employments." They were to avoid "state-matters" and "controversies of the Church."[1] Fifty years later Lord Halifax went into much greater detail about the "weaker sex" and the "reasonableness of masculine dominion."

> You must first lay it down for a foundation in general, that there is inequality in the sexes, and that for the better economy of the world, the men, who were to be the law givers, had the larger share of reason bestowed upon them, by which means your sex is the better prepared for the compliance that is necessary for the better performance of those duties which seem to be most properly assigned to it. This looks a little uncourtly at the first appearance, but upon examination it will be found that Nature is so far from being unjust to you that she is partial on your side. She hath made you such large amends by other advantages, for the seeming injustice of the first distribution, that the right of complaining is come over to our sex; you have it in your power not only to free yourselves, but to subdue your masters, and without violence throw both their natural and legal authority at your feet. We are made of different tempers, that our defects might be mutually supplied. Your sex wanteth our reason for your conduct, and our strength for your protection: ours wanteth your gentleness to soften and to entertain us.[2]

1. Florence M. Smith, *Mary Astell* (1916), pp. 38-39.
2. H. C. Foxcroft, *The Life and Letters of George Saville*, (1898), Vol. 2, p. 394. By permission of Longmans, Green and Company, Inc.

The Ladies Calling, an anonymous pamphlet apparently written by a man about 1700, urged women to study "the art of economy and household managery," needlework, writing, and languages, to dress "moderately," to keep silence in church, and to remember that the chief state of woman is "obedience to authority." "God and Nature do attest the particular expediency of this."[3] We offer one more statement of men's claim to superiority, an excerpt from a letter of Lord Chesterfield to his son in 1748:

. . . Women then are only children of a larger growth; they have an entertaining tattle and sometimes wit, but for solid reasoning and good-sense, I never knew in my life one that had it, or who reasoned or acted consequentially for four-and-twenty hours together. Some little passion or humor always breaks in upon their best resolutions. Their beauty neglected or controverted, their age increased or their supposed understandings depreciated instantly kindles their little passions, and overturns any system of consequential conduct that in their most reasonable moments they might have been capable of forming. A man of sense only trifles with them, as he does with a sprightly, forward child; but he neither consults them about nor trusts them with serious matters, though he often makes them believe that he does both, which is the thing in the world that they are proud of; for they love mightily to be dabbling in business,—which, by the way, they always spoil,—and being justly distrustful that men in general look upon them in a trifling light, they almost adore the man who talks more seriously to them, and who seems to consult and trust them: I say, who seems; for weak men really do, but wise ones only seem to do it. No flattery is either too high or too low for them; they will greedily swallow the highest and gratefully accept of the lowest; and you may safely flatter any woman from her understanding down to the exquisite taste of her fan . . .[4]

Sex Mores

Just as the Middle Ages witnessed the development of chivalry with a highly formalized code of behavior, so did the sixteenth century witness the rise of another set of conventions, in this case pertaining to Platonic love. This was ideally a "more spiritual relation between the sexes" than was cus-

3. Smith, *op. cit.,* p. 44. By permission of Columbia University Press.
4. Edward G. Johnson, ed., *The Best Letters of Lord Chesterfield* (1902), pp. 91-92. By permission of A. C. McClurg and Company.

tomarily experienced either in marriage or out. Ordinarily a matter-of-fact relationship obtained between husband and wife. Between man and mistress there might be real romance or merely physical passion. But Platonic love was described in one case as "not an amity that polluted their souls, but an amity made up of a chain of suitable inclinations and virtues."[5] In a letter to Margaret Blagge, John Evelyn described this new type of heterosexual relationship:

> Friendshipp is beyond all relations of flesh and blood, because it is less materiall . . . The privileges I claim are that I may visitt you without being thought importunate; that I may now and then write to you to cultivate my stile; discourse with you to improve my understanding; read to you to receive your Reflections; and that you freely command me upon all occasions without any reserve whatsoever; you are to write to me when I am absent, mention me in your prayers to God, to admonish me of my failings, to visitt me in sickness, to take care of me when I am in distresse, and never to forsake me, change or lessen your particular esteeme, till I prove unconstant or perfidious, and noe man's friend; in a word, there is in Friendshipp something of all relations, and something above them all. These, Madam, are the Laws, and they are reciprocall and eternall.[6]

Clearly the kind of experience that John Evelyn described was different from the usual relations of men and women in his day. It involved mutual respect, loyalty, and frankness. It contained neither masculine domination nor adoration of the lady. In it physical attraction was considered unimportant or presumed to be absent. However, in actual fact there were wide variations. On the one side poets gave expression to sentiments that closely resembled those of chivalry. Thus Edmund Spenser wrote in his *Hymns in Honor of Love and Beauty:*

> *Such is the powre of that sweet passion*
> *That it all sordid baseness doth expell.*

. . . . .

5. Elizabeth Godfrey (pseudonym), *Social Life under the Stuarts* (1904), p. 179. By permission of E. P. Dutton and Company, Inc.
6. *Ibid.*, p. 171. By permission of E. P. Dutton and Company, Inc.

For loue is Lord of truth and loialte,
Lifting himself out of the lowly dust,
On golden plumes up to the purest skie,
Above the reach of loathly sinful lust.

.   .   .   .   .

But they which loue indeede, look otherwise,
With pure regard and spotless true intent,
Drawing out of the object of their eyes,
A more refyned forme, which they present
Unto their mind, voide of all blemishment,
Which it reducing to her first perfection,
Beholdeth free from fleshes frayle infection.[7]

Platonic academies arose, which were much like medieval courts of love. Outwardly all was beautiful and pure; behind the scenes men and women often gave way to those passions whose existence they publicly denied. So to some persons Platonic love was a lofty ideal, to others a cloak for sordid sensuality.

Quite apart from the pretenses of Platonic love, there was vice open and unashamed. It has been estimated that eighteenth-century London had at one time 50,000 prostitutes, not counting mistresses kept by men of wealth. In the villages it was said that the habits of many traders' and poor farmers' daughters were "astonishingly lax." In every community were some illegitimate children. On the other hand, the general reputation of English girls credited them with "discretion and modesty." What were the actual ratios of those who observed and those who violated the scriptural code we have no means of knowing. But we do know that the mores dealt unequally with the sexes. While unfaithfulness of a husband was not to his credit, it brought only mild condemnation. But infidelity of a wife was a heinous offense. Young men were rather expected to sow their wild oats, while their sisters were sup-

7. Edmund Spenser, *Hymns in Honor of Love and Beauty,* lines 190-191, 176-179, 211-217.

men expected to visit these prostitutes.

posed to remain chaste. Some of the frankest statements of "the double standard" were made by Lord Halifax, who was in no sense a roué nor a defender of vice.

First, then, you are to consider, you live in a time which hath rendered some kind of frailties so habitual that they lay claim to large grains of allowance. The world in this is somewhat unequal, and our sex seemeth to play the tyrant, in distinguishing partially for ourselves, by making that in the utmost degree criminal in the woman which in a man passeth under a much gentler censure. The root and excuse of this injustice is the preservation of families from any mixture that may bring a blemish to them; and whilst the point of honour continues to be so placed, it seems unavoidable to give your sex the greater share of the penalty. But if in this it lieth under any disadvantage, you are more than recompensed by having the honour of families in your keeping.[8]

Lord Halifax went on to advise women that if they found their husbands *in flagrante delicto,* they must feign ignorance thereof. In no case should they bring charges against an adulterous husband.

. . . Remember, that next to the danger of committing the fault yourself, the greatest is that of seeing it in your husband. Do not seem to look or hear that way.

. . . Besides, it is so coarse a reason which will be assigned for a lady's too great warmth upon such an occasion, that modesty no less than prudence ought to restrain her, since an indecent complaint makes a wife much more ridiculous than the injury that provoketh her to it . . . Be assured that in these cases your discretion and silence will be the most prevailing reproof; and an affected ignorance, which is seldom a virtue, is a great one here.[9]

The Family Cycle

Marital Selection

While there were many changes going on in England from the sixteenth to the nineteenth century, the procedures

8. Foxcroft, *op. cit.,* Vol. 2, p. 395. By permission of Longmans, Green and Company, Inc.

9. *Ibid.,* pp. 395, 396. By permission of Longmans, Green and Company, Inc.

involved in mate selection were not suddenly or drastically altered. To be sure, there was an increase in the number of clandestine marriages, but most matches continued to be arranged by parents or guardians, not infrequently for financial considerations. Often the bride and bridegroom were not acquainted before their wedding. In his *Advice to a Daughter*, written in 1687, the Marquis of Halifax said:

> It is one of the disadvantages belonging to your sex, that young women are seldom permitted to make their own choice; their friends' care and experience are thought safer guides to them than their own fancies, and their modesty often forbiddeth them to refuse when their parents recommended, though their inward consent may not entirely go along with it. In this case there remaineth nothing for them to do but to endeavour to make that easy which falleth to their lot, and by a wise use of everything they may dislike in a husband, turn that by degrees to be very supportable, which, if neglected, might in time beget an aversion.[10]

An early nineteenth-century document suggests that the mores of marital selection still had not changed much. "Indeed, without an unusual share of natural sensibility, and very peculiar good fortune, a woman in this country has very little probability of marrying for love."[11]

Not only did parents do most of the choosing; they sometimes made the arrangements while the prospective bride and bridegroom were small children. Records of the Diocese of Chester in the sixteenth century describe the marriage of a boy aged three. "He was hired for an apple bie his uncle to go to the Church," where he was held during the ceremony by this same uncle.[12]

> If the parent of either child is mercenary, a money-bargain is made for it: the father of a boy of two, gets from an older girl's father, "monie to bie a pece of land," and executes a Bond to repay the money if his boy doesn't marry the girl. In another case, the boy's father is in debt, "and, to get

10. Foxcroft, *op. cit.*, Vol. 2, pp. 393-394. By permission of Longman's Green and Company, Inc.

11. Dr. John Gregory, *A Legacy to his Daughters* (1808), quoted by Madlyn E. Hayward in an unpublished Master's thesis, Washington University (1936).

12. Frederick J. Furnivall, ed., *Child Marriages, Divorces, and Ratifications in the Diocese of Chester*, A.D. *1561-6* (1897), p. xxii.

somme money of William Whitfield, to the discharge of his debtes, maried and bargained his sonne to the said Whitfield's daughter." Again, a girl of 3 or 4 is married to a boy of 7 "biecause her frends thought she shuld have had a lyvinge bie hym," and her father-in-law is under Bond to marry them. So again, a girl's father says that she married a boy of her own age, 11-12, "biecause she shuld have had bie hym a prety bargane, yf they cold have lovid, on the other." Another girl of 11 is married to a boy of 9, because, on her father's death, the boy's father gets the landlord's leave to take on the girl's house. Another girl of 8 is married to a boy of 10, because the boy's father feard "lest he shuld lose his parte of his lyvinge" in a tenement which he held in common with the girl's protector . . .

Other children are married "bic the compulsion of their frendes"; another "by a wile," the girl being invited by a relation of the boy's to come and make merry, and then married to the boy against her consent. But in one case a girl arranged her own marriage. She was "a bigge damsell, & mariageable," that is, past 12, and evidently fancying a nice boy of 10-11, "intised hym with two Apples, to go with her to Colne, and to marry her."[13]

After these infant betrothals and weddings the bride and bridegroom usually continued to live separately with their own parents, meeting from time to time for meals or holiday celebrations. Depending upon the socio-economic level, a married boy might be sent to school or to service; his wife might also be placed out as a servant. Some of these child marriages apparently turned out satisfactorily, but in other cases we are told that "dislove fell betwene them." A late seventeenth-century judge held that betrothals and marriages prior to the age of seven were "utterly void." But they became valid if, after passing the age of seven, the children called each other husband and wife, or if, without "words of ratification," they "laye together, imbrace, or kiss each other, or give and receive Gifts and Token."[14] Aside from the mercenary motives previously noted, there were cases in which a father wished to protect his child and possibly his estate "from a strange guardian's sweating." In other cases the fathers of boys were eager to "marry them when young, no doubt to stop them running on the loose."[15]

Evidently such practices did not go unnoticed or unques-

13. *Ibid.*, pp. xv-xvi.
14. *Ibid.*, pp. xxxv-xxxvi.
15. *Ibid.*, pp. xli-xlii.

tioned. Some pamphleteers and poets condemned parents who forced their children "into wedlock out of sordid motives," or who matched "a lively young woman unwillingly with an infirm and decrepit person."[16] It appears that there were increasing numbers of cases in which the young people were already acquainted and attracted to each other. Even for most of these the formalities were still attended to by her parents, but the arrangements were acceptable to the bride and bridegroom. In other cases the young couple ran away and had a ceremony privately performed without banns or license. Such clandestine marriages were solemnized in unauthorized chapels and even in prisons. These elopements and private ceremonies represented the beginning of a revolt against parental control of marital selection. Between the two extremes a position was taken by some that, while a child might not make his choice, he might at least veto his father's selection.

In Shakespeare we find a linking of romantic love with marriage:

> His lovers look forward to marriage as a matter of course, and they neither anticipate its rights nor turn their affections elsewhere. They commonly love at first sight and once for all. Love-relations which do not contemplate marriage occur rarely and in subordination to other dramatic purposes . . . The course of love rarely runs smooth; but rival suitors proposed by parents are quietly resisted or merrily abused, never, even by the gentlest, accepted. . . . Married life, as Shakespeare habitually represents it, is the counterpart, *mutatis mutandis*, of his representation of unmarried lovers. His husbands and wives have less of youthful abandon; they rarely speak of love, and still more rarely with lyric ardour, or coruscations of poetic wit. But they are no less true.[17]

Married Life

After they were married most women continued to engage in productive labor. There were not many idle ladies, although their numbers apparently increased after the Restoration (1660). The wife of a gentleman was a supervisor and director

16. William S. Davis, *Life in Elizabethan Days* (1930), p. 100.
17. C. H. Herford, *Shakespeare's Treatment of Love and Marriage* (1921), pp. 18-19. By permission of Ernest Benn, Ltd.

of servants' tasks. In addition she herself participated in the actual work of brewing, candle making, and other domestic functions. She shared with her husband the discipline of children and servants. The yeoman's wife performed harder manual labor. In describing her duties Byrne quotes Fitzherbert's *Book of Husbandry:* "It is a wives occupation to winnow all manner of corns, to make malt, wash and wring, to make hay, shear corn, and in time of need to help her husband to fill the muck wain or dung cart, drive the plough, to load hay, corn and such other." She took charge of dairy work. She also would "go or ride to the market to sell butter, cheese, milk, eggs, chickens, capons, hens, pigs, geese and all manner of corn."[18] If the wives of gentlemen and yeomen were so well occupied with useful activities, we may be sure that women on lower socio-economic levels were not idle!

The married woman's ambition was to make a good home for her family, where order and good cheer flourished along with religion. Her tasks were many and often arduous, but it apparently never occurred to her that she was downtrodden or leading a hard or narrow life. Occasionally she had some outside activity such as working for a farmer, keeping a shop, running a school, or making lace for sale. Occasionally she managed her husband's estate or even served as churchwarden or overseer of the poor.

By playing roles of economic importance women must have commanded some respect even though their services were taken for granted. But their traditional status was still inferior to that of men. This is demonstrated again and again in the literature of the period. Thus in *The Taming of the Shrew* Shakespeare makes the conquered Katherine say:

> *I am ashamed that women are so simple*
> *To offer war where they should kneel for peace,*
> *Or seek for rule, supremacy and sway,*
> *Where they are bound to serve, love, and obey.*[19]

18. M. St. Clare Byrne, *Elizabethan Life in Town and Country* (1925 and 1934). p. 133. By permission of Methuen and Co., Ltd.

19. William Shakespeare, *The Taming of the Shrew*, Act V, Scene ii.

Children

In the sixteenth, seventeenth, and eighteenth centuries both birth rates and infant mortality rates were high. One eighteenth-century estimate was that seventy-five percent died before reaching the age of five. Thus there was a continuation of the situation described in the preceding chapter. Glimpses of child life, of parent-child relations, and of training given in the early modern period are afforded by such works as Caxton's *Book of Curtesye,* Hugh Rhodes' *Boke of Nurture,* and Richard Weste's *Book of Demeanor.* In Caxton's book, printed about 1477, these instructions were given to boys: On rising they were to cross themselves three times, repeat the Pater Noster, Ave Maria, and Apostle's Creed; they were to comb their hair, wash their hands, face, ears, and nose, clean and pare their nails, and take care of their clothes. In passing along the street they were to greet their peers "wyth ryght frendly chere," and their superiors "wyth humble obeysaunce." They should not throw stones at fowl or beast, and so on and on didactically in verse.[20]

From Hugh Rhodes' *Boke of Nurture or Schoole of Good Maners,* reprinted in 1577, we learn more of the things that children were taught to do and to avoid. Like other courtesy books this was in verse. We offer brief samples of the poetry and summarize other parts of the work.

> *Obedience learn you in your youth.*

> *Vnto your Elders gentle be,*
> *   agaynst them say no harme.*

> *Reuerence to thy parentes deare,*
> *   so duety doth thee bynde:*
> *Such children as vertue delight,*
> *   be gentle, meeke, and kynde.*

---

20. Frederick J. Furnivall, ed., *Caxton's Book of Curtesye* (1868).

Agaynst thy parentes multiplye
no wordes, but be demure.

Rise at six o'clock in the morning, thank God for your good rest, clean your nose, brush and sponge your clothes, clean your shoes, wash your hands and face, wish your mates good morning, pay your respects to your parents.

When that thy parents come in syght,
doe to them reuerence:
Ask them blessing if they haue
bene long out of presence.

If you dine with your master, let him begin first; don't press up too high, but take the place assigned to you. At table don't pare your nails. If your master speaks to you, take off your cap and stand up. Try your soup before putting bread in it; if another shares your dish, don't crumble bread in it, as your hands may be sweaty. Cut nice bits of bread to put in your broth, and don't sup that too loudly. Don't dip your meat in the common salt-cellar, wipe your spoon clean before putting it down, and take care that it be not stolen. Burnish no bones with your teeth. Belch near to no man's face; don't scratch your head at meals; don't spit over the table, or pick your teeth with a knife. Wipe your mouth when you drink. Don't blow your nose on your napkin. Don't fill your mouth too full, or blow out your crumbs. Don't blow on your soup or drink, "for if thou be not whole of thy body, thy breath is corruptible." "Cast not thy bones under the Table." Don't stretch at the table, nor cut the table with your knife. When leaving the table say to your companions, "Much good do it ye," bow to your master and withdraw.[21]

Formal education was limited since there were no public schools and the few private schools were available only to children of the upper classes. Teaching the children of peas-

21. Frederick J. Furnivall, ed., *The Babees Book* (1868).

ants and craftsmen was supposed to do more harm than good. "They had better learn some good mystery [trade]." However, families of modest means might send their boys to a "dame school" conducted in a cottage. These "of gentler condition" might attend an elementary school where they would learn their letters, the Lord's Prayer, and a short catechism. In homes of the upper classes tutors prepared boys for grammar school, teaching them letters, singing, playing a musical instrument, and perhaps a bit of French or Italian. At grammar school boys learned to read, memorized certain Psalms and rituals, studied Latin grammar and a "book of short sentences conveying high moral lessons." Girls received less schooling than boys. It is said of Shakespeare's daughters that one could barely sign her name and the second could only make her mark. After all, the important thing for a girl was to learn how to manage the kitchen, laundry, and dairy, to sew, and to care for the sick. If her station in life seemed to warrant, she might be tutored by a "decayed gentlewoman," learning her letters, catechism, Bible stories, popular dances, and how to play the lute (like a mandolin) or virginal (something between a harp and a piano). But girls and boys alike in the majority of homes had little or nothing in the way of formal schooling.

In general children were "regarded by the normal parent as miniature but troublesome men and women: the more nearly and the more quickly their behaviour approximated to the adult the more they were to be commended. Childhood, like the diseases incident to it, was a thing to be got over as quickly as possible."[22]

As we have already seen, many children died in early life, boys were often apprenticed, marriages were commonly arranged, and new families started the cycle over again. Sometimes a son or daughter, most likely the eldest son, remained in the parental home. In these three-generation households

22. M. St. Clare Byrne, *op. cit.*, p. 176. By permission of Methuen and Co., Ltd.

the old folks gradually tapered off their useful activities, while the middle generation took on more responsibility and authority. There might be a warm relationship between small children and their grandparents. But otherwise members of the family seem to have taken each other for granted and made little display of affection.

Family Controls

Struggle of Church and State for Control of Marriage

Within the early modern English household we have seen that control was largely in the hands of the husband-father-master, whether the family were rural or urban, upper, middle, or lower class. As to external controls there was continued conflict and confusion over what is a valid marriage and how, if at all, it might be dissolved. Thus while it seems that most weddings involved an ecclesiastical ceremony, both civil and canon law showed a number of variations. The rule for Catholics was set forth at the Council of Trent in the middle of the sixteenth century. While decreeing that all marriages previously contracted merely by verbal consent should be considered valid, it ordered that thereafter all marriages must be solemnized in the presence of a priest and witnesses. The publication of banns was also required unless a license was secured from the bishop. During certain seasons, Lent in particular, weddings were forbidden.

From Henry VIII's break with Rome until Cromwell's protectorate ecclesiastical ceremonies were the rule. A statute in 1540 specified that marriages solemnized by the Church and consummated should take precedence over unconsummated pre-contracts not celebrated in church. This was repealed in the reign of Edward VI and spousals *per verba de praesenti* were again held to be "very matrimony." However, if such a marriage contract were not followed by a religious ceremony a woman might forfeit her dower and the children

would be rendered illegitimate. Thus was continued the confusion which we noted in the preceding period—certain marriages were binding but not in good standing; husband and
wife were legally united but their children were bastards. The
Anglican Church held that children could be legitimized by a
religious ceremony after their birth, but the civil law ruled
this out.

The Civil Marriage Act of 1653, passed by the Puritans
under Cromwell, required a civil ceremony before a justice
of the peace after presentation of the certificate from the
parish register that banns had been published. If either party
were under twenty-one, proof of parental consent must also be
presented. The wedding ceremony consisted of a simple formula
to be repeated by the man and the woman and was accompanied by handfasting. The use of a ring was forbidden. After
the Restoration this law was displaced by the legislation which
preceded it, but civil marriages continued to be legal, despite
the efforts of some vengeful Royalists to have them declared
null and void.

In 1694 a direct tax was imposed on all weddings. In 1695
the requirements of banns or a license of the bishop was reen-
acted with the fixing of heavy penalties for violations. But
there were loopholes. Some clergymen were not covered by the
exact terms of the laws. Presently it was found that ministers
in the Fleet and other prisons for debt were performing wedding ceremonies. Some of them were only technically prisoners
and actually had quarters outside where they hung out their
signs, "Marriages performed here." Some advertised in newspapers and scattered handbills. Their fees were small, no banns
or parental consent were required, and publicity was avoided.
As a result "Fleet parsons" performed thousands of ceremonies
every year.

In the face of the inevitable confusion, scandals, and hardships accompanying these clandestine marriages, there was
strong agitation for legal reform. By the Hardwicke Act of 1753
all weddings, except those of Quakers, Jews, and members of the
royal family were to be performed only after publication of
banns or issuance of a license, only during the morning hours

eight to twelve, only in an Anglican chuch or chapel, and only before an Anglican clergyman. Two or more witnesses were required and a register must be kept. Parental consent was demanded unless the banns had been published. Precontracts were finally abolished along with prison weddings. While this was in many respects a reform measure, it expressed bigoted intolerance of Catholics and Protestant Dissenters that was not corrected until passage of the Civil Marriage Law of 1836.

In general the laws pertaining to legal separation, divorce, and annulment underwent little change during this period of English history. It appears that a wife who considered herself cruelly treated might claim separate maintenance. But if at any time her husband offered to be reconciled and she refused, he was no longer under obligation to support her. If a husband deserted, his wife could sue for "restitution of conjugal rights."

The Catholic Church, in the Council of Trent, restated its position that marriage was one of the seven sacraments and hence could not be dissolved, not even on account of "heresy, or irksome cohabitation, or the affected absence of one of the parties."[23] However, "matrimony contracted but not consummated" could be "dissolved by the solemn profession of religion by one of the married partners."[24] The Church reserved the right to establish impediments such as consanguinity and affinity, and on the basis of these to declare marriages null and void (*divortium a vinculo matrimonii*). It also declared that for many causes husband and wife might be legally separated from bed and board (*divortium a mensa et toro*), but that in no case might either remarry during the lifetime of the other.

Under the Protestant regime divorce was legally possible, but it was seldom granted and remarriages were of doubtful validity. Divorce suits were brought in the bishops' courts on the grounds of impotence, refusal to have intercourse, adul-

23. Canons and Decrees of the Council of Trent, "On the Sacrament of Matrimony," Canon IV; quoted by S. P. Breckinridge, *The Family and the State* (1934), p. 11.

24. *Ibid.*, Canon VI; quoted by Breckinridge, *op. cit.*, p. 11.

tery, and cruelty. Persons of wealth and influence sometimes secured divorce through a special act of Parliament. But the number of divorces was not large. Legal complications and costs automatically barred the masses from this means of escaping unhappy marriages. Even persons on the higher socioeconomic levels were hindered by the stigma attached. Lord Halifax wrote in 1687: "The causes of separation are now so very coarse, that few are confident enough to buy their liberty at the price of having their modesty so exposed."[25] Annulment was doubtless restrained by the same social pressure, but was granted in some cases of fraud, abduction, and child marriages.

In general the Anglican Church was unwilling to depart very far from the Catholic position. Moreover, many of the Protestant Dissenters were equally conservative. But others argued for more liberal provisions. In Bullinger's *The Christen State of Matrimonye,* published in 1541, we read that ". . . divorce is permitted of god for the welth and medicine of man and for amendment in wedlock."[26] Another writer called it "the rod of marriage." John Milton said divorce was a "law of moral equity." In fact, he wrote a small book, *The Doctrine and Discipline of Divorce Restored to the Good of both Sexes.*

As early as 1552 a Parliamentary Commission recommended the abolition of *divortium a mensa et toro* and the granting of absolute divorce for adultery, desertion, cruelty, "and in cases of such violent hatred as rendered it in the highest degree improbable that the husband and wife would survive their animosities and again love one another."[27] However, nothing came of this report. For three centuries more English divorces were difficult to secure, and the social if not the legal status of divorced persons was a handicap.

25. H. C. Foxcroft, *The Life and Letters of Sir George Saville, Bart., First Marquis of Halifax* (1898), Vol. 2, p. 394. By permission of Longmans, Green and Company, Inc.

26. George E. Howard, *A History of Matrimonial Institutions* (1904), Vol. 2, p. 72. By permission of the University of Chicago Press.

27. *Ibid.,* p. 78. By permission of the University of Chicago Press.

Tradition, Law, and Public Opinion

The general status of women was fixed partly in tradition and partly in law. Under the common law as formulated by Blackstone in 1765, "A woman upon marriage dissolved her legal personality into that of her husband."[28] However, it was the marriage rather than her sex which occasioned the cancellation. "The wife could not retain her earnings, enter into contracts, make conveyances, or bear witness in court apart from her husband. . . ."[29]

Passing from law to popular sentiment and the beginning of public opinion about the status and roles of the sexes, we find that the concept of husband and wife as friends made its appearance in Owen Feltham's *Resolves*, published about 1628. "It is the crown of blessings, when in one woman a man finds both a wife and a friend."[30] In 1694 Mary Astell sought to establish a school for girls arguing that "such an education will put the stability of marriage on a basis . . . furnished by veneration and esteem."[31] In 1700 she wrote: "And if a Woman can neither Love nor Honour she does ill in promising to Obey."[32] Thus were some new notes being struck and our present conception of marriage relationships anticipated. However, such views as these were exceptional even in the eighteenth century. The conventional position was forcefully expressed by Hannah More. In an essay *On the Danger of Sentimental or Romantic Connexions* she condemned those who "consider fortune, rank, and reputation, as mere chimerical distinctions and vulgar prejudices."[33] She attributed such

28. John Sirjamaki, *The American Family in the Twentieth Century* (1953), p. 23. By permission of Harvard University Press.

29. *Ibid.*

30. Smith, *op. cit.,* p. 79. By permission of Columbia University Press.

31. Mary Astell, *A Serious Proposal to the Ladies for the Advancement of Their True and Greatest Interest* (1694), p. 111; quoted by Smith, *op. cit.,* pp. 55-56. By permission of Columbia University Press.

32. Mary Astell, *Some Reflections upon Marriage Occasioned by the Duke and Duchess of Mazarine's Case* (1700), p. 52; quoted by Smith, *op. cit.,* p. 88. By permission of Columbia University Press.

33. Hannah More, *Essays for Young Ladies* (1777), p. 82.

folly to "pernicious reading" and "imprudent friendships." She described the course of romantic love most contemptuously, referring scornfully to "violent intimacy . . . wrought to the highest pitch by a secret and voluminous correspondence . . . filled with vows of eternal amity," and complaining against "the groveling spirit and sordid temper of the parents."[34]

Against the subordination of women and the unromantic character of arranged marriages Mary Astell voiced a mild protest. In her anonymous pamphlet, *A Serious Proposal to the Ladies,* published in 1694, she said:

> . . . instead of inquiring why all women are not wise and good, we have reason to wonder that there are any so. Were the Men as much neglected and as little care taken to cultivate and improve them, perhaps they would be so far from surpassing those whom they now despise, that they themselves would sink into the greatest stupidity and brutality . . . Women are from their very infancy debarr'd those advantages with the want of which they are afterwards reproached and nursed up in those vices which will hereafter be upbraided to them.[35]

But hers was only a mild rebellion as is shown by the following passage:

> If the woman is already married there is no remedy: she must abide by what she has done. If the man is foolish and wicked, she can only despise even though she may obey. Though he may love her at marriage, passion often cools into indifference, neglect, or perhaps aversion. There is left to the wife in either case only a life of devotion that she may make her trials in the world prepare her better for the next. The woman who seeks relief in the gayeties of a court brings worse troubles upon herself.[36]

Not for another century was a thoroughgoing feminist to appear upon the scene. In 1791 Mary Wollstonecraft published her *Vindication of the Rights of Woman* protesting strongly against the long continued subjection of her sex. The following passages indicate the general character of her protest

34. *Ibid.,* pp. 88-90.
35. Mary Astell, *A Serious Proposal to the Ladies for the Advancement of Their True and Greatest Interest* (1694), pp. 7, 17; quoted by Smith, *op. cit.,* pp. 51, 52. By permission of Columbia University Press.
36. *Ibid.,* pp. 17-18; quoted by Smith, *op. cit.,* p. 83. By permission of Columbia University Press.

against conventional English marriage and her vision of an equalitarian relationship in which spouses would be lovers and companions:

> Riches and hereditary honors have made cyphers of women to give consequence to the numerical figure; and idleness has produced a mixture of gallantry and despotism into society, which leads the very men who are slaves of their mistresses to tyrannize over their sisters, wives, and daughters. This is only keeping them in rank and file, it is true. Strengthen the female mind by enlarging it, and there will be an end to blind obedience; but as blind obedience is ever sought for by power, tyrants and sensualists are in the right when they endeavor to keep women in the dark, because the former only want slaves, and the latter a plaything. The sensualist, indeed, has been the most dangerous of tyrants, and women have been duped by their lovers, as princes by their ministers, whilst dreaming that they reigned over them . . .
>
> Would men but generously snap our chains, and be content with rational fellowship instead of slavish obedience, they would find us more observant daughters, more affectionate sisters, more faithful wives, more reasonable mothers—in a word, better citizens . . .
>
> If marriage be the cement of society, mankind should all be educated after the same model, or the intercourse of the sexes will never deserve the name of fellowship, nor will women ever fulfill the peculiar duties of their sex, till they become enlightened citizens, till they become free by being enabled to earn their own subsistence, independent of men; in the same manner, I mean, to prevent misconstruction, as one man is independent of another. Nay, marriage will never be held sacred till women, by being brought up with men, are prepared to be their companions rather than their mistresses; for the mean doublings of cunning will ever render them contemptible, whilst oppression renders them timid.[37]

Thus social control *within* the family continued to be largely patriarchal. But social control *over* the family was in process of passing from tradition to church, to state, to public opinion, with none of these ever dropping entirely out of the picture.

Family Functions

In general the functions of the family did not change greatly in a thousand years. In all these centuries the nuclear

37. Mary Wollstonecraft. *A Vindication of the Rights of Woman* (1792), pp. 28-29, 164, 182-183.

or conjugal family was the agency of procreation and early
child rearing; the household was the economic unit; the patrilineal kinship group determined status. In Anglo-Saxon times
and in the early Middle Ages the kinship group, i.e., the clan,
exercised considerable social control and provided for the
needs of unfortunates. But gradually both police and protective
functions were transferred to the parish. Education and training
of older boys and youths went on either in their own households or in those of masters to whom they were indentured or
apprenticed. Girls learned domestic arts, manners, morals,
religious doctrines and practices from their mothers and other
female relatives. Whenever, during this period, serious thought
was given to the functions of the family, procreation was
stressed. "The Family must be kept up, the antient Race preserved."[38] We have seen too that marriage was regarded as a
means of regulating sexual behavior. It was a "physic against sin
and unchastity." Hence we may say in brief that the family as an
institution was slowly changing throughout the thousand years
from King Alfred to George III. But during those ten centuries in England it was altered less than it was to be in the
next hundred and fifty years on the North American Continent.

REFERENCES

Aries, Philippe, *Centuries of Childhood: A Social History of
Family Life,* trans. by Robert Baldick. New York: Alfred A. Knopf,
Inc. and Random House, Inc., 1965.

Astell, Mary, *Some Reflections Upon Marriage Occasioned by
the Duke and Duchess of Mazarine's Case.* London: J. Nutt, 1700.

Breckinridge, Sophonisba P., *The Family and the State.* Chicago:
University of Chicago Press, 1934, pp. 10-27.

Byrne, M. St. Clare, *Elizabethan Life in Town and Country.*
London: Methuen and Company, Ltd., 1925 and 1934.

Davis, William S., *Life in Elizabethan Days.* New York: Harper
and Brothers, 1930.

38. Mary Astell, *Some Reflections Upon Marriage* (1700), p. 35.

Foxcroft, H. C., *The Life and Letters of Sir George Saville, Bart., First Marquis of Halifax*. New York: Longmans, Green, and Company, 1898, 2 volumes.

Furnivall, Frederick J., ed., *The Babees Book*. London: Early English Text Society, No. 33, 1868.

——, *Caxton's Book of Curtesye*. London: For the Early English Text Society by N. Trübner and Co., 1868.

——, *Child Marriages, Divorces, and Ratifications in the Diocese of Chester, A.D. 1561-6*, London: Early English Text Society, 1897, Original Series No. 108.

Godfrey, Elizabeth (*pseudonym*), *Social Life under the Stuarts*. New York: E. P. Dutton and Company, 1904.

Goodsell, Willystine, *A History of Marriage and the Family*. New York: The Macmillan Company, 1934, Chapter VIII.

Herford, C. H., *Shakespeare's Treatment of Love and Marriage*. London: T. F. Unwin, Ltd., 1921.

Hole, Christina, *English Home Life, 1500 to 1800*. London: Batsford, Ltd., 1947.

——, *The English Housewife in the Seventeenth Century*. London: Chatto & Windus, 1953.

Howard, George E., *A History of Matrimonial Institutions*. Chicago: University of Chicago Press, 1904, Volume I, Chapters IX-X; Volume II, Chapter XI.

Johnson, Edward G., ed., *The Best Letters of Lord Chesterfield* (Philip Dormer Stanhope). Chicago: A. C. McClurg and Company, 1902, Chapter XXVI, "General Character of Women."

More, Hannah, *Essays on Various Subjects, Principally Designed for Young Ladies*. London: J. Wilkie and T. Cadell, 1777.

Powell, Chilton L., *English Domestic Relations, 1487-1653*. New York: Columbia University Press, 1917.

Sirjamaki, John, *The American Family in the Twentieth Century*. Cambridge, Mass.: Harvard University Press, 1953.

Smith, Florence M., *Mary Astell*. New York: Columbia University Press, 1916.

Visiak, E. H., *Milton, Complete Poetry and Selected Prose*. Glasgow: Glasgow University Press, 1937, pp. 628-670, "The Doctrine and Discipline of Divorce."

Wollstonecraft, Mary, *A Vindication of the Rights of Women*. Boston: By Peter Edes for Thomas and Andrew, 1792.

13 The Colonial Family in North America

When the English colonists came to America in the seventeenth and eighteenth centuries they of course brought with them the customs, traditions, and laws of the mother country. However, under pioneer conditions some of the folkways and mores underwent considerable change. Moreover, they were altered in different ways in the North and the South. As a matter of fact there were unique developments in each of the colonies, but for our purposes it may be sufficient to deal with New England and the South as regions. This is not the place to recapitulate the early history of white settlement in North America, but it is well to remind ourselves that in the beginning life was hard, houses were crude, food was scarce, disease carried off large numbers, and the margin of survival was narrow. Nevertheless there was land to be had, to be worked by the patriarchal father, to be passed on when he so decided to mature sons; and the agricultural-based extended family, the type that was having hard going in a disorderly rural England of the seventeenth century, could through a few generations' existence in New England regain its traditional form.[1] As time

1. Philip J. Greven, *Four Generations: Population, Land, Family in Colonial Andover, Massachusetts* (1970). Recent researches in social and demographic history along the lines of Greven's strongly question the long accepted notion that colonists merely transferred a stable community-oriented patriarchal extended family system from one shore to another. Overlooked has been the forces for disorder and declension of rural family life in seventeenth-century England, and the social and economic conditions favoring the growth of large, orderly (and authoritarian) families and households in the towns and villages of New England. Likewise, not all towns suffered the large and growing mortality rate characteristic of England at the time. Greven found in seventeenth-century Andover, Massachusetts, that "(demographic) evidence reveals that people were extraordinarily healthy, lives were unusually long, and women exceedingly fecund." (p. 269.) See also John Demos, *A Little Commonwealth: Family Life in Plymouth Colony* (1970), and Edmund S. Morgan, *The Puritan Family* (1966).

passed the material conditions of life improved, security increased, and the growing population enjoyed a richer social life.

NEW ENGLAND

The Pilgrims and others who settled in New England usually established villages in which they lived compactly together. Thus they not only continued an ecological pattern familiar in the old country; they also facilitated defense, neighboring, and that democratic institution known as the town meeting. Religious liberty for themselves was one of their objectives in coming to America, but they were often intolerant of other faiths. With their religion was associated a rather stern code of behavior, which reflected the hard conditions under which they lived. The climate was rigorous, the Indians were sometimes hostile, the settlers brought few of this world's goods with them, and medical knowledge and skill were very limited. But the New Englanders were determined people, courageous and undaunted in the face of great difficulties and privations. In keeping with all this, marriage and family life were serious business.

Family Structure

The New England Household and Its Economy

Like their English forefathers and contemporaries, the colonists assumed that all persons should be members of family groups. All adults were expected to marry, and the usual pattern of family life was patriarchal. Starting with small groups of parents and children, households often grew by the addition of indentured or wage-earning servants, unattached female relatives, and sometimes married sons with their wives and children. The head of the house was held responsible for the support and conduct of its members. In fact kinsmen were expected to assist one another in time of need, whether living under the same roof or not. However, it appears that the towns took no chances on residents' caring for newcomers who were related. Thus in Dorchester in 1670 notice was given to Henry Merrifield "to discharge the towne of his daughter Funnell which hath been at his hous about a weeke; unless he gitt a note under the hands of the Selectmen of Melton that they will receaue her again if need be . . ."[2] The early diaries, journals, town records, and other accounts leave us somewhat in doubt as to the strength of the ties that bound kinsmen together.

Still very few of the colonists lived otherwise than as members of family groups. But there were some who lived in households without full participation in the privileges associated with blood and marriage. The small numbers of unmarried adults were viewed askance. "Antient maids" of twenty-five were described as a "dismal spectacle." Single men were treated almost as criminal suspects. Connecticut in 1636 ordered "that no young man that is neither married nor hath any servant nor is a public officer, shall keep house of himself without the consent of the town."[3] Hartford taxed "lone men" twenty shillings a week "for the selfish luxury of solitary living." Plymouth enacted similar legislation. In addition to unmarried adults, married persons living apart from their spouses were regarded as "exposed to great temptations." Unless they could show good reason to the contrary, it was ordered in New Haven that they "shal by the first opportunity repair to their said relations."

Status of the Sexes

In colonial New England the position of women represents a slight gain in legal status. For example, Demos notes

2. Robert W. Kelso, *The History of Public Poor Relief in Massachusetts* (1922), p. 38. By permission of the author.
3. J. Hammond Trumbull, ed., *The True Blue Laws of Connecticut and the False Blue Laws Invented by the Rev. Samuel Peters* (1876), p. 104.

that in Plymouth the wife would be expected to participate freely and legitimately in family decisions to transfer land; moreover, it was the *joint* responsibility of both spouses to arrive at decisions involving the "putting out" of children into foster families.[4] in another case apropos the legal rights of women he finds that the Court of Plymouth occasionally granted liquor licenses directly to women.[5] As we shall see a little later, wives as well as husbands could initiate divorce proceedings. It also seems significant that single women enjoyed about the same property rights as single men. In the early days at Salem town lots were granted to single women as well as to men. But Endicott wrote that the custom should be abandoned in order to "avoid all presedents & evil events." Resistance to change, or at least the inertia of custom, was most evident in the restrictions, previously noted, on the inheritance, management, and disposal of property by married women. Their subordination is displayed most strikingly in cases like these: a man brought suit to collect ten pounds due his wife as wages; a woman's second husband sued for one third of her first husband's estate; Robert Crocker was ordered to pay five pounds to Thomas King for breach of promise to marry the latter's wife. On the other hand husbands had to pay their wives' debts, meet fines imposed upon their wives, and provide general maintenance. These obligations may be regarded as a sort of compensation for claiming the property of married women.

In the field of religion the status of women was definitely one of subordination to men. While Mrs. Anne Hutchinson was worrying the rulers of Massachusetts, the synod of ministers resolved:

That though women might meet [some few together] to pray and edify one another, yet such a set assembly [as was then the practice in Boston] where sixty or more did meet every week, and one woman [in a prophetical

4. John Demos, *A Little Commonwealth* (1970), p. 88.
5. *Ibid.*, p. 90.

way by resolving questions of doctrines and expounding scripture] took upon her the whole exercise, was agreed to be disorderly and without rule.[6]

John Winthrop's conception of women's place was clearly expressed in a journal entry of 1645.

Mr. Hopkins, the governor of Hartford upon Connecticut, came to Boston, and brought his wife with him, (a godly young woman, and of special parts), who was fallen into sad infirmity, the loss of her understanding and reason, which had been growing upon her divers years, by occasion of her giving herself wholly to reading and writing, and had written many books. Her husband, being very loving and tender of her, was loath to grieve her; but he saw his error, when it was too late. For if she had attended her household affairs, and such things as belong to women, and not gone out of her way and calling to meddle in such things as are proper for men, whose minds are stronger, etc., she had kept her wits, and might have improved them usefully and honorably in the place God had set her . . .[7]

Women were punished much as men and for similar offenses. In addition they suffered severe penalties for "unlawful maternity" and witchcraft. Mrs. Anne Hutchinson was condemned not merely for novel theological opinions, which rendered her "not fit for our society," but also for holding meetings, "a thing not fitting for her sex."

Women's work and authority was centered in the home, but it included a wide range of activities from tending babies to tilling the soil. Moreover, there were women who carried on trades and businesses outside the home. Eighteenth-century advertisements show that they were teachers, wax workers, and jelly-makers, and that they dealt in groceries, wines, and musical instruments. Several women published newspapers, one acted as her own attorney, and another is said to have run a blacksmith shop.

No doubt large numbers were genuine partners and companions of their husbands, sharing work and danger. Calhoun quotes from letters, diaries, and various documents evidence

6. Alice M. Earle, *Colonial Dames and Goodwives* (1895), pp. 113-114. By permission of The Macmillan Company.

7. James K. Hosmer, ed., *Winthrop's Journal* (1908), Vol. II, p. 225. By permission of Barnes & Noble, Inc.

that real affection was present in many cases. Yet even here we find love tempered by the assumption of male supremacy. Minister Clapp, President of Yale, 1740-1766, wrote this about his wife:

And if it happened at any time that we seemed not altogether to agree in our opinion or inclination about any lesser matter we used to discourse upon it, with a perfect calmness and pleasancy; but she did not choose to debate long upon any such thing but was always free and ready enough to acquiesce in the opinion or inclination of her husband . . . She always went through the difficulties of childbearing with a remarkable steadfastness, faith, patience, and decency . . . Indeed she would sometimes say to me that bearing, tending, and burying children was hard work, and that she had done a great deal of it for one of her age (she had six children, whereof she buried four, and died in the 24 year of her age), yet would say it was the work she was made for, and what God in his providence had called her to, and she could freely do it all for Him.[8]

Such passages as this suggest not only masculine dominance, but possibly sexual exploitation as well. Calhoun definitely makes this inference when he speaks of colonial women as "instruments of male gratification" and a "vicarious sacrifice to the peopling of a continent."[9] This seems to us to be putting it much too strongly, but we can hardly ignore the evidence of sexual subordination. On the other hand, there is scant evidence that women considered themselves "degraded" or that they felt resentful of their lot.

Widows and Orphans

In 1698 Boston was said to be "full of widows and orphans," but it is doubtful that there were many such persons unattached to some natural household. In the cases of

8. Reprinted by permission of the publishers, The Arthur H. Clark Company, from Calhoun's *Social History of the American Family*, Vol. I (1919), p. 90.
9. Reprinted by permission of the publishers. The Arthur H. Clark Company, from Calhoun's *Social History of the American Family*, Vol. I (1919), p. 105.

widows and widowers remarriage was both useful and prompt. The first marriage in Plymouth was that of Edward Winslow, a widower for seven weeks, and Susanna White, a widow for twelve weeks. One governor of New Hampshire married a widow of only ten days standing, and the amazing case is cited of Isaac Winslow who proposed to Ben Davis' daughter the same day he buried his wife. The difficulties of living alone were great; the property and experience of widowed persons may have been attractions. Even so, future disposition of their respective properties would be subject to contractual agreement before marriage.[10]

Half-orphans usually acquired stepparents, as has just been implied. Full orphans were either cared for by kinsmen or indentured. In addition the children of thriftless or otherwise dependent parents were commonly bound out as apprentices. Sometimes whole families, whether broken or intact, were "vendued to the lowest bidder" and incorporated into the latter's household.

Marital Selection

In marriage, as in household organization and economy, there was persistence of laws and customs brought over from England, and there were innovations. The Old World struggle of Church and state for control of marriage continued in the colonies, but with this interesting difference. In New England civil marriages were the rule and divorce was permitted. In the South the Church was nominally in control, but the scarcity of clergy, especially in the back country, led to the authorization of civil ceremonies and even to common-law marriages. Arranged matches were not so common in America as in England, but permission to marry was supposed to be obtained from fathers or masters. Nevertheless, under frontier conditions there was a growth of independence.

10. Demos, op. cit., p. 85.

In pioneer villages it was obviously impossible to seclude girls; hence there were many natural contacts between the sexes. Adolescent friendship and courtship were further aided by the singing schools. Some matches may be traced to matrimonial advertisements in Boston papers. In any case courtship was not expected to be dragged over a long period. It was something "to be got over with decent haste and not too much sentiment."[11] More than once, it is said, "a lonely Puritan came to the door of a maiden he had never seen, presented credentials, told his need of a housekeeper, proposed marriage, obtained hasty consent, and notified the town clerk, all in one day."[12] However, it was rarely as simple a matter as this statement might lead us to suppose. A young man was required by the laws of several colonies to secure the consent of his prospective father-in-law before beginning the courtship, and this was not always easy to obtain. Aside from personal likes and dislikes, fathers of eligible maidens looked into young men's economic statuses. The young men in turn looked out for their own interests and bargained for dowries. A third and powerful factor was the authority of the father over the settlements of land to his offspring. Many young male descendents of first-generation colonists, Greven notes, found their prospective marriage dependent upon "the willingness of fathers to permit sons to leave the parental homestead and to establish themselves as married adults, usually in houses of their own built on family land, designated as the married son's responsibility."[13]

Violations of marriage laws were punished. At Plymouth in 1660 Arthur Howland, Jr., was fined five pounds for making love to Elizabeth Pence without her father's permission. He was evidently a persistent young man, for we learn that

11. Willystine Goodsell, *A History of Marriage and the Family* (1934), p. 372.

12. Reprinted by permission of the publishers, The Arthur H. Clark Company, from Calhoun's *Social History of the American Family*, Vol. I (1919), p. 52.

13. Philip J. Greven, *Four Generations* (1970), p. 75. By permission of Cornell University Press.

in 1667 he was fined another five pounds because he had "disorderly and unrighteously endeavored to obtain the affections of Mistress Elizabeth Pence."[14] Not only did fathers give or withhold consent to begin courtship; they sometimes took the initiative. Thus Emanual Downing wrote in 1640 that he wanted his son, James, to marry a niece of Mr. Endicott. He said that he had made a "verie good match" for his niece, getting her married to a young man with an estate of 400 or 500 pounds.[15] However, the young folks sometimes had ideas of their own and, either on their behalf or for the peopling of the new land, a magistrate might intervene to keep an obstinate father from "unreasonably denying any child timely or convenient marriage."[16] Several cases might be cited of children defying their fathers' will and of suitors securing judgment against stubborn elders. In case a girl's father should grant permission to marry and later change his mind the young man may bring suit to recover damages "for his time and expense." Cases were also taken to court in order to force a recalcitrant or dilatory father-in-law to deliver a promised dowry. Finally there were ordinary breach-of-promise suits, brought sometimes by the man, sometimes by the woman, and sometimes by her father.

Despite their small numbers and the ties of kinship and affinity that bound many of them together, the early New Englanders laid down strict rules about forbidden degrees within which marriage would not be permitted. In this they were continuing the regulations of the Anglican church, but in their statutes reference was made directly to the Old Testament, specifically to the eighteenth chapter of Leviticus. Persons mating within the prohibited degrees of consanguinity and affinity were punished by having to wear on their cloth-

14. John A. Goodwin, *The Pilgrim Republic* (1879), p. 598. By permission of Houghton Mifflin Company.

15. William B. Weeden, *Economic and Social History of New England*, 1620-1789 (1890), Vol. I, p. 219.

16. George E. Howard, *A History of Matrimonial Institutions* (1904), Vol. II, p. 166. By permission of the University of Chicago Press.

ing the capital letter I for incest. In 1705 Massachusetts forbade the intermarriage of white and Negro persons; in 1786 this prohibition of miscegenation was extended to Indians, and all such interracial marriages were declared void. This law was not repealed until 1843.

Because of the high death rate many marriages involved widows and widowers. There are instances of a man thrice widowed marrying a woman twice or thrice bereaved. Widows were apparently attractive because of their experience and sometimes their property. The economic motive appears clearly in a letter quoted by Calhoun.

> Our uncle is not at present able to pay you or any other he owes money to. If he was able to pay he would; they must have patience til God enable him. As his wife died in mercy near twelvemonths since, it may be he may light of some rich widow that may make him capable to pay . . .[17]

It would be a mistake to assume that romantic love was wholly absent from colonial New England, but it was obviously restricted and hampered by the habit of driving hard bargains which, in turn, was traceable partly to the narrow margin of survival and partly to the stern code of Puritanism. How much the latter may be attributed to study of the Old Testament we cannot tell, but the laws of forbidden degrees were taken directly from the Pentateuch.

Having decided that they wished to marry, having got over the hurdle of parental consent, and being assured that they were eligible to marry each other, a couple's next step was usually the celebration of a public betrothal. It was not at all like an announcement party in our day, but more like an Anglo-Saxon *beweddung*. In Plymouth this observance was called precontract. It included the "promise of marriage in due time" and often the preaching of a sermon. In other parts of New England this custom was followed, but was not required by law. However, it was everywhere stipulated that

17. Reprinted by permission of the publishers, The Arthur H. Clark Company, from Calhoun's *Social History of the American Family*, Vol. I (1919), pp. 57-58.

there be publication of intention to marry. In Plymouth the banns had to be read three times in meeting, or, if there were no meeting, they had to be posted in a public place for fifteen days.

Since marriage was regarded as a civil contract it was natural for the Pilgrims to make the wedding ceremony a function of the magistrates rather than of the clergy. Massachusetts in 1646 provided "that no person whatsoever in this jurisdiction, shall joyne any persons together in Marriage, but the Magistrate, or such other as the General Court, or Court of Assistants shal Authorize in such place, where no Magistrate is neer."[18] A similar law was enacted in Plymouth, and not until 1692, when the two colonies were merged, were clergymen authorized to solemnize marriages. Connecticut and New Haven colonies specified that wedding ceremonies should be performed by magistrates. Rhode Island did likewise, making, however, an exception in favor of Quakers and clergymen of the Church of England. In 1733 Rhode Island extended this privilege to "settled and ordained ministers and elders of every society and denomination of Christians." Despite these prohibitions some ceremonies were performed by unauthorized persons and occasionally couples even went to the point of marrying themselves. For such "disorderly marriages" fines were imposed in Plymouth, but Rhode Island treated them as *de facto* marriages, in the spirit though not the words "illegal but not invalid." In 1665 the latter colony adopted a statute outlawing clandestine marriages, but providing that any persons reputed to live together as man and wife should not come under the new penalties even though "there may have been some neglect of the due observation of the rules."

There was no prescribed marriage ritual. Any appropriate words might be used. In the earliest years it was customary for the wedding to take place at the bride's home with a minimum of festivity.

18. Howard, *op. cit.*, Vol. II, p. 133. By permission of the University of Chicago Press.

In accordance with the principle that marriage was a civil contract, all the New England colonies required the registration of marriages, as well as of births and deaths. It is to this fact that we can attribute the relatively adequate and accurate vital statistics over a long period of time in New England.

Once married, with or without the occasion of romantic love, there was an infinitely more important love that was recognized, used in the language of home and pulpit, and was observed to be more than a fortunate accident. *Conjugal* love was "a duty imposed by God on all married couples, and a solemn obligation that resulted directly from the marriage contract."[19] But like all emotions that might lead to excess in their overt expression, the love of the husband and wife was deemed best when kept from the public, but existing as a quality of relationship about which each spouse in thinking of the other would need have no doubts.

Children

The figures available to us make it clear that both the birth rate and infant mortality were high. Housing was crude, sanitation was poor, food often improper and inadequate, quarantine was imperfect, knowledge of hygiene was limited, and medicine was mixed with astrology and necromancy. Hence children died in large numbers from diseases. Both birth and death were often accepted fatalistically as expressions of divine will, hardly subject to human control. In general it might be said that children were prized as "providential accidents," but they came into the world via "original sin," displaying "natural depravity." John Robinson, the Pilgrim preacher, said in an essay on children: "Surely there is in all children (though not alike) a stubbernes and stoutnes of minde arising from naturall pride which must in the first

19. Edmund S. Morgan, *The Puritan Family: Essays on Religion and Domestic Relations in Seventeenth Century New England* (1944), p. 12.

place be broken and beaten down that so the foundation of ther education being layd in humilitie and tractableness other virtues may in their time be built thereon."[20] Children were "to be seen and not heard," and not seen too much either! In some households they were made to stand through meals, eating whatever was handed to them. They were taught it was sinful to complain about food, clothing, or their lot in life. Courtesy of a formal sort was insisted upon. Corporal punishment seems to have been liberally employed. Use was made of birch rods, canes, "flappers" (leather strap with a hole in the middle), and at school dunce stools and caps and placards bearing humiliating names.

Thus the effort was made to break the will of children and keep them in subjection at home and at school. But discipline was not left entirely to the home and the school. Stern laws were enacted requiring strict obedience and fixing severe penalties for violation. For example, a Connecticut statute reads:

> If a man have a stubborn and rebellious son of sufficient years and understanding, viz. sixteen years of age, which will not obey the voice of his father or the voice of his mother, and that when they have chastened him will not harken unto them, then may his father and mother, being his natural parents, lay hold on him and bring him to the magistrates assembled in court, and testify unto them that their son is stubborn and rebellious and will not obey their voice and chastizement, but lives in sundry crimes, such a son shall be put to death.[21]

Religious training was given in a grim and almost morbid spirit. Children were warned of the wrath to come and the danger of being consigned to eternal torment. Cotton Mather took his little daughter Katy into his study and "sett before her the sinful Condition of her Nature." Samuel Sewall wrote in his diary on January 13, 1696, that his daughter Betty had become depressed so that she burst out crying without apparent reason. When asked by her mother why she did so, she

20. Alice M. Earle, *Child Life in Colonial Days* (1899), p. 192. By permission of The Macmillan Company.

21. J. Hammond Trumbull, ed., *op. cit.*, pp. 69-70.

replied that "she was afraid she would go to Hell, her sins were not pardon'd." Jonathan Edwards is reported to have "conversed with his children singly and closely about the concerns of their souls." Children were drilled in *The Shorter Catechism* or some similar book. They were sometimes required to read the Bible straight through, chapter by chapter, not even omitting Leviticus and Numbers. In keeping with all this, children were frequently taken to funerals and sometimes acted as pallbearers. The morbid outlook on life which supported these practices is suggested in Sewall's comment on his visit to the family tomb where he saw the coffins of his father, mother, cousin, and six children. " 'Twas an awful yet pleasing Treat."

A Connecticut law represents the standard of home training for colonial New England:

> The selectmen of every town . . . shall have a vigilant eye over their brethren and neighbors, to see first, that none of them suffer so much barbarism in any of their families as not to endeavor to teach themselves or others their children and apprentices so much learning as may enable them perfectly to read the English tongue, and knowledge of the capital laws, upon penalty of twenty shillings for each neglect therein; also, that all masters of families do once a week at least, catechise their children and servants in the grounds and principles of religion . . .
>
> And further, that all parents and masters do breed and bring up their children and apprentices in some honest lawful calling, labor, and employment . . . And if any of the selectmen, after admonition by them given to such masters of families, shall find them still negligent . . . the said selectmen, with the help of two magistrates, shall take such children or apprentices from them and place them with some masters for years, boys till they come to twenty-one and girls to eighteen years of age complete . . .22

While an important part of the educational function was performed in the home there were schools from an early time. These were primarily for boys, but sometimes girls were admitted during hours not devoted to the teaching of boys. One farmer said, "In winter it's too far for girls to walk; in summer they ought to stay at home to help in the kitchen."23 A

22. Trumbull, *op. cit.*, pp. 78-79.
23. Earle, *op. cit.*, p. 96. By permission of The Macmillan Company.

Connecticut town voted not to "waste" its money in the education of girls. Whether taught at home or in school girls learned chiefly to "sew, floure, write and dance." Some were taught to read and "cipher," but many were quite illiterate. Boys studied the three R's, plus Latin and Euclid. Neither boys nor girls had much time for play, although they had some toys and games. Boys played hopscotch, tag, marbles, and leapfrog; they went swimming and skating. But much of their time was spent doing chores, working in the fields, helping with spinning and the making of cider, soap, maple sugar, and other domestic industries.

We should not infer that all New England children were unloved and exploited. We must remember that the conditions of life were hard and that the younger generation had to contribute very early to the common welfare. However, there is no gainsaying that they grew up in an atmosphere that was Puritanic both literally and figuratively.

Broken Homes

In the section on Family Structure we observed that death frequently came to New England homes leaving widows, widowers, half-orphans, and orphans. In addition homes were sometimes broken by divorce or annulment. For the first time in our studies we have information about the actual frequency of divorce and annulment. At Plymouth, during its seventy-two years of existence as a separate colony, six divorces were granted. Three suits were brought by the husband, two by the wife, and one by the wife's father. Three were granted "on scriptural grounds," one for bigamy, one for nonsupport, and one for "eloping from the colony." In Massachusetts from 1639 to 1692 there were forty cases, twenty-seven brought by women, thirteen by the men. The results: twenty-five marriages dissolved, four annulled, two petitioners granted leave to remarry, five petitions denied, and four decisions not clearly specified. Desertion was alleged in sixteen cases, adultery in nine. From 1692 to 1739 we find no records. From 1739 to 1760 there were eleven cases, five brought by the husband, six by the wife. The results were three divorces *a vinculo,* two separations from bed and board, two annulments, one leave to marry, and three cases uncertain. After 1760 the number increased greatly. Between that date and 1786 there were ninety-six cases before the Governor and Council, forty brought by men and fifty-six by the women. The most frequent charges: adultery in sixty-eight cases, desertion in twenty-one, failure to provide in fifteen, cruelty in eleven. Others were having a bastard, venereal disease, wasting estate, and bigamy. Adultery was the sole ground in only seventeen cases, two or more causes being usually alleged. The decrees dissolved seventy-five marriages, annulled five, granted separate bed and board in seven, and leave to remarry in two. Three petitions were denied, one each dismissed, deferred, and accommodated. One outcome was not clear.

Family Controls

From the foregoing it is evident that custom and law combined to emphasize two aspects of the early New England family system: (1) everyone was expected to live as a member of some household; (2) the family was viewed essentially as an economic institution headed by an authoritarian father. In these respects New England followed closely in the steps of the mother country.

Marriage and Divorce

In the discussion of marital selection we indicated the legal controls over who might marry whom and under what conditions. These were not greatly different from those obtaining in the old country. But in the matter of dissolving marriages New England parted company with the mother country. Absolute divorces were more easily secured, but divorces "from bed and board" were rare in the northern colonies. In Massachusetts the legal grounds for divorce included female (not male) adultery, desertion "a year or two" with evidence of intention not to return, and cruel usage by the husband. In some cases involving unexplained absence of seven years the spouse was granted permission to marry again, without receiving a formal divorce. Until 1754 there were no legal separations *a mensa et toro*. Decrees of divorce were granted by popular assemblies as well as by legal tribunals.

Other New England colonies differed little except in detail. The Connecticut law of 1667 authorized the court of assistants to grant a bill of divorce to either husband or wife, with the privilege of remarriage, for adultery, fraudulent contract, three years' wilful desertion, or seven years' "providential absence." The Rhode Island law made specific mention only of adultery, but by implication recognized other grounds of divorce. In addition to divorce, colonial legislation provided for annulment on the grounds of bigamy, marriage within forbidden degrees, or impotence at the time of entering upon marriage.

Property and Its Inheritance

With reference to property rights and inheritance the northern colonists started with English laws and customs, which gave preferential treatment to male heirs, especially to eldest sons. But the New Englanders moved gradually toward a more nearly equal distribution of property. Fathers could and did exercise considerable discretion through making of wills in which a variety of arrangements was made. An early Massachusetts law provided that "when parents dye intestate, the Elder sonne shall have a double portion of his whole estate real and personal, unless the Generall Court upon just cause alleged shall judge otherwise."[24] In the New Haven

24. M. Robert Cobbledick, "The Property Rights of Women in Puritan New England," in George P. Murdock, ed., *Studies in the Science of Society* (1937), p. 108. By permission of Yale University Press.

Colony the law provided that if a will were improperly drawn or could not be "legally proved," the court was to follow "as neer as they rationally may, the scope, and aim of the testator." If a man died intestate, the court was to appoint an administrator and require of him a bond. After payment of debts the property was to be divided thus: one third to the widow and two thirds to the children, "with due respect to the eldest son, who is to have a double child's portion of the whole estate, real and personal."[25]

In 1656 New Haven extended the dower to include "money, goods, and chattels." For a short time Massachusetts did likewise, but the usual provisions were like those just quoted. In addition to her dower a widow recovered real estate which was her own but had been in the hands of her husband, also any obligations due her, and her "paraphernalia." A widower had the life use, not of one third, but of all of his deceased wife's property if they had had a child legally eligible to inherit his mother's estate. This was known as "curtesy of England."

In view of the many remarriages it is interesting to note that a widow and her prospective husband might be required to post a bond to assure the carrying out of the terms of a will or of a court order dividing her deceased husband's estate. A court sometimes intervened to make provision for children, if this had not been done in a will.

Sex Mores

Colonial New England had a stern code of sexual behavior. In keeping with the general hardness of life, the frowning on frivolity, and the attention to certain scriptural doctrines, the Puritans and their neighbors sought to prohibit all sexual activity save for procreation within marriage. But violations of the code were numerous. Perhaps the very efforts at repression, the inevitable gossip about scandals, the public confes-

25. Trumbull, *op. cit.*, pp. 266-268.

sions and punishments combined with natural human urges and the lack of other pleasures to stimulate an unhealthy interest in sex.

We have no means of comparing the relative frequency of sex offenses in colonial days with those of contemporary New England, but we do have some information about penalties imposed. Thus in Middlesex County, Massachusetts, from 1726 to 1780 there were 523 single women, 160 married couples, and 31 wives punished for sexual offenses. In the records of the Groton church it appears that from 1761 to 1775 the parents of one third of the children baptized made public confession of premarital intercourse.

Fornication was usually punished less severely than adultery. In Connecticut unmarried persons guilty of having sexual relations were "enjoined to marriage," fined, or whipped, or all three. Some offenders were made to stand in the pillory; others were branded on the cheek. If a young married couple should have a child "too soon," they were forced to make public confession in church to save the infant from eternal perdition. If an unbetrothed woman bore a child, she was whipped, fined, or imprisoned, even though she was known to have been seduced and deserted. If the father of her child was identified, he was in most cases unpunished, though he might be ordered to contribute to the child's support.

For adultery the original penalty, except in Plymouth and Rhode Island, was death. The records show that the law was no idle threat, for some offenders were actually executed. At Plymouth in 1639 a woman was sentenced to be "whipt at a cart tayle," "weare a badge upon her left sleeve," and if she went out without the badge to be "burned in the face with a hott iron."[26] The custom of the "scarlet letter" became law in Plymouth in 1658 and in Massachusetts in 1794. Rhode Island specified that an adulterer should be

. . . publickly set on the Gallows in the Day Time, with a Rope about his or her Neck, for the Space of One Hour; and on his or her Return from

26. Howard, *op. cit.,* Vol. II, p. 172. By permission of the University of Chicago Press.

the Gallows to the Gaol, shall be publickly whipped on his or her naked Back, not exceeding Thirty Stripes; and shall stand committed to the Gaol of the County wherein convicted, until he or she shall pay all Costs of Prosecution.[27]

If a betrothed woman was guilty of intercourse with a man other than her fiancé, both she and her companion were punished as adulterers. If an engaged couple were guilty of premarital sex relations, the civil court usually imposed a penalty about half that inflicted on persons not betrothed. As we have seen, the church also punished them by insisting on public confession. It is evident that a good many were "guilty of incontinence with each other after precontract before marriage."[28]

The mores of early New England included one very interesting custom known as "bundling." This is variously accounted for, but very likely began as a necessary phase of hospitality. A stranger was taken in for the night; a bed was shared regardless of the sex of its occupants. When a young man went courting the scarcity of candlelight and firewood made it natural for him and his intended to carry on their conversation under the bed covers, usually without removing their clothes. It appears that further intimacies did not necessarily follow. This custom seems to have been most widely practiced among the poorer folk and during the second half of the eighteenth century.

Other minor matters included the prohibition against the "loose and sinful custom" of men and women riding together from one town to another "upon pretense of going to lectures," but actually "to drink and revel" in taverns. "Mixed dancing" was generally condemned and in 1684 Increase Mather preached a strong sermon against "Gynecandrical Dancing." Even the May Pole was attacked as a form of vice. Along with all this censorship and "pathological publicity" Calhoun says there

27. *Ibid.*, p. 173. By permission of the University of Chicago Press.
28. *Ibid.*, p. 180. By permission of the University of Chicago Press.

was an "epidemic of sickly sentimentality . . . with excessive talk on love, matrimony, and 'Platonicks' even between comparative strangers."[29]

In New England we see a continuation of the trends noted for England in the preceding chapter. But in coming across the Atlantic, families were separated from their large kinship groups; they started life anew as nuclear families and households, which were parts of a community of other nuclear families and households. Hence it was natural that some of the old customs should be weakened or dropped.

Thus we see evidence of a slight movement away from the conception of family property held in trust by the male head, and a tendency to recognize individual rights. This tendency did not develop very far, but its very appearance is significant. As we proceed we shall note other evidences of incipient individualization, but we must not forget that a person was still regarded primarily as a member of a family group. Moreover, in the colonies as in England, the basic domestic unit was the often crowded household; it was not the small nuclear family nor the extended kinship group, although both of these were recognized parts of the social system. Also, in the colonies as in England, the household had very inclusive functions—educational, religious, protective, regulatory, procreational—but with heavy emphasis on the economic. We shall see that these inclusive functions of the household were even more accentuated in the Colonial South.

THE SOUTH

On the whole the culture of the South was much the same as that of New England, but still there were important differences between the two regions. In the South people settled less frequently in villages and more often on isolated planta-

29. Reprinted by permission of the publishers, the Arthur H. Clark Company, from Calhoun's *Social History of the American Family*, Vol. I (1919), pp. 136-137.

tions and farms. There were many Cavaliers and few Puritans. Many of the earliest settlers were detached males seeking their fortunes, instead of families seeking homes. There was marked stratification which involved social distance between first families, yeomen, a pioneer fringe of poor whites, indentured servants, and Negro slaves. Gradually there was built up a social system reminiscent of feudalism and chivalry, though actually very different from anything ever developed in Europe.

The Southern Household

On the large plantations of the coastal lowland and on the frontier each household was a relatively self-sufficient group, producing a large part of its own food, clothing, and other necessities, erecting buildings, making tools, training the children, caring for the sick, dispensing homemade justice, and providing amusement. These southern households were often much larger than those of New England, and they were more isolated.

As is the North, everyone was supposed to be a member of some such group, and all adults were expected to marry. After the first few years bachelors became scarce and at no time were there many "ancient maids of desperate expectations." In general unmarried adults were regarded as "pitiable encumbrances." But, as in New England, bachelors were sometimes viewed as enjoying unwarranted privileges and menacing the social order in which all free men belonged in families. In keeping with this spirit Maryland imposed a tax on bachelors.

In such a household system the experiences of bereavement, widowhood, and infanthood were quite different from those encountered in the small family system of a contemporary city. Being in a large group of kinsmen and other close associates must have meant a diffusion of affection and dependence, and provided a broader basis of security. Death took away loved ones, but less frequently broke up homes. Instead of the orphan going away to live with someone, he commonly stayed on in the same household of which he was already a member. However, there were cases in which children deprived of one or both parents were "bound out," and a few were placed in orphan asylums. Widows and widowers also generally continued in the household, but the younger ones were likely to remarry soon.

The maintenance of the large household was facilitated by the laws and customs of inheritance. In general these were much alike throughout all the English colonies. But in the South male heirs had greater advantages than in New England. At first the trustees of Georgia Colony restricted the transmission of real estate to males. Later this ruling was modified so as to give a widow life use of part of the property and to permit daughters to inherit, if there were no male heirs. Gradually the custom of leaving the manor house and principal lands to the eldest son paved the way for legal establishment of primogeniture in Virginia. In Maryland property might be distributed by will, but in case of intestacy the estate went to the eldest son. Thus lands were kept in the same male line for many generations. Families were identified both with the name and with the estate.

Southern Chivalry and Sex Mores

The phrase "southern chivalry" suggests a social code quite distinct from anything found in New England. It has come to represent a tradition of graciousness, romance, respect, and solicitude for women, which presently developed in upper-class families, but which at first was not much in evidence anywhere, and was never general among the common people. We shall describe later the marriage market of early Virginia, the economic considerations emphasized in many a premarital agreement, and the assumption of responsibilities by women of all social classes, all of which indicate clearly that "putting woman on a pedestal," except in the ritual of courtship, was far from universal, and hardly present at all in the early years.

But certain factors contributed toward the adulation of

women of the aristocracy. First of all was their scarcity value. Then with the development of great plantations, the accumulation of wealth, and the delegation of menial labor to slaves and bond-servants, came the cultivation of "social graces." Chivalry of the South was, of course, unlike that of medieval England in many respects, but there were not a few similarities. Neither system was incompatible with marital infidelity, but while the original chivalry gave especially to women the privilege of freely bestowing their favors, southern chivalry closely guarded the purity of upper-class women, while condoning promiscuity on the part of their husbands. Both types of chivalry were obviously class institutions. In the South the courtesy, protection, and service rendered to women of the aristocracy were rarely shown to yeomen, poor whites, and Negroes.

Even among the first families women often occupied an inferior position. We have noted the restrictions on inheritance, and we shall find that they received little education. Popular attitudes were in keeping with these practices. Col. William Byrd in telling of visits to Virginia homes made such comments as these: "We supped about nine and then prattled with the ladies . . . Our conversation with the ladies was like whip-syllabub, very pretty but nothing in it."[30] A book called *The Ladies Calling*, published in 1673, described the peculiarly feminine virtues as modesty, meekness, compassion, affability, and piety. Another book entitled *The Gentleman and Lady Instructed*, published in 1723, cautioned women not to "wade too deep into controversy," for such studies "lie out of a Lady's way." *The Virginia Gazette* in 1737 advised women for the "advancement of matrimonial felicity" never to dispute with their husbands, whatever might be the occasion. "Generally it was stated that the husband should guide, defend and provide for the wife, while she was to serve him in subjection, be

30. Alice M. Earle, *Colonial Dames and Goodwives* (1895), p. 189. By permission of The Macmillan Company.

modest in speech and dress, and be a good housewife."[31] It was held that "while marriage was for man a pleasant duty, it was woman's reason for existence."[32]

In actual practice we find evidence of conjugal devotion, loyalty, and affection in some cases, and of discord and discontent in others. Colonial newspapers published many notices of voluntary separations and refusal of a man to be responsible for his wife's debts. These advertisements sometimes carried charges, usually against a wife, charges of being "fond of men's company," "refusing to cohabit as a wife," scandalizing her husband," or "eloping from his bed and board." Journalists commented with "reflections on unhappy marriages," which they attributed to such causes as "female extravagance," neglect of domestic duties, and the like.

In contrast with these wives who were charged with failure to fulfill their marital duties, most women appear to have been faithful wives and mothers, hard-working housekeepers, and, in the absence of their husbands, managers of farm or business. Women of the aristocracy, as well as their less favored sisters, sometimes assumed great responsibilities.

It was in the sex mores that male dominance and female subordination were most clearly displayed. Premarital chastity and marital fidelity of white women, especially upper-class women, were supreme values. But white men were relatively free and Negro women were available for exploitation. Thus there were not only different requirements for male and female, but also for Negro and white. In the *Lady's Magazine* for August, 1771, appears this statement:

A licentious commerce between the sexes . . . may be carried on by men without contaminating the mind, so as to render them unworthy of the marriage bed, and incapable of discharging the virtuous and honorable duties of husband, father, friend . . . the contamination of the female mind

31. Julia C. Spruill, *Woman's Life and Work in the Southern Colonies* (1938), p. 163. By permission of the University of North Carolina Press.
32. *Ibid.*, p. 136.

is the necessary and inseparable consequence of an illicit intercourse with men . . . women are universally virtuous or utterly undone.[33]

Women were warned against jealousy and advised to conceal knowledge of their husbands' infidelity. An inquisitive wife who tried to pry into her mate's "left-handed connections" was considered more contemptible than he, provided, of course, that he kept his affairs reasonably private. It was reported that governors of Maryland and Georgia openly kept mistresses and numerous North Carolina gentlemen acknowledged illegitimate children. Cases of adultery and bastardy sometimes got to court, but the parties involved were of the lower classes. "Nice" people shut their eyes to such affairs, as they did to violation of laws against miscegenation.

The statutes of southern colonies were milder than those enacted in New England—no death sentence, no scarlet letter, and no pillory. However, Virginia imposed fines and whippings. Maryland ordered that persons guilty of adultery or fornication should be censured and punished as the governor and council might see fit, but "not extending to life or member." If the offending woman were a bond servant she was to be held in servitude one or two years beyond the expected time of her release. Her male companion might be made to pay damages to her master. If he were single and a freeman and had promised to marry the girl, the Maryland law of 1658 said "that then hee shall performe his promise to her, or recompense her abuse, as the court before whom such matter is brought shal see convenient, the quality and condition of the persons considered."[34] If the master himself were the child's father, he could claim no extra services from the woman, but the parish could extend her servitude an extra year. Similar legislation was adopted in Virginia and North Carolina.

33. *Ibid.,* p. 72. By permission of the University of North Carolina Press.

34. Reprinted by permission of the publishers, The Arthur H. Clark Company, from Calhoun's *Social History of the American Family,* Vol. I (1919), p. 313.

The southern colonists were less severe than New England in dealing with premarital incontinence. However, punishment was sometimes inflicted even though the couple was legally married before the birth of a child. Occasionally public confession was demanded, but evidently not so frequently as in Massachusetts.

A further word should be said about irregular sex relations involving white and black. The usual relation was quite casual, compliance of the slave woman being effected by prestige of the white male. But there were also cases of enduring mutual attraction. Such concubinage naturally aroused jealousy on the part of white women, who sought revenge and restoration of their holds on husbands by arranging sale or marriage of female slaves. Jealousy sometimes centered on the mulatto offspring, especially if the master showed them attention and favors. When white men displayed attachment to colored mistresses and their children, attempts were sometimes made to prove the masters' mental incompetence. Frazier holds that "all classes of whites in the South were involved," masters, overseers, and "poor whites."[35]

Marriage and Its Control

As in New England, marital selection involved a mixture of romantic and practical considerations.[36] The early settlers in Virginia, being mostly young bachelors, became restless and unwilling to put themselves into the hard work of hewing homes out of the wilderness. So Sir Edwin Sandys arranged for the shipment of young women from England to become wives of the "adventurers." The men were to pay for the girls' passage 120 pounds of tobacco each. In this and other colonies white bond servants often became the wives of settlers.

35. E. Franklin Frazier, *The Negro Family in the United States* (1939), p. 77. By permission of the University of Chicago Press.

36. An excellent depiction of growing up and getting married in eighteenth-century Virginia is found in Edmund S. Morgan's *Virginians at Home* (1952).

All through colonial times girls married at an early age. She who remained single at twenty was reckoned a "stale maid." Men too usually married while very young. But, as in New England, there were numerous weddings of widowers and of widows; hence some brides and some grooms were more advanced in years.

After the establishment of family life in the South parental consent was generally a prerequisite of courtship and marriage. The proprieties among upper-class folks rendered the opening of courtship rather tedious and matter-of-fact. The initiative was always supposed to be taken by the man. For a maiden to acknowledge that she was in love was not "consistent with the perfection of female delicacy."[37] Girls were advised to choose "men of sense," and young men were urged to select wives who were "agreeable, sensible, and of 'equal' family and fortune."[38] There was open bargaining over property that might be involved in a marriage, and formal contracts were sometimes drawn. In keeping with these economic considerations there were suits for breach of promise, usually brought by disappointed swains. Clearly, romantic love had not yet become the chief basis for marriage.

Marriages were prohibited within the Levitical degrees. For each sex there were thirty grades of kinsmen or in-laws who were forbidden as mates. Servants were denied the right to marry at all without their masters' consent. Miscegenation of white with Indian or Negro was quite generally forbidden. Nevertheless many mulatto children appeared as a result of illicit unions. Matings of slave with slave ranged from very casual unions to cases of permanent monogamy, depending largely on the policy of the master.

In all the southern colonies except Maryland the Church of England assumed dominance, and its rules requiring solemnization of marriage by an Anglican clergyman were enforced

37. Spruill, *op. cit.*, p. 220. By permission of the University of North Carolina Press.
38. *Ibid., p.* 153.

with varying degrees of success. This, of course, was in marked contrast with the practices of New England. The Virginia law of 1657-58 provided that "ministers only shall celebrate marriages." They might do so only after the publications of banns three different Sundays in the parish churches where the parties lived. In lieu of banns a license might be secured from the governor, and after 1661 from the county clerk. Such licenses were not to be issued "without certificate under the hands of the parents, masters or guardians."[39] By the act of 1705 a bond was required, but parental consent was necessary only in the case of minors. A record of all marriages solemnized was ordered to be kept by the clergy of each parish. This monopoly on weddings lasted in Virginia until 1794. But in spite of strict laws there were clandestine marriages and not a few couples ran away to Maryland where legislation was more liberal.

Having Catholic proprietors, Maryland naturally did not support the Anglican Church or its regulations pertaining to matrimony. But in contrast to the general rule of the Catholic Church, Maryland legalized civil ceremonies as early as 1658. Persons wishing to be married had the option of a magistrate or minister. Curiously this liberty, after lasting all through the Colonial period, was taken away during the Revolution.

In the Carolinas it was evidently considered that an Anglican ceremony performed by a clergyman of that church was the normal procedure, but due to a scarcity of ministers the governor of North Carolina and members of his council were authorized to join persons in wedlock. In South Carolina an act of 1706 gave a monopoly of solemnizing matrimony to the established clergy, but in the back country this was quietly disregarded. Toward the end of the eighteenth century Presbyterian ministers were singled out from other dissenters and authorized to perform wedding ceremonies. Finally this priv-

39. George E. Howard, *A History of Matrimonial Institutions* (1904), Vol. II, p. 233. By permission of the University of Chicago Press.

ilege was extended to "regular ministers of the gospel of every denomination." The history of marriage laws in Georgia was much the same.

As a matter of fact, access to civil officers and to clergy of any sort was for many people very difficult. Hence not a few couples proceeded to live as man and wife without any ceremony at all. Their action was open and unashamed, their friends and relatives considered them to be married, and under varying circumstances the law accepted them as such. All this was in keeping with the traditional consent *per verba de praesenti* and the agreement *per verba de futuro* followed by *copula carnalis*. It rested on the legal theory that "marriage is nothing but a contract; and to render it valid, it is only necessary, upon the principles of natural law, that the parties should be able to contract—willing to contract, and should actually contract."[40] Thus arose what is still called "common-law marriage."

Once a marriage was entered into by religious or civil ceremony or by "common law" it was presumably indissoluble. Throughout the southern colonies no legal provision was made for divorce *a vinculo* or *a mensa et toro*. No court was given jurisdiction over such matters nor can we find a record of any absolute divorce by legislative act. However, there were separations by mutual consent, and, without specific legal authority, courts sometimes granted alimony. Now and then a marriage was annulled. In the back country it appears that separations as well as marriage were more freely arranged than in the older settlements near the coast. Among slaves marriages were frequently disrupted without great concern for the interests of spouses or their children.

Children

It is obvious that children in the southern colonies grew up under varyng circumstances, depending on the social class

40. From an 1821 decision of the Kentucky Court of Appeals, quoted by Ernest R. Groves, *The American Family* (1934), p. 349.

into which they were born.[41] On the higher levels they enjoyed such comforts as the age provided and they received the attention of nurses, tutors, and governesses. The young children of small farmers were cared for chiefly by their own mothers. But very early they began to assume responsibilities and to share the work of house, barn, and field. Children of indentured servants and of slaves must have received rather haphazard attention. No doubt they were soon included in the working force.

As in New England the birth rate was consistently high and apparently the death rate followed the same trend. Dr. Brickell wrote in 1737:

> The women are very fruitful, most houses being full of little ones, and many women from other places who have been long married without children, have removed to Carolina and become joyful mothers, as has often been observed. It very seldom happens they miscarry, and they have very easie travail in the child-bearing . . .[42]

We are hardly justified in assuming that childbearing was always as easy and happy an experience as portrayed by Dr. Brickell. But we do recognize a fatalistic attitude toward birth and death which is further illustrated by the statement of a Quaker who had just buried his tenth child:

> It was some exercise to me thus to bury my children one after another; but this did a little mitigate my sorrow, that I knew . . . it was safer and better for them, and they more out of danger, being taken away in their infancy and innocency . . .[43]

All this sounds much like New England. But there were other ways in which children were differently regarded and

41. Morgan, *Virginians at Home,* Chap. 1, pp. 5-28.
42. Reprinted by permission of the publishers, The Arthur H. Clark Company, from Calhoun's *Social History of the American Family,* Vol. I (1919), p. 287.
43. Spruill, *op. cit.,* p. 54. By permission of the University of North Carolina Press.

treated in the South. Especially in upper-class families there was less personal care of children by their mothers. Instead, there was the previously mentioned succession of nurses, tutors, and governesses. There were far fewer schools than in New England, and it is said that only three white men out of five could sign their own names, and only one white woman out of three. On the lower economic levels child labor was almost universal. In their own homes or elsewhere as indentured servants or slaves, children early did their share of heavy work. Virginia received several shiploads of "friendless boyes and girlcs," evidently kidnapped from their homes and sent over to provide cheap and docile labor for the American planters. Perhaps in compensation for this exploitation, perhaps merely as part of the religious spirit of the day, parents and masters were expected to have their children baptized and catechized.

The Slave Family

Obviously the buying and selling of slaves made for impermanent relations between the sexes. Another factor was the fact that not until 1840 were the numbers of women equal to those of men. In some cases where the sex ratio was reversed it is said that Negro males were set up as stallions. There were cases of intercourse between Negro men and indentured white women, some of which may even have been stimulated by masters with a view to increasing the number of mulatto slaves. Finally, Negro women were the occasional bedmates and sometimes the continuing concubines of white masters.

All these things interfered with the usual types of conjugal family organization, i.e., father-mother-children. This is not to say that all white masters were inconsiderate of their slaves, or that there were no formalities or no permanent unions. We simply mean that stable marriage groups came into being and continued under great handicaps.

Under these circumstances the mother and her offspring constituted in many cases the continuing group. The father was sometimes absent, sometimes irresponsible. The mother was the most dependable and the most important figure in the family. Often the affection between her and her children was very strong. At other times there was apparent rejection of her children. If they were not the product of an enduring relationship with their father, if she could not keep them with her, it is not surprising that "maternal feeling was choked and dried up." Sometimes she got a substitute satisfaction through caring for the master's children, displaying in herself the "mammy" stereotype.

FUNCTIONS OF THE COLONIAL FAMILY

On the whole colonial families performed a wide range of functions for their members. Of course the slave family had no important economic, educational, or religious responsibility, but it was in many cases a center of affection. Both in New England and in the South, but especially in the South, the most important economic unit was the household rather than the family. Under the direction of the father and master many sorts of work were carried on—tilling the soil, raising livestock, erecting buildings, and making and repairing vehicles and implements. His wife often supervised spinning, weaving, sewing, cooking, preserving, soap making, and other domestic arts. The household was very nearly a self-sufficient economic unit. It also gave children a large part of their education, general, vocational, and religious. More often in the North than in the South there were public or private schools; hence southern homes were relatively more important educational agencies than were those of New England. The same was true of recreation. But in matters of religion we have the impression that the New England family was more active than the southern. Most of the differences we have noted are bound up with the general differences between village and plantation life, plus the contrasts between Puritan and Cavalier.

In both regions the procreational function was stressed.

The white men sought an increase of population that the plantations might "spread into the generations." The family was also viewed as an agency for the regulation of sex. For the "avoiding of fornication," marriage was urged upon those "that have not the gift of continency." At the very outset Virginia promoted marriage as a means of holding men in the colony and of making them contented with their lot. But throughout the colonies companionship was valued, "the mutuall comforting of each other." There are many evidences of affection in families, both northern and southern. However the expression of such feeling was commonly restrained and formal. A New England sea captain was severely punished for publicly kissing his wife on Sunday, having just returned from a long voyage. It is possible that there was less repression of marital affection in the South, but there may have been just as much formality imposed on the relations between parents and children. Wherever families were large, mothers probably had little time for any but their youngest children. Fathers and sons worked together, but there apparently were not many occasions for the expression of tender emotions. Among Negroes the affectional function appears to have been relatively more important than among whites, primarily because the slave family had so few other functions. But among the blacks affection was not always in evidence, for reasons noted in the preceding section.

In general it is correct to say that the family was a much more important *institution* in colonial times than today. Its functions were much more inclusive, almost everyone was a member of some family group, and there were fewer agencies of other kinds to threaten the family's hold on its members.

REFERENCES

Andrews, Charles M., *Colonial Folkways, A Chronicle of American Life in the Reign of the Georges*. New Haven: Yale University Press, 1919.

Bruce, H. Addington, *Women in the Making of America*. Boston: Little, Brown and Company, 1928.

Calhoun, Arthur W., *A Social History of the American Family*. New York: Barnes and Noble, Inc., 1945, 3 volumes.

Cobbledick, M. Robert, "The Property Rights of Women in Puritan New England," in George P. Murdock, ed., *Studies in the Science of Society*. New Haven: Yale University Press, 1937, pp. 107-116.

Demos, John, *A Little Commonwealth: Family Life in Plymouth Colony*. New York: Oxford University Press, 1970.

Ditzion, Sidney, *Marriage Morals and Sex in America*. New York: Bookman Associates, 1953.

Earle, Alice M., *Child Life in Colonial Days*. New York: The Macmillan Company, 1899.

———, *Colonial Dames and Goodwives*. Boston: Houghton Mifflin Company, 1895.

Farber, Bernard, *Guardians of Virtue: Salem Families in 1800*. New York: Basic Books, Inc., 1972.

Fithian, Philip Vickers, *Journal and Letters, 1767-1774*. Princeton: Princeton University Library, 1900.

Frazier, E. Franklin, *The Negro Family in the United States*. Chicago: University of Chicago Press, 1939.

Goodsell, Willystine, *A History of Marriage and the Family*. New York: The Macmillan Company, 1934, Chapter IX.

Goodwin, John A., *The Pilgrim Republic, on Historical Review of the Colony of New Plymouth*. Boston: Houghton Mifflin Company, 1879.

Greven, Philip J., *Four Generations: Population, Land, and Family in Colonial Andover, Massachusetts*. Ithaca and London: Cornell University Press, 1970.

Groves, Ernest R., *The American Family*. Philadelphia: J. B. Lippincott Company, 1934.

Hosmer, James K., ed., *Winthrop's Journal*. New York: Charles Scribner's Sons, 1908.

Howard, George E., *A History of Matrimonial Institutions*. Chicago: University of Chicago Press, 1904, Volume II, Chapters XII-XV.

Kelso, Robert W., *The History of Public Poor Relief in Massachusetts*. Boston and New York: Houghton Mifflin Company, 1922.

Morgan, Edmund S., *The Puritan Family: Essays on Religion and Domestic Relations in Seventeenth-Century New England.* Boston: Published by the Trustees of the Public Library, 1944. Published as *The Puritan Family* by Harper Bros., 1966.

————, *Virginians at Home: Family Life in the Eighteenth Century.* Williamsburg: Colonial Willamsburg, Inc., 1952.

Spruill, Julia C., *Woman's Life and Work in the Southern Colonies.* Chapel Hill: University of North Carolina Press, 1938.

Trumbull, J. Hammond, ed., *The True Blue Laws of Connecticut and the False Blue Laws Invented by the Rev. Samuel Peters.* Hartford: American Publishing Company, 1876.

Van Doren, Mark, ed., *Samuel Sewall's Diary* (abridged from a three-volume edition published by the Massachusetts Historical Society). New York: Macy-Masius, 1927.

Weeden, William B., *Economic and Social History of New England, 1620-1789.* Boston: Houghton Mifflin Company, 1890, 2 volumes.

Part Three

14 Transition to the Modern American Family

Since the English colonies along the Atlantic seaboard became a nation, many changes have taken place in the institution which we call the American family. These have been accompanied by many other changes which, in a popular sense, may be said to have "caused" the changes in family life. At least the latter can not be understood except in relation to the former.

To begin with there has been immense territorial expansion spreading the American people over areas as diverse as Florida and North Dakota, Pennsylvania and Texas, Alaska and Hawaii. To fill in these "wide open spaces" the population has grown from 4 million to 210 million; of this the urban portion has increased from less than one tenth to over two thirds. Ten metropolitan centers alone contain some 45 million people. While part of the population increase represents the excess of births over deaths, another large part is due to immigration. Forty million immigrants have come from Ireland, Germany, Scandinavia, Italy, Poland, the Orient, Latin America, Africa, and indeed every part of the world. Thus we have become a somewhat heterogeneous people living in quite diverse geographic regions. On the other hand, improvement in transportation and communication, together with constantly changing economic opportunity and demand for labor in different areas, have kept our people on the move and have facilitated the processes of acculturation and assimilation. Out of the "melting pot" is coming a quasi-homogeneous, certainly a very different, American people with new patterns of marital selection, child rearing, and all the other elements that go to make up the institution we call the family. Finally, we must mention the greatly increased wealth and heightened level of living. Poverty and hardship have not been abolished, but most American families enjoy facilities of which their grand-parents never dreamed. The transition from log house, fire-place, hand churn, washing kettle in the back yard, wool from the sheep's back to the children's back, and home-produced foods—from all these marks of pioneer life—to steam-heated apartment, electric lights, vacuum cleaner, garbage disposal, packaged foods from delicatessen and supermarket, ready-made clothes, automobile, radio, and TV—this transition has been accompanied by great changes in use of time, changed roles of all ages and of both sexes, changed structure and function of the family.

Family Structure

One important change has been the decline of the large family household and much greater emphasis on the smaller nuclear family. There are, of course, many kinship groups characterized by frequent contacts, occasional reunions, mutual aid, tradition and family pride. But, in general, the ties that once united three or four generations of kinsmen and cousins are less evident than a century ago. To increasing numbers of Americans "family" means husband and wife, parents and children. Many factors have contributed to this transition. First there has been physical mobility, a pushing west to ever new frontiers, moving from farm to city, and in the twentieth-century migrations associated with two world wars and a great depression. Along with all this there has been the mingling of peoples of diverse ethnic and religious groups, including much intermarriage. When Catholic marries Protestant or Irish mar-ries German the chances of detachment from the kinsmen of both are greatly increased. When members of the younger generation obtain an education well beyond the level of their elders, enter new occpuations, receive incomes never dreamed of by their kinsfolk, or move from farm to city or from Arkansas to California, there are very likely to be breaks in family ties. On the other hand, some people settle down in a given area and remain long enough to build up a new extended family. Hence the transformation is by no means complete, and the likelihood of nuclear families existing autonomously and in isolation from other consanguinal and affinal kin is quite remote.

While the nuclear family has become more important it has also become smaller. In 1790, when the first United States census was taken, the median-sized household (not the same as nuclear family) was 5.7, in 1965 it was 3.7, and in 1972 it was 3.1. In those early days a household often included grandparents, in-laws, other relatives, "hired hands," apprentices, and sometimes lodgers. In 1970 there was less than one such person for every two families. There has been an especially sharp decline in domestic servants and dependent elders. Thus today the household and the nuclear family are nearly identical. All but about two percent of married couples maintain homes of their own.[1] While birth registration was far from complete during much of our history, there is much evidence that the birth rate has gradually declined, except for a fluctuating increase between 1945 and 1956. The current birth rate in 1973 is nevertheless above the level necessary to maintain a stable population for the next several decades, even though women are averaging only about two children in the course of their childbearing years. The reason lies in the fact of a large proportion of youth now in the population, and we can expect an increase in the total number until the end of the century, despite a slowly dropping birth rate.

There has been a gradual change in the roles and status of the sexes, particularly of women. During most of the nine-

---

1. *The American Almanac: The Statistical Abstract of the United States* (1973), p. 39

teenth century women were, with few exceptions, homemakers, sexual mates, teachers of the young (at home), nurses of the sick (at home), and guardians of the aged, infirm, and otherwise handicapped (at home). Although none of these roles has completely disappeared, the last three have fallen into the background. Today over forty-one percent of wives are gainfully employed outside the home, and the number is likely to continue to rise.[2] Some wives are supplementing their husband's income; some are the sole support of their families; some are career women. Among women not gainfully employed outside the home, some are social butterflies, and others are busy with civic, philanthropic, and religious activities, but a great many are genuine partners in the conduct of family affairs and are real companions of their husbands, sharing pleasures and woes, achievements and failures.

Recently we have witnessed the emergence of a social movement to "liberate" American women from the bonds of their perceived second-class citizenship—in many states they are discriminated against in securing credit cards, cashing checks, making loans, ordering and charging catalog items, owning certain kinds of property, in the marriage vows, and in a variety of ways reminiscent of earlier male-dominated centuries, but scarcely compatible with modern democratic precepts and usages. The goals of the protest group center around equality of treatment from males and the securing of equal rights before the law. The social consequences of such proposed reforms would be far-reaching in respect not only to the role of woman in society and in male-female relations, but also for changing family, particularly intrafamily, role relationships. But whatever the developments over the immediate future it is evident that among those sectors of American society where the new activist-oriented woman's liberation movement has made its greatest strides, among middle-class and more educated persons, marriages are changing willy-nilly toward either an equality-based or a consensus lacking loosely

2. *Ibid.*, p. 219.

arranged companionship in which traditional conventions, usages, and marriage folkways are constantly being reviewed, renegotiated, and sometimes hopefully or resignedly abandoned.

The roles of husbands appear to have changed much less. In the nineteenth century most husbands (as farmers, small town merchants, and the like) were managers of an economic enterprise in which other members of the family participated. Today a man is most often the principal, though not always the sole, source of income. He spends more time out of the home than in former days. His wife and children know less about his vocational activities and the sources of the family's sustenance.

Along with these changing roles have come challenges to the earlier male dominance. Still in many families most decisions, most initiative, the planning of major moves, the management of finances, and other activities involving power are in the hands of the husband-father. On the other hand, there are many families in which these functions and the associated power rest with the wife-mother. Sometimes there is a partnership with a sharing of initiative and responsibilities. All too often there is conflict and something of a power struggle. Perhaps even more often there is confusion and ambivalence, with both husband and wife uncertain as to division or sharing of labor, authority, and responsibility. These uncertainties contribute to instability in many American families.

The *percentage* of broken homes appears to change very little from year to year, but the percent broken by death has declined, while the percent broken by divorce has grown. During the nearly hundred years for which nationwide data are available divorce has increased rather steadily, the only breaks in the rising rate being in the early 1930's and the middle 1940's. No matter how the rate may be computed, there has been a marked rise in the ratio of divorces to marriages, to the total population, and to ten-year averages.[3] In 1971 there were thirty-four divorces granted for every 100 marriages in the

3. Ray E. Baber, *Marriage and the Family* (1953), pp. 446-447.

United States.[4] Most divorces occur in the early years of marriage, but many also appear in middle age. The relative frequency of divorce is greater for familes without children than for those who have some. In addition to divorces there is a large number of informal separations, which are often permanent, and there are desertions of varied duration. Together, these separations are probably more numerous than divorces. Finally there is a small number of annulments. Perhaps it would be no exaggeration to say that today from one third to one half of all marriages are doomed to failure. In any case family stability is not one of the outstanding characteristics of the modern United States.

The structure of family relationships is often disturbed and sometimes drastically changed by crises other than marital conflict and death. Prolonged unemployment of the husband-father, especially when other members of the family find jobs, often means a shift of prestige and power. The man's status may pass from head of the family to that of idler around the house, to that of a nuisance, and finally to that of a reject. Serious illness or chronic disability may also threaten the stability of family structure. If the husband-father is the patient, the wife as sickroom attendant may withdraw her attention from the children. When the woman becomes the manager, guidance and discipline of the children may be weakened. Illness or serious handicap of a child may make it difficult for the mother to meet the needs of her husband and may increase sibling rivalries. Finally, illness of the wife-mother may subject both husband and children to neglect or "undersupport."

Family Cycle

Changes in the family cycle have been computed from the United States Census by Paul Glick.[5] From 1890 to 1950 the

4. *The American Almanac, op. cit.,* p. 50.
5. Paul C. Glick, *American Families* (1957); Paul C. Glick and Robert Parke, Jr., "New Approaches in Studying the Life Cycle of the Family," *Demography,* 2 (1965), pp. 187-202.

median age at first marriage declined for both men and women,[6] as did their age at birth of the first child and at marriage of the last child. However, the age at which either husband or wife was widowed, and the age at which the survivor died, both increased. This means a relatively shorter period of child bearing and a shorter period of child rearing, in spite of the extension of "infancy"—more correctly economic dependency— through the high school years. Finally, there is, on the average, a longer period during which husband and wife might be called "postgraduate parents," with at least sixteen years between the first marriage of the last child and the death of the spouse.

In marital selection the rule is "free choice" on the basis of romantic love by the youth and maiden directly concerned. Marriages are often across ethnic and religious lines, as well as across more hazy class lines. Frequently a young person selects a mate not known to his or her kin. In colonial times the sequence was generally parental permission, brief courtship, banns, wedding. Today for the high school and college sets it is dating, "pinning," engagement, wedding. For others there may be no equivalent of "pinning" or engagement; they may go directly from dating to marriage. Dating itself has passed through several changes in the cycle of fashions. In an earlier time it was exclusive and pointed directly toward marriage. From about the turn of the century to World War II there was much "playing the field," gradually more exclusive dating, engagement, wedding. Today "going steady" is again in vogue, but it is wondered if the boys and girls, from junior high school to university can remember who it was they were "going steady with" last year.

As noted, since late in the nineteenth century and until recently the average age at first marriage has been slowly but steadily declining. Many young married people are still in school, some of them subsidized by their parents. For some there is an extended "companionate" before arrival of the

6. In the last two decades it has levelled off. See below.

first child. During this time it is common for either or both to
go to school or have a job or both. But others are not so
careful, and pregnancy interrupts the girl's schooling or
employment. Financial difficulties often ensue, and some young
careers are stopped before they get under way. About a fifth of
first-married females are pregnant before marriage.

Children are less numerous than they were a century ago,
but the decline in numbers has been much less than is popularly supposed. Since World War II the number has increased.
The actual care and rearing of children differs considerably
from that of earlier times, but it also differs greatly now as
between social classes and ethnic groups. Though most of the
nineteenth century children spent a large part of their time
in the home, tasks were assigned at an early age, and an important part of the preparation for adult life was gained from sharing household and farm work with the parents. Today children spend much more time in school and in organized groups.
Small children have been subjected to waves of fashion as to
rigid or permissive training. School children enjoy earlier independence as to spending money and dates, but cling to economic dependence longer than a hundred years ago. There is a
good deal of ambivalence on the part of both parents and children as to their relations.

In a study by Miller and Swanson[7] the development of
parent-child relationships in the United States has been traced
through four broad periods. From the mid-eighteenth century to the Civil War there was a decline in efforts to
"break the child's will," which we noted in colonial times.
From the Civil War to World War I there was a decline in
corporal punishment and the arbitrary use of parental authority. Between the two world wars there came an era of formal
and rigid schedules in the name of science. Finally, since
World War II there has been more permissiveness with reference to such matters as weaning, toilet training, and discipline.

7. Daniel R. Miller and Guy E. Swanson, *The Changing American
Parent* (1958), Chap. 1.

In a society like that of the United States in the early 1970's there are, of course, many variations, by social class, by religion, and by ethnic group. In some families children are regarded as assets for display, as future help in making a living, as support in old age, continuers of the family line, or a projection of parental ambitions. In other families there is more emphasis on children as liabilities—a disturbance of adult routine, interference with the mother's social life or career, and added expense. In some families there is marked ambivalence about children. Some parents display a martyr complex, punishing themselves in the name of "setting a good example," and in general acquiring the reputation of being "good parents," while resenting their "great responsibility." Finally, there are parents who regard each child as a "bundle of potentialities," a growing personality with his own life to lead after passing through a gradual transition from complete dependence to relative independence, but still integrated into the family and other social groups.

The period of adolescence seems, in our society, to be particularly trying. The teen-agers may demand both independence—with freedom to make choices and be just "like the rest of the gang"—and dependence—expecting father to pay the bills and get them out of trouble with school authorities, employers, or the law. They often assert the right of sexual freedom without expecting to assume responsibility—physical, economic, psychological, or social—for the consequences of their acts. Those who drop out of high school are most likely to become unemployed.

After the children are grown and have left home, the man is likely to carry on much as before. His job, business, or profession still occupies most of his waking hours. But the woman who has been a devoted mother often finds herself stranded. She may putter around and fill the day with small chores that can be completed in two to four hours. She may take up new church, charitable, or civic activities. She may shop, play bridge, converse on the telephone, or worry about her health. On the other hand, the woman who has kept up her hobbies or vocational activities may have little difficulty in making the transition. In fact, with increased leisure, husband and wife may do more things together and enjoy a second companionate period.

To summarize, the life cycle of an average middle-class family in the contemporary United States progresses from marital selection, a stage involving dating, "going steady," "pinning," engagement, and, finally, wedding. This commonly extends from the early 'teens to the early twenties. In the eighty years from 1890 to 1970 the median age of a husband at his first marriage dropped from twenty-six to twenty-three, of his wife from twenty-two to twenty. In most recent times, the first child has usually appeared in a year; thus the first "companionate" was not very long. The period of child-bearing was on the average short, under nine years. But from the birth of the first child to the marriage of the last child was about twenty-eight years, a long period of child rearing and support. The "second companionate" ran, on the average, about sixteen years, followed by widowhood of nine years, if the husband survived, sixteen years if the wife survived. Three out of four wives survive their husbands.

Family Controls

In the peoples and cultures that we have examined, from the Todas of India to the English colonists in North America, there appears to have been in each—except perhaps in the Roman Empire—a large degree of uniformity and stability, which is much less evident in the twentieth-century United States. In those other cultures social control seems to have been fairly effective in making people conform with respect to marriage, child rearing, sex relations, and other aspects of family life. So far as we can discover, individual persons and individual families had to make relatively few decisions in these matters. There was a well defined pattern to follow and few alternatives were available. In contrast, today there are many alternatives among which to choose. Social control is not absent, but it is more flexible, and probably less effective.

First, let us consider controls *over* the family. The laws of various states specify that before getting married one must have attained a minimum age (thirteen to eighteen for girls; fourteen to eighteen for boys) and must have parental consent in the earlier years. In most states a license and a ceremony performed by clergyman or magistrate are required. In about twenty states common-law marriages are recognized, but these do not involve the absolute freedom popularly imagined. In thirty states a couple must wait from two to five days after applying for a license. In forty-five states some kind of a physical examination is required. In all states marriage between specified near relatives is prohibited. In addition to legal requirements, churches exercise varying degrees of control over their members. Some, like the Roman Catholic Church, Mormons, and Orthodox Jewish, have very specific rules; others are less definite, but put pressure on their young people to marry within the faith and conform to its expectations about married life and child rearing. Finally, there are many informal controls applied by and through kinsmen, friends, neighbors, and others whose approval and acceptance one needs. What "they say" has not wholly lost its force.

As for divorce, all states specify the circumstances under which a marriage may be broken. However, such regulations vary greatly from state to state. Some churches forbid divorced persons to remarry. Various elements in the population take quite diverse attitudes toward divorce and toward persons whose marriage has been legally ended.

Still other controls over the family are expressed in compulsory school attendance, juvenile court laws, child labor laws, and laws requiring financial support of certain relatives. Public sentiment sometimes supports the legal controls and sometimes opposes them. Thus the much vaunted freedom of Americans is actually considerably curtailed, even in such intimate matters as those we have been discussing.

Besides controls over the family, there are controls *within* the family. Obviously the newborn child is controlled almost completely. As he grows up his parents regulate his activities in varying degrees and try to teach him the rules of the game as played in their social circles. In adolescence, children exercise some control over their parents when they cite, for example, what other parents let their children do in dating, driving a car, and so forth. In the later years of life the direction of control is still further reversed. Grown children, themselves parents, may plan and regulate the lives of their elders. Again, there is great diversity of method and results. But within the family, social controls are constantly in operation when choices and decisions are being made.

Functions of the Family

The term *function,* as we have noted, is used in several different ways. Some mean by it what they think the family *ought* to do or accomplish. Some refer to what goes on when members of the family are interacting with each other. Still others have in mind their own observations as to what the family *does* for its several members. Finally, some are chiefly interested in what happens when you find one kind of family life rather than another. Here we are concerned with the second and fourth uses—interaction and one kind of family as opposed to another. Also we shall concern ourselves separately with the nuclear and the extended family.

Already we have pointed out that over the centuries the large or consanguine family has greatly diminished in the United States. Some people do not even know the names of uncles, aunts, and first cousins. But for others, such as the Boston "Brahmins" and "First Families of Virginia," kinship is still taken very seriously. Even there, however, social control and economic provision have largely slipped away from the extended family; the chief remaining function is that of status-giving.

The nuclear family too has lost some of its functions. First of all, the economic activities of the nuclear family have been reduced. Usually the living is "made" away from the home. If there be more than one income producer, the sources are likely to be quite separate, with wages or other prerequisites regarded as personal rather than familial. Most often the man is chief provider, but the woman is chief spender or purchasing agent. Such household activities as baking, canning, laundering, gardening, and making and repair of clothing have been steadily slipping out of the American home, and when youth are at home the stereo set, radio, and TV often shield the parents from their children—and each other.

As to educational functions the public elementary school has been supplemented in one direction by kindergarten and nursery school, in the other by vocational and academic high schools, colleges, and universities. Less and less of the training of youth remains in the home.

As to recreation, gone is the day when an entire family climbed into a wagon or surrey to spend the day together at a picnic, "all-day meeting with dinner on the ground," or shopping trip to the county seat. Instead, Johnny goes to Boy Scouts, Mary to Campfire Girls, father spends leisure time at the Elks Club, corner tavern, or pursuing a solitary hobby, mother has her pet charity, bridge club, or goes window-shopping. For a time it seemed that radio, TV, and automobile might reunite the family, but three radios and two TV sets in every house and two cars in every garage have put an end to that dream.

Once upon a time families—Catholic, Protestant, and Jewish—had family prayers, grace before meals, and religious instruction in the home. These have not quite vanished, but they are greatly reduced.

We have already commented on the partial assumption of protective and correctional functions by courts and other public or semipublic agencies. It would appear that the only family function to expand, at least in relative importance, is that of providing affection and intimate response between husband

and wife, parents and children. Perhaps this is what Burgess meant when he spoke of the American family as undergoing a transition "from institution to companionship." Whether or not the companionship is being achieved it is clear that egalitarian norms stressing a fair share in the costs and benefits of family life are becoming increasingly dominant in American society. Suzanne Keller aptly summarizes the problem: The equality of spouses . . . collides with the continuing greater economic responsibilities, hence authority, of the husband. The voluntary harness of love chafes under the constraint of numerous obligations and duties imposed by marriage, and dominance patterns by sex or age clash with these new demands for mutuality, reciprocity, equity, and individualism.[8]

Can we say, then, that because the modern American family is weakened, our society is degenerating? In view of the variety of ways in which man can adapt himself to his natural and social environment, such a statement seems quite unwarranted. We can only say that in modern urban society the family is no longer the social group which performs most of the functions necessary for man's survival. Its chances of disappearing are as unlikely as it is that the traditional multifunctional family will return.

We live in a changing world and are increasingly aware of the fact. We have not been urbanites for long, and many of our present values are rooted in the past, in a cultural tradition which was not urban. We see the world in terms of those earlier values; they color and largely determine our outlook. We cannot understand a world in which the family is not the basic social group and we tend to see in its narrowing role the potential destruction of everything which we value. But man's values and outlook gradually alter with his changing situation. The period of transition is difficult, but once the change is accomplished, once new values and attitudes have taken the

8. Suzanne Keller, "Does the Family Have a Future?," *Journal of Comparative Family Studies*, 2 (1971), p. 6. Reprinted by permission of the publishers.

place of the old, all will doubtless seem natural and well. To an ideal observer man may be better or worse than before, but he himself, since he is the product of the new training and the new institutions, will not feel that these are strange and abnormal. Man's culture changes; man persists.

REFERENCES

Adams, Bert N., *The American Family*. Chicago: Markham Publishing Company, 1971.

The American Almanac: The Statistical Abstract of the U.S. New York: Grosset & Dunlap, Inc., 1973.

Baber, Ray E., *Marriage and the Family,* second edition. New York: McGraw-Hill Book Company, 1953.

Burgess, Ernest W., and Locke, Harvey J., *The Family from Institution to Companionship*. New York: American Book Company, 1953.

Calhoun, Arthur W., *A Social History of the American Family from Colonial Times to the Present*. Cleveland: The Arthur H. Clark Company, 1919. Also New York: Barnes & Noble, Inc., 1945, Volume 3.

Farber, Bernard, *Family: Organization and Interaction*. San Francisco: Chandler Publishing Company, 1964.

Glick, Paul C., *American Families*. New York: John Wiley & Sons, 1957.

——, and Parke, Robert, Jr., "New Approaches in Studying the Life Cycle of the Family," *Demography*, II (1965), pp. 187-202.

Keller, Suzanne, "Does the Family Have a Future?," *Journal of Comparative Family Studies*, 2 (Spring, 1971), pp. 1-14.

Kenkel, William F., *The Family in Perspective,* second edition. New York: Appleton-Century-Crofts, 1966, Chapters 9-13.

Kephart, William M., *The Family, Society, and the Individual,* second edition. Boston: Houghton Mifflin Company, 1966.

Kirkpatrick, Clifford, *The Family: As Process and Institution,* second edition. New York: The Ronald Press Company, 1963.

Miller, Daniel, and Swanson, Guy, *The Changing American Parent*. New York: John Wiley & Sons, Inc., 1958.

Sirjamaki, John, *The American Family in the Twentieth Century*. Cambridge: Harvard University Press, 1953.

15 The Contemporary Black American Family

The developing and contemporary American family has been treated as if it were fashioned from whole cloth cut solely from the fabric of Western civilization.* If, in a general sense this is true, two specific corrections should be added: First, there were indigenous Americans, Indian peoples, here before the American colonists, and it is difficult to argue that their tribes, and even nations, had no effect on the cultural and institutional development of American society. The second, equally important correction, concerns the impact upon and contributions to the American "way of life" by peoples of African ancestry, first as slaves, later as citizens. However much recognized, the extent to which the mainstream of American culture has been influenced by additions from this group remains yet to be adequately measured. Blacks in America, like any ethnic group here for centuries, have helped *compound* a new society. Moreover, because of the eventual destruction of virtually all African cultural heritage—to be discussed below—it can be argued that they have in a sense become "purer" Americans culturally than the majority whites, who still retain important and salient ties to the peoples and countries of Europe.

A reverse consideration underlies the inclusion of this final chapter. As a distinctive group brought into American society under different circumstances from the bulk of the population, blacks have not always found an open road to acculturation and have made adaptations that sometimes have removed them from the mainstream of the developing society.

---

* The authors wish to acknowledge the many useful suggestions and criticisms made for this chapter by Ellen H. Biddle, Peter Manning, and C. T. Pihlblad.

Such adaptations may become organized in cultures, or sub-cultures, and provide a functionally autonomous way of life for their members. Or they may remain *ad hoc* and makeshift, unorganized, discontinuous usages and folkways that have not yielded to what William Graham Sumner called "the strain for consistency." The implications of this consideration will be clarified below in the major sections that describe and elaborate a typology of black family organization.

The following chapter, then, deals with the varying forms or profiles of the American black family, seen first historically and then currently. Necessarily, the historical development will be brief and intended to serve only as a backdrop to assist in the understanding of modern development. Without some reference to its history, one cannot fully comprehend the present social, cultural, and political developments in the American black community. On the other hand, an attempted full explanation that merely rakes up the ashes of the past would be equally inadequate.

Because blacks are now proportionately more urban than the majority whites, and because it will be in urban life that their acculturation and/or differentiation will be increasingly significant, we will focus on black families who reside in, but do not necessarily come from, essentially urban settings.

Historical Backdrop

Blacks today make up between eleven and twelve percent of the population of the United States and constitute the nation's largest and most visible minority group. Their introduction to America in 1619 was not as slaves but as servants. Foreign in their folkways and mores, different in color, the Africans were not assimilated easily into the white colonial society. It eventually became both psychologically and economically expedient to give them slave status. Through the first half of the seventeenth century the English colonists, who, in contrast to the Spanish and Portuguese, had little or no experience with institutionalized slavery, fashioned a system of their own.[1] Slaves were defined as something less than human and consequently not to be taken into or given the protection of the colonists' social, political, and religious institutions. Instead they were incorporated into the economy as property on the same basis as livestock, their value set by their utility. By the end of the seventeenth century, the institution of slavery was an accomplished fact in Virginia, Maryland, and the Carolinas, and Georgia followed a half century later. Although slavery spread through the middle colonies and into New England, it was not economically profitable. The slave codes were progressively less harsh from south to north, and slavery became less attractive to northern colonists than was the slave trade itself.

The bulk of the slaves and the predominance of the slave economy were then in the southern colonies. The plantation system, with its large number of field hands cultivating extensive agricultural holdings, cast slavery into a mold that persisted for well over two centuries in the South. Slaves as chattels could be utilized rationally without regard for human or social bonds and sentiments. The majority of the males were used in the fields, domiciled separately and moved about as they were needed. Only under special circumstances—as house servants or artisans—were they permitted to take wives and to

1. Slave trade in the seventeenth and eighteenth centuries was largely in the hands of Dutch, French, and English companies. During the eighteenth century the English dominated this increasingly profitable form of trade. Although Negro servants were found in most European countries, England included, the institution of slavery did not take root there. See John Hope Franklin, *From Slavery to Freedom, A History of American Negroes* (1956, 1967); also, his "A Brief History of the Negro in the United States" in *The American Negro Reference Book,* John P. Davis, ed., (1966), pp. 1-95. The basic reference work on the history of the Negro family is still E. Franklin Frazier's *The Negro Family in the United States* (1939). For differences between slavery in Latin America and the American colonies see Frank Tannenbaum, *Slave and Citizen: The Negro in America* (1947). For a substantial bibliography see Elizabeth Miller, *The Negro in America: A Bibliography* (1966).

establish families. In such cases the opportunity for personal
contact and the establishing of personal bonds between master
and slave could take place—always within, however, the limits
set forth by the widely separated statuses.

Whatever social organization may have prevailed in their
native Africa, whatever family arrangements, forms, and
usages found in the mores of the preexistent cultures, these
were stripped from, or eventually lost, to the blacks brought
to America. Dispersion of social groups, separation of husbands from wives and families, a callous disregard for kindred
relationships, all but destroyed the African cultural and social
heritage. The memories of such heritage dimmed with the
passing centuries.[2] The sporadic appearance of pan-African
movements in the United States, however, indicates they have
not been completely extinguished.

The status of the male slave suffered more than that of the
female. In nearly two and a half centuries of slavery the black
male could expect less consideration by whites as a human
being, less social status, less responsibility, more alienation
from white society, more violent treatment, and a more
demeaning appraisal of his personality. Black-white sexual
involvements were proscribed, but when they did occur, the
punishment for black male-white female sexual relations was
much greater than for those in which white males had relationships with black females. Thus the mixing of races that
occurred during the period of slavery was predominantly at
the initiative of the white male.

The upshot of the differential treatment of the black male
slave was the establishment of a social role, reinforced often
by personality type,[3] that made for economic, social, and per-

2. The point of view that the African cultural heritage was not
destroyed by slavery is presented in Melville Herskovits' *The Myth of the
Negro Past* (1941).

3. Stanley M. Elkins, *Slavery* (1959). A review of historical projections
and modern research findings and formulations on the American Negro
personality is found in Thomas F. Pettigrew's useful *A Profile of the
Negro American* (1964).

sonal instability. It is this legacy of slavery that overshadows the development of the contemporary black family. As a historico-cultural force it operates to undermine the development of male black ego-strength and to hinder the development of a form of family organization in which the father's role can be clearly identified and stand as a model in the socialization of his children.[4]

Obviously the status of the black female slave never fell so low as that of her male counterpart. Nevertheless, she was the victim of a deliberate imbalance, inasmuch as young vigorous males were preferred by plantation owners and as long as the importation of slaves was permitted were imported disproportionately. The unnatural imbalance in the black male and female populations continued until the middle of the nineteenth century. Thus among nearly all slaves in America, the women were necessarily shared by men—the opposite of the polygynous pattern that prevailed in many African tribal cultures from which slaves were recruited. Marriage for field hands was uneconomical and prohibited, but for house and yard servants and for artisans it was sometimes permitted but without legal sanction. Since children were economic assets to the owners, the female slave could look forward to having children in substantial numbers and possibly a succession of mates rather than a permanent spouse. Children, then, were frequently born into a family consisting of mother, other siblings, and quite possibly maternal aunts and grandmothers.

Slave mothers might develop strong maternal attachments to their children or grow to be indifferent toward an increasing number of offspring whose fathers were often absent or perhaps unidentifiable. Indeed her own children could well prove to be an added burden to a mother charged with the responsibility of the care and nurturing of the white children in the master's house. For the most part, then, their role as breeders, nurses, and household servants put mothers in a strategically better position than male slaves. Further, their

---

4. Pettigrew, *op. cit.*, pp. 3-55.

sexual exploitation by white owners and their sons introduced a personal relationship that had no counterpart for the
black male.

Female slaves, in short, usually found themselves heading
families without fathers, often burdened with heavy domestic
responsibilities in two families, and with higher performance
standards set for them by the white society than for black
males. Their coping abilities to adjust were both tested and
developed in and by slavery. The net result of more than three
centuries of differential treatment, both during and after
slavery, has been an overburdening of women with responsibility for the care, socialization, and, if necessary, the subsistence of their families.

Emancipation from slavery was a crisis in the life of the
black that tended to destroy his traditional ways of thought
and action.[5] Thousands of freedmen found themselves in an
unorganized state, set free by decree but without norms or
institutions to give continuity and direction to their lives.
Those families that had managed to develop stability during slavery held fast, but families loosely held together broke
apart. Men wandered about, often looking for family members
from whom they had long been separated. Some sought land
for farms or work to achieve these goals and a stable family
life to sustain the prosperous farm life that they desired.
Others formed casual marital and familial attachments, to be
severed as they continued to wander. Between 1865 and 1915
most movement consisted of milling about in the rural south.

Wars and economic booms stimulated the northward
migration of blacks. Many migrated ahead of their families to
find work and get established. Like most immigrants, they
settled in the center of cities in areas of minimal services and
choice. Families followed to find themselves in an environment
that was strange, exacting, and often hostile. Lacking institutional supports, short on communal controls, and suffering
chronically from weak economic underpinning, the black fam-

5. Frazier, *op. cit.*, p. 89 ff.

ily faced the grim problem of survival and reorganization. The magnitude of the problem can be appreciated when one recognizes the crises facing a slavery-disorganized people—upheavels caused by mobility, exchange of rural for urban environment, economic survival, the need to gain social acceptance, and to develop a positive self-image.[6] To cope with the vagaries of their social, political, and economic environment, black Americans through the years have developed a variety of forms of family organization. We have distinguished four types: (1) *traditional matriarchal*, (2) *traditional small patriarchal*, (3) *acculturated middle majority* and (4) *adaptive urban matricentric*. The first two are essentially historical in origin; the remainder we have constructed to characterize current profiles of black family organization.[7]

Traditional Matriarchal Black Family

In the matriarchal family the mother, or perhaps, the maternal grandmother and daughter, holds dominant influence over property, authority, and household affairs. The Billingsleys have distinguished three subtypes[8] of the matriarchal family pattern: (1) father absent, (2) a father or series of fathers temporarily present, and (3) father constantly present. In the last case, although the father is present, he usually cannot be the breadwinner or assert parental authority because of his precarious status in the labor market. All three of these

6. For a detailing of these problems see Nathan Glazer and Daniel P. Moynihan, *Beyond the Melting Pot* (1963), pp. 24-85.

7. The latter two types are closely related to the "externally adapted" and the "acculturated" family types developed by Jessie Bernard. They derive from current black life styles that are somewhat reflective of, but also cut across, economic classes. See Jessie Bernard, *Marriage and Family Among Negroes* (1966), Chapter 2, pp. 27-66.

8. Andrew Billingsley and Amy Tate Billingsley, "Illegitimacy and Patterns of Negro Family Life," in Robert W. Roberts, ed., *The Unwed Mother* (1966), pp. 131-157.

subtypes find their roots in traditional black family organization. We have noted that by virtue of his occupational status and restricted personal freedom, the slave husband was at best a sometime husband. After emancipation the achievement of a strong parental role was extremely limited, if not blocked, by his inability to maintain the status of breadwinner for the family. With her acceptance of the dominant role in the family, the female in the mother-centered family came to develop a "keen sense of personal rights,"[9] accompanied by a grim realization that males could not always be trusted to accept normal parental responsibilities. These handicaps are also the legacy of slavery and its aftermath.

Small Patriarchal Black Family

The black sociologist E. Franklin Frazier in his unrivaled study of the black family has traced the development of the patriarchal family from early slave days.[10] Slaves who had won or bought their freedom could also buy freedom for wife and family. Such an act would establish a propritary interest in their family. To the extent that a plot of farmland was obtainable, or a breadwinning job available, the free or emancipated black could then establish the basic economic flooring for a stable black middle-class family. And, with his economic dominance would come, in Frazier's words, "the downfall of the matriarchate." Thus, in both a rural environment, where the father-headed farm family with all members holding an interest in the successful operation of the farm enterprise was characteristic, and in the urban areas, where the father's job gave him status and authority, a stable patriarchal family could emerge. Both this form and the matriarchal type, then, reflect

9. Ernest W. Burgess, Harvey J. Locke, and Mary Margaret Thomes, *The Family: From Institution to Companionship* (1963), p. 89.

10. E. Franklin Frazier, *op. cit.* See particularly Chapters IX and X, pp. 163-214.

the adaptability of American blacks to the crises and disjunctions of slavery and emancipation. Both these types developed over centuries; the remaining two, which are more recent in their origin, build upon and to some extent derive from the older forms. They will be examined in greater detail.

The Acculturated Middle Majority Black Family

Jessie Bernard has traced the institutionalization of marriage among blacks from emancipation to the present. Legislative efforts of the states to legalize marriages and make them a matter of record were reinforced by military authorities, the Freedman's Bureau, the church, and the schools. Marriage sanctioned by these diverse institutions took on a positive value to blacks: as a status symbol, as an evidence of equality with whites, as a source of dignity lent to the alliance by minister and church, and as a joyous occasion in the wedding itself.[11] In Bernard's words:

> Thus, the outside world came increasingly to impinge on the Negro world. With the advent of child-welfare programs and public-health activities, all kinds of documentary proofs of relationships came to be required, and the old casual patterns became anachronistic. People had to prove that they had been born, had married, had borne children, had died. The intrusive hand of the official recorder appeared even in the backwoods, and once-spontaneous—even impulsive—human interrelationships were forced to take on the stern permanence of a written form.[12]

The consequence, in the decades following emancipation, was a reciprocal process: external norms exacted compliance, and the compliant behavior, in turn, became valued and eventually supported by internal or indigenous norms.

When norms are internalized in such a manner that they become associated with the ego, or personality, *acculturation* has occurred. From the standpoint of the group, acculturation

11. Jessie Bernard, *op. cit.*, p. 9 ff.
12. *Ibid.*, p. 12. Reprinted by permission of the publishers, Prentice-Hall, Inc., Englewood Cliffs, N. J.

implies the incorporation of cultural forms and usages into its areas of strongest collective belief as to what ought to and must be done. For the individual to violate such norms is to invite sanctions from the group, and probably, to engender on his part a feeling of guilt and anxiety.[13] For the majority of black Americans the history of the past century has been presumably a history of acculturation, a gradual process of accepting and internalizing and contributing to the norms of the middle majority of American whites. Secondarily, it has been a history of adaptations, some drawn from slave times, which may have run obliquely or counter to the normative mainstream of our society. Finally, there has been the expressive cultural infusion that has contributed to the making of the modern American life style.

Family Structure

The *acculturated middle-majority* black family accepts monogamy as the proper marriage form; the ideal of a permanent mate is qualified realistically by the recognition that marriages can fail, and the divorce is an acceptable, if regrettable, alternative to a permanently unhappy marriage relationship. The nuclear family group consisting of husband, wife, and children living in their own home and managing domestic affairs without pressure or influence from parents—the primary relationship—represents the ideal in household arrangements. The tendency toward establishing a stable residence conflicts with the desire to leave deteriorated or inferior dwelling areas behind in search of more suitable housing. Thus, when it can be attained, the single dwelling in the suburb or the better-class apartment as far away from the slums as possible remains the residential goal.

The size of the family is likely to be smaller than that found in the adaptive urban matricentric black family. Nevertheless

13. *Ibid.*, p. 27 ff.

a concern for parents is expressed in a willingness to share the domicile if the parents clearly cannot manage their own housing needs. Both sides of the family will be included in the extension of effective kinship relations, but such bilaterality is not likely to extend to more distant relatives. Close in-laws, grandparents, aunts, uncles, and cousins round out the effective kinship circle. Perhaps most important in household organization by comparison with the adaptive type is the tendency to afford more physical privacy and greater areas of inviolate life space for its members. The family, in a social psychological sense, seeks to close in on itself.

Family Cycle

Mate selection for the acculturated middle majority tends to be achieved at a somewhat later age than for the adaptive group. The process usually begins with casual dating in high school, possibly going steady in the senior year, and marriage only after at least high school education has been completed. For others, the serious going together will take place in college. Also, for a few females the husband will have been met first as a member of the armed forces. A standard pattern seems to be that of dating, going steady, becoming engaged, and being married with considerable ceremony in church, or at least before a minister, with friends and relatives from both sides of the couple present. Black females, in view of a disadvantageous sex ratio, tend to find the process of mate selection complicated. Their image of the ideal mate may emphasize occupational stability, stable personality, and "good prospects." In turn, the male may be selective, and somewhat disposed to seek a mate of light color. Some males seem not to want to marry at all, but in the long run blacks are a more married group than are whites.[14] Although racial intermarriages are proportionately very small in our society, when they do occur they are dominantly between a black male successful

14. *Ibid.*, pp. 79-85.

in his career and a white female. In sum, marriage for both sexes is considered a serious venture, not to be undertaken lightly nor without consideration of a number of contingencies. Sociologically, it is made more complex by demographic and other factors specific to blacks.

Traditionally, motherhood has meant more to black women than wifehood, and the maternal role has in most cases entailed heavy responsibility. In the acculturated family, a sharing of responsibility for socialization of the children is present. Children are wanted, but family size is likely to be restricted. Parents project high hopes for their children's futures, expect to provide them educational and cultural advantages they themselves might not have enjoyed, and are willing to plan and make sacrifices on their children's behalf. It is not part of this pattern for the wife's mother, the children's "granny," to become the principal socializing and caretaking female of the household. When mothers work—a higher proportion of black females are in the work force and working than are white females—they often employ paid baby sitters or send their children to day-care schools rather than use parents for the job.

Children are wanted, socialized, presented with definable male models by the father, given emotional support from mothers, and encouraged to achieve. Since education is so highly valued, both sexes are encouraged to absorb all the learning they can. While it is currently the case that black females have more education than males, this imbalance does not reflect an ideal of the acculturated family. In any event, the number of college graduates among blacks is rising at a faster rate than the overall increase in the total nonwhite population.[15] Success models in various walks of life are becoming more available for both sexes and are communicated to the members of the acculturated family in both black and white media.

15. Joseph H. Douglass, "The Urban Negro Family" in *The American Negro Reference Book, op. cit.,* p. 341.

Both parents are quite likely to be present during their offsprings' infancy and childhood. Bernard has noted that the most common type of black household is one in which there is a male head and his wife, and that most children under fourteen live in families of this type.[16] Although their cultural heritage may have little to offer in support of the arrangement, husbands will assay the instrumental (disciplinarian) role and the wife the affective (emotional support) role. The discipline, however, is not likely to be harsh and both parents may be overindulgent.[17]

In view of the restricted range of opportunity and the discriminatory practices, which have a stronger impact on the black male, the wife may find herself with equal if not better occupational life chances. But, when both husband and wife have a college education or when both are prepared for a business or professional career, husband-wife relations develop on the basis of common interests, congeniality, and mutual respect for the individuality of the other.[18] The result is an added equalitarian dimension to acculturated family organization.

Yet it would be incorrect to characterize the acculturated middle-majority black family as predominantly or perfectly equalitarian. Compelling evidence on the matter is lacking, just as it is for the middle-majority white family pattern. What seems to be evident is a joint dedication of husband and wife to establish a stable family, to prosper economically, and to bring forth a succeeding generation of children who will suffer fewer of the disadvantages experienced by their parents. It is unlikely at this point in time that the acculturated family

16. Bernard, *op. cit.*, p. 118.

17. For a harsh, possibly overdrawn, indictment of middle-class Negro life, including indulgence of children, see E. Franklin Frazier, *Black Bourgeoisie,* (1957, 1962). For a more recent, balanced, but not uncritical depiction see St. Clair Drake, "The Social and Economic Status of the Negro in the United States" (1967).

18. Ernest W. Burgess et al., *op. cit.*, p. 91. See also Andrew and Amy Tate Billingsley, *op. cit.*, pp. 152-155.

has developed a system of role specialization and a division of labor and authority to such extent that neither spouse attempts to dominate the other.

Parents in the acculturated family may expect their children to choose their own mates, establish households of their own—married couples living with parents will be a temporary expedient—and avail themselves of whatever economic opportunities may develop. Adults whose children have left home will have diminishing chances of spending their last years in a three-generation family. The maternal grandmother's dominant position will soon have vanished, and grandparents of either sex or side of the family will have equal chances to achieve the favor of their children or children-in-law. However, their chances of spending their last days away from their children and grandchildren, in low-cost public housing, or in retirement communities, or alone in substandard housing, at present, are increasing, Opportunities for their developing an aged subculture can only be speculated upon; there seems little research knowledge available on the subject. Increased longevity *is* a fact, and the special needs of the black aged loom as a matter for increasing public concern. One irony of the situation of the aged black is that since there is no discrimination in old-age benefits, the sixty-five-plus black often finds his, or more likely her, economic status improved.[19] In any event the aged seem likely to lose some claims on the legitimacy of their involvement in children's and grandchildren's lives. The acculturated family members, including many low-income blacks, unfortunately, may find loneliness the most pressing problem of their last years.[20]

19. Jeanne L. Noble, "The American Negro Woman," in *The American Negro Reference Book, op. cit.*, p. 525.

20. Village and small-town, low-income blacks are often left behind by their migrating offspring. Isolation, loneliness, and neglect may be more extreme among these people than for those in central cities.

The Adaptive Urban Matricentric Black Family

One associates the acculturated black family with better urban dwelling areas, usually away from the core of the central city, and with the suburbs. Conversely, turning toward the center of the American city, or the center of its black community, one finds a type of black family quite divergent from the acculturated type, a family revealing characteristically different organizational and personal elements. We have already given this family type, or cluster of tendencies, the name *adaptive urban matricentric* black family. To describe this type most clearly we have chosen first to examine its habitat and some of the social processes that have led to its creation.

The Ghettoized Black Community

After emancipation, particularly after the turn of the century, the movement of blacks was to the cities of the South and North. Black communities grew rapidly in size. Yet by World War I they were still a small fraction of the total population, usually well under five percent. For the most part, but not universally by any means (Harlem, for example), black migrants and older black residents were usually restricted in their dwelling areas to the poorer or poorest section of town. Often these areas had been abandoned by European immigrants and their succeeding generations eager to move toward more desirable places of residence. The labor needs and boom atmosphere of industrial cities during World Wars I and II attracted increasing numbers of rural Southern immigrants of both races. More recently, agricultural technology and large-scale farming have pushed small farmers off their lands and diminished the market for unskilled rural labor. In all, some 2.75 million blacks left the South between 1940 and 1960, and by 1964 the black population outside the South had increased five-fold since 1910.[21] Most of the blacks moving north and west have crowded into the slums of some two dozen cities from Boston to San Diego. Increases in the last three decades have been phenomenal. Blacks now comprise at least one quarter of the total population of nearly all major cities; yet most have found dwelling areas restricted to the central city, the areas of decreasing aesthetic, physical, economic, and political quality, areas of high social and personal disorganization as revealed by nearly any index.

"Ghettoization" is the word coined to describe the living arrangements of urban blacks. Disturbingly, the residential segregation of blacks has increased in the past decades. Karl and Alma Taeuber constructed segregation indices for 109 American cities and in comparing these for 1940, 1950, and 1960 found that segregation was increasing or had increased in most metropolises, with older southern cities, hithertofore less segregated, now following the pattern of northern urban black ghettoization.[22] G. Franklin Edwards, black sociologist, notes that the central city *cores* inhabited by blacks are "inferior in terms of housing, quality, recreational facilities, schools and general welfare services."[23] Further, ". . . all of these deficiencies contribute to crime, delinquency, school dropouts, dependency, broken families, excessive deaths, and other conditions which represent the pathology of the ghetto."[24] Of the latter one might specify illegitimacy as a crucial development in light of the substantial increase in black illegitimate births over the past several decades. Possibly one third or more births in black ghettos are of this character.

This rise in illegitimacy must be viewed against the

21. Charles Silberman, *Crisis in Black and White* (1964), p. 30. See also Chapter II, pp. 17-35.

22. Karl E. Taeuber and Alma F. Taeuber, *Negroes in Cities* (1965), pp. 37-43; also "The Negro Population in the United States" in *The American Negro Reference Book, op. cit.*, pp. 96-160.

23. G. Franklin Edwards, "Communities and Class Realities," in *The American Negro*, Volume 2, *Daedalus* (Winter, 1966), p. 4.

24. *Ibid.*

decreasing ability of the urban slum black male to maintain steady employment and sustain the role of married head of the household.[25] Unemployment, particularly severe in slum areas, falls most heavily on the unskilled, the young, the high school dropouts. Black urban populations are younger than white and contain potentially more able-bodied workers. Paradoxically, next to "urbanized" American Indians, they contain the highest proportions of unemployed. Insufficient education, lack of employment, underemployment, and, for many, depleted energies and ego stamina needed to cope with the frustrating urban environment are prime factors affecting urban black family organization. This is particularly the case in the inlying cores of metropolitan central cities.

Matricentric Adaptation

The three central factors seen as providing the basis for a mother-centered urban black family are, then: (1) ghettoization, and consequent *isolation* of blacks in central city cores; (2) economic insecurity, partly a function of sluggish national economic growth, partly caused by job discrimination, and partly a consequence of labor-saving technology claiming unskilled and low-skilled black males as heaviest casualties; and (3) a growing disparity between black female and male occupational life chances, with the male having fallen behind.[26]

In the face of these contingencies, the pattern of response by the blacks of the ghetto has been to combine elements of a traditional form of family organization—the matriarchal family —with indigenously developed adaptations. The characteristics of this adaptive family form will now be examined. Significantly, this alternative form will exhibit behavioral patterns

25. Two central references which have been drawn upon here are Daniel P. Moynihan's *The Negro Family: The Case for National Action* (1965); and Lee Rainwater's "Crucible of Identity" in *The American Negro*, Volume 2, *Daedalus* (Winter, 1966), pp. 172-216.

26. Daniel P. Moynihan, *op. cit.*

that are not supported by deeply held norms. The adaptations, in Jessie Bernard's terms, are essentially external.[27] They represent things people *can* do to get them past daily contingencies and life crises, but not necessarily what, in keeping with general normative prescriptions, they feel they *ought* to do.

Family Structure: Marriage Institution

A fragile monogamy severely compromised by even less permanently institutionalized marital attachments characterizes the marriage institution of the adaptive urban matricentric family. The black female is the pivotal figure; it is she who makes, often has to make, the decision to accept or demand a marriage partner. But, since a shortage of eligible adult and young adult males disposed to marry is also chronic in the core areas of the black urban communities the female may have to settle for less than the best in a mate. Conversely, the male may and can play the field. A tendency for the more economically stable or prosperous urban blacks, as well as for most whites, to avoid involvement with core-area blacks and to permit institutions to grow and develop independently, often tangentially to the main stream of American culture, has contributed to the distinctiveness of the subculture that is emerging in the central cities. And, in consequence, the opportunities for expediential variations and deviations are greater for slum-dwelling blacks than for their acculturation-oriented brethren.

The tenuous character of the black husband's role leads to the building of the effective household unit around wife, her children, and often her mother. These arrangements are not necessarily defined as ideal; they may often be makeshift. For example, after having been absent for weeks or months a hus-

27. Jessie Bernard, *op. cit.*, p. 27.

band will often return home and try again to be the head of the household.[28] But by doing so he may jeopardize his wife's welfare allowance for their dependent children.

Family Structure: Family and Kinship

A modified extended family[29] built around the mother-daughter relationship and usually extending through three generations is the modal form of organization for the adaptive family. The very large matriarchal family with a number of daughters, children, and possibly husbands under one roof, presided over by the wise and authoritative "granny" is infrequently encountered. Neither is the completely isolated nuclear family, with husband, wife, and a few children, separated by choice from kin ties and local attachments, very much in evidence. Rather, when looking across the broadest continuous segment of the family life cycle, one finds in the adaptive family one or more married daughters, sharing with the mother under a common roof the responsibility for support and socialization of the children. The father, in such a family, occasionally present, often itinerant or permanently absent, plays the weakest or most incidental role of all the adult

28. Note that it is not held that *all* slum dwelling or central city blacks of lower socio-economic classes elect the matricentric family pattern; nor do all middle and upper class blacks find themselves in the acculturated type. These quite different family types represent modal tendencies, one more grounded in normative elements than the other. Middle class mothers may still cling to the matriarchal role. On the other hand, some unemployed or casually employed fathers become adjusted to their economic contingencies and play dominant, often authoritarian, paternal roles. See for example, "The Culture of Unemployment: Some Notes on Negro Children" by Michael Schwartz and George Henderson in Arthur B. Shostak and William Gomberg, eds., *Blue Collar World* (1964), pp. 459-468.

29. See Eugene Litwak's "The Use of Extended Family Groups in the Achievement of Social Goals: Some Policy Implications" in *Social Problems,* 7 (Winter 1959-60), pp. 177-186.

principals. The patronymic is respected but its meaning lies essentially in the respectability conferred on children and not as a device for reinforcing patriarchial authority.

Residence, in the long run, tends to follow the neolocal-matrilocal pattern. Ideally, the first residence of the married couple will be outside the wife's mother's household but not necessarily far from it. Children have great freedom and are encouraged frequently to visit aunts, grandmothers, great-grandmothers. If such relatives are nearby, the pattern of visiting both for children and adults is informal, selective, and, to some extent, haphazard. If they are distant the family itself may make extended visits. Households are, in terms of access and life space, very much open—to relatives, friends, acquaintances, friends of friends, and so forth. Relatives, particularly maternal, introject themselves into the operations of each other's families; older generations feel free, if not obligated, to offer advice to the younger, and not infrequently a child will be sent to live with a maternal aunt or grandmother.

The emergence of moderately extended kin networks in black urban areas has only just come to the attention of sociologists.[30] Kin-related households, from two to possibly a dozen, form communication and interpersonal relationships networks that reflect both consanguinity *and* affinality. Core social relations will be those of mother-daughter and sister-sister, but sisters-in-law and mothers-in-law may also be participating members or "knots" in the kin network. These networks seem to proliferate where neighborhoods have a larger percentage of single dwellings and where husbands and wives, or wives and children, attempt to set up and maintain independent households. Here we may have a compromise form of family, residentially nuclear, but caught up in a network of matrilineal ties which can serve to provide support and sociability to members of the elementary family units. This

30. Interesting pioneer work in this area has been done by P. J. Epling, under U. S. Public Health Service Grant #1 SOL-FR-05442-01. Los Angeles. University of California, 1964.

adaptation remains to be studied; its presence bears out the fact of flexibility in form and function of central city core black families.

Family Life Cycle: Mate Selection

Marriages in the adaptive urban matricentric black family take place at a somewhat earlier age than for blacks generally. Mate selection is a serious matter, but it is preceded by a number of steps involving peer-group associations. Rainwater found that adolescents tend to become deeply involved in their peer-group societies beginning as early as the age of twelve or thirteen, and they continue to be involved even after first pregnancies and first marriages.[31] Both sexes become heavily committed to peer-group activities and are introduced to a wide range of experiences. Adult black society, in contrast to white, is much less closed to black adolescents. The behavior of the latter "more often represents an identification with the behavior of adults than an attempt to set up group standards and activities that differ from those of adults."[32]

Boys and young men seek to enhance status and self through participation in street games. In verbal contests those male youths who can claim and demonstrate success in gaining sexual favors from and dominance over females are much admired. They are thus ranked according to their success in seduction, and to survive in the peer group they must develop an ability to "make out" in talk, if not physically, with the opposite sex.

The girls, according to Rainwater "are propelled toward boys and men in order to demonstrate their maturity and attractiveness." But not wishing to be taken advantage of or

31. Lee Rainwater, *op. cit.,* p. 183. The remainder of this section follows closely this excellent research report. See also the related research of Rainwater's colleague David A. Schulz, reported in *Coming Up Black: Patterns of Ghetto Socialization* (1969).

32. *Ibid.,* pp. 183-184.

to get into trouble, they approach sex relations ambivalently, and few, if any, are disposed toward outright sexual promiscuity. The boy seeks to build up his "rep" and the girl seeks to limit her sexual relations to as few boys as possible. Competitiveness, aggression, ambivalence, status striving, physical enjoyment, and persuasion all in one way or another enter the picture.

Life Cycle: Pregnancy and Parenthood

The second stage in the formation of families, notes Rainwater, is that of premarital pregnancy.[33] If the girl is fortunate, the step may be avoided. But premature pregnancy is not the catastrophe that it would be for acculturated middle-majority blacks. Parents, who have been cautioning the daughter against such hazards and now find their fears justified, nevertheless know what to do. Usually the girl will continue to live at home and her mother will take the major responsibility for rearing the child—or children. Pregnancy becomes a measure of maturity for the girl, but once the baby is in the care of the grandmother, who may well be only in her middle or late thirties, the unwed mother can resume activities with her peer group.

Inasmuch as it is not necessary to have a man around the house in order to have and rear children, the decision to marry may be considered apart from the necessity to give the child a father. But the designation of the child's father is felt necessary—for the sake of the child. Not to know who one's father is seems "the ultimate in illegitimacy."[34]

For the youth to father a child means the creation of a new bond between himself and the girl. It is asymmetrical, however, in the sense that his claims for affection and fidelity

33. *Ibid.*, pp. 185-187.
34. *Ibid.*, p. 186.

are the more binding. In any event, and as with most groups in the broader society, marriage challenges peer-group loyalties and constitutes a threat to its cohesion.

Marriage, as noted, is approached ambivalently. The security of her own home is appealing to the girl, and the contingencies and uncertainties of setting up an independent household are often intimidating. The long peer-group associations have not socialized either boy or girl sufficiently to permit adult parent roles to be firmly internalized. Past histories of marriages of friends and relatives give little comfort to the couple. And, finally, the young male must face the prospect of uncertain occupational life chances. Thus, marriages are likely to be impulsive; prudent judgment and prolonged consideration, in most cases, would militate against the step. Once married, and on their own, the young couple find it indeed hard to prevent marital disruption.

Life Cycle: Parents at Work

A steady job at good wages in desirable work surroundings is a rarity for black males of the central-city core area. The wife's chances for congenial employment are considerably better. Most wives in the adaptive family work after marriage. Eventually the wife finds herself burdened with increasing responsibilities for household management, socialization, *and* breadwinning. The wife, therefore, is as likely to send her husband away as he is to desert a family that, from the beginning, he was never too confident of heading. Rainwater has found wives showing little respect for husbands who have fallen into unemployment. It is almost a marital maxim that if the husband cannot win bread he cannot take up the house and life space of the wife. If she does not make this plain he nevertheless accepts this as the code of his group. As the husband is increasingly less present in the house, the street and tavern claim more of his time. Philandering, drinking, and getting into scrapes become substitute activities for his former life style, which, though more desired, is now almost impossible to attain. Eventually he appears at home only after drinking; at such times argument and violence become the final elements of discord as the marriage shatters. Or the husband may quietly drop out of the picture and join thousands of other homeless males who are lost to the ongoing society and are often missed by its last and least personally involved representative, the census taker.

Life Cycle: Role of Women

The life cycle for the female who becomes the focal point of the adaptive family type has two prolonged stages. Following a relatively brief and—as much as possible—sheltered childhood, she finds herself involved deeply in her peer group for as long as two decades. Heterosexual association, sexual exploitation, pregnancy, even marriage, figure prominently in this stage, but the overriding consideration is the dominance of peer-group commitment. As she enters the job market and as her children grow up, she finds the mother-manager-breadwinner role demanding more of her time. Her adolescent children ignore her most of the time, and, following her example, enter the street and peer culture well before puberty. Before she has had time to establish and sustain—and be sustained by—the mother role, she faces the pregnancy of her own daughters. Her maternal role has been overlaid by her continued peer-group associations, and, like childhood in comparison with the larger society, is relatively short. But as a woman in her late thirties, she will probably have to face two or three more decades of responsible involvement with daughter's children and even grandchildren.

What must give way is the engrossing outside life of the peer group. Clubs, associations, "sets," the street, cabarets, friends' homes, movie houses, and shops can no longer monopolize her time. By now a mate or several husbands have come and gone. Home life, more time-consuming and engrossing, is made more congenial, with male companions or a "friend" who lives in but does not present the complications of a husband.

Life Cycle: The Aged

In past centuries blacks had a shorter life expectancy than whites. During the last half-century this discrepancy has been decreased although despite medical and sanitational advances, blacks are not progressing as fast as might be expected in the areas of infant mortality, health, and longevity. The smaller proportion of aged blacks and the "baby boom" in which blacks shared in the 1940's has made black Americans a younger population group than the white. Additionally, the black birth rate exceeds that of whites, and a one percent or higher increase in their share of the general population each decade is not unlikely. It is interesting to note that urban white poor tend to be predominantly the aged; for the ghetto blacks the situation is reversed.

The "over-sixty-five" blacks who have adapted their family life in the manner described will in most cases have been principals in more than one family. The mother will have members of several descending generations still involved in her life and will probably be living with or quite near some primary descendants. Their home, notes Rainwater, can become a kind of court at which other families gather and to which they bring their friends for sociability, and as a by-product provide amusement and entertainment for the mother.[35] Rainwater goes on to note that grandmother may provide homes for daughters and their children, and the childrens' children without much return in the material sense; yet she does receive a "sense of human involvement, a sense that although life may have passed her by she is not com-

35. Rainwater, *ibid.*, p. 196.

pletely isolated from it."[36] By current American standards, however, the demands made on grandparents, particularly on grandmothers, by offspring and grandchildren would be called excessive; nevertheless the return, in the form of family involvement, in being *of* as well as *in* family gatherings, may offer compensation for which no rational calculus exists. And, as noted above, the less demanding "boyfriend" for the aging mother replaces the unsuccessful husband.[37]

Older males become less involved with their blood relatives, but as boyfriends to husbandless women may achieve a quality of emotional involvement and gratification that their ascribed status as father, husband, and kinsman might never have provided. If they are not too old they will also have access to their own mother's household. But their claims on descending generations of primary relatives are few and have no great normative sanction.[38]

Problems of the Two Family Types

Socialization and Identity

Since a primary function of the family is the socialization of the young so that they develop a firm sense of who they are and what they can and perhaps should do in an ongoing society, we might examine the manner in which this problem is met in the two family types.

36. *Ibid.*
37. *Ibid.*, pp. 192-199.
38. A study of knowledge of grandparents' occupations among high school seniors found that black students knew significantly fewer than did the white, but of those occupations they did know, maternal grandparents scored significantly higher. There was, however, little difference between black males and females in knowledge of grandfather's occupation. See C. T. Pihlblad and Robert W. Habenstein, "Social Factors in Grandparent Orientation of High School Youth," in Arnold M. Rose and Warren A. Peterson, eds., *Older People and Their Social World* (1965), pp. 163-180.

In the adaptive urban matricentric family, the absence or weak presence of the father hampers the development of the masculine ego. Mothers hold most of the power to award or withhold emotional gratification and often find difficulty in giving equal shares of response and recognition to the male children. In default of a strong father figure, and immersed in an expressive or acting-out subculture, male youth exchange the mother-dominated restricted family life for the peer group, street activities, and the colorful, sometimes violent, tenor of life of the adult world. Both male and female find themselves inside a large world they cannot completely adapt to their needs, a world that frustrates ambition, confidence, respect for others, and ultimately self-respect. Females must adopt a sense of wariness, males of opportunism—to "make out" at any point in time, but with little sense of life continuity. It is thus, as Rainwater observes, such gratifications as the children in the matricentric family can obtain must be procured deviously, and without necessarily adding to one's self-respect.

Yet there *is* survival and at some periods there may be more than precarious existence. The young children, for example, experience a rather casual upbringing—far different from the intense, anxious concern of middle-class parents for their infants. This may have its advantages. At a different level of concern, if the work force continues to absorb more females and reject more males, the coping qualities found in matricentric families may deserve closer study and greater appreciation. Perhaps most impressive is the continued human involvement of adult and aged females in an active, ongoing, family-centered world, and the utilization of makeshift substitute husbands—boyfriends—as old age companions. Thus, what are difficult problems at one stage in the life cycle give way to reasonable adaptations and inventive solutions in another. For a youth-centered, achievement-oriented society, however, the matricentric adaptation to urban black life conditions remains an alternative of dubious continuing value.

The acculturated middle-majority family bears a responsibility for socialization that is difficult to overestimate. The necessary product, a person of firm ego, with a well developed sense of adult role-identification and a strong enough sense of morality and purpose to propel him into leadership for just causes, is defined as worthy and necessary across nearly *all* levels of black society. The peer group, school, and other formal groups may or may not play supportive and integrative roles. Since the institutional realms representing the middle-majority white society have yet to work out appropriate means of adult socialization of the black members who come within them, an even stronger ego identity for the latter may be required. Thus the responsibility is thrust back to the family and other primary agencies. And, it should not be forgotten that the equalitarian impulses of acculturated family members have yet to become organized into a viable system of role differentiation and tension management.

Conversion at Mass Level?

Finally, at the mass-behavior level, there is evidence that with respect to consumption of goods and services economically successful black Americans are moving toward the middle-majority white life style, and giving up rapidly what has been called the Negro market. The newer consumption patterns of blacks, with more stress on life insurance, retirement funds, house purchases, and general upgrading of living standards, suggest a value conversion toward family, home and community status. Although less heralded than other changes in the social world of the black American, these new consumer changes might well mark one of the more important bases for the development of a further acculturated black family.

Nevertheless the evidence for polarization of the two family types remains impressive. Particularly notable is the increasing concentration of poverty in the predominantly black-inhabited central-city cores. The process is marked not only by the migration of more successful blacks toward the perimeters of black residential areas—seeking to expand these

—but also by the migration of industry to the city's suburbs and beyond. Since newly located industries are likely to be more automated than those left behind, the number of low-skilled employees needed decreases. Not only do central-city blacks suffer unemployment, but those retaining their jobs must face the prospect of a longer journey to work or moving of their household. And those searching for work, in addition to color discrimination, are further disadvantaged by having to seek work farther and farther from home. These socio-economic-logistic factors operate to isolate further and economically depress those blacks who are already most vulnerable to the vicissitudes of a dynamic society. For many the situation is desperate.

The adaptive urban matricentric family is a fusing amalgam of many social elements. To some extent it contains elements of a *genus of family found wherever there are poverty-stricken people*. It also reflects the adaptation of historical practice to modern exigency. In addition, indigenously developed folkways are obviously present. Finally, the adaptive family draws from, and is immersed in, an expressive church, club, cabaret, and, more recently, protest *mass* black culture. The elements do not combine into an institutionalized family type; rather, they hang together in a dynamic state of quasi-organization, continually subject to the play of economic and social forces. Thus, the adaptive, nonacculturative elements of family organization, in the last analysis, are likely to persist just to the extent that prejudice, discrimination, and economic disadvantage remain the lot of the central-city black.

REFERENCES

Bernard, Jessie, *Marriage and Family among Negroes*. Englewood Cliffs, N. J.: Prentice-Hall, Inc., 1966.

Billingsley, Andrew, and Tate, Amy, "Illegitimacy and Patterns of Negro Family Life," in Robert W. Roberts, ed., *The Unwed Mother*. New York: Harper and Row, 1966, pp. 131-157.

Burgess, Ernest W., Locke, Harvey J., and Thomes, Mary Margaret, *The Family: From Institution to Companionship.* New York: The American Book Co., 1963.

Douglass, Joseph H., "The Urban Negro Family" in John P. Davis, ed., *The American Negro Reference Book.* Englewood Cliffs, N. J.: Prentice-Hall, Inc., 1966, pp. 160-196.

Drake, St. Clair, "The Social and Economic Status of the Negro in the United States," in Talcott Parsons and Kenneth B. Clark, eds., *The Negro American.* Boston: Beacon Press, 1967, pp. 9-16.

Edwards, G. Franklin, "Communities and Class Realities," *The American Negro,* Volume I, *Daedalus* (Winter, 1966), pp. 1-23.

Elkins, Stanley M., *Slavery: A Problem in American Institutional and Intellectual Life.* Chicago: The University of Chicago Press, 1959. Also published in Universal Library Paperback edition with introduction by Nathan Glazer. New York: Grosset and Dunlap, 1963.

Epling, P. J., *Memorandum on Urban Negro Kin Networks.* U.S. Public Health Service Grant No. 1 SOL-FR-05442-01. Los Angeles, University of California, 1964.

Franklin, John Hope, "A Brief History of the Negro in the United States" in John P. Davis, ed., *The American Negro Reference Book.* Englewood Cliffs, N. J.: Prentice-Hall, Inc., 1966.

———, *From Slavery to Freedom, A History of American Negroes.* New York: Alfred A. Knopf, 1956, 1967.

Frazier, E. Franklin, *Black Bourgeoisie.* Glencoe, Ill.: Free Press, 1957. With a new preface by the author, Collier paperback A5347, 1962.

———, *The Negro Family in the United States.* Chicago: The University of Chicago Press, 1939. Also published in a revised Phoenix Books edition with a foreword by Nathan Glazer. Chicago: The University of Chicago Press, 1966.

Glazer, Nathan P., and Moynihan, Daniel P., *Beyond the Melting Pot.* Cambridge, Mass.: The M.I.T. Press, 1968.

Litwak, Eugene, "The Use of Extended Family Groups in the Achievement of Social Goals: Some Policy Implications," *Social Problems,* 7 (Winter, 1959-60), pp. 177-186.

Miller, Elizabeth, *The Negro in America: A Bibliography.* Cambridge, Mass.: Harvard University Press, 1966.

Moynihan, Daniel P., *The Negro Family: The Case for National Action.* Washington, D. C.: U.S. Government Printing Office, 1965.

Noble, Jeanne L., "The American Negro Woman" in John P. Davis, ed., *The American Negro Reference Book.* Englewood Cliffs, N. J.: Prentice-Hall, 1966.

Pettigrew, Thomas F., *A Profile of the Negro American.* Princeton, N. J.: D. Van Nostrand Company, Inc., 1964.

Pihlblad, C. T., and Habenstein, Robert W., "Social Factors in Grandparent Orientation of High School Youth" in Arnold Rose and Warren Peterson, eds., *Older People and Their Social World.* Philadelphia: F. A. Davis Company, 1965.

Rainwater, Lee, "Crucible of Identity," in *The American Negro,* Volume II, *Daedalus* (Winter, 1966), pp. 172-216.

Schulz, David A., *Coming Up Black: Patterns of Ghetto Socialization.* Englewood Cliffs, N. J.: Prentice-Hall, 1969.

Schwartz, Michael and Henderson, George, "The Culture of Employment: Some Notes on Negro Children" in Arthur B. Shostak and William Gomberg, eds., *Blue Collar World.* Englewood Cliffs, N. J.: Prentice-Hall, 1964, pp. 459-468.

Silberman, Charles, *Crisis in Black and White.* New York: Random House, 1964.

Staples, Robert, ed., *The Black Family: Essays and Studies.* Belmont, Calif.: Wadsworth Publishing Company, Inc., 1971.

Taeuber, Karl E., and Alma F., "The Negro Population in the United States" in John P. Davis, ed., *The American Negro Reference Book.* Englewood Cliffs, N. J.: Prentice-Hall, 1966, pp. 96-160.

Tannenbaum, Frank, *Slave and Citizen: The Negro in America.* New York: Alfred A. Knopf, 1947.

16 Profiles of the Canadian Family

Canada is a large, modern nation state which today comprises ten provinces and two vast northern territories, all of which combine to make up nearly 4 million square miles of land characterized by a great diversification of soil, terrain, and climate. Since most of Canada lies above 45° north latitude, it has to be included among the cold climate countries of the world. A vast majority of its 21 million inhabitants cluster in a narrow belt above the border of the United States, with the southeast quadrant containing the largest concentration of cities, towns, industries, and centers of business, commerce, and government.[1]

Despite its great land mass, Canada is a country of predominantly urban dwellers. About seventy percent of its people live in cities, towns, and villages, another twenty percent are in rural nonfarm areas, while less than ten percent are farm dwellers. Its forests, oil, and mineral deposits, arable farm lands, hydroelectric sites, productive coastal waters, and other natural resources have been exploited by local, national, multi-national, and other types of corporations and businesses. Modernity is expressed in increasing industrialization and urbanization, and in concomitant suburban growth, in the rapid development of transportation, utilities, and communication sectors of the economy, and in a national consciousness of the social and cultural needs of a pluralistic nation.

1. *Canada Year Book 1970-71: Statistical Annual of the Resources, Demography, Institutions, and Social and Economic Conditions of Canada* (1971).

SOCIETY AND FAMILY

The Inhabitants

The inhabitants of Canada present a remarkable picture of demographic differentiation. Historically this has been brought about by the overlaying of indigenous native peoples and earlier settlers with waves of ethnic groups migrating from central and western Europe and the British Isles, and to a lesser extent from the United States. The Dominion Bureau of Census shows the mother tongues of Canadian residents to include more than twenty-eight languages. About one out of every six migrants to leave Europe over the past century and a half come to, settle in, or stay awhile and move on from Canada.[2] For all the centuries of settlement there has been both a large influx and a corresponding fairly large outflow of migrants, all carrying with them distinctive linguistic, cultural, and socio-economic-political traits. Canadian society, then, is a mosaic of social groups, many with strong ties to another homeland or mother country; it is also a country whose traditions of egalitarianism and pluralism are bisected by a vertical, elitist-dominated system of socio-economic stratification.[3]

Despite this wide spectrum of ethnicity, there is a concentration of Canadians of British origin and of French Canadians whose forty-four percent and thirty percent proportions of the total population respectively account for almost three fourths of those with European backgrounds. The remaining quarter are led by Germans (5.8 percent), Ukrainians (2.6

2. Pierre Canu, E. P. Weeks, and Z. W. Sametz, "The People," in *Economic Geography of Canada* (1964), Chap. III; reprinted in abridged form in *Canadian Society: Sociological Perspectives,* third edition, Bernard R. Blishen, Frank E. Jones, Kaspar D. Naegle, and John Porter, eds. (1968), p. 23.

3. John Porter, *The Vertical Mosaic: An Analysis of Social Class and Power in Canada* (1965).

percent), Italians (2.5 percent), Dutch (2.4 percent), and
Scandinavians (2.1 percent). None of the remaining dozen or
more nationalities show totals of more than two percent.
Those of Asiatic background comprise about one percent of
the total population, and the native Indian and Eskimo peoples with their one-and-a-half percent round out the varied
ethnic pattern.[4]

Two large scale modern socio-political movements serve as
dynamic counter forces within the Canadian political system.
One is a growing dualism that puts English and French Canadians more or less consciously in a competitive power relationship, and the other a growing nationalism that seeks to
integrate all Canadians into a truly modern, economically-
independent nation state. Of longer duration is the generally
shared social value embracing pluralism—the willingness of
any one group or people to seek an amicable accord with any
other, whatever the hue or creed. The persistence of this
value, however, leads to an emphasis on *accommodative* at the
expense of *assimilative* social processes. The consequence, as so
many Canadians have observed, is a "salad bowl" rather than
a "melting pot."

"*The*" Canadian Family

The salad bowl figure of speech may have been uppermost
in Canadian sociologist Frederick Elkin's mind when, in 1964,
he stated flatly, "There is no one Canadian family. With its
distinctive geography and history, Canada is much too heterogeneous to have one or ten or twenty distinctive family types.
As the geographical setting, and as the social class, religious,
ethnic, occupational, and other groupings vary, so too do our
families."[5] To attempt an extended analysis of Canadian families as they exist in their distinctive cultural and socio-

4. *Canada Year Book 1970-71, op. cit.,* p. 237.
5. Frederick Elkin, *The Family in Canada: An Account of Present
Knowledge and Gaps in Knowledge about Canadian Families* (1964, 1970),
p. 31. This is the single most important review of the literature of Canadian
family studies.

economic-political contexts would be far beyond the scope of this work.[6] In keeping with the historical and ethnographic themes of the earlier chapters of this book, we propose to outline in some detail the characteristics of two interesting and instructive family types that have developed in different parts of Canada through the past several centuries. The first is the outport fisherfolk family of coastal Newfoundland, and the second is the French-Canadian *habitant* family found in the rural villages of Quebec. Although the historical perspective dominates, in both cases some attempt will be made to assess the direction and impact of modern forces for change.

THE NEWFOUNDLAND OUTPORT FAMILY

Newfoundland, an island sea province of Canada, along with its larger arctic adjunct, Labrador, constitutes about 150,000 square miles of wind, rain, fog, and, in winter, snow-swept glaciated terrain. The majority of its half-million inhabitants still cluster in a few cities and in towns and small "outport" villages along its 6,000 miles of rocky coastline. Small portions of the island, particularly the valleys leading to the sea, are minimally arable, but such little farming as exists is for the most part small scale, as inclement weather, the presence of swamps, or tree- and moss-laden muskegs and soil thinly deposited on solid rock severely restrict agriculture.[7]

A proliferation of tree growth, mostly coniferous, has always provided inhabitants of the deep bays and inland areas with wood for fuel and timbers and lumber for house and boat construction. More lately substantial pulpwood opera-

6. An impressive effort to gather the relevant reports and theories about Canadian family organization is found in *The Canadian Family* (1971), K. Ishwaran, ed. The growth of interest and research in family studies has been given impetus by the establishment of The Vanier Institute of the Family, Ottawa, Ontario, Canada.

7. Up-to-date materials on Newfoundland will be found in the *Canada Year Book 1970-71*.

tions have been developed. Cornerbrook on the west coast, for example, boasts one of the world's largest paper mills (absentee owned). The province, including notably Labrador, is rich in ores, mostly iron, but copper, zinc, lead, asbestos, and lately fluorspar have been mined on the island proper.

The Outports

But it is the coastline with its thousands of coves, bights, or unprotected small bays, inlets, fiords, and its dozens of larger bays, deep water harbors, and occasional shallow sandy lagoons that originally attracted early French and English settlers. However, before permanent settlements were established and the aboriginal Beothuks[8] decimated or assimilated, the shores were dotted with primitive fisheries—shore bases where fish could be "made" (cured) on "flakes" or racks, blubber from seals and whales rendered, and catches handled on the "stages" or platforms and in sheds, and where ships could put in for safety, repair, and fresh water. The shore crews that manned the fisheries might originally have been Basque or Portuguese whose ships had visited the cod-rich waters off Newfoundland even before Columbus put to sea.[9] But it was the French and English shipbased and shorebased crews in the sixteenth and seventeenth centuries who made the short step to founding more permanent, but for many decades "illegal," settlements up and down the coasts. Farley Mowat, a contemporary Newfoundland writer, elaborates:

> During the early centuries of Newfoundland's discovery and occupation, the common man in Europe was in peonage—if not outright bondage.

8. Forgotten long ago, having left few cultural traces on modern Newfoundlanders except that Memorial University at St. John's has adopted the Beothuks as their sports totem.

9. Dr. Anne Stine's excavations at L'Anse aux Meadows on the Great Northern Peninsula provide archaeological evidence of Norse attempts to colonize North America circa the mid-tenth century. For an easily accessible account see Helga Ingstad, "Vinland Ruins Prove Vikings Found the New World," *National Geographic*, 126 (1964), pp. 708-734.

His very life was forfeit at the whim of those who governed him. The poverty of the damned was the general lot of most except the upper ranks. The hardships of hacking out a free life on the granite coasts of Newfoundland were no greater than those a man had to face at home in Europe, and in all likelihood were considerably less. And in Newfoundland, as in no other part of North America, there was only the natural hostility of wilderness with which to deal: the Beothuks made no real effort to resist the alien interlopers, as did their brothers on the continental mainland.[10]

The Spanish, French, and English mixed the commercial attraction of fishing off the banks of Newfoundland with exercises in demonstrating their sea power. After the Spanish war fleets had been destroyed, England, who dates her first Newfoundland contact as 1497, with John Cabot's landfall at St. John's, and "possession" of the island with Sir Humphrey Gilbert's announcement of the same in 1583, vied with the French for fishing, bait catching, and shore-basing areas for more than a century. A partial solution to the control and use of the island and its waters came about in 1713 with the Treaty of Utrecht which gave England sovereign right to the island, but permitted the French fishing and bait-catching privileges on the north and west coasts (where in their "Terre Neuve" they had already established many small coastal settlements).

Since then the British, after many years of discouraging permanent settlements and viewing the fisheries and the waters off the island as mainly beneficial to England's commercial and naval power interests (Newfoundland's waters were for many years training grounds for cadets of the British Navy), have exercised varying forms of control over the island and its inhabitants. Major changes were the achievement of dominion status in 1855, a return to direct British control during the Great Depression of the 1930s, and the joining of Newfoundland into the confederation of Canadian provinces in 1949 after two referendums. In all this time the "French

10. Farley Mowat and John de Visser, *The Rock Within the Sea: a Heritage Lost* (1968), not paginated. By permission of Little, Brown and Company.

Shore" fishing rights problems were never more than partially solved. The United States has by no means been a newcomer to fishing the Grand Banks and, principally during and after World War II, has maintained large scale defense installations on the island. Other European countries including England as usual, France, the two Germanies, Portugal, and Russia, usually with highly technologized "factories of the sea," have similarly filled the waters off the island with their fleets. These countries operate under a complex set of treaties, agreements, international codes, and laws that control somewhat tenuously use of the island's fabulously rich offshore fishing waters.

The People of the Inshore Fisheries

Our attention is drawn, however, to the inshore or close-to-shore fishing people, particularly those of Scotch, Irish, English, French, and Channel Islands ethnic amalgamation, who distributed themselves in hundreds of small villages around the long Newfoundland coastline. These are the out-port villagers whose cultural ties are mainly to the British Isles; they are highly egalitarian and individualistic, yet family- and kin group-centered, living in self-contained households, communicating with a spare, direct language, and displaying a character and temperament shaped by centuries of isolated community life. It was, and for many still is, a life in which fishing is everybody's business, where men and their grown sons spend more time in their boats and dories than in their homes during the fishing season, and where domestic life revolves around them when they come in from the sea.

This is a distinctive type of Canadian family, but one that shares general characteristics with families throughout the world where men put out daily in small boats to fish in local waters, and whose fortunes are tied in with the providence of the sea. It is a family whose operations and organization are closely and intricately interwoven into the local economy, subject almost exclusively to local social controls. While recent change has had serious effects on economy, family, and habitat, the Newfoundland outport fisherfolk family has until lately retained an almost classic form, and what follows in this section pertains to it as it persisted until the middle of the present century. We will use the historical-present mode of describing this family.

Family Structure

The Outport Village Family and Its Economy[11]

The patricentric, patrilocal, extended family, with nuclear units clearly visible within or nearby, represents the typical Newfoundland family. While variation exists, particularly from one coastal area to another, students of maritime cultures will find the type described here as both logically consistent in its inner workings and easy to find in the historical and present reality of outport life.

The patrilocal and patricentric extended family is not only the typical mode of outport family organization, but also is a major component of the total village economy.[12] The pri-

---

11. This section leans heavily on the monographs produced under the auspices of The Institute of Social and Economic Research, Newfoundland Social and Economic Studies. Memorial University, St. John's, Newfoundland. Most relevant for our purposes have been *Brothers and Rivals: Patrilocality in Savage Cove,* by Melvin M. Firestone (1967); *Cat Harbour, a Newfoundland Fishing Settlement,* by James Faris (1966); *Craftsman-Client Contacts: Interpersonal Relations in a Newfoundland Fishing Community,* by Louis J. Chiaramonte (1970); and the independently written moving tribute *The Rock Within The Sea: A Heritage Lost,* by Farley Mowat and John de Visser, *op. cit.* Mary Sparkes' ethnographic study, as yet unpublished, of "Bay Port," a Great Northern Peninsula outport village that no longer has fishing central to its economy, becomes increasingly important when we consider recent changes in outport life. Many long conversations and travels around the island with Raoul Andersen, Fred Evans, and Alan Sparkes, Newfoundlanders by birth or adoption, have helped lend substance to this section.

12. Firestone, *op. cit.* See particularly "The Patrilocal Extended Family," Chap. III, pp. 45-83. This is one of the most comprehensive chapters on the Newfoundland outport village family thus far in print.

mary categories of persons typically linking family and economy are the fathers as head of the extended family, the young adult sons who may or may not be married and who fish with him in his boat, and the local merchant, a representative of the type of mercantile company that first appeared with the breaking up of feudal society.[13] The merchant supplies the family fishing enterprise with all necessary fishing paraphernalia and the family members with comestibles and other necessary commodities on a "company store" or credit system base; he has by agreement prior right in buying the caught fish. If the catches are good and there is a surplus of credit for fish sales over the amount on the merchant's books for the supplies advanced, the company account will either be credited ahead for future purchases or a cash settlement will be paid to the family head. The advantages of the company account inhere objectively in the guarantee of necessities for family sustenance and the family fishing enterprise during periods of poor fishing or economic recession, and subjectively in the interpersonal relationship to the company merchant—a mixture of institutionalized contractual and interpersonal social bonds.[14]

Supplementary sources of income or value in kind are gathered or produced by all family members. The search for fuel is unending—a large wigwam-shaped stack of logs, limbs, and long roots outside each house signifies readiness for a cold, wet, and snowy winter. (Dry, cold, subzero temperatures are as uncommon in winter as are warm, dry, sunny days in summer.) Seals are hunted as are wild game and sea fowl. Sheep,

13. For an elaboration of the merchant credit system see Cato Wadel's *Marginal Adaptations and Modernization* (1969), pp. 9-25.

14. The merchant-client relationship can easily become exploitative, on either side of the counter. The merchant must answer to his conscience, but as a company representative he also has the role of profit-maker for the firm he represents. Unpaid bills of short standing are indicative of the relationship of continuing trust and willingness to do business with each other. But like merchants everywhere the outport merchant has his share of long overdues and uncollectibles.

goats, and occasionally cows are kept along with barnyard fowl. Small hay pastures are tended with care as hay making, given the damp uncertain weather, is difficult. Small gardens are planted with turnips, carrots, and potatoes—the most common root crops. Other small domestic economies, canning and preserving, weaving, knitting, carving, and knotting all add to the pantry and purse. Working in the woods remains an important ancillary income-producing activity when there is no fishing. All in all, however, it is fishing that undergirds the family economy, and for this reason the interrelationship of family, kinship, and crew needs further description.

Fishing Crew Structure

As already noted, two generations, a father and several of his adult sons linking families of procreation and orientation, make up the typical fishing crew. The arrangement is described by Firestone:

> The family which inhabits a house is ideally a part of a larger group, the patrilocal extended family. When brothers grow up they are expected to fish with each other and their father. After a father dies the oldest brother becomes the leader, and the group may be referred to by his name ("Jack's crew") just as it was considered to be his father's when he was living. When the brother's children grow up there will in most cases be a split and each brother will fish with his sons. This group is referred to as a *crowd* or *crew*. The head of this group is the *skipper* . . . the father, or in his stead the oldest brother, is the leader and director in all affairs of the group and is superior, too, in authority and prestige. On the other hand the brothers, or junior brothers if the father is deceased, are in general behavior always a group of equal partners under the authority of the skipper.[15]

The company account supplies the crew as an economic unit, but in addition there are subaccounts for each married man who is entitled to an equal "share" against which his household expenses may be charged. "It does not matter how many children each brother has," observes Firestone, "he gets but his

15. Firestone, *op. cit.*, p. 45. By permission of the Institute of Social and Economic Research, Memorial University of Newfoundland.

single share. Thus, equal division among all adult brothers and their father is considered the basic economic arrangement."[16]

Fishing is done within a few miles of the shore. Nets are placed in "berths," the rights to which have been established traditionally and are honored by other village crews. The boats are small, under twenty-five feet, invariably under-powered, and can be worked out of by three or at most four men. Usually the crew makes two trips a day, hauling in and resetting the nets and bringing the fish into the stage where they will be cleaned and prepared for drying on flakes, salt-ing, or iced and shipped. Wives and daughters, as well as young boys, work at "making" the fish; with their boots, oil-skins, and sou'westers, the females would be hard to distin-guish at a distance.

Females and the Domestic Drama

Despite her supporting activities in respect to the family fishing enterprise, the role of wife and mother is played out in the home. There is a dramatic quality to fisherfolk living that revolves around the pragmatic but nevertheless heroic act of the family provider(s) daily putting out to sea in poten-tially dangerous waters in small, usually overloaded, scarcely safe boats. Each day the men in the family will rise early, gulp mugs of strong tea, eat thick slabs of homemade bread dolloped with butter or seedy bakeapple jam, don oilskins and boots that hang near the kitchen stove, and make their way to their boats. Inshore fishing is a chilling, bone-tiring occupation. And it is dangerous; "lost at sea" is a phrase as common to fisherfolk discourse as "killed on the highway" is to the conversations of urbanites. Yesterday's successful trips guarantee nothing against the day. Inured against chilling water and cold winds but nevertheless susceptible to rheuma-tism, arthritis, and other crippling diseases, developing ulcers over daily indeterminables, fishermen grimly acknowledge it

16. *Ibid.*, p. 46.

is at best a young man's occupation. "Your health's your most precious asset, me son," observes a retired skipper who has so early lost his.

The operations and social center of the home are located in the kitchen. With its large stove—a central source of warmth for the house—sink, table, day bed or bench, hooks and pegs for hanging wet clothes, and an adjoining pantry, it provides a place for the mother to cook and preside over other family members, sometimes in competition with the grandmother, who may sit on the day bed and hold court for the quiet but intensively observant children who pass freely in and out of everyone's kitchens. The evening card game players often span three generations, and despite the presence of a more pretentiously furnished parlour or sitting room, the game will be played on the same kitchen table where all meals are eaten.

As with all established family systems there is a daily rhythm of activities, comings and goings, transactions, and social gestures. With outport fisherfolk, getting on with the daily household activities is relatively simple, involving a rudimentary division of labor along lines of age, sex, and marital status. But the life is not humdrum. Let the wind pick up, clouds gather, or fog begin to rise and adult faces around the home will show concern. The anxious mother looks out the window to sea hoping to catch a glimpse of the returning crew an hour before they are due. Children run to the point to sight returning kinfolk and run back twice as fast to report the good news. The rhythm and drama of the occupation of the inshore fisherman is far removed from that of the farmer who with his team is seldom out of the sight of the family, and whose certainties in life are assured by the land on which he walks.

Marriage Institution

Wives may be sought within or in a nearby village. Consent of the father of the groom-to-be is considered essential.

The bride ordinarily moves into the husband's family home, and the family is thus expanded by another of several affinals, nearly always daughters-in-law. It is, of course, further extended by the new couple's children. Four generations under one roof are not uncommon but the usual number is three. By a process described later in this chapter most married sons establish independent nuclear family households on a portion of the old family home site within a few years.

Marriages provide excitement and color in a society that ordinarily sees little of either. The drama of sea fishing is for the most part latent. But weddings, called "times," are openly and enthusiastically participated in by all members of the village, including some "strangers" (people not well known, or not living in local kinship groups) and occasionally a dignitary or political aspirant. Banns will have been published three times before the wedding. Firestone[17] lists the usual complement of centrally involved persons as the *bride's boys* and the *bride's girls* who do the work involved in the wedding reception and who act as ushers and bridesmaids during the wedding. The *best bride's girl* and the *best bride's boy* will sign the marriage certificate as witnesses, with the *father giver,* who may not be the father but an uncle or older brother of the bride, the minister, and parents playing a lesser role.

Once the more formal and ceremonial phases of the wedding are accomplished the "time" begins to develop a characteristic collective excitement. As the couple emerge from the church, guns are fired into the air. Should the "tea" or wedding reception be held in the school house, or possibly a community center, the hall will be festooned with paper ribbons, pompons, and other home-fashioned decorations. The bridal party will eat at the first table and afterwards everyone present eats as often and as much as he cares to. Drinking at weddings is nearly as common as music and dancing. The men of the village pass around bottles of rum, the children run excitedly around the dance floor and outside the hall, bedtimes forgotten.

17. *Ibid.,* p. 76.

Everybody participates in "set" dances with all eyes on the bride and groom during the first dance. *Haste to the Wedding* has been traditionally the opening tune.[18] The principals slip off early to their room in the groom's family home or a room in the village kept secret from most, but the "time" goes on throughout the night.

Family and Kinship

The elemental unit of family organization is the nuclear family consisting of husband, wife, and offspring, whether or not the married couple live within or near the family home. Depending upon the stage of the family life cycle, this unit may have a higher or lower degree of visibility and independence. From the very beginning the practice, as noted above, has been for maturing brothers to participate in an integrated household economy centering around crew fishing. Each married son, after several years' living in the family home, will seek to establish his family independently in a home of his own. He will usually be given a portion of the old family home site on which to erect his own house.

The physical contiguity of the sons' homes to the original homestead, the close working association of brothers, the tendency for wives, mothers, and unmarried daughters to play supporting roles in family enterprise and organization, the use of the patronymic, and the continuity of life over the generations have helped produce a moderately extended *kin group*[19] with dual organizational aspects. The presence of *patrilines* will be apparent, i.e., a limited number of families related by kinship ties to the second or third degree, and sharing a common name.[20]

18. *Ibid.*, p. 77.
19. Mary Sparkes, unpublished study of "Bay Port" (1974). The study is of the modern outport village family, but the kin group's presence reflects a mode of family organization that goes back centuries.
20. Firestone, *op. cit.*, prefers the term to "sib" or "agnates."

The less formal or visible but nevertheless functional set of kin-related sociability and socializing bonds emerges out of the constant interaction of mothers, sisters, daughters-in-law, aunts, and grandmothers, who (along with children as socializers and couriers) develop communication networks of gossip, comment, and reproof, and who take responsibility in various shared ways for developing effective modes of socialization and control. Not so well developed as the dual descent system of the Todas, the matriarchal dimension of the extended kin groups of outport villages gets elaborated and expressed and becomes operational through what might be called the "kitchen-centered" social bonding of affinally and consanguinally related females.

The central kinship relationships seen in dyadic form are that of: father-son, marked by respect and obedience; brother-brother, a close relationship involving cooperation, continuity of association tempered by a latent rivalry that seldom breaks out into destructive competition; grandmother-mother as coprincipals of the kitchen; mother-young daughter, a close but less enduring relationship since the daughter normally marries out and becomes part of her husband's family; and mother-daughter-in-law, a relationship that usually sees ambivalence and strain giving way to a viable incorporation of incoming wife into the established kin group. The spousal relationship incorporates intimacy and affection, love of children who are deeply cherished, and some strain occasioned by the competing closeness of brother-brother relationship, and by an abiding familism that restricts the autonomy of the nuclear family group. Still, an individuality flourishes, an individuality of the sort that is expressed in the drive to manage by one's self, and to merge selves in cooperative behavior only where strictures of kinship make it appropriate.

Household Property and Inheritance

Land, buildings, boats, other capital goods, and paraphernalia of the fishing enterprise are the property of and are inherited through male descent. Similarly, fishing berths, where the nets are regularly located, are passed down through the males of the extended family. Women may inherit domestic goods, but little else. At the death of the parents the homestead is never sold to nonkin; rather, it is passed on to the son who has chosen to live with and care for his elderly parents in their later years. Most likely this will be the youngest son, and if there is any cash to be passed on he will also be the recipient.[21] It should be added that traditionally the land was not granted, so there would be no deeds to land or recording of ownership. But by common consent of the villagers, home site boundaries, often marked with low stone walls or fences, are known and respected without question.

Family Cycle

Childhood

Children are born into family households that may include two ascending generations and possibly collateral kin in the form of aunts, uncles, and even cousins. This is particularly the case for the firstborn; however, collateral kin will in any event be close by on adjoining or near-adjoining property. Newfoundland families are large[22] and the houses are by comparison small. Children will always share a room, sleeping several to a bed. The youngest child shares a bed with his parents until supplanted by a younger sibling or until he is about three years old. "The fear of isolation in the dark" says Firestone, "somewhat due to the fear of spirits (ghosts), is perhaps, like the threat to the child that the fearful fantasy will take him away from family and local society, a reflection on the intimacy that permeates social relations."[23]

21. *Ibid.*, p. 52.
22. Averaging somewhat larger, in persons per household and per family, than any other province in Canada. See *Canada Year Book 1970-71, op. cit.*, pp. 71-78.
23. Firestone, *op. cit.*, pp. 69-71.

As everywhere, outport children play without being taught, running in small packs wide-eyed and excited when playing, seldom destructive, but with a penchant for throwing stones at nearly everything that moves, avidly pursuing games of war, exploring cliffs, and making an occasional brave assault on some suspected haunt of the "boo man."

Children are likely to have godparents, at the least a godfather. The consequent usual small reciprocities and friendships that deepen into a substantial form of ritual kinship not only contribute to the welfare and add breadth and depth to the child's interpersonal relationships, but serve to "knot" the network of community social relations by bringing nonkin related groups together.[24]

Children grow up as active participants in the household economy and play must be subordinated to pragmatic matters of everyday existence. Yet parents are loath to bring an early end to childhood, perhaps out of awareness of the hard life that stretches ahead. But always errands are run, small chores accomplished, and during the season fish are helped "made." In creating and sustaining a household economy children will have a role to play, and there will be no dearth of role models, given the availability of such in the kinship group.

Schooling is a local matter, although schools have always been in the hands of the churches, and missionary teachers are usually sent in from the outside. But the content of schooling tends to be pragmatically and realistically oriented to the needs of the outport adult to come. A broader maritime wisdom is absorbed from male adults whose fishing ventures may have taken them "on the Labrador," or away from the village through shipping on large trawlers that cruise in a variety of waters, or by episodes of work in maritime cities followed by return to the smaller, folk-like society. The youth may not grow up worldly-wise, but he will know that the world is wide and that alternatives to permanent residence in the village do exist. He may be

24. John Szwed, *Private Cultures and Public Imagery: Interpersonal Relations in a Newfoundland Peasant Society* (1966), pp. 71-78.

of the sea, but he is not chained to it as is the traditional peasant to the land. Newfoundland has always exported impressive proportions of its youth, females no less than males, but under the ordinary expectable operations of the combined patri-centric and sibling-centered family system where all males inherit a home site and share in the family enterprise, no son grows up expecting to be required to seek his future elsewhere.

Adulthood

Many adult activities have already been described. The husband, because fishing is a summertime activity, will usually find many other things to do to supplement the family income. Home is a base of operations from which, if necessary, he may be absent for shorter or longer periods of time. The wife and mother is home-bound. Visits outside the village are few, and nearly impossible during the winter. The home, family, and kin group orientation means security and comfort, friendliness and camaraderie. In a society not far removed from subsistence level people learn to cooperate when they must, but also to exhaust their own efforts before seeking help. "The crew members of a boat keep their plans and activities to themselves" says Newfoundland ethnographer Mary Sparkes, "so that in good luck and bad their neighbors cannot be said to have had a hand in their lot, an important facet in village harmony, especially during trying times for a family." The men learn not to intrude or to interfere, not to offer help or advice that may well backfire, not to plan for or insinuate themselves into the lives of others, and to shy away from direct speech and expression of conflicting points of view in the presence of persons they do not know well. Contractual relationships such as the building of a boat will be approached indirectly, and a long roundabout conversation will ensue before an agreement is reached.[25]

25. Chiaramonte, *op. cit.* This little work is completely given over to an analysis of the process of making and fulfilling craftsman-client contracts in a Newfoundland fishing community.

To be an adult is to be self-sufficient. "Fixing me trawl" also means minding one's own business. Brothers grow up under the tutelage and authority of a benign patriarchal father. Their wives are less likely to have parental or sibling bonds close at hand to sustain and integrate social and personal life. They stay at home, with their primary bond at first spousal, later to be shared or crosscut with attachments to children. In the necessarily close association with mother and father-in-law and other affinals the process of sharing and expressing basic human sentiments with all its subjective gratifications, and later the pride of accomplishment in establishing an independent household, balances the personal costs of leaving the family of orientation behind. The values of home life, fidelity, and sociability permeate traditional outport household settings. The result has been continuity and consistency in norms, values, and meaning in life.

The Elderly

Old age interlocks biological and social processes. For the male it begins with his inability to coextend patriarchal controls with physical performance, particularly to withstand the rigors of inshore fishing and to exercise daily command of the fishing enterprise. Decisions at sea are vital both to the catch and to the safety of the crew. When the father turns over the "skipper's" role it signalizes a significant turning point for himself in the family cycle. He and his wife will continue to remain active, but their needs and abilities will be located in a new family context, with the youngest son remaining in the homestead to organize and increasingly to exercise the authority relinquished by the father. The aged mother moves gradually away from the dominance of the home; yet, if she does not organize and direct, she still presides over much of the daily family activity. She has much to give in the way of wisdom and experience. She is the repository of traditional values and understanding, and culinary skills that threaten to be lost if not passed on, and there is, too, the warmth and cheer of her presence. If the homestead through the years goes through cycles that see the children grow and move neolocally to their own homes, it nevertheless remains the sentimental focus of all descending generations, even after the old folks die. Death itself is an expectable and nonmysterious fate, its onset usually slow and discernible in increasing physical impairments and generally failing health. The old folk die at home, attended and cared for until the end. Sons, daughters, grandchildren, and other primary relatives are not alienated from the dying; the funeral, simple, neighborly, and dignified, ceremoniously marks the rent in the social fabric, and shows the folk manner of helping to pick up and reweave the loose ends.

Functions and Controls

The traditional Newfoundland outport village society, from its beginning nearly a half-millenium ago, has chronically experienced geographical isolation, long winter periods that have prohibited sea travel, virtually no roads, and the most rudimentary institutionalized social services provided by the local church through the auspices of external government or extant political power. In population clusters, each of only a few hundred, contacts were necessarily face-to-face, continuous, and primary, with roles structured out of the practical needs in the day-to-day existence of a fisherfolk culture. In such society the folkways carry the sanction of past performance—they have "worked" with the evidence simply that through the centuries the outport has held its own. Adaptations to the harsh exigencies of isolated coastal living show clearly in the values, norms, and flexibility of various social creations. Priests or clergy who made intermittent stops at a village would marry those who both wanted and had to get married. Rituals might be conducted for retroactive effect, as for those buried without baptism, or lay persons might temporarily perform ceremonies ordinarily the province of the specialist. The midwife, if the village had one, delivered the children, and children as they grew up found they were learning to perform useful and necessary roles, with an audience composed of an extended kin group in addition to primary relatives and their peers.

The family, seen in its larger dimension as a three-generation extended family household, stood as the central social institution. If necessary it could survive solely by its own resources. It could migrate inland into the woods in winter to escape the freezing blasts of winds and snow off the seas. If a father were lost at sea the children would have male adults, usually uncles or grandfathers to relate to; foster parentage was common. Within the family the pervasive ethic of division of labor, sociability, and inhibition of impulse obtained. It is characteristic of the outporter to inhibit speech and action. Impulsiveness is discouraged, as is more patent deviation from family and local norms.

The family is a primary agency of social control. Since so much interaction involves kin of one degree or another, the extended family will mobilize a variety of persons who intercede personally, often by indirection, by using approbation, exemplary tales, or by distraction from a hurtful area, and by social activities and games, gatherings, and "times." The end goal, not always realized or understood, is a person quiet, reticent, indrawn, and nonaggressive in larger social contexts, who shies from a quickly constructed consensus and who dislikes direct contracting for, or the conducting of, affairs removed from the kin group. A variety of aphorisms and folklore assist him in defining situations, as do habit and usage. Mowat has said that the world of the outport man is the world of waters, that his thoughts lie constantly with it and "like a true mammal of the sea his real existence is aquatic; all else is peripheral to him."[26] But he is also a man of society and perforce human, the humanity of his life centered in his primary family, with a rich context of constantly developing kinship involvements within and about the family homestead.

26. Mowat and de Visser, *op. cit.*, not paginated.

Recent Changes and Trends

Since Confederation only a quarter-century ago incipient forces and rationally conceived plans for change have gathered headway, more rapidly in the communication, economic, and political-jural sectors, with changes in family structure and organization lagging somewhat behind. The central or basic foundation of change lies in the growing awareness of village people in most parts of the world that there are alternatives to lives that require an inordinate investment of time and labor to support existence. No matter how valued the traditional mode, if it can be achieved only by struggle at the subsistence level, we can expect that the promise of social change will receive increasing attention to the extent that the quality of life is conceived to be improvable.

In her study covering several part-years of participant observation of "Bay Port" on the Great Northern Peninsula, Mary Sparkes has examined in some detail the process involved in the changing outport village.[27] The introduction of a province-wide system of all-weather roads as part of an ambitious plan of the provincial government to bring Newfoundland into the twentieth century in one great leap, and the consequent shift of transportation from sea to land, marks the onset of social and economic change. The mobility provided by the car and serviceable roads permitted a wider range of social contacts. New patterns of work took the males away from the sea, many of them permanently, locating them in the traditional occupations of lumbering, woodcutting, and construction, operating increasingly farther from the sea, and also in the new enterprises that sprang up in the context of the transportation boom. As the boat gave way to the bulldozer and the truck, the face of the outport economy changed toward a wage-based, cash-dominated system, accompanied by an increasing emphasis on cash and credit buying of mass-produced commodities, the staple fare of an urban civilization.

27. Sparkes, *op. cit.*

Along with the boom in transportation came the near revolution in communication. Virtually isolated through the winter months, the outport villagers were mostly dependent upon what communication might come with sea transportation. A first big step was the radio-telephone, with perhaps one outlet to a village. Public broadcasting, home radios, telephones, and lately TVs further shattered cultural isolation. And the roads would bring an infinitely greater number of people to and through the outports: visitors, job and business enterprise seekers, tourists, and service and welfare functionaries, all in one way or another multiplying the social contacts of the residents. The result has been a laminating of the traditional culture with layers of urban and mass values, embracing change in nearly all areas of life. The family, too, has responded adaptively, serving in some ways to restrain a rapid reordering of institutional arrangements and in other ways to encourage them.

In folk or folk-like societies the sentiments and affective attachments of people to each other and to their way of life are deeply structured and unquestioned. Internalized as part of the outport personality these sentiments influence the ways in which the social reality of the outport world is conceived and the requisite social roles played. Inasmuch as these Newfoundlanders have in the past grounded so much of their everyday existence in family and kinship, it should not be surprising that today such features of family organization as patrilocality, strong fraternal bonds, and strength in the patriarchal aspects of family authority, matched by strong sentiments that attach to the complex of motherhood and mother dominance of the home, are still in evidence. These and other traditional family elements remain integrative but, as Mary Sparkes is careful to point out, in their operation they are more than just a force for resistance to change.[28]

For upon closer inspection one sees that the incentive to develop a better standard of existence, to improve one's lot, the determination to "go up" in the scale of social improve-

28. *Ibid.*

ment, is also a product of family and kinship socialization. The roots of individual enterprise are cultivated in family contexts. The socializaticn process has long functioned to produce a peculiar blend of personality characteristics in the outporter: self-reliance, individual effort, and the ability to make do in the face of high odds but to become enterprising when they even out. The other side of the coin is gregariousness, family- and kin-centeredness, and a tendency to take refuge in the social meanings indigenously developed within family, kin group, and community.

The Newfoundland outport family is caught up in forces that move people everywhere toward modernity—modernity in institutions and full participatory rights in the social felicity promised by the urban mass society. The usual indices are already apparent: individual enterprise (though still embedded in the kin group), smaller families, modern or modernized houses with all the conveniences and rooms full of department store or catalog-ordered furniture, egalitarianism making inroads on familism, and the rise of an increasingly free-standing nuclear family unit whose members are pragmatically discarding traditional values and are poised for geographical, occupational, and social mobility, with the "heritage of the sea" dimming in their personal histories.

THE TRADITIONAL FRENCH-CANADIAN HABITANT FAMILY

French Canada begins with the colony of New France in 1584, but the expansion of French colonialism in southeastern Canada proceeded slowly through the sixteenth and early seventeenth centuries. For the most part the growth consisted in small rural settlements following the *rang*[29] pattern strung

29. The *rang* system will be described later. A well developed treatment is found in "The *Rang*-Pattern of Rural Settlement in French Canada" by geographer Pierre Deffontaines, translated and included in *French Canadian Society*, Marcel Rioux and Yves Martin, eds. (1964), Vol. 1, pp. 3-18.

along the great St. Lawrence River, oriented by waterway to the slowly developing commercial and trading centers of Montreal, Trois Rivières, and Quebec, the latter coming to serve as an administrative center for both secular monarchical and religious authorities. It was to these and to other, later towns that many of the earlier rural settlers, both noble and common, would return for shelter from the frightening Canadian winters. In spring the *hivernant,* later *habitant,*[30] would return to his farm, or *seigneurage.*[31] For the peasant and artisan the practice might not be so common nor so lasting, and many came to rough it out the year round. In any event the term *habitant* came to mean the man of the countryside and the soil, living a family-, kinship-, and community-centered, religion-dominated, primarily agricultural way of life.

Other roles and life styles competed. The *voyageur* participated by boat and canoe in the exploration of the hinterland, and the *coureurs de bois* cleared, settled, and later worked for pay in the vast Canadian woodland. In an age of fur trade both might become hunters and trappers. However, the *habitant* had skills with the ax as well as the hoe, and would often spend the colder portions of the year away from home working in the woods to supplement family income. Nor would he be stranger to the paddle canoe, as the primary settlements nearly always consisted of narrow ribbons of family-owned lands, each terminating at the river's edge. While roads were yet to be built the river was the mode of transportation *par excellence.* The point to be made here is that no matter how much a son of the soil he might be, the *habitant* from the beginning differed from his native French peasant counterpart in that he had alternatives and oppor-

30. The interpretation is from Jean Charlemagne Bracq, *The Evolution of French Canada* (1924), p. 241.

31. Brief treatments of the *seigneurial* system are found in Deffontaines, *op. cit.,* pp. 4-6, and in Horace Miner, *St. Denis: A French Canadian Parish* (1939, 1963), pp. 6-8.

tunities for social and geographical mobility.[32] A vast hinterland beckoned. "Even today," says Gérald Fortin, "the forest has an almost magic attraction for urban and rural Quebecers alike. It is both a symbol of challenge and of liberation."[33]

The "nobility" came often as down-and-outers who might recoup fortunes in the fur trade, as merchants, army officers, or as *nouveau riche* in the form of freshly titled and often untitled *seigneurs*. Most were anxious to effect the life of the landed gentry, but they found themselves spending as much time as possible in town in preference to functioning as noblemen of the "manor."[34] A shortage of wives for all classes was chronic, and females, whether they sought to reproduce the fashionable society left behind at court and in cities, or to produce large families for God and country in the rural areas, could capitalize on their scarcity and take on more encompassing and influential roles.[35]

The clergy might not have been the best of its kind to depart France, but the strength of organized Catholicism left behind—more powerful than that of the monarchy—either sustained them in their resolve or challenged them to an unusual and productive vigor. For several hundred years the center of New World Catholicism remained Quebec, and until recently more priests were trained there than in any other city in North America.[36]

32. For a persuasive statement on the *habitants'* access to a more affluent way of life and a more ebullient life style, at least before the British Conquest, see W. J. Eccles, *Canadian Society During the French Regime* (1968), pp. 70 ff.

33. Gérald Fortin, "Woman's Role in the Evolution of Agriculture in Quebec," in *The Family in the Evolution of Agriculture* (1968), p. 28.

34. See Eccles, *op. cit.* and Bracq, *op. cit.* Miner quotes Parkman (1880) as concluding that "only half of the *seigneurs* were of the *noblesse,* and many of these sold their fiefs to persons of very humble social rank," *op. cit.,* p. 7. Although *seigneurs* were supposed to remain on and develop the land and build settlements, many gave up country living when they found out how much effort it actually took to make a seigneurial system work.

35. Fortin, *op. cit.,* pp. 27 ff.

36. Bracq, *op. cit.,* pp. 212 ff.

Society in New France thus was shaped by the values and institutions imported from France, and by the peculiar Canadian environment.[37] Both the church and the monarchy had interests in producing a country worthy of bearing the name of France, and at least one author has termed the solicitude and paternalistic intervention of these powers as constituting in effect an "aristocratic welfare state."[38] New France may have had elements of feudalism permeating its major institutions but the result was not a simple extension of feudalism to a new continent. Fur trader, merchant, *seigneur, habitant* —all came under a monarchical and ecclesiastical concept of guidance, support, and control that differed widely from the decentralization of the traditional feudal order. Such system as there was mixed theocracy with monarchy in a colonial enterprise dominantly mercantilistic, class rather than caste oriented, and leavened with the new ethos of an adventurous group of Frenchmen bent on peopling and devising a New France of at least partially their own making.[39]

It was a different society that emerged out of the English Conquest of New France. The British military victory on the Plains of Abraham in 1759 brought to a conclusion the process of changing the status of New France from an important preoccupation of French monarchs to a pawn in an international chess game played among powerful warring nations. The treaty concluded in Paris in 1763 ceded France's major North American possessions to England. Faced with minority status in what was then New France and is now mostly the province of Quebec and part of New Brunswick, the English used draconian measures to pacify the "aliens" who outnumbered them more than a dozen to one. A contemporary authority on French-Canadian history, Mason Wade, drawing on the work of an earlier historian, Abbé I. Caron, notes that while there could be little doubt that most of French colonial

37. Eccles, *op. cit.*, pp. 11-46.
38. *Ibid.*, p. 14.
39. *Ibid.*, particularly pp. 12 ff.

society was severely shaken by the conquest and that soldiers, officials, and the nobility who were deprived of their old opportunities for soldiering and fur trading were forced to emigrate, ". . . the clergy remained at their posts, and since their position alone among the elite was not affected by the conquest, their prestige as leaders of the people was strongly reinforced. The great mass of population, the *habitants,* were little disturbed by the change of rule."[40]

Attempts by the British to assimilate the majority population (70,000 at the time of the conquest) were soon abandoned, and in the Quebec Act of 1774 recognition was granted to the major institutions of the French-speaking community: its civil laws, its seigneurial system, its Roman Catholic religious organization.[41] It is at this juncture in French-Canadian history that their current subcultural identity was firmly established.[42] The leadership role of the Catholic church has remained decisive through the ensuing centuries, and even today in Quebec remains a strong if muted influence in all matters affecting the French-Canadian commonweal.[43]

The Rang *and the Parish*

The *rang* pattern of rural settlement provided a geographical and socio-ecological arena within which a set of community relations partly preformed in rural feudal France emerges and takes a distinctive French-Canadian form. Deffontaines writes:

The French Canadian therefore had to plan his own type of settlement and devise his dwelling, knowing little of the country, its geographical features, its waterways, its natural routes, its soil varieties. In a word, he

40. Mason Wade, *The French Canadians* (1968), Vol. 1, p. 50.

41. *Canada 1971* (1970), p. 33.

42. Laurence French, "The French Canadian Family," manuscript prepared for *American Minority Family Life Styles,* Robert W. Habenstein and Charles Mindel, eds. (1974).

43. The role of the church is also described briefly in a later section on the parish.

had to people and exploit a country, to initiate a process which in the old countries of Europe took many centuries and constantly required numerous modifications.[44]

The Canadian seignorial ·system with its individual holdings made way for the success of the small farmstead.[45] Each farmstead consisted of a narrow strip, nearly 800 feet wide and a mile and a half long, fronting on the river and extending at a ninety-degree angle up from the shore to the higher and usually wooded hinterland. Clearing the land and establishing the homestead began at the waterfront, and the settlers worked their way uphill clearing the land for gardens, meadows for hay—often with the stumps remaining—and establishing woodlots farther above. Whatever variation in width, the length remained constant, and rent, which tended to be very low, was calculated on width of the river lot only. *Seigneurs* were expected to clear, maintain, and settle their land; thus each *seigneurage* became in effect a practical act of land distribution and a method of colonization that retained residual aspects of a "peasant-noble" relationship. A notable exception, however, was that the Canadian *seigniory* was not a political institution;[46] the *seigneur* could have no voice in the direction of the government and he could not call upon the *habitant* for military service. Vassalage, if it existed at all, existed in a highly attenuated form.

The *rang* system thus provided relatively uniform-sized river lots with exploitable hinterlands for peasant-status settlers who, although they were subject to some aspects of traditional feudalism, found themselves rather free to develop a robust, possibly affluent, but certainly culturally consistent, integrated, and meaningful community and family life. Writes Eccles:

44. Extract taken from Deffontaines, *op. cit.*, p. 3, and reprinted with permission of the publishers, McClelland and Stewart, Ltd., and Université Laval Quebec in whose sponsored publication *Cahiers de géographie* 5 (1953) the article first appeared.
45. *Ibid.* p. 5.
46. *Ibid.*, p. 4.

The Canadian in the lower ranks of society did not have to labour, scrimp, cheat, and hide his little hoard from the tax collector in order to buy a small parcel of land, or purchase exemption from onerous medieval obligations. He could obtain as much land as he could work on payment of modest seigneurial dues, and a tithe of 1/26 of his wheat crop . . . they lived well, enjoying the right to hunt and fish, privileges that were stringently denied their European counterparts. In that age, wood and leather were vital commodities, the Canadians had ample supplies of both. In the eighteenth century Intendant Hocquart remarked that no one starved in Canada. Of few lands in Europe could this have been said.[47]

The *rang* system, further notes Deffontaines, had two advantages that cannot easily be obtained both at once: it allowed the settlers to possess large land tracts and at the same time, because of the layout of the lots, it afforded protection from isolation.[48] Isolation was avoided in part because of family and extended kinship organization, but also because of the custom of the *premier voisin,* or the first and nearest neighbor. To the *habitant* "the *premier voisin* comes even before a relative; he is invited to all family gatherings, is consulted about important decisions and helps out in all large projects."[49]

The *rang,* which was a secular, indigenous, French-Canadian creation, would be established before the parish and thus in a significant way constitute the major social-geographical unit. But while the *rang* had aspects of social innovation, the parish, as Falardeau notes, was one of the key religious institutions which the pioneers brought with them to New France.[50] The parish might begin with only the property on which a church was built. Through time and by gifts, purchases, and subdivision, particularly for the retired old folks, or *emplacitaires,* there would slowly be both expansion

47. Eccles, *op. cit.,* pp. 71-72. By permission of Harvest House, Ltd., Montreal, Que., Canada.

48. Deffontaines, *op. cit.,* p. 11.

49. *Ibid.,* p. 12.

50. Jean-Charles Falardeau, "The Seventeenth Century Parish in French Canada," in *French Canadian Society,* Marcel Rioux and Yves Martin, eds. (1964), Vol. 1, p. 23.

of church land and a village growth upon it.[51] A well-filled cemetery would be evidence of a long established church village. While French Canadians and their rural-minded clergy resisted urban growth, it was inevitable that a growing economy would produce and in part become the consequence of concentration of commercial, business, and professional interests and functionaries. But in the earlier periods the municipal interest of *habitants* such as it was remained of a strictly parochial character. "All the problems of village life," notes Falardeau, "such as the organization of schools, were solved adequately by the few agents of the local parochial church, especially by the *fabrique*."[52]

There can be no doubt that rural French Canada from the very beginning has felt most comfortable when virtually all matters pertaining to societal behavior have been under the aegis of the Catholic church. To say that the *habitant's* life has been religion dominated is less correct than it is to say it has been so permeated with religious doctrine that life thereby gains its meaning, in nearly all contexts.

Turning now to the rural French-Canadian family, the traditional family of the *habitant*, we will focus on the proto-typical form that emerges out of the early history of the colonization of New France. Like the Newfoundland outport family it has retained its elements of organization through a number of centuries—most were there fifty years ago and many are to be found even today.[53] We shall avoid the argu-

51. Deffontaines, *op. cit.*, p. 16.

52. *Ibid.* The *fabrique* is a type of church board consisting of three elected lay persons who meet with the curé to handle financial and other matters of the church.

53. Horace Miner's excellent ethnographic study of St. Denis in the late 1930s, *St. Denis, A French Canadian Parish* (1939), catches the parish in moments of change between the old and the new. Still the old dominates, and it is easy to identify the traditional organizational structures and the institutions as they held firm through the eighteenth, nineteenth, and early twentieth centuries. The remaining portion of this chapter that deals with the rural French-Canadian family is rather completely given over to a summary of Miner's exemplary field study.

ment as to whether *the* French-Canadian family has all along been predominantly urban and commercial, or rural and local economy-oriented. Given the great St. Lawrence and other major rivers for transportation, a river-frontage-based system of land holdings and settlements, and an enormous hinterland to conquer, settle, and exploit, and given a *seigneurage* system that made minimal economic and personal service demands on the *habitants,* one can see how mobility, social contacts, opportunity, and the promise of affluence would make a truly folk or peasant society that kept people chained to soil and master virtually impossible. Yet the tendency of rural settlements to draw in on themselves as self-isolating enclaves, to build a total round of life, and to give meaning to this life through domestic and local institutions, the emergence in other words of a virtually closed *rang*-parish-family system, cannot be denied in light of historic and more modern ethnographic evidence. It is with this orientation that we shall be describing the French-Canadian *habitant* family of several generations ago. As before, the "historical present" mode of presentation will be employed.

Family Structure

Mate Selection and Marriage

Marriage is less an individualistic than it is a family and kinship matter. Eligible mates do not exist randomly in the community but are located in groups of families or cliques that are held together by bonds of kinship, obligation, and often political partisanship. One marries someone known through long association as a member of such ingroups. Cousin marriages are common, and even though, as Miner observes, the church frowns on marriages of second cousins and closer, dispensations will be granted by the curé who will usually have adapted to the local endogamous-like mode of mate selection.[54]

54. *Ibid.,* p. 78.

Nor is marriage taken lightly. Courtship takes place within the contexts of lively parties and group social activities, and also in the more subdued atmosphere of the girl's home where more serious chatting with the parents is in order. Courtship, often lasting only a few months, provides a means for both principals and parents, particularly the latter, to work out the details of the marriage and the "establishment" of the son. Marriage is by contract and with dowries, and no child would marry against the wishes of his parents.[55] According to Bracq, "The pre-matrimonial arrangements are still like those of Old France where the father asked, in a formal way, the hand of her who was to become his daughter-in-law."[56] The contract having been approved, the sacramental seal of religion must be laid upon the marriage. After the banns are read the marriage will be held in the church, with the curé of the bride's parish performing one of his more pleasant duties. With dancing and feasting beginning at the home of the groom, moving from house to house on different nights, the wedding can go on for days. Writing of the tone and mood of rural French-Canadian marriages, Bracq observes:

> Their gay nature never displays itself more felicitously than on these occasions. They never feel that their marriage is a misalliance. As a rule it is free from fear and never has the dark prospect of divorce. They make no dissection of their happiness. Self-analysis is not common.[57]

A short honeymoon to Quebec or Ste. Anne de Beaupré is the usual pattern, but even today the *habitants* are not known for wanting to be long alone outside kinship groups. Ralph Piddington, in a recent study of kinship in a French-Canadian parish near Winnipeg, tells of an informant and his wife who went to Chicago for their honeymoon and stayed at a hotel. On the day of their arrival a murder was committed in an

55. *Ibid.*, p. 69.
56. Bracq, *op. cit.*, p. 195. Still known as "la grande demande."
57. *Ibid.*

adjoining bedroom. The wife said, "I don't like this place; we have relatives in Milwaukee; let's spend the rest of our honeymoon there," which they did.[58]

Family and Kinship

"The main characteristics of the French-Canadian family," observes a close student of French-Canadian society, Philippe Garigue, "can be said to be an extensive kinship recognition only partially weakened by geographical scattering, an extensive exchange of services among recognized kin, a strong sense of household, unity, and a large sibling group."[59] Enough perhaps has been said about kinship groupings, but both early and modern studies of French-Canadian kinship reveal an impressive degree of kinship recognition in both rural and urban settings. The wife in our period will have no difficulty remembering several hundred kin, where they are, and the degree of relationship, with such knowledge extending to affinal as well as to consanguineal relatives. The scattering of kin reflects an inexorable relationship between a constantly expanding population, a finite amount of arable land, and a disposition on the part of the *habitants* not to divide farms among their offspring.

Families, as already noted, are large, enormous by American standards, with nine, ten, or more children preferred. The fact that the church approves and urges early and fertile marriages is probably not so decisive as the need for a large number of family members working together as a productive agricultural unit in order to sustain their domestic economy. Given a low level of technology (and rural French Canadians have long been resistant to large-scale or corporate farming),

58. Ralph Piddington, "A Study of French Canadian Kinship," in *The Canadian Family*, K. Ishwaran, ed. (1971), p. 462.

59. Philippe Garigue, "The French-Canadian Family," in *Canadian Dualism*, Mason Wade, ed. (1960), p. 197.

five, six or more persons of sufficient age to participate one
way or another in farm work have always been considered
nescessary for the successful operation of a family farm.

Familism is a key descriptive term appropriate to French
Canadians everywhere. Rural families are highly familistic
and from an outside view decidedly patriarchal. The father
occupies center stage, exercising authority and making decisions in the best interests of the family. By traditional belief
he is the stronger and more capable of the sexes. When one
observes the father leading the more adult members of his
family into church, seated at the head of the dinner table, or
talking politics in the company of adult males, there is the
temptation to overemphasize his importance. Gérald Fortin,
a student of French-Canadian family and culture, balances the
scales in arguing that the role of the mother has necessarily
been important if for no other reason than that the father was
so often away, and that even when the *coureurs de bois* became
farmers they were not able to take away from the mother all
the functions she had traditionally played.[60]

Although the continual presence of the father in a traditional type of
farming seemed to favor the emergence of a patriarchal form of family
structure, it was always a modified type of patriarchy in which the father
had to allow the mother to exercise a fair amount of leadership if not
authority. While the father's authority in matters pertaining to farm operations was hardly ever questioned, the mother retained the role of a spiritual
and moral guide and acted as a mediator in affective matters . . . as she was
more educated than her husband she became the repository of spiritual,
intellectual and moral values. Being more directly concerned with these
problems she also tended to follow the teachings of the clergy more readily
and to accept the values they conveyed.[61]

Household Economy, Inheritance, and Kinship

The family and the systems of labor are intimately identified.[62] As already pointed out, farming has never been con-

60. Fortin, *op. cit.*, p. 27.
61. *Ibid.* Courtesy of the Vanier Institute of the Family, Ottawa,
Ontario, Canada.
62. Léon Gérin, "The French-Canadian Family—Its Strengths and
Weaknesses" in *French Canadian Society*, K. Ishwaran, ed. (1971) p. 462.

ducted on more than a modest scale. Varieties of garden vegetables are planted, and diversified crops, hay, corn, wheat, and
other grains, are grown on a double rotational system—two
successive harvests of grain alternate with fallow or unplowed
land, or more rarely with pastureland.[63] The homes tend to
be spacious and the barns long, up to 100 feet. Roofs are
thatched "because the straw does not cost anything, and if
we stopped doing this it would be necessary to use wood
which is very expensive . . ."[64] The household economy is
sustained through the hard work of many family members;
even the family dog will pull a cart. Sons will work with the
father and begin to absorb some of his occupational personality; daughters learn domestic arts, weaving, baking, and
household management. Grandparents are at hand to participate in such ways as they can in the ongoing economy and to
contribute to the socialization of the young. Relatives seem
to be everywhere, but each farm is run independently.

The "stem family" studied by Le Play, while it does not
provide a clear model, is instructive in understanding the
family of the *habitant*.[65] The nuclear unit of parents and
offspring exists within a larger group, *la famille*, which
includes grandparents, aunts, uncles, and cousins. This group
is considered to have unity in time and space and is held
together by symbols of property.[66] The central principle that
applies to marriage and inheritance is that the homestead and
family farm will go to one inheriting son, and that without
a farm a son is not considered sufficiently established to be
eligible for marriage and to live in the community. Since in
the French-Canadian families the succession of children will
begin when the mother is in her mid-twenties, the earliest
born will have reached young adulthood while the parents
are still vigorous and have no reason to turn over farm and
homestead to a son. If the family is prospering, attempts will

63. *Ibid.*
64. *Ibid.*
65. Pierre G. Le Play, *L'Organization de la famille* (1884).
66. Linda W. Phelps, "The French Family: A Cultural Analysis"
(1969). Unpublished manuscript.

be made to acquire farms within the parish for the earliest born, but they will not ordinarily inherit, and the family farm will not be divided.

The practice is to relinquish the farm to a middle son, one deemed the most intelligent, responsible, provident, and likely to maintain or increase its prosperity. He in turn will have the responsibility for helping establish the younger brothers who will not inherit. If they have not been established locally through the efforts of the parents the older brothers will leave the community. They may then look for other nearby settlements where they have relatives, or migrate to more distant urban or rural settings. Daughters may be sent to convents to receive their *diplomes* after they complete local schools. Also, dowries must be built up, as these figure importantly in the mate selection process. Those who do not marry locally—and chances are about even that they will not —may remain as maiden aunts in the families of their brothers, or also migrate.

Family Cycle

Childhood

"The birth of the child causes no particular excitement because no atmosphere of novelty surrounds it," observes Horace Miner. "Babies are a continual part of the average household for fifteen out of every thirty-four years."[67] For the mother much of married life must seem an endless series of pregnancies. The "revenge of the cradle"[68] must lose some of its savor when it seems to the *habitant* mother that she must bear the burden of keeping French Canada's birth rate high.

But children are never rejected however many in a fam-

67. Miner, *op. cit.*, p. 169.
68. The term springs from French-Canadian political ideology. The English Canadians are to be displaced from power by sheer growth of French-Canadian population. A large family not only reflects traditional rural socio-religious norms, it becomes a political act as well.

ily; on the contrary, they are frequently spoiled with parental affection, particularly in their infancy. Baptism is of course essential, to be carried out within twenty-four hours after birth. The child must be named, godparents—usually closely related to the child—chosen, and the "bearer" at the baptismal ceremony designated. The simple ceremony and the baptismal party restricted to the father and child, godparents and bearer, is important, and again puts an ecclesiastical seal on a turning point in the family life cycle.[69]

The child remains close to the mother throughout early childhood. An elder sister may be entrusted with his care, but the mother is in the background as a sympathetic person to whom appeal may be made in case of injury or wrong.[70] Given the size of families, the child nearly always finds itself in a context of multiple sibling relationships. The older children, as Miner indicates, segregate themselves from the younger and take minor responsibilities seriously. Even in play adult roles are imitated:

> A lad of three or four will mount an empty wagon and drive and work imaginary horses for hours on end. Toys reproduce in miniature objects associated with adults. A girl will tend her doll as her mother tends the baby. Already gender distinctions, marked in the manner in which the parents dress the children, begin to be accentuated by different behavior patterns . . . The development of a gender personality constitutes a large part of the growth of personality.[71]

Until about six years of age the child is more likely engaged in imitative play, in playing at roles of adults, but is still confined in play and other activities to the household and vicinity. After six the child learns *le petit catéchisme,* takes first communion in a group of age mates, and begins to enter more fully the religious life of the community. School instruction and family education are conjoined as the youth works his way through the grades and closer toward young adult-

69. Miner, *op. cit.,* pp. 174-175.
70. *Ibid.,* p. 176.
71. *Ibid.,* p. 177. By permission of the University of Chicago Press.

hood. The explicit purpose of the parish school is to make
the children into good Catholics and good citizens, the two
being synonymous in the local culture.[72] As age and sex separation continues, there emerges an increasingly distinct division of labor. The girl helps her mother and older sister more
and more, the boy his father and brothers.

Young Adulthood

Grande Communion and graduation from school are
important rites of passage in moving the young from adolescence into young manhood and womanhood. The young man,
Miner explains, finds his religious and secular obligations and
privileges increasing. His range of contacts broadens, he
attends parties involving neighbors and extended relatives,
and he now finds himself part of the group of unmarried men
of the community. Boys begin to smoke, girls look at parties
as occasions to catch the attention of a potential mate, and
the interests of both shift toward the economic and social
realities facing them as future married adults. While the
father will have traditional responsibility for the establishment of the children, "the parent is supposed to help his offspring, not guarantee a livelihood. If the economic possibility
of such parental help is slight, it devolves upon the child to
look out for himself."[73] Recalling that one son will inherit
the farm and homestead, others will all along have been eval-
uated by the parents, who have been looking for other ways
that establishment might take, i.e., college education, priest-
hood, commercial training. Likewise, it is well known that
the daughters who receive college education have a better
chance of getting married, and that an ample dowry harms
no one's chances for marriage.

It seems fairly obvious that the young adult who does not
inherit will have a relatively heavy burden of responsibility

72. *Ibid.*, p. 184.
73. *Ibid.*, p. 199.

for making his own way in the world. For the inheriting son the responsibilities are no less heavy, but they can be anticipated. He has long worked in close association with his father, and the running of the farm will follow the pattern already set by a succession of fathers. The older daughters are likewise learning to assume the adult female role and by the time of marriage young adulthood will merge into full adulthood without trauma.

Adulthood

Adulthood proper begins with marriage. The seriousness of the new status is marked by a change toward more somber clothing for the woman, while the male grows a moustache and henceforth associates with other married adults. A family is immediately started. The wife is busy in her homemaking role; the husband in addition to his farm work will be expected to be active in local civic and religious affairs. He must not only pay head tax, but will be expected to "buy" a pew in the church and to contribute to school upkeep and road projects.[74] A catalog of *habitant* values would include thrift, prudence, religiosity, concern for those close by, and an indifference to the world at large, except for the knowledge that groups of relatives and important religious shrines—both worth occasional visiting—are located somewhere in it. Little can be done about the rest. One day blends into another, as do the seasons. After three decades of mature adulthood two segments of the life cycle yet remain: old age, which may continue another decade or two, and death that terminates life but by no means obliterates the social being.

Old Age

The period of old age for the *habitant* begins with turning over the farm and homestead to the inheriting son. As long

74. *Ibid.,* pp. 217-218.

as a hoe may be lifted or a potato peeled there is meaningful activity for the elderly, and whatever disengagement from social roles there may be, it cannot be said to derive from an indifferent society. Since the three-generation household is an expectable segment of the life cycle, grandparents will have grandchildren to live with and to indulge. All extended kin groups will have their share of the elderly, including a few great-grandparents in their eighties. The fact of age in rural society is as common as it is inexorable. Religious duties are lightened but as old age sets in awareness of death increases. Old people spend a great deal of time and thought in religious matters, prayers, and contemplation.[75]

Death activates a set of mourning and funeral practices that have the effect, as Miner points out, of asserting the solidarity of the groups. For the *habitants* there is no alienation from death or the dead. Religious involvement begins with the last rite, the church bells toll (differently according to age and sex of the deceased), and wakes are held for at least two nights before the burial. The wake combines social and religious activity, with friends and relatives going into the room containing the corpse and saying three rosaries before returning to their conversation.[76]

On the morning of the funeral the mourners will gather at the house of the deceased for prayers and then attend the funeral. Whatever the "class" of funeral—depending upon the money paid—all the dead are buried from the parish church. Traditionally, mourning observances, which include wearing mourning dress and altering one's behavior, have been elaborately scheduled for all relatives of the dead. These follow principles of closeness of kin and vital relationship to society. Thus, mourning falls hardest upon a woman who has lost her husband; it is of shorter duration for both the old and the young, more so for the very old and for infants. Miner calculates

75. *Ibid.,* p. 219.
76. *Ibid.,* p. 223.

that through the life cycle a person spends an average of about twelve years in mourning, with a maximum of around twenty years should he be a tenth child married to a tenth child.

> Burial will be in the church cemetery. The priest and choir conclude the service at the grave, and those parishioners who have gone to the cemetery crowd up to look in. It is not unusual for a member of the deceased's immediate family to request the undertaker to remove a coffin ornament. The undertaker jumps down onto the coffin, still in his high hat, and pries off a crucifix, name plate, or handle. The souvenir of the departed one thereafter adorns the family salon.[77]

An anniversary service at which an artificial coffin is used reenacts the funeral in all its particulars, up to the point where the body is removed from the church. The consequence of the "second burial," Miner concludes, is that the dead is further cut off from society. Even this is not a complete severance, as his kinsmen continue to wear mourning and to pray for him for a time after this ceremony.[78]

Disjunction and Continuity

Thus far in stressing stability of form and continuity in process we have presented a somewhat static and at the same time uncritical picture of the *habitant* family. Part of the reason may be the lack of commonly expected disjunctions in family and community. Divorce, for example, is prohibited, and desertion a phenomenon that seldom occurs. Juvenile delinquency would hardly be an apt term to apply to the occasional overstepping of conventional proprieties by youth. The disorganized, disoriented, and nonconforming find it easier to leave than to stay. The mentally deficient are rather casually cared for in their families. Crime in most of its aspects is something read about in the newspaper. Nevertheless, the full span of human emotions is present in the *habitant* personality and many of them come out in discourse,

77. *Ibid.*, p. 227.
78. *Ibid.*

argument, and expostulation. Sides are taken on local, sometimes national issues, often by extended kinship groups. Ingroups imply outgroups, and when the traditional figure of injustice, the English-Canadian establishment, is not being taken to task, fallouts can and often do occur at much more local levels. The organizing function of such conflicts should be recognized. Gossip, rumor, hearsay, superstition, folk wisdom, including some incredible traditional cures and remedies (fried onion in the ear for earache, etc.) which Miner catalogued in his parish study, and an indifference toward pre- and neonatal care with high infant mortality as a consequence, are some common characteristics of traditional peasant cultures everywhere and need no special comment. Their persistence in the face of burgeoning rationalism and the growth of science suggests that the imponderables and life cycle crises, the "junctures and turning points" as E. C. Hughes terms them, have in the main been dealt with efficaciously if non-rationally by the rural French Canadians.

A more immediate phenomenon is the friction that develops between father and sons, usually involving the older ones and most particularly the eldest, whom the father accuses the mother of preferring.[79] The authority of the father tends to be unbending, and the traditional practice of having sons and daughters at home or away giving up their wages when they work, to be distributed by the father in the best interests of the family, meets with resistance. Colette Moreux has termed the interfamily power arena a "fragile equilibrium."[80] The mother and all the women, she finds in a modern study, unite against the men, and the wife as "mother" takes possession of the things and the people of the house.[81] Earlier quoted references seem to support the retrospective projection of these instabilities back into our earlier twentieth century time frame.

The major disjunctive process, at least seen superficially as such, is the dislodgment from the parish of young men and

79. Colette Moreux, "The French-Canadian Family," in *The Canadian Family*, K. Ishwaran, ed. (1971), p. 142.

80. *Ibid.*, pp. 140 ff.

81. *Ibid.*, p. 143.

women whose parents could not get them properly established. True, two brothers may somehow become neighbors, but in more cases than not males and females, after rather intense and lengthy child, youth, and young adult socialization, will be faced with a new and strange role, that of migrant. Settlement of nearby areas becomes increasingly difficult, and arable lands for farming must be sought farther and farther from the home parish. The New England states in the past century and a half, particularly between 1860 and 1930 when there was an open Canadian-United States border, absorbed a very substantial number of migrants who for the most part stayed in the small mill towns as an amenable, non-visible work force, and who established a Franco-American subculture containing most of the institutions of the communities left behind.[82] When western Canada was opened to settlement, French Canadians from Quebec, New Brunswick, and "Acadia" moved out to establish ethnic villages in the open and undeveloped areas, and urban enclaves in the growing cities, both patterns recapitulating earlier migrations.

Interestingly, though modes of farming and the worlds of work of the new migrants may differ from the traditional domestic household-centered economy of the St. Lawrence Valley *habitant,* most of the structural features posited by Garigue as common to French-Canadian families in all settings persist: kinship extension, large sibling groups, family identity, reciprocity of service, religious integration of most aspects of life, and a proclivity to scatter as surplus community population to other kin-oriented and organized parishes, enclaves, and village communities.[83] Piddington finds, for example, an astonishing ramification of kinship in St. Jean-Baptiste, located between Winnipeg and the United States border, where it would not be outlandish to have an informant reply to a kinship query, "He is my brother-in-law because his second wife is my wife's sister; he is also my uncle because his first wife was my mother's sister; and he is also my cousin, like

82. French, *op. cit.*
83. Garigue, *op. cit.*

everybody else."[84] Piddington's findings support those of Garigue's in Montreal and in a northern French-Canadian ethnic mining community.[85] French's work on the New England Franco-American subculture shows a recapitulation of traditional kinship patterns,[86] and Moreux finds kinship groups in a suburb of Montreal visible and important in transmitting culture and reinforcing social controls.[87]

Using a macrosociological level of analysis we may conclude that the *habitant* family sustains its traditional form and pattern of operation while scattering a well socialized human product that is programmed to reproduce the familism and kin-centeredness left behind. At the personal level, if the cost of growing up in the large *habitant* family is to have to face making it on one's own elsewhere, the benefit derives from the certainty that there are other places near and far to which the sentiments of kinship service, loyalty, affection, and affiliation may be transported. In a society rapidly coming under the influence of technology and translocal values, norms and controls, these truly social factors we have been concerned with in both sections of the chapter must be taken into account as forces independent in their own right.

REFERENCES

Bracq, Jean Charlemagne, *The Evolution of French Canada*. New York: The Macmillan Company, 1924.

Canada Year Book 1970-71: Statistical Annual of the Resources, Demography, Institutions, and Social and Economic Conditions of Canada. Ottawa: Dominion Bureau of Statistics, 1971.

Canada 1971. Ottawa: Dominion Bureau of Statistics, 1970.

Canu, Pierre, Weeks, E. P., and Sametz, Z. W., "The People," in *Economic Geography of Canada 1964*, Chapter 3; reprinted in abridged form in Bernard R. Blishen, Frank E. Jones, Kaspar D.

84. Piddington, *op. cit.*, p. 457. Piddington used this example from an earlier study of a St. Lawrence island community conducted by Marcel Rioux.

85. Garigue, referred to in Piddington, *op. cit.*, pp. 449-450.

86. French, *op. cit.*

87. Moreux, *op. cit.*

Naegle, and John Porter, eds., *Canadian Society: Sociological Perspectives*, third edition. Toronto: Macmillan of Canada, 1968.

Chiaramonte, Louis J., *Craftsman-Client Contacts: Interpersonal Relations in a Newfoundland Fishing Community.* St. John's, Newfoundland: The Institute of Social and Economic Research, Newfoundland Social and Economic Studies, Memorial University, 1970.

Deffontaines, Pierre, "The *Rang*-Pattern of Rural Settlement in French Canada," translated and included in Marcel Rioux and Yves Martin, eds., *French Canadian Society.* Toronto: McClelland and Stewart Limited, 1964, Vol. 1.

Eccles, W. J., *Canadian Society During the French Regime.* Montreal: Harvest House, Ltd., 1968.

Elkin, Frederick, *The Family in Canada: An Account of Present Knowledge and Gaps in Knowledge about Canadian Families.* Ottawa: The Vanier Institute of the Family, 1970.

Falardeau, Jean-Charles, "The Seventeenth-Century Parish in French Canada," translated and included in Marcel Rioux and Yves Martin, eds., *French Canadian Society.* Toronto: McClelland and Stewart Limited, 1964, Vol. 1.

Faris, James, *Cat Harbour, A Newfoundland Fishing Settlement.* St. John's, Newfoundland: The Institute of Social and Economic Research, Newfoundland Social and Economic Studies, Memorial University, 1966.

Firestone, Melvin M., *Brothers and Rivals: Patrilocality in Savage Cove.* St. John's, Newfoundland: The Institute of Social and Economic Research, Newfoundland Social and Economic Studies, Memorial University, 1967.

Fortin, Gérald, "Woman's Role in the Evolution of Agriculture in Quebec," in *The Family in the Evolution of Agriculture.* Ottawa: The Vanier Institute of the Family, 1968.

French, Laurence, "The French Canadian Family in America," in Robert W. Habenstein and Charles Mindel, eds., *American Minority Family Life Styles.* New York: Holt, Rinehart and Winston, 1974.

Garigue, P., "The French-Canadian Family," in Mason Wade, ed., *Canadian Dualism.* Toronto: University of Toronto Press, 1960.

Gérin, Léon, "The French-Canadian Family—Its Strengths and Weaknesses," in Marcel Rioux and Yves Martin, eds., *French Canadian Society.* Toronto: McClelland and Stewart Limited, 1964, Vol. 1.

Hughes, Everett C., *French Canada in Transition.* Chicago: The University of Chicago Press, 1943; Toronto: W. J. Gage and Company, Limited, 1943.

Ingstad, Helga, "Vinland Ruins Prove Vikings Found the New World," *National Geographic*, 126 (1964), pp. 708-734.

Ishwaran, K., ed., *The Canadian Family: A Book of Readings*. Toronto and Montreal: Holt, Rinehart and Winston of Canada, Limited, 1971.

Miner, Horace, *St. Denis, A French Canadian Parish*. Chicago and London: The University of Chicago Press, 1939; first Phoenix edition, 1963.

Moreux, Colette, "The French-Canadian Family," in K. Ishwaran, ed., *The Canadian Family: A Book of Readings*. Toronto and Montreal: Holt, Rinehart and Winston of Canada, Limited, 1971.

Mowat, Farley, and de Visser, John, *The Rock Within the Sea: A Heritage Lost*. Boston and Toronto: Little Brown and Company, 1968. Published as an Atlantic-Little, Brown Book in association with The Atlantic Monthly Press.

Phelps, Linda, "The French Family: A Cultural Analysis." Unpublished Manuscript, 1969.

Piddington, Ralph, "A Study of French-Canadian Kinship," in K. Ishwaran, ed., *The Canadian Family: A Book of Readings*. Toronto and Montreal: Holt, Rinehart and Winston, 1971.

Porter, John, *The Vertical Mosaic: An Analysis of Social Class and Power in Canada*. Toronto: The University of Toronto Press, 1965.

Rioux, Marcel, and Martin, Yves, eds., *French Canadian Society*. Toronto: McClelland and Stewart Limited, 1964, Vol. 1.

Sparkes, Mary, "Bay Port" (tentative title), Columbia, Missouri: Master's Thesis, Department of Sociology. University of Missouri, 1974.

Szwed, John, *Private Cultures and Public Imagery: Interpersonal Relations in a Newfoundland Peasant Society*. St. John's, Newfoundland: The Institute of Social and Economic Research, Newfoundland Social and Economic Studies, Memorial University, 1966.

Vanier Institute of the Family. Ottawa, Ontario, Canada.

Wade, Mason, *The French Canadians: 1760-1945*. London: Macmillan, 1968, Vol. 1.

Wadel, Cato, *Marginal Adaptations and Modernization*. St. John's, Newfoundland: The Institute of Social and Economic Research, Newfoundland Social and Economic Studies, Memorial University, 1969.

17 The Mexican American Family

There are approximately 9 million people of Spanish ethnic origin living in the United States.[1] Of these whom we know mostly as Puerto Ricans, Cubans, Central and South Americans, and Mexican Americans the latter group constitutes a large majority, over 5 million persons, most of whom cluster in five southwestern states: Texas, New Mexico, Colorado, Arizona, and California. While we speak of Spanish ancestry, nearly all Mexican Americans carry some evidence of the mixing of the Spanish conquerors with indigenous native populations, some of whom, such as the Mayans, Aztecs, and Toltecs, had developed advanced civilizations of their own. The destruction of these civilizations, their art and artifacts, and the decimation of their people by genocidal medieval Christian conquistadors marks one of the least savory chapters in the history of the New World.

New Mexico leads in the proportion of Mexican Americans to the total state population, but Texas, which has traditionally dominated numerically and California, to which members of this minority group are migrating in rapidly growing numbers, are presently the front runners. Los Angeles county approaches 1 million Mexican American inhabitants and must be recognized as an unofficial capital, as are New York City for Puerto Rican migrants and Miami, Florida for Cubans. While only ten percent of the Mexican Americans in the United States live outside the southwest, an increasing number of "dropout" migrants have moved into midwestern towns and metropolitan areas, so that nearly every major city has its newer Latin additions. Some of the latter, depending upon economic contingencies, will reestablish *barrio*-like enclaves, but others in their move up the ladder of social-

1. *Statistical Abstracts of the United States 1972*, p. 33.

economic class will filter into the residential areas that have traditionally housed upper blue collar and white collar populations.

Increasingly, the movement of Mexican Americans is rural to urban, and in the southwest east to west. Many forms of farm labor relying on migratory workers are still performed predominantly by Mexican Americans, and the swing of family-centered groups out of Texas up through the northern states, harvesting fruit and vegetables as they come into season, is still a common phenomenon. Several factors operate currently to diminish such labor: the competition of crews of black workers in the eastern states now dominating harvesting from Florida to upstate New York; the disinclination of younger generations of Mexican Americans to live a substantial portion of their lives constantly on the move; and, perhaps by far the most important in long range implications, the increasing technology of agriculture in all its forms and a consequent reduction in human labor needed for work in the fields.

As slavery provides an important key to the understanding of the American Negro minority, so does the labor utilization of Mexicans and Mexican Americans provide an important category of analysis for understanding the growth and deterrents to growth of a distinct and viable Mexican American subculture or, for that matter, a successful assimilation into the American cultural mainstream. Immigration has been closely tied into southwestern labor needs, but these needs have been in the main defined by the "Anglos" who, in the wake of the Mexican American War of the mid-nineteenth century, through confiscation, displacement, and settlement, came to dominate the land and its economy. American military conquest provided land-hungry settlers with carte blanche for aggrandizement and created almost instantaneously a new, subjugated, exploitable minority group. As agricultural production became large scale and labor intensive, immigration policies tended to accommodate labor needs. Until quite recently job-starved Mexican nationals worked competitively and at lower wage scales than Mexican Americans, crossing and recrossing the border continuously. Even today border towns on the Mexico side are crowded with nationals who commute to factories and service industries in the United States. And, although the *bracero*[2] program is defunct, the influx of "wetbacks" still provides a significant sub rosa input of Mexicans into the American labor force. The point to be made very briefly, but which must be made, is that Mexican Americans, because of the proximity of Mexico, the fluidity of the border, and what must in all candor be termed an exploitative, labor-depressive, "Anglo"-dominated agricultural system, have never been able to participate in the familiar social process by which European immigrants through the generations become socially mobile and assimilated into the mainstream of American society. This fact must be kept in mind as we turn to a discussion of the structure of the Mexican American family.

The difficulty in defining and generalizing about the Mexican American, Spanish American, *Chicano,* Latin, or Latin American family is recognized by all authorities.[3] There is some consensus that a rather traditional type of family closely resembling that of the Mexicans of town and village continues to exist all along the border areas, and particularly in South Texas. Recognizing the difficulty of attempting to write of *the* Mexican American family we shall restrict our purview for most of this chapter to the tradition-oriented family found particularly in border towns and small isolated vil-

2. The *bracero* program was developed by agreement of the United States and Mexico during World War II when labor supply for field work was uncertain. Selected Mexican workers were permitted to work under contract to the U. S. The program continued into the 1960s, much to the distress of Mexican Americans who stood only to lose by the competition of imported labor.

3. A thoughtful discussion of the terminological problem is found in John Burma's "Introduction" to *Mexican Americans in the United States: A Reader* (1970).

lages throughout the southwest. In the concluding portion we will turn to the changes in and the changed Mexican American family.

Traditional Mexican American Values

The Mexican American family has existed within, has drawn cultural meanings from, and made contributions to a system of values that sets itself apart from the familiar Anglo-Saxon Protestant ethic.

Following psychologist Nathan Murillo, these major cultural values are, in highly summarized form:

a) Material objects are usually seen as necessities and not ends in themselves.

b) Work is viewed as necessary for survival but not as a value in itself.

c) Higher value is assigned to activities other than work in the Mexican culture.

d) It is much more valuable to experience things directly through intellectual awareness and through emotional experience rather than indirectly through past accomplishments and accumulation of wealth.

e) The time frame between Mexican Americans and Protestant-ethic Americans is quite different.

f) The Anglo is taught to value openness, frankness, and directness, while the traditional Latin approach is to use diplomacy and tactfulness when communicating with another individual.

g) The Anglo-American style of kidding can be offensive to the Mexican American who interprets and reacts negatively.

h) The Mexican American has a penchant towards utilizing his "full range of psychological senses to experience things about him . . . to touch, taste, smell, feel or be close to an object or person on which his attention is focused."[4]

Family Structure

Familism and Family Solidarity

Within this constellation of cultural values an overriding assumption is that the family remains the single most important social unity. The theme of family honor and unity diffuses throughout Mexican American society, irrespective of social class variation or geographical location. The upper class rancher and the lowly crop picker both think of themselves first as family members and second as individuals.[5] It is a familism that extends beyond husband, wife, and children to relatives on both sides. In center city enclaves the ideal of familism persists even when the dominance of the male role becomes weakened. It is the main focus of obligations and also a source of emotional and economic support, as well as recognition for accomplishment.[6] William Madsen, a student of Mexican Americans in South Texas, writes:

The family is a sanctuary in a hostile world full of envy and greed. The Mexican-American child who has been humiliated by Anglos at school knows that he will receive love and understanding from his mother. The wife who has been abused by her husband can seek help and guidance from

4. Nathan Murillo, "The Mexican American Family," in *Chicanos: Social and Psychological Perspectives,* Nathaniel N. Wagner and Marsha J. Haug, eds. (1971), Chap. 10, pp. 99-102.

5. William Madsen, *The Mexican-Americans of South Texas* (1964), p. 44.

6. *Ibid.*; Murillo, *op cit.,* pp. 103-105. Joan Moore feels, however, that familism seems to be declining in the big cities of the southwest. See her *Mexican Americans* (1970), pp. 116-118.

her parents. Any Latin boy with a brother knows he need never stay alone in a fight. As long as one member of the family has a house and food, none of his close relatives will lack shelter or meals.[7]

But, obligations to the family provide the other side of the coin. Individualism and individual needs must accommodate to the collective needs of the family—as these needs come to be defined by the patriarchal father. "The strength with which a person is bound to his family," observes anthropologist Arthur J. Rubel, "so overshadows all other bonds in importance that it contributes to the atomistic nature of the neighborhood."[8]

One reason that Mexican American family organization can encompass a full set of primary roles with ramified age and sex differentiation is its size. Mexican families by ordinary American standards are quite large. "They are so large," remarks Joan Moore, "as to make Mexican participation in the ordinary material rewards of American life much more marginal than that of most other populations identified by the census."[9] High fertility and the presence of many young families assure continued growth of the number of Mexican Americans, at least through the remainder of the century.

Family and Kinship

The Mexican American family in the first instance exists as a sharply definable nuclear unit of husband, wife, and children. The specificity of roles is reinforced by the denotative kinship terminology used among family members, contrasted with the generally classificatory system operating in the more inclusive kinship system.[10] The family is highly monogamic and, as indicated above, strongly patriarchal. While the enveloping extended kinship system is

7. Madsen, *op. cit.*, p. 44.
8. Arthur J. Rubel, "Across the Tracks" (1966), in *Mexican Americans in the United States: A Reader*, John Burma, ed. (1970), Chap. 3, p. 211.
9. Moore, *op. cit.*, p. 57.
10. Rubel, *op. cit.*, p. 211.

bilateral and mother's and father's kin of generally equal importance, special recognition is given to mother's sisters. Both sets of grandparents are revered but not the siblings of grandparents. First cousins are especially important collateral kin and, as Rubel indicates, "are said to be somewhat like one's sisters and brothers."[11]

Ritual Kinship: Compadrazgo

An important integrative social usage that has prevailed through several centuries is a form of ritual kinship involving the special linkage of two persons or groups as *compadres*. While the *compadrazgo* may take a number of forms, notably coparenthood, by providing fictive kinship linkages, its effect is to generate social and interpersonal cohesion and thus to reduce the potential extrafamilial conflict that might arise in a highly family-centered society. Coparenthood, which is considered the most important, links two families through the baptismal ritual. The godparents, *compadres,* will have been chosen with care from outside the kinship circle and the male, the most important *compadre,* will hopefully be a man of goodness, status, and respect in the community. The bond having been established ritually, the interaction henceforth will be carried on between the younger person and his coparent in the context of prescribed formality and mutual respect. They are expected to visit each other and cultivate a close relationship. And, in any kind of trouble, *compadres* have the right to call on each other for help and advice.[12]

The Marriage Institution

The traditional norms of Mexican American culture prescribe endogamy, formal courtship, chaperonage, permission

11. *Ibid.* This paragraph paraphrases Rubel's description of Mexican American family structure.
12. Madsen, *op. cit.,* p. 47.

from both sets of parents to marry, and a great circumspection in courtship behavior. The services of a go-between, *portador,* may be secured by the parents. Madsen elaborates:

> A proper *portador* is a respected member of the community who may be an older woman of good family or a man of good reputation. The *portador* makes the proposal to the girl's parents and they take the matter for consideration for a period of at least two weeks in order to discuss it with their daughter. A polite refusal delivered to the *portador* carries no offense to the boy's family. The *portador* who brings back an acceptance is rewarded with a handsome gift.[13]

Rubel tells of an earlier custom of exchanging potential spouses, the girl spending several months on trial at the home of the boy's parents and vice versa (*intercambio*). After the proposal had been accepted the boy would send food or money to the girl's parents for several months, and after thus demonstrating ability to provide would marry and live at the home of the girl until he could establish a separate household.[14]

Parental involvement in courtship and marriage continues, but not without resistance of the younger generation. Elopements have increased, but the common pattern is for a period of engagement followed by an elaborate wedding.

> The approaching wedding of a daughter is publicly announced at a dance sponsored by *her* parents, and there at the dance the parents of the girl are introduced to the gathering by the master of ceremonies. Their obligations toward her met, *they* are honored as well as she. The financial outlay for such an announcement is considerable, but after all, it is a life's work to prepare a daughter to become a worthy wife and mother.[15]

The lavishness of the wedding, as Madsen notes, varies with social class.

> Lower class marriages are customarily celebrated with an outdoor barbecue and beer party. Wedding celebrations among the elite sometimes fill the ballrooms of the largest hotels where champagne and imported French delicacies are served in addition to a towering wedding cake. Regardless of

13. *Ibid.,* p. 56. By permission of Holt, Rinehart and Winston.
14. Rubel, *op. cit.,* p. 216.
15. *Ibid.,* p. 217. By permission of University of Texas Press.

these differences, the symbolism is the same. By uniting their children in marriage, the two families have become *compadres* to each other. It is a relationship that endures as long as the marriage.[16]

Residence of the newlyweds tends to be matrilocal. The bride's mother is not anxious to lose a daughter from the intimate circle of familiars upon whom she is forced to depend for friendship, confidences, and assurance.[17] The groom, who has been restive under the authority and control of the *jefe de la casa,* is assured whatever freedom that can come from geographical separation, and at the same time he will have fewer qualms about a wife continuing her associations with mother and intimates than reconstructing a set of social and personal relationships in a strange setting. Mothers-in-law fare no better in the Mexican than in the Anglo-Saxon tradition, and the wife would prefer to avoid her spouse's mother. Finally, the marriage behind and the residence established, the groom settles down as the authoritarian head of household, a role for which he has served a lengthy, often trying apprenticeship.

Role Behavior and Life Cycle

Again, the role prescriptions described in this section emanate from, and emphasize the norms and values of, traditional Mexican culture. As such they should be seen to have operated either as acknowledged cultural ideals or to have persisted in common everyday experiences and so taken for granted as to have been seldom thought about consciously. Their closest approximation to reality would be found along the border areas, particularly in South Texas.

Childhood

The Mexican American infant is wanted, cherished, pampered, and thoroughly "spoiled."

16. Madsen, *op. cit.,* p. 57. By permission of Holt, Rinehart and Winston.

17. Rubel, *op. cit.,* pp. 217-218.

The small child is regarded as an *angelito* as yet uncontaminated by human sin and error. He receives adoring affection from mother and father alike. The father may drop his dignity to cradle a child, care for his needs, or even crawl on hands and knees to play with him. Such behavior is confined to the home.[18]

But awareness of gender comes early. The son-father relationship soon becomes asymmetrical and remains so throughout the life of both. The father very early in the child's life exemplifies the patriarchal parental role and the socialization process is long and difficult, as the son must constantly try to measure up to the demands and expectations of his father. A certain amount of distance and formality develops once the son is judged to have reached the ability to reason and to accept responsibility. The father must hold his own in male society, not only for himself, as a *macho,* but as the representative of his family unit. The lessons of male childhood are as demanding as they are endless. The mother, acting as a buffer between father and son, tends to indulge the latter, only to contribute to the tension when her favoritism is suspected or becomes apparent to the father.

Father-daughter relations throughout the latter's childhood are less distant and severe. "This is partly because the daughter is not expected to emulate him in any way," says Peñalosa, "nor is she at all a threat to his male status."[19] Mother-daughter relationships during early childhood are very close, with the mother dominating in much the same way as the father does the son. The daughter receives the most attention from the mother, even more than the son. "Because of the close relationship prevailing between mother and daughter on both emotional and household chore level," continues Peñalosa, ". . . the daughter ordinarily manages full identification with the mother."[20]

18. Madsen, *op. cit.,* p. 51. By permission of Holt, Rinehart and Winston.

19. Fernando Peñalosa, "Mexican Family Roles," *Journal of Marriage and the Family,* 30 (Nov., 1968), p. 686.

20. *Ibid.,* p. 687.

By the time childhood gives way to the teens both son and daughter have experienced no difficulty finding appropriate role models. The differentiation process has been reinforced in innumerable ways. Boys are expected to emulate fathers, to learn masculine ways, and to gain independence from maternal solicitude and pampering. Since a succession of children is the expectable occurrence, the boy will find himself dislodged from the favored position by the next born, and his narcissistic needs threatened.[21] The dynamics of coming of age for the male center around the psychogenic, emotional needs generated in infancy and reinforced by maternal solicitude, with these in turn coming into conflict with the clear cultural demands for manliness, independence, and maturity.

The adolescent male is encouraged and given the freedom to move about and gain experience in an expanding social world, the world which he must someday master as representative of his own family. Ordinarily he will join in with informal youth groups, *palomillas,* which afford him an opportunity to test his manliness against his peers. Thus he begins to develop a reputation centered on skill, knowledge, experience, and ability, from which his social status and prestige in the community is eventually derived.[22]

The adolescent female must learn a culturally defined role of an opposite yet complementary character to that of male *machismo.* Her social world is constricted and is home and mother-centered—but there is much more to it than learning housewifery. The female occupies a virtually sanctified position in Mexican and Mexican American society. Revered as a symbol of purity, she must grow up virginal, compassionate, submissive, aware that in the meaning of things she exists to complement but never to compete with the manly male. She finds herself less likely to be in conflict with her mother than the son with his father as she enters, in effect, a sisterhood made up of all the females of the extended kin group. Within

21. *Ibid.,* p. 686.
22. Murillo, *op. cit.,* p. 105.

it ambivalence, mistrust, and suppressed hostility toward the dominant male (whatever the psychogenic roots) are learned and/or reinforced. Biologically impelled toward males, yet long instructed that in the weakness of her sex she is incapable of resisting male exploitation, her refuge lies in early marriage and entrance as quickly as possible into the fully expressive, if sexually suppressed, role of motherhood.

Adult Roles

Perhaps enough has already been said about the traditional male role in Mexican American culture. A deeper look into the symbolic underpinning of the role, however, may be instructive. Octavio Paz, one of Mexico's greatest writers, has analyzed the *macho* or masculine role as incorporating superiority, aggressiveness, insensitivity, and invulnerability, all subsumable under one word, *power*, ". . . force without the discipline of any notion of order: arbitrary power, the will without reins and without a set course."[23] Beneath the more public or cognitive meanings of honor, strength, and masculinity lie subjective, symbolic associations leading back to and rooted subconsciously in earlier histories of two rather frightful peoples, the warring, sacrificing Aztecs, and their medieval Spanish conquerors.[24] Spelled out in day-to-day role activities, however, *machismo* calls for an aloof authoritarian head of family, directing its activities, arbitrating disputes, policing behavior, and, as already indicated, representing the family to community and society.

23. Octavio Paz, "The Sons of La Malinche," in *Introduction to Chicano Studies,* Livie Isauro Duran and H. Russell Bernard, eds. (1973), p. 24. "The Sons of La Malinche" was originally a chapter in *The Labyrinth of Solitude* (1961).

24. Aztecs slaughtered hundreds of thousands of victims in propitiatory rituals; the Conquistadors killed the necessary thousands it took to subjugate the Indian civilizations and, through spreading disease to and by starvation, torture, executions, and working enslaved natives to death, assisted in the decimation of *millions* more.

The adult female finds security in motherhood, a sainted role, to be differentiated from the spousal role. The latter is clearly the more difficult for its focus is on husband-wife inter-action in all its concrete reality. Twin ambivalencies present themselves: the husband, having long been socialized in the tradition of the sexual conquest of "bad" girls and the ascetic veneration of the "good," finds it difficult to assimilate sexual intercourse with the wife as an act of mutuality involving grati-fication and fulfillment equally shared; the wife, aware from earliest socialization that as a weaker female she cannot trust herself in sexual matters, denies herself or makes no sexual advances toward the spouse. The husband, free to continue the social activities enjoyed before marriage, finds conquests of other females ego building, and, as he makes no effort to deny such activities to his friends, they become just another means of demonstrating *machismo*.

The effect, as indicated above, is to take the husband out of the home and to consign the wife to an early and perma-nent role of motherhood. Each child becomes the object for expression of strong affective sentiments, themselves generated in the wife's childhood socialization. The wife and mother vies with all other family members in possessiveness toward the children, her rationalization being that only she can properly serve and minister to their needs. The latter include formal religious education and the providing of an appropriate reli-gious atmosphere in the home. In a sense the home becomes an extension of the Catholic church with its mixture of indigenous folk beliefs, and the mother symbolically becomes the embodi-ment of the Virgin of Guadalupe.

Grandparenthood has always been a well established status and, as already noted, grandparents are revered by their own adult children and by grandchildren alike. But prestige is not coterminous with power, and the authority of the father takes precedence. Children may go to their grandparents with ques-tions they might be afraid to bother the father about, but if there are decisions to be made the children will be referred to their father. Reporting child's-eye views of life in an urban *barrio* in Houston, Mary Ellen Goodman and Alma Beman report that grandmothers as well as mothers fill many domestic roles in the child's world, but again when small rules are disobeyed discipline falls to the mother.[25] Still, grandmothers will compete actively for the attention and affection of grandchildren, more so than the grandfather, understandable in relation to the intimacy world of children and females. "In contrast to the father and his relationship to the children," Murillo points out, "the mother continues to be close and warm, serving and nurturing even when her children are grown, married, and have children of their own."[26]

Social Integration and Social Problems

Function and Strain

Let us now briefly review the Mexican American family as a functioning unity. In rural and *barrio* society familism, as a normative prescription emphasizing family needs and family reputation over all other matters, provided the *context of meaning* for intrafamilial behavior and gave reality and importance to the roles all its family members would play. This meaning has long been grounded in tradition and undergirded by a symbol system incorporating elements of two medieval cultures, Spanish and indigenous native. Moreover, the social and interactive arena within which the drama of everyday family life would be played and individual family roles enacted was constricted, embracing in the first instance the nuclear family of husband, wife, and children, and in the second extending only moderately to include close collateral and lineal relatives. Beyond that, neighboring and community participation was or could easily become erratic, and unsystematized in

25. Mary Ellen Goodman and Alma Beman, "Child's-Eye Views of Life in an Urban Barrio," in *Chicanos: Social and Psychological Perspectives, op. cit.,* p. 112.

26. Murillo, *op. cit.,* p. 104.

the sense of an incomplete articulation of wider social roles. Community life would be beset by contingencies that are present when constituent family members, age and sex groups turn in on themselves, retreat to the sanctuary of their homes, and find difficulty in establishing social networks.

Yet within this arena an exchange and balance of expected behaviors operated smoothly enough to guarantee family continuity for generation after generation. Only one role called for serious, sustained, critical involvement with social systems external to the family, that of husband, provider, and protector of the family name. Assuredly economic contingencies were ever present, and the hazards of a personal contest system whereby one's *macho* was always on the line would make the male role difficult but seldom impossible. The embracing system of cultural values detailed at the beginning of this chapter always provided a rationale for Mexican Americans to downgrade the demands of the Western Protestant ethic. The centrality of the work ethic for Anglo Americans has as its reciprocal a residual anxiety attached to one's being physically present in the home when there's work to be done elsewhere. It is clear that the strictures to find meaning in life through vocational activity are neither so meaningful for Mexican Americans nor so all-embracing as they have been for Anglo Americans. The home is the social and personal center of gravity for the people of the *barrio* and the *hacienda* alike. And, it must also be remembered, each home is a religious sanctuary serving as a physical and spiritual extension of the church, centering around the wife as Holy Mother and objects of religious significance that are found everywhere in Mexican American homes.

Finally, a number of social arrangements or mechanisms have served to link families to each other and to assure at least a modicum of social integration at the extrafamilial level. These we recall as the woman's kin and sociability groups, the husband's drinking companions, the *palomillas*, i.e., peer groups for youth, the *compadre* relationships generated through the *compadrazgo* system, and the pervasive religious community, sensuously and symbolically glorifying the miracle of the Holy Family in fiestas, other religious observances, and through the services of the Catholic ministry.

Disjunction and Change

Our last task will be to look at the internal weaknesses of the traditional Mexican American family in the context of social change.[27] Conflicts within any family are of course inevitable, but their genesis and importance will vary significantly. Husband-wife discord in Mexican and Mexican American families has never been uncommon. The asymmetrical nature of the husband's role, with his prerogative to express himself personally, socially, and sexually in the community at large, while the wife must stay at home, mind the family, and serve the husband in all his needs, gives rise to a sense of injustice on the part of the female—particularly in a world society where modernity increasingly prescribes equality of the sexes. The enshrinement of womanhood clashes with the particularity and individuality of each wife as a person with human needs. Given the increasing vocational opportunities for women,[28] as well as the demands of external institutions, agencies, schools, secondary associations, City Hall, etc., the wife finds herself with an expanded secular role to play.

The higher the family income the more likely there will be a departure from traditional ethnic norms.[29] The *macho* role of the husband includes his function as provider, but in a world of rising expectations and standards of living, the long-

27. Cf. Chap. 15, "The Family, Variations in Time and Space" in Leo Grebler, Joan W. Moore, and Ralph Guzman, *The Mexican-American People* (1970), pp. 350-377.

28. *Ibid.*, p. 206. Mexican American female participation in the labor force remains low, much lower, for example, than for Negro females. In the southwest areas, California, particularly Los Angeles, their participation is highest.

29. *Ibid.*, p. 582.

standing depressed occupational status of the male[30] frustrates the breadwinner's role and often leads him into heavy drinking, rows with friends and neighbors, and abusive behavior at home. The tendency to withdraw rather than to challenge authority and status reported by most students of Mexican-American culture suggests that the *macho* role is not correlatively supported by ego strength. In any event, mistreated wives still have as one recourse a further retreat into the inner sanctum of religion or the emotionally supportive group of female intimates. However, it is not unknown for the wife to fight back, to scorn the husband for his weakness and improvidence. Divorce, anathema to the Catholic church, provided no way out, but desertion always has. Husbands who migrate to look for work may not return; others simply flee the family. Technology and the urban tropism have moved persons and families everywhere, but geographical mobility does not insure better job opportunities. When the occupational base of the provider is undermined or jeopardized it is a sociological truism that family form and solidarity are likewise threatened. *Machismo* might coexist with uncertain employment in the small village and the *barrio*, but the city apartment or flat does not provide the same climate of refuge as did the village *casa*. *Mañana* has only a hollow echo. Desertion rates are increasing, and when divorce statistics are combined with separation statistics the result is as dismaying as it is indicative of the deterioration of family unity.[31] The Mexican American family in this regard fares no

30. Labor force participation for Mexican American males is lower than for Anglos and is concentrated in the middle and lower ranges of the occupational hierarchy. Unemployment rates, by the same token, are higher. The absorption of rural migrants into urban labor markets becomes an increasingly critical problem.

31. *Op. cit.*, pp. 130-131. In their Mexican American Study Project at Los Angeles Grebler, Moore, and Guzman found that "When separations and divorces are combined, Anglo women show the lowest incidence, Spanish-surname females rank next, and non-whites by far the highest."

better than the American black. Significantly, both groups at
the low income level have a large proportion of female household heads.

Education, in the context of small parochial schools taught
by members of a religious teaching order,[32] seldom if ever
operated to separate children from their parents. Family solidarity and the virtues of family life would as a matter of
course be emphasized in parochial education. The predominance of formal public school education has meant that greater
opportunities and resources could be made available to children of Mexican Americans and provide the means for breaking out of the culture of poverty cycle. But consensus seems
to favor the proposition that the American public school system has been particularly deficient in its impact on Spanish
and Mexican-Spanish vernacular-speaking children and their
families. For one, the confusing and ego damaging experiences
in school lead to early dropping out, despite the general high
value that Mexican peoples in the abstract have placed on
intelligence and learning. The child's personal problem of
thinking in one language and being asked to learn by thinking
in another is compounded by the experience of bringing the
foreign language into the home, of using it or some variety of
it with brothers and sisters in front of noncomprehending
parents. Also, as Murillo and others have indicated, the child
often finds himself caught up in the clash between authoritarian values embedded in the family structure and the democratic ideals learned at school.[33] Again, children may be kept
home from or even taken out of school by parents who put
matters involving the family as a whole over the needs of any
member. Migratory workers' children are virtually guaranteed
discontinuous and abortive schooling.

32. Parochial schools never figured very prominently in Mexican
society and were banned by the Constitution of 1912. In the United States
a continuing effort has been made by the Catholic church, particularly
since World War II, to build and bring Mexican Americans to parochial
schools. Possibly a fifth of all Mexican American youth attend such schools.
33. Murillo, *op. cit.*, p. 105.

The desires of the young to escape the domination of the old gets expressed in both conflict and avoidance. As much as possible the father will be avoided by the older offspring. The mother, where and if possible, will be dominated by both sons and daughters—particularly the former, who vie for the favorable treatment that was once their birthright. Brothers of varying ages avoid each other except in the presence of an external threat from a nonfamily source. The young wish to date and marry freely. Chaperonage, the *portado,* even parental consent for marriage may be relegated to the category of "old-fashioned." Elopements are common and intermarriages are on the increase. The division of labor breaks down as older children stay on in school and/or are diverted from household chores by homework and school activities. The increase in the number of working mothers makes for further complications.

All familial roles and the contexts of family interaction, it seems, are undergoing change. Some internal tensions arising in the wake of a changing society have already been discussed. However, a few of the macrolevel changes noted earlier remain to be elaborated. One of these is the revolution taking place in agricultural technology. Mechanization and the application of rational, corporation-style modes of organization in the planting, growing, harvesting, and marketing of agricultural products have meant a continuing reduction of stoop labor. For Mexican Americans who have always been heavily employed in this kind of work, mechanization poses a threat to their livelihood more significant than that presented by the *braceros* and the wetbacks who competed when labor was more scarce. Not only does the market for farm labor lessen but a concomitant development, that of increasing marginality and economic hazard of small scale farming, has made it difficult for Mexican Americans to succeed as farmer-entrepreneurs. Lack of capital and credit, the crushing forces of corporate competition, labor militancy, jurisdictional disputes and strikes, all in one combination or another loom up as obstacles to the maintenance of the family farm and the farm family.

The "pull" of urban centers—Los Angeles, San Antonio,

Chicago, Kansas City—then, must be seen partly as a consequence of the "push" occasioned by the lack of promise for any kind of economically based good life in village and country. Inner cities have always been the point of urban entry for migrants, and when the migration is large scale the reproduction of familiar institutions is expectable. However, the urban *barrio* remains to be more thoroughly studied, not merely for the replication of traditional social structures but for adaptations and changes that represent responses to new environmental problems.[34]

Certainly one of the important "inputs" into the urban mix is the demographic fact that Mexican Americans have the highest birth rate of all the larger minority groups, and that in view of a decreasing death rate, the proportion and concentration of urban Mexican Americans in American society can only increase. The matter of physical concentration is crucial but must be seen against some evidence of dispersion and assimilation into the American mainstream. It can be shown that opportunities to do better in the labor force are increasing, and the elaboration of a social class as against an earlier caste system is advanced as a corollary development. Thus the future of the Mexican American is held by some to lie in the realm of blending into Anglo American society, with a tincture effect occurring as Mexican culture is absorbed into the American mainstream. That such assimilation, even if it were desirable, is in the realm of possibility is doubted by the thousands of politicized Mexican Americans who have redefined their problem as victimization through suppression and exploitation. The conception of *la Raza* and the redesignation of Mexican Americans as "Chicanos"—a political stratagem— represent the frustration responses of Americans of Spanish-Mexican ancestry whose hopes for an equal sharing of the

34. One excellent sociological study has been carried out by Anthony G. Dworkin, part of which is readably summarized in his "No Siesta Mañana: The Mexican American in Los Angeles," in *Our Children's Burden*, Raymond W. Mack, ed. (1968), pp. 387-439.

affluence of the world's richest nation still remain remote in their minds. Thus the counter-assimilation moves and the power sought by militant leaders are based on the proposition that the bulk of Mexican American urban migrants will remain concentrated in the center of the nation's cities.

Conclusion

The Mexican American family differs historically from the black American family because of its early and continued unity. For Negroes slavery, emancipation but with exclusion as a separate and inferior race, and a wide variety of forms of social and economic discrimination could scarcely produce other than a fragile monogamy with the male provider facing an uphill struggle for status, authority, and ego strength, both inside the family and out. Despite conquest and subjugation Mexicans—and later Mexican Americans—have always enjoyed nuclear family unity: husband, wife, and child, with other primary collateral and affinal relatives usually close at hand. If neither group could experience economic verisimilitude in the past, it has been the Mexican and Mexican American family that could relegate such matters to a secondary order of value and still keep its unity of organization. Both groups remain part of a great underclass of American society. Should it be their collective fate to pile up in the disintegrating and blighted urban centers the prospect for family change will increase just to the extent that adaptations and accommodations, or breakdowns, are generated in face of family, community-, and minority-wide crises. For the Mexican American family there will undoubtedly be a number of structural changes, the most significant of which will be the equalization of spousal roles. Females may find opportunities for education, work outside the home, job careers, social contacts, mobility of thought and person, and identity and ego building in urban society increasingly irresistible. The male role will not necessarily erode, but adaptations to a changing, strengthened female role will occur in the context of the opportunity structure for both vis à vis the labor marketplace. The middle-majority Anglo American life style, built out of conjoining occupational opportunity for males and females alike and with high standards of remuneration and consumption, presents an evocative if not particularly praiseworthy model. For the activist *Chicano* seeking to restore the integrity of *la Raza*, the model may represent only a capitulation to the blandest of middle class values and the betrayal of the Mexican Americans' unique birthright. The argument may indeed be academic if their occupational life chances on the whole remain indifferent or become worsened. The future of the Mexican American family will to a large extent hinge on the reality of the Anglo maxim that there is always room at the top.

REFERENCES

Burma, John, ed., "Introduction" to *Mexican Americans in the United States: A Reader.* Cambridge, Mass.: Schenkman Publishing Co., Inc., 1970.

Choldin, Harvey, and Trout, Grafton D., *Mexican Americans in Transition: Migration and Employment in Michigan Cities.* East Lansing, Michigan: Department of Sociology, Rural Manpower Center, Agricultural Experiment Station, Michigan State Universty, 1969.

Diaz-Guerrero, Rogelio, "Neurosis and the Mexican Family Structure," *American Journal of Psychiatry* (December, 1955), pp. 411-417.

Dworkin, Anthony J., "No Siesta Mañana: The Mexican American in Los Angeles," in Raymond W. Mack, ed., *Our Children's Burden.* New York: Random House, 1968, pp. 389-439.

Goodman, Mary Ellen and Beman, Alma, "Child's-Eye Views of Life in a Urban Barrio," in Nathaniel N. Wagner and Marsha J. Haug, eds., *Chicanos: Social and Psychological Perspectives.* St. Louis: The C. V. Mosby Company, 1971.

Grebler, Leo, Moore, Joan W., and Guzman, Ralph, "The Family, Variations in Time and Space," in Grebler et al., *The Mexican-American People.* New York: The Free Press, 1970, Chapter 15.

Heller, Celia S., *Mexican American Youth: Forgotten Youth at the Crossroads.* New York: Random House, 1966.

Ludwig, Ed and Santibañez, James, eds., *The Chicanos: Mexican-American Voices.* Baltimore, Md.: Penguin Books, Inc., 1971.

Madsen, William, *The Mexican Americans of South Texas.* New York: Holt, Rinehart and Winston, 1964.

Mittlebach, Frank G. and Moore, Joan, "Ethnic Endogamy—the Case of Mexican Americans," in John Burma, ed., *Mexican Americans in the United States: A Reader.* Cambridge, Mass.: Schenkman Publishing Company, Inc., 1970.

Montiel, Miguel, "The Social Science Myth of the Mexican American Family," *El Grito,* III (Summer, 1970), pp. 56-63.

Moore, Joan W., "Colonialism: The Case of the Mexican American," in Livie Isauro Duran and H. Russell Bernard, eds., *Introduction to Chicano Studies: A Reader.* New York: The Macmillan Company, 1973.

Moore, Joan W. with **Cuellar, Alfredo,** *Mexican Americans.* Englewood Cliffs, N. J.: Prentice-Hall, Inc., 1970.

Murillo, Nathan, "The Mexican American Family," in Nathaniel N. Wagner and Marsha J. Haug, eds., *Chicanos: Social and Psychological Perspectives.* St. Louis: C. V. Mosby Company, 1971, Chapter 10.

Paz, Octavio, *The Labyrinth of Solitude: Life and Thought in Mexico,* trans. by Lysander Kemp. New York: Grove Press, 1961.

———, "The Sons of La Malinche," in Livie Isauro Duran and H. Russell Bernard, eds., *Introduction to Chicano Studies.* New York: The Macmillan Company, 1973.

Peñalosa, Fernando, "Mexican Family Roles," *Journal of Marriage and the Family,* 30 (November, 1968), pp. 680-689.

Ramirez, Manuel, III, "Identification with Mexican Family Values and Authoritarianism in Mexican Americans," *The Journal of Social Psychology,* LXXIII (1967), pp. 3-11.

Rubel, Arthur J., "Across the Tracks," in John Burma, ed., *Mexican Americans in the United States: A Reader.* Cambridge, Mass.: Schenkman Publishing Co., 1970, Chapter 3.

Samora, Julian, ed., *La Raza: Forgotten Americans.* Notre Dame, Ind.: University of Notre Dame Press, 1966.

Statistical Abstracts of the United States. Washington, D.C.: U.S. Department of Commerce, 1972.

Tharp, Roland G. et al., "Changes in Marriage Roles Accompanying the Acculturation of the Mexican-American Wife," *Journal of Marriage and the Family,* XXX, No. 3 (August, 1968), pp. 404-412.

INDEX OF NAMES

447

INDEX OF SUBJECTS